Branches

{ kiln
firing

↓

Tar

{ boiling

↓

Pitch

gum

{ distilled

Turpentine   Rosin

Tapping the Pines

Tapping the Pines

The Naval Stores Industry in the American South

ROBERT B. OUTLAND III

 LOUISIANA STATE UNIVERSITY PRESS   *Baton Rouge*

Designer: Amanda McDonald Scallan
Typeface: Whitman
Typesetter: Coghill Composition Co., Inc.
Printer and binder: Thomson-Shore, Inc.

Library of Congress Cataloging-in-Publication Data

Outland, Robert B.
Tapping the pines : the naval stores industry in the American South / Robert B. Outland III.
    p.   cm.
    Includes bibliographical references (p.   ) and index.
    ISBN 0-8071-2981-X (hardcover : alk. paper)
1. Naval stores industry—Southern States—History.   2. Naval stores industry—Southern
States—Employees.   I. Title.
HD9769.N33U66   2004
338.1′738959′0977—dc22

                                                              2004006758

To Barbara

CONTENTS

ILLUSTRATIONS

Charts and Maps

Photographs

FOLLOWING PAGE 206

Burning a tar kiln in North Carolina

"Box" cutting near Ocilla, Georgia

Worker chipping a face

"Turpenting in the South Atlantic Country"

Scraping the face

A North Carolina turpentine distillery

Naval stores dock, Savannah, Georgia

Plant and yards of Yaryan Naval Stores Company, Brunswick, Georgia

ACKNOWLEDGMENTS

As long and as hard as I have worked toward the completion of this book, I could never have accomplished what I have without the selfless help of many individuals and institutions. More than a decade ago, Tim Silver suggested labor in the naval stores industry as a potentially valuable topic. Later, Gaines Foster offered unlimited assistance in my efforts to explore the subject more broadly. As a model mentor he allowed me to pursue my own ideas, critiqued my arguments and prose thoroughly, and respected my opinion when it differed from his own (as it often did). Carville Earle's advice to incorporate in my analysis work from the fields of geography and forestry significantly contributed to the study's depth. Paul Paskoff and Charles Royster lent valuable research suggestions and noted ways to improve my argument's clarity. Portions of this book, which were previously published in the *Journal of Southern History,* the *North Carolina Historical Review,* and *Atlanta History,* appear thanks to the permissions graciously granted by the journals' respective editors. The dedicated staff at Louisiana State University Press was an absolute delight to work with, especially Sylvia Frank Rodrigue. As editor in chief she had faith in my work and kept her promise to move the manuscript through the approval and launch phases in a timely manner.

In my research, which took me on fascinating adventures across the southeastern United States, I accumulated debts to the staffs at the Coastal Georgia Historical Commission, St. Simons Island, Georgia; the Darlington County Historical Commission, Darlington, South Carolina; the Department of Special Collections, George A. Smathers Libraries, University of Florida; the Florida State Archives; the Forest History Society, Durham, North Carolina, especially Cheryl Oakes; the Georgia Agrirama, Tifton, Georgia, especially Johnny Johnson and David King; the Georgia Department of Archives and History; the Georgia Historical Society; the Horgett Rare Book and Manuscript Library, the University of Georgia; the Lake County Historical Society, Tavares, Florida; the Lowndes County Historical Society, Valdosta,

Georgia; the Manuscripts Department, Mitchell Memorial Library, Mississippi State University, especially Mattie Sink; the McCain Library and Archives, University of Southern Mississippi; the North Carolina State Archives; the Pensacola Historical Society, Pensacola, Florida; the St. Augustine Society, St. Augustine, Florida; the South Caroliniana Library, University of South Carolina; the Southern Historical Collection, the University of North Carolina at Chapel Hill; the National Archives; the Special Collections Department, Woodruff Library, Emory University; and the Special Collections Library, Duke University, especially William Erwin. Residents of St. John County, Florida—Elliott Maguire, Jo Meldrim, and Prince K. Reed—kindly provided their firsthand knowledge of the twentieth-century naval stores industry. The Interlibrary Loan staff at Louisiana State University's Middleton Library processed my endless requests for obscure material.

My family contributed in all ways to the work's completion. My in-laws provided much-needed diversions, especially exceedingly festive family gatherings (folks celebrate everything in South Louisiana). My parents' limitless encouragement and willingness to spend a small fortune on my education have left me humbly indebted. I can only attempt to repay them by doing the same for my own children. As for Robby and Mary, who persistently diverted their father's attention from his work, this book was completed despite them. However, their sparkling clear blue eyes (like their mother's), genuine smiles, and boundless enthusiasm for exploring the big wide world have been constant, powerful, and valuable reminders that researching and writing place a distant second and third in life's priorities. Finally, I thank my wife, Barbara, whom I met in graduate school and who has lived with this project from its uncertain beginning to its gratifying end. She has endured my absences on research trips, my boring explanations of longleaf pine physiology, and my ranting about chapter disorganization. After more than minor persuasion, she proofread the majority of my chapters and in so doing caught the most embarrassing mistakes before someone less forgiving did. Most of all she provided limitless love and support through a process that taxed her every bit as it did me. For all these things I am eternally grateful.

Tapping the Pines

Introduction: A Southern Industry

Just before his death from pneumonia in 1889 at the young age of thirty-nine, Henry Grady, *Atlanta Constitution* editor and the New South's most renowned booster, detailed his region's strengths and progress for readers of the *New York Tribune*. As one example of the South's numerous efforts at economic advancement, he explained that "The long-leafed pine, now standing in Southern forests, would yield, at $10 a thousand feet—the crudest form in which it can be rendered—$500,000,000 in excess of the total taxable value of the South, including cities, railroads, farms, personal property, everything. That is an enormous possession! But that does not satisfy the New South. Made into furniture, that pine would bring $50 instead of $10 a thousand feet. And so, in something over four hundred and fifty factories, she is turning it into furniture."[1]

What Grady described were two different types of industry, one that extracted and processed raw material and another that finished it. Each was centered in different parts of the South's two principal areas of manufacturing, the piney woods of Georgia, Florida, and southern Alabama and Mississippi, which specialized in timber products, and the Carolina piedmont, which possessed not only furniture factories but tobacco factories and cotton textile mills. Those industries located in the Carolinas ultimately fulfilled Grady's hopes for the South while the ones in the lower South failed. One hundred years after his death the Carolina piedmont possessed the expected characteristics of industrial development—relatively high population density, a large percentage of residents employed in manufacturing, and a low poverty rate. The piney woods South, by comparison, had a largely rural population, few people employed in manufacturing, and a high rate of poverty, especially among African Americans. Unlike the industries that devel-

1. *The New South: Writings and Speeches of Henry Grady* (Savannah: Beehive Press, 1971), 149.

oped in the Carolina piedmont, those located in the piney woods brought little change.[2]

An important part of the timber products trade, the southern naval stores industry furnishes an alternative picture of southern industrialization than that usually provided by historians of the South, who have focused on finished-product industries such as furniture, tobacco, and especially textiles. These scholars find a dramatic difference between the Old South and the New. They describe a region emerging from the ravages of the Civil War ready to cast off its dedication to forced labor and agriculture and shift its resources toward the construction of factories located in towns and employing free, if inadequately paid, wage laborers. However, naval stores production, the South's oldest industry, perhaps reflects the nature of development in the region better than any other form of manufacturing. It thus serves as a superior vehicle through which to explore several broad issues regarding the area's development both before and after the Civil War—industrial growth, the transition from slave to free labor, environmental change, twentieth-century reform efforts, changes in the rural countryside, and the extent of change from the antebellum to postbellum years.

The significant attention southerners paid to naval stores production, especially after the 1820s, demonstrates that they were far from uninterested in manufacturing. That the South failed to fund industrialization to the extent that the North did is clear. On the eve of the Civil War the South produced only 15 percent of the value of manufactured goods in the United States. Yet southerners did not ignore industry, and during the late antebellum period they began significant initiatives into economic development outside of agriculture. Spurred by the Panic of 1837, which depressed cotton prices until the mid-1840s, investment in manufacturing rose from $53 million in 1840 to $93.6 million in 1850 and jumped to $163.7 million by 1860. Between 1850 and 1860 the value of manufactured output rose 79 percent. Southern investors built railroads, operated ironworks, and wove textiles, but most of them extracted and processed raw materials or agricultural products. They established and operated rice, sugar, wheat, and corn mills, saw mills, cotton gins, tobacco factories, hemp factories, salt works, coal mines, and turpentine operations. Large planters controlled a significant percentage of the South's new industry; 20 percent of manufacturers owned more slaves than the average slaveholder. Although such large slaveholding investors were a small minority of planters—only 6 percent—they controlled 23 percent of manufacturing capital. In North Carolina, where the naval stores

2. Edward L. Ayers, *The Promise of the New South: Life after Reconstruction* (New York: Oxford University Press, 1992), 23; Rodger Doyle, *Atlas of Contemporary America: A Portrait of the Nation* (New York: Facts on File, 1994), 12, 120–1, 131.

industry first developed on a large scale, planters enthusiastically invested in manufacturing and, in fact, constituted the majority of its backers. In the Tar Heel State, 33 percent of all manufacturers owned more slaves than average slaveholders, and many owned two to three times as many bondsmen. By 1860, the nearly 4,000 hands who labored for North Carolina's roughly 1,600 naval stores establishments produced turpentine and rosin valued at well over $5,000,000, 32 percent of the state's total manufacturing output value. Moreover, in the postbellum years, many of the former slaveholding North Carolina operators helped spread enthusiasm for naval stores production across the piney woods South. Although the business represented only a small portion of the industrial economy of other southern states before the Civil War, by the last decades of the nineteenth century naval stores manufacturing ranked among the top five industries in North Carolina, and in South Carolina, Georgia, and Florida as well.[3]

Not only was naval stores production a prominent southern industry, it also possessed the general characteristics typical of manufacturing in the South, say recent historians. James C. Cobb explains that most industries in the postbellum South, like those before the war, comprised operations that were largely undercapitalized and involved extracting and processing agricultural products and raw materials—such as gum turpentine. Cobb also notes that southern industry shared these characteristics with southern agriculture. The two "remained locked in a mutually dependent relationship in which the weakness of one reinforced the weaknesses of the other." The New South, David Carlton finds, did not conform to the prevailing image of

3. Much of North Carolina's high rate of planter investment in industry was a result of the state's prominence in naval stores production. In 1860, North Carolina's total capital investment in industry amounted to $9,693,703, of which $2,059,780, or a little more than 21 percent, was in naval stores production. That same year the state produced $16,678,698 in manufactured goods, of which $5,355,780, or 32 percent, was naval stores. Moreover, 42 percent of the state's manufacturing establishments made these products. William J. Cooper, Jr., and Thomas E. Terrill, *The American South: A History* (New York: Alfred A. Knopf, 1990), 323; Fred Bateman, James Foust, and Thomas Weiss, "The Participation of Planters in Manufacturing in the Antebellum South," *Agricultural History* 68 (April 1974): 279–80, 284, 286–90, 292, 294, 296–7; James C. Cobb, *Industrialization and Southern Society, 1877–1984* (Chicago: Dorsey Press, 1984), 5; Mary A. DeCredico, *Patriotism for Profit: Georgia's Urban Entrepreneurs and the Confederate War Effort* (Chapel Hill: University of North Carolina Press, 1990), 1–2, 10–2, 16, 18–20; United States Department of the Interior, *Manufactures of the United States in 1860* (Washington, D.C.: 1865), 2–14, 57–82, 168–204, 285–94, 420–38, 552–79; United States Department of the Interior, *Report on the Manufactures of the United States at the Tenth Census* (Washington, D.C.: 1883), 88–9, 103, 105, 141, 160–1, 173–4; United States Department of the Interior, *Report on the Manufacturing in the United States at the Eleventh Census* (Washington, D.C.: 1895), 30–3; United States Department of Commerce and Labor, *Manufactures, 1905*, Part 2 (Washington, D.C.: 1907), 6, 158, 170, 556, 800, 1020.

an industrial society, but rather remained predominantly rural and relied on low-wage and nonunionized labor—again, both common in the naval stores industry. Moreover, as F. Ray Marshall finds, the lives of agricultural and industrial workers in the South, especially those involved in forest industries, usually diverged very little. Both types of laborers lived and worked in rural areas, inhabited substandard houses, worked for paternalistic bosses, and received company scripts that they spent in company stores. The characteristics of the southern industry and industrial workers offered by Cobb, Carlton, and Marshall do not fully apply to cotton textile production. Although the textile industry used the South's most important raw commodity and employed low-skilled workers, it did not extract or process the fiber but rather produced a finished product in a highly mechanized facility typically located in at least a moderate-size town. These traits, however, perfectly describe naval stores manufacturing, which typically took place in rural areas where few other opportunities for economic development existed, where capital commanded a high price, and where pines grew in abundance and sold for little. The industry used crude techniques that maximized the short-term returns of both capital and labor and employed methods and work rhythms that in many ways resembled agriculture more than industry. Furthermore, naval stores production relied on a variety of systems of forced labor, which supports recent scholarship that argues that slavery, peonage, and convict leasing, rather than hindering the southern economy, helped to modernize it. Turpentining can therefore be studied as a prototypical southern industry.[4]

It certainly provides a better means of examining the region's growth than does cotton textile production, which not only was unrepresentative of most southern industry but was not even the New South's most important

4. Because of naval stores manufacturing's primitive production characteristics, disagreement has persisted as to whether naval stores operations constituted industry or an unusual form of agriculture. Throughout the nineteenth century, the United States government classified naval stores products as manufactured commodities, but, as is discussed in a later chapter, in the 1930s it reversed itself and designated them as agricultural products. The confusion arose because the techniques for refining turpentine closely mirrored manufacturing, but the schedule and methods of harvesting raw turpentine resembled those in agriculture. Naval stores production first demanded multiple and systematic sweeps through pine forests to prepare trees for the collection of raw turpentine and to keep the resin flowing during the harvest season, just as agricultural fields required periodic trips through them for plowing, planting, and hoeing. Moreover, the harvest of raw turpentine involved several operations on the same tree each season, just as tobacco harvests involved picking leaves from the same stalk at different times. Cobb, *Industrialization and Southern Society*, 11, 16; David L. Carlton, "The Revolution from Above: The National Market and the Beginnings of Industrialization in North Carolina," *Journal of American History* 77 (September 1990): 446; F. Ray Marshall, *Labor in the South* (Cambridge: Harvard University Press, 1967), 87.

industry until after the First World War. Edward Ayers maintains "while the cigarette, furniture, and textile industries made impressive strides in the New South, most Southern industrial workers labored in forests and mines rather than in factories. Those extractive industries became increasingly dominant throughout the New South era, outstripping the growth of more heavily mechanized enterprises." Until 1920, economist Gavin Wright finds, the South's timber products industry—raw timber, lumber, and naval stores production—was the region's largest in terms of both employment and value added. Indeed, a map of southern industry in 1900 included in Ayers's *Promise of the New South* reveals that the percentage of families with a member engaged in manufacturing was the highest across the rural pine region of south Georgia, Florida, and the Gulf coast of Alabama and Mississippi—where the timber products industry was most concentrated—not in the more town-oriented Carolina piedmont, which possessed the majority of the South's textile mills. Moreover, Ayers argues "lumber, more than any other industry, captures the full scope of economic change in the New South, its limitations as well as its impact."[5]

Nevertheless, naval stores and other timber products production have received little attention in studies of the South. Wright believes that scholars have largely ignored the rural-based timber industry because it was of an extractive and therefore transient nature and, in most areas of the South, consequently made no lasting contribution to local development. But in a significant portion of the South, timber and naval stores operations were—despite their mobility—the largest and most influential businesses for half a century. Furthermore, their failure to bring lasting development to rural areas constitutes an important legacy and helps explain why the southern pine belt remains relatively devoid of industry and cities today. Naval stores alone, it must be admitted, did not represent the most important industry in even the piney woods South; lumber did. But as a part of the larger timber products trade, with which it shared common characteristics, the naval stores industry serves as a valid example of southern economic change.[6]

Despite the importance of naval stores to the history of the South, few people today even know what naval stores are. Since ancient times, naval stores have been vital commodities for shipbuilding. Originally defined to include all materials used in ship construction and maintenance—hemp, flax, masts, spars, planking, tar, and pitch—the term "naval stores" by 1800 referred only to tar, raw turpentine, and their derivatives: spirits of turpen-

5. Ayers, *Promise of the New South*, 23, 105, 123; Gavin Wright, *Old South, New South: Revolutions in the Southern Economy since the Civil War* (New York: Basic Books, 1986), 159.

6. Wright, *Old South, New South*, 159, 161.

Tar
Decay

Pitch
water
proofing

Resin
is not
Pitch

tine, rosin, and pitch. Tar, produced by firing pine branches and logs in slow-burning kilns, and pitch, made by boiling tar, were used primarily for nautical purposes. To reduce decay, seamen slathered heavy applications of tar on the standing rigging that held masts in place and painted lighter coats on the running rigging used for raising and adjusting sails. Tar was also used as axle grease for wheeled vehicles, rust protective for cannons, and a preservative for fence posts. Livestock wounds that received an application of tar stood a lower chance of infection, and seeds coated with the sticky, resinous substance proved unappetizing to hungry birds and rodents. Pitch, applied to the sides and bottoms of wooden ships, prevented leakage. The other principal naval stores product, spirits of turpentine—a substance distilled from gum secreted by living conifer trees to protect wounds to their trunks and also known as resin or gum—had relatively few uses before the nineteenth century. It was an ingredient in the paint that coated the sides of ships above the water line and was also employed for a variety of medicinal purposes—as an external rub, a laxative, and a flea repellent. Turpentine also served to waterproof leather and cloth. The residue that remained in the still after the raw turpentine finished distilling, called rosin, possessed even fewer applications before 1800. Over the course of the nineteenth century, however, turpentine and rosin came to be used for a multitude of purposes. Spirits of turpentine became an important solvent in the growing rubber industry and an essential ingredient in a widely popular lamp oil. It was also employed in the manufacture of such diverse products as adhesives, pharmaceuticals, disinfectants, and shoe polish. Rosin was used as paper sizing and in the production of soap, floor covering, and paving material. These new applications expanded the demand for turpentine and rosin and spurred the naval stores industry's rapid expansion across the South during the nineteenth and early part of the twentieth centuries.[7]

In chronicling that expansion and analyzing the neglected southern naval stores industry through three interrelated dimensions—business, labor, and environment—this study addresses many of the connected issues historian Gerald Nash asked historians of the South to consider over three decades ago. Nash believed that "the growth of business and industry, readjustments in agriculture, the changing nature of the South's transportation system, its

---

7. Michael Williams, *Americans and Their Forests: A Historical Geography* (New York: Cambridge University Press, 1989), 83; Carroll B. Butler, *Treasures of the Longleaf Pines: Naval Stores* (Shalimar, Fla.: Tarkel, 1998), 3; Percival Perry, "The Naval Stores Industry in the Ante-Bellum South, 1789–1861" (Ph.D. diss., Duke University, 1947), 200–1; G. Melvin Herndon, "Naval Stores in Colonial Georgia," *Georgia Historical Quarterly* 52 (December 1968): 426; Percival Perry, "The Naval Stores Industry in the Old South, 1790–1860," *Journal of Southern History* 34 (November 1968): 511.

financial institutions, and its labor force all require further detailed investigation before we obtain a clearer conception of the tortuous course of industrialization in the twentieth-century South." Nash also argued that the region's timber industry, the role of government in the process of industrialization, and the use of applied science also deserved attention. In response to Nash's suggestion, this work explains the role of transportation improvements in the naval stores industry's expansion, the place of the factorage house in financing and even directing production, the adaptation of different labor systems to the unique manufacturing requirements, the application of forestry research, especially after 1900, and both state and federal governments' sometimes contradictory roles in shaping all of these elements. This study is not intended as an economic history in the methodological sense of the term, but rather as a broad analysis of a business and the region and people it impacted.[8]

Because southern industry shaped the lives of a significant number of people, despite its failure to meet the claims of southern boosters, this study examines not only the abstract labor systems employed in the industry, but also the day to day reality of workers and their families involved in the business. It analyzes work patterns—task difficulty, labor expectations, supervision, and incentives—as well as life in the camps, houses, and juke joints. Thomas Armstrong, who employs a similar approach in his study of the work experience and residential and family patterns of Georgia lumber workers, admits that, for the historian, concerns over meeting task requirements or maintaining a camp shanty (household) might seem mundane, but "for the workers these were often the questions which had daily meaning in their lives."[9]

This study also explores the part played by the environment—the piney woods—in shaping the experiences of laborers and producers who lived and worked in the region as well as the naval stores industry's development and how, in turn, the industry and its workers altered the environment. It serves to show that "social and environmental history," as environmental historian Alan Taylor argues, "are fundamentally compatible and mutually reinforcing" and together can show the "systematically unequal distribution of the rewards and burdens extracted from the environment." Such a pattern was deeply rooted in the southern naval stores industry's colonial past and persisted well into the twentieth century.[10]

8. Gerald D. Nash, "Research Opportunities in the Economic History of the South after 1880," *Journal of Southern History* 32 (August 1966): 314, 320–1.

9. Thomas F. Armstrong, "Georgia Lumber Laborers, 1880–1917: The Social Implications of Work," *Georgia Historical Quarterly* 67 (winter 1983): 436.

10. Alan Taylor, "Unnatural Inequalities: Social and Environmental Histories," *Environmental History* 1 (October 1996): 7–8, 16.

CHAPTER 1

ORIGINS OF A NAVAL STORES ECONOMY

OVER THE COURSE of the eighteenth century, North Carolina developed into the largest colonial producer and Britain's principal supplier of naval stores. England had manufactured its own naval stores supplies since the Middle Ages, but, no longer able to do so in the seventeenth century, turned to other western European sources for tar, pitch, and turpentine. For much of the 1600s, England found the quality and price of imported naval stores to be satisfactory. But by the beginning of the eighteenth century, wars and mercantilist trade policies scuttled this arrangement. Therefore, in 1704 England created an incentive program to encourage its North American colonies to increase their then-small output of naval stores. After a slow start, the program succeeded, and for most of the remainder of the colonial era, England enjoyed a steady, abundant supply of naval stores, most of them produced in North Carolina. For a variety of economic, environmental, and geographical reasons, North Carolina was particularly well suited for making naval stores. Although other colonies with similar capabilities produced tar, pitch, and turpentine, in them alternative commodities proved more profitable and crowded out naval stores products. North Carolina, with few other staple crops, therefore, never lost its hold on the naval stores trade once it achieved dominance after the 1720s. In fact, North Carolina produced so many naval stores that it ultimately became known as the "Tar Heel State."[1]

In the Middle Ages, England had supplied its own ship materials. As the

---

1. Hugh Talmage Lefler and Albert Ray Newsome, *North Carolina: The History of a Southern State* (Chapel Hill: University of North Carolina Press, 1954), 90.

country's merchant fleet and navy grew larger, its population increased, and its iron industry expanded; however, England's forest resources rapidly dwindled, causing wood product prices to climb. Ships required wood for lumber, planking, and masts, homes needed wood for heating, and iron forges burned charcoal, or carbonized wood. Coal proved to be an adequate substitute for heating, and iron manufacturers found alternative wood sources in Ireland. Shipbuilding supplies were more difficult to obtain. At the beginning of the seventeenth century, English shipyard managers sought materials from Prussia, the most important exporter of naval stores at the time. Soon, Sweden established itself as the primary European supplier. Sweden—whose territory by the late seventeenth century included not only what is today Sweden, but also Finland, Estonia, Livonia, and parts of northern Germany—made the highest-quality tar. Using Scotch pine, tar makers there employed a labor-intensive process that involved removing the bark of the tree from the base to a height of eight feet and leaving only four inches on the north side to sustain the tree's life. After standing this way for a year, the pines were cut and their pitchy bottom sections burned in a ground kiln. The process was both wasteful of timber resources and yielded little profit. For forest owners with tracts close to markets or transportation centers, significantly greater profits could be had from sawing timber into lumber. Only in the more remote areas where shipping charges for bulky lumber proved prohibitively expensive did owners find tar a profitable choice. Even there, tar manufacturing paid little, and farmers turned to it primarily as an income supplement.[2]

Despite production inefficiency, the Swedish tar makers offered England a reliable supply of a high-quality product at reasonable prices. The exclusion of forest products from the enumerative clause of the Navigation Act of 1660 suggests that England did not consider its dependence on Swedish naval stores a problem. In the mid-seventeenth century, however, a single firm, the Stockholm Tar Company, tightened its grip on the entire Swedish tar trade, and by the 1690s it possessed enough power to fix tar prices at home and abroad. As a result of the monopoly, between 1689 and 1699 prices more than doubled (from 5 pounds 15 shillings to 11 pounds for twelve

2. Kustaa Hautala, "European and American Tar in the English Market during the Eighteenth and Early Nineteenth Centuries," *Annales Academiæ Scientiarum Fennicæ* 130 (1964): 7–9; Sinclair Snow, "Naval Stores in Colonial Virginia," *Virginia Magazine of History and Biography* 72 (1964): 78; Mikko Airaksinen, "Tar Production in Colonial North America," *Environment and History* 2 (1996): 116; Stephen Innes, *Creating the Commonwealth: The Economic Culture of Puritan New England* (New York: W. W. Norton, 1995), 243; Robert Greenhalgh Albion, *Forests and Sea Power: The Timber Problem of the Royal Navy, 1652–1862* (Cambridge: Harvard University Press, 1926), 97, 123.

barrels). England scrambled to find a cheaper source. Improved trade relations with Russia following Peter the Great's visit to England in the 1690s, combined with Russia's rising naval stores production, offered hope for an alternative tar supplier. However, the tsar raised Russia's price to capitalize fully on this highly demanded product.[3]

In the early 1700s, England's problems in securing reasonably priced naval stores worsened. During the Great Northern War, the Russian army overran Finland, which resulted in a drop in the latter's naval stores production. England had imported 30,117 barrels of Swedish tar and pitch in 1701, but only 6,654 barrels arrived the following year. The War of the Spanish Succession, in which the English, Dutch, Austrians, and Prussians fought France and Spain from 1700 to 1713, led to a massive naval buildup that increased demand and pushed naval stores prices to record levels. By 1703, the cost of twelve barrels of tar had risen to twenty-two pounds, double its price before the war. At the same time, the Stockholm monopoly further tightened its control of the market. It no longer sold naval stores directly from Stockholm, but only through its factors abroad and only at the price and quantities set by the company. Moreover, all supplies sold to England were delivered exclusively aboard company ships. Not only did Stockholm force Britain to pay exorbitant prices for naval stores, but also British shipping interests lost a valuable cargo. England's cheap and stable naval stores supply had ended.[4]

England's dependent position in the early eighteenth century resulted from years of failed endeavors to develop naval stores production in its colonies. From the beginning of their efforts in North America, English financiers hoped their new colonies would produce, among other commodities that could be sold to England, naval stores. In 1585, Ralph Lane, the governor of the fledgling colony on Roanoke Island, reported "that what commodities soever Spaine, France, Italy, or the East parts do yeeld unto us in wines of all sortes, in oils, in flaxe, in rosens, pitch, frankenscence, currans, sugars & such like, these parts do abound with ye growth of them all." Prospects

3. Thomas R. Cox et al., *This Well-Wooded Land: Americans and Their Forests from Colonial Times to the Present* (Lincoln: University of Nebraska Press, 1985), 28; Justin Williams, "English Mercantilism and Carolina Naval Stores, 1705–1776," *Journal of Southern History* 1 (May 1935): 172; Hautala, "European and American Tar," 9–11, 22–3; Margaret Shove Morriss, "Colonial Trade of Maryland, 1689–1715," *Johns Hopkins University Studies in Historical and Political Science*, n.s., 3 (1914): 53.

4. Hautala, "European and American Tar," 19–20; Williams, "English Mercantilism," 173; Walter Allen Knittle, *The Early Eighteenth Century Palatine Emigration: A British Government Redemptioner Project to Manufacture Naval Stores* (Philadelphia: Dorrance, 1936), 114; Peter H. Wood, *Black Majority: Negroes in Colonial South Carolina from 1670 through the Stono Rebellion* (New York: W. W. Norton, 1974), 111.

for naval stores also appeared promising with Thomas Harriot's exploration of the Carolina coast. He claimed that "Pitch, Tarre, Rosen and Turpentine. There are those kinds of trees which yeeld them abundantly and great store." But any attempts by the Roanoke colonists to produce naval stores ended with the colonists' mysterious disappearance. However, the Jamestown colony, founded in 1607, met with early success in tar manufacturing. In 1608 the settlement was resupplied with a second group of colonists, among them Poles who knew the methods of tar and pitch making. With the English apprenticed to the Poles, Jamestown managed to include several barrels of naval stores among its first exports. But despite hopes that Virginia would become an important source for these products, the new colony soon lost interest in tar and pitch and cast its lot with another staple, tobacco, a crop that could deliver more substantial returns. When British officials pushed Virginians to produce naval stores—particularly tar—the colonists complained that there were no horses or other means to transport the wood necessary for production. Moreover, they argued, the threat of Indian attack made work in the forest too dangerous. Parliament tried to encourage tar production by allowing naval stores to be imported free of the four-shilling two-pence duty to which other commodities were subject. The effort apparently failed because, in 1682, the Virginia colonial government made its own attempt to increase production. That year the General Assembly declared tar legal tender in the colony, with each thirty-two-gallon barrel carrying a value of fifteen shillings. But like Parliament's, Virginia's attempt to encourage production met with little success. By 1698, the only place in the colony where naval stores were produced in any significant quantity was Elizabeth City County, and its products never exceeded 1,200 barrels annually.[5]

More than the Indian threat or a lack of horses, three significant disadvantages in profitably selling naval stores to overseas markets discouraged colonial production. First, shipping distances between North America and Britain vastly exceeded those between the Baltic and Britain and therefore resulted in significantly higher shipping costs for colonial suppliers, despite colonial measures to lower them. In an effort to hold down transport expenses, the Virginia General Assembly in 1640 set a standard shipping rate charge of six pounds per ton on products traveling from Virginia to England. Although the act was primarily designed to reduce the excessively high rates

5. David B. Quinn and Alison M. Quinn, *The First Colonists: Documents on the Planting of the First English Settlements in North America, 1584–1590* (Raleigh: North Carolina Department of Cultural Resources, Division of Archives and History, 1982), 22, 51; Snow, "Naval Stores in Colonial Virginia," 78–81, 91; Thomas Gamble, "Early History of the Naval Stores Industry in North America," in *Naval Stores: History, Production, Distribution, and Consumption,* ed. Thomas Gamble (Savannah: Review Publishing and Printing, 1921), correction of page 17.

for shipping tobacco, it applied to naval stores as well. Despite the act, though, by 1704, the cost of shipping naval stores from Virginia had climbed to eight pounds per ton. Exporters from the Baltic states paid only two pounds. Second, colonial labor costs also exceeded those in the Baltic states because of a worker shortage. Third, the colonists lacked experience in tar making, which resulted in lower productivity and a poorer-quality product than that made in Europe. For all three reasons, naval stores never became the predominant export of any colony during the seventeenth century. Virginians produced some naval stores, but concentrated on tobacco. The Carolinas exported a combination of beef, pork, rice, and naval stores, but not significant quantities of the latter before 1700. In the seventeenth century, New England became the first center of American naval stores production, but its exports failed to supply more than a small fraction of England's needs. New Englanders tended to favor lumbering and shipbuilding as more profitable enterprises for wood products and limited tar and pitch production to quantities required for their own needs.[6]

The Whig government, which controlled Britain in the early eighteenth century, felt new pressure to force colonial naval stores manufacturing. Coming to power in the Glorious Revolution of 1688, the Whigs strongly supported mercantilist policies that emphasized exporting the largest possible amount of products while importing as little as possible. Under their control in 1696 Parliament created the Board of Trade, which determined that the empire's mercantilist structure was not operating up to its potential. Not only were the colonies failing to supply adequately the raw materials for British manufacturing, but also the northern colonies actually posed a threat to the English wool industry. A shift to a more mercantilist-oriented trade policy, the Whigs believed, would help strengthen English manufacturing, increase the volume of English shipping, and develop the outer regions of the empire. Colonial naval stores production could help achieve all these ends.[7]

A combination of these three factors—the Scandinavian tar monopoly, Whiggish mercantilist support, and the threat of developing colonial manu-

6. Hautala, "European and American Tar," 42; Snow, "Naval Stores in Colonial Virginia," 91; Donald Fraser Martin, "An Historical and Analytical Approach to the American Gum Naval Stores Industry" (Ph.D. diss., University of North Carolina, 1942), 43–5; A. Stuart Campbell, Robert C. Unkrich, and Albert C. Blanchard, The Naval Stores Industry (Gainesville, Fla.: Bureau of Economic and Business Research, College of Business Administration, University of Florida, 1934), 8; Airaksinen, "Tar Production," 120; Innes, Creating the Commonwealth, 272; Wood, Black Majority, 110.

7. Williams, "English Mercantilism," 170–1; Hautala, "European and American Tar," 20; Knittle, Palatine Emigration, 122.

facturing—prodded Parliament to respond. In 1704 it passed "An Act for Encouraging the Importation of Naval Stores from America," legislation that one historian has described as "one of the most interesting and significant mercantilist experiments made by England during the whole colonial period." Encouragement took the form of bounties, or price subsidies, which compensated for the high shipping charges associated with transatlantic export. Effective January 1, 1705, and lasting nine years, the Navy Department would pay a bounty of four pounds per ton on tar and pitch, three pounds per ton of rosin and turpentine, six pounds per ton of hemp, and one pound for each ton of masts, yard-arms, and bowsprits. The Admiralty, however, had the right of refusal for up to twenty days of any colonial naval stores sent as part of the program. The act also made naval stores enumerated commodities; colonists could export tar, pitch, and turpentine only to British ports and aboard British or British colonial ships. Few colonists grumbled about the restriction; in essence the bounty act created a receptive market for colonial naval stores by forcing the British Navy to purchase them at inflated prices.[8]

The War of the Spanish Succession delayed the bounty act's effectiveness because the resulting high wartime freight rates, as much as four times those from Sweden, rendered the subsidy's compensation inadequate. While Swedish exporters paid only 5 shillings to ship a barrel of tar to England, Carolina colonists paid 1 pound 2 shillings, New England 18 shillings, and New York 16 shillings. Between 1708 and 1710 tar exports actually dropped. However, with the end of hostilities in 1713 and a subsequent decline in shipping costs, American tar achieved prominence in the British naval stores market and soon came to dominate it. Britain had imported only 177 barrels, or one-half of a percent, of its naval stores from the colonies in 1701. By 1714 the colonies supplied 11,639 barrels, or 25 percent. A year later the mother country imported nearly one-half of its naval stores from America, two years later a majority, and six years later 90 percent of its supply. Between 1716 and 1724 England received an annual average of 61,488 barrels of tar and pitch from the colonies and an annual average of only 12,849 from the Baltic. By 1725 the colonies provided England with more than it required for yearly use, so much so that England became a net exporter of naval stores, selling to Holland, Flanders, Germany, Spain, Portugal, and Ireland. Most importantly, Britain's import volume released it from its dependence on Sweden and, in fact, drove down the costs of the Swedish products.[9]

8. Williams, "English Mercantilism," 169; Charles Christopher Crittenden, *The Commerce of North Carolina, 1763–1789* (New Haven: Yale University Press, 1936), 37–9.

9. Hautala, "European and American Tar," 45–7; Martin, "American Gum Naval Stores Industry," 49; Herndon, "Naval Stores in Colonial Georgia," 427; Williams, "English Mercantilism," 175, 177–8.

Although highly successful in stimulating naval stores production, the 1704 act did not foster the industry where Whig administrators had wanted. They intended the act to boost naval stores manufacturing in the northern colonies whose export products actually competed with England's. New England and New York, with a climate similar to England's, produced commodities that could just as easily be made in the mother country. Much of the northern colonies' produce, consequently, had to be exported to other colonies. The mercantilists especially hoped that if New England could shift from wool to naval stores production, not only would competition with English woolen works diminish and an alternative source of tar and pitch open, but the colonists could use the profits from naval stores to purchase England's woolens. The act, in fact, called for bounties to be paid only on naval stores produced in the New England and middle colonies. But by the end of seventeenth century, New Englanders had relentlessly cut timber, especially pine, until its depletion curtailed even limited naval stores activities. The southeastern colonies, in contrast, possessed an abundance of longleaf pines, a species that yielded much more oleoresin than New England pines. Therefore, most of the tar, pitch, and limited amounts of turpentine that left northern ports originated from the southern colonies, especially Carolina. Southern producers exported naval stores through such northern ports as Philadelphia, New York, and Boston so they could collect the bounty. The British overlooked the origin of most naval stores because they were pleased with the volume they received. England remained determined, however, to build a northern naval stores industry, so determined that in 1709 it sent three thousand Palatine immigrants to New York and instructed them to produce naval stores. The effort failed when it lost its financing and the Germans, who were not accustomed to burning tar kilns, found they could prosper as farmers instead.[10]

While few pines grew in the northern colonies by the early eighteenth century, making naval stores manufacturing exceedingly difficult (as the Palatine immigrants discovered), an expansive pine forest covered the coastal plain of the southern colonies. In much of this area, longleaf pine, the best pine species for making naval stores, made up 80 percent of the trees. Only river bottom lands, where hardwoods and other pines grew, broke up this almost pure longleaf growth. A nineteenth-century traveler through the

10. Williams, "English Mercantilism," 168; Cox et al., *This Well-Wooded Land*, 28; Hautala, "European and American Tar," 15, 21, 42–3, 70–1; Snow, "Naval Stores in Colonial Virginia," 82; Knittle, *Palatine Emigration*, 120, 122, 128, 226, 133; Airaksinen, "Tar Production," 119; Martin, "American Gum Naval Stores Industry," 59–60; Carl E. Ostrom, "History of Gum Naval Stores Industry," *Chemurgic Digest* 4 (July 15, 1945): 219.

southern forest observed that "its features are monotonous in the extreme, varied only by alternate swamp and piney woods; the former bordering the water-courses, the latter covering the sandy ridges between." Stretching for nearly twelve hundred miles, from near Norfolk, Virginia, through the Carolinas, eastern Georgia, the Florida panhandle and northern peninsula, and southern Alabama and Mississippi, to portions of Louisiana and Texas, the longleaf pine forest of the southeastern coastal plain and Gulf South regions covered an estimated sixty million to ninety million acres. André Michaux, the French botanist who explored the United States' forests in the late eighteenth century, found only three significant areas in the southern pine belt where longleaf did not dominate, one in the Neuse River vicinity in North Carolina, another north of Columbia, South Carolina, and the third just north of Augusta, Georgia.[11]

The longleaf pine is particularly well adapted to the southern environment. As a pioneer tree species, the longleaf is first to appear on land where wind, water, fire, or human or animal activity has disturbed vegetation. In the absence of further disturbance, it gives way to a mixed forest of gum, oak, and other hardwood species. The mixture of hardwoods represents the natural climax forest for the southeastern United States' coastal plain. But in areas that experience frequent fires, caused either by lightning or humans, the longleaf remains dominant. Although hardwoods and other pine species are easily damaged or killed by fire, the longleaf's reproductive and growth characteristics render it well-suited to not only survive but to thrive in frequently burned over areas. Although it produces seed only at long intervals, usually no more than once every seven years, it does so in abundance. When the seeds reach maturity, the cone dries out and its scales spread apart, freeing the winged seeds, which then float to the ground. Although the relatively large size of the seeds permits foraging animals and birds to find them with ease, their weight enables them to penetrate undergrowth and reach the forest floor where they can germinate. The tops of new longleaf pines emerge in early winter but achieve little height growth. They remain at a low grass stage for three to ten years, depending on grow-

11. Porte Crayon, "North Carolina Illustrated: The Piney Woods," *Harper's New Monthly Magazine* 14 (May 1857): 745; Albion, *Forests and Sea Power*, 269; R. D. Forbes, *Timber Growing and Logging and Turpentining Practices in the Southern Pine Region* (Washington, D.C.: United States Department of Agriculture, 1930), 7; Edward Buckner, "Prehistory of the Southern Forest," *Forest Farmer* 54 (July-August 1995): 21; Thomas C. Croker, Jr., "The Longleaf Pine Story," *Southern Lumberman* (December 1979): 69; S. W. Greene, "The Forest That Fire Made," reprint from *American Forests,* Austin Cary Memorial Forestry Collection, Department of Special Collections, George A. Smathers Libraries, University of Florida, 2; F. André Michaux, *The North American Sylva* (Philadelphia: D. Rice and A. N. Hart, 1857), 107.

ing conditions, which puts the longleaf at a disadvantage to other tree species, especially other pines. Slash and loblolly pines, for example, grow considerably faster at an early stage and can crowd out the squat longleaf seedlings. But the longleaf's slow growth gives it superb fire resistance. Until the first autumn after germination, very young longleafs are as susceptible to fire as other species. However, after that, when the stem reaches six inches tall, the longleaf is well protected from fire by a covering of heavy eight- to fifteen-inch needles that grow in bundles of three. At this stage, the seedling grows a deep root system in which it stores a reserve food supply. In the event it loses its crown of needles in a fire, the seedling can draw on the energy stored in the root to grow a new set. Once the grass stage ends, the longleaf begins rapid height growth for two or three years, and is once again susceptible to fire. If it survives, though, it develops a layer of heavy bark, from one-quarter to one-half inch thick, that can protect it from most fires for the rest of its life. From this point on the longleaf requires fire to eliminate the competing tree species. In fact, it is seldom successful in wet areas, where fires occur infrequently. In such places other tree species shade the longleaf out during its short, grass stage years.[12]

The southeastern forests endured frequent fires. Some had natural causes. The heat and humidity the region experienced during the warmer months encouraged thunderstorms and lightning that sparked fires. But because most lightning strikes were accompanied by precipitation which moistened the forest floor, the fires they started often burned slowly, low to the ground, and, consequently, rarely spread. On occasion they could smolder until extinguished by the next rain. Lightning, however, was only a secondary cause of the fires that created the longleaf pine forest. Native Americans were responsible for most of the fires in the southeastern forest. "It was in large measure owing to the Indian and his Grandfather Fire," explains Stephen J. Pyne, historian of fire in America, "that the forest primeval had already been widely cleared, converted, and otherwise managed." Environmental historian Albert E. Cowdrey maintains that in the hands of native Americans, "fire became central to the maintenance of a human-centered ecology." Burning served as a means of sustaining a balance in the forest

12. Timothy Silver, *A New Face on the Countryside: Indians, Colonists, and Slaves in South Atlantic Forests, 1500–1800* (New York: Cambridge University Press, 1990), 18; Buckner, "Prehistory of the Southern Forest," 21; Albert E. Cowdrey, *This Land, This South: An Environmental History*, rev. ed. (Lexington: University Press of Kentucky, 1996), 15; Forbes, *Timber Growing*, 7–11, 25; Howard E. Weaver and David A. Anderson, *Manual of Southern Forestry* (Danville, Ill.: Interstate Printers and Publishers, 1954): 38–9; Lenthall Wyman, *Florida Naval Stores* (Tallahassee: State of Florida, Department of Agriculture, 1929), 5; Greene, "Forest That Fire Made," 2–3; Michaux, *North American Sylva*, 107.

that supported the Indian economy. It was the only way for Indians to maintain their population in the temperate forest that developed in eastern North
America at the end of the last ice age. By the time vegetation in a temperate
forest reaches its most mature stage, it has developed a two- or three-layer
canopy that shades the ground enough to prevent grass and undergrowth
development. Such a forest sustains relatively low plant and animal populations, making human habitation difficult for all but the smallest communities. Since the beginning of the Holocene period, which began ten thousand
years ago and marks the disappearance of the mega fauna, Indians relied on
bison, deer, elk, and other grazing animals as their source of protein. To
encourage the growth of grasses and shrubs on which this game could feed,
Native Americans periodically burned the undergrowth to keep the forest
open, a common practice among both pastoral and farming cultures. Indians
also used fire to herd their prey together for easier hunting and to improve
their own quality of life in the forest. Fire drove off mosquitoes, flies, snakes,
and other pests. It also improved the production of edible berries, eased nut
gathering by clearing away debris, opened the forest for better travel, boosted security by giving better visibility, unlocked nutrients for trees and
grasses, and discouraged larger forest fires by clearing away their fuel, forest
debris.[13]

The accumulation rate of ground litter—leaves, needles, branches, and
twigs—varies with forest type. In pine forests it tends to collect more rapidly
than it does in hardwood or mixed forests, but the volume at any given time
depends on the burning frequency. Pyne explains that "under natural conditions the intensity and frequency of fire varies according to the work required of it: The greater the litter, the more intense the fire; the more
frequently litter is built up, the more frequent the fire." By keeping accumulation to a minimum, Indians, who may have fired the southern coastal plain
woods as often as twice a year, ensured that fire had only enough fuel to
burn slowly and at ground level. Besides fuel accumulation, other factors
that contributed to fire intensity include precipitation patterns, relative humidity, wind speed and direction, ground slope, and temperature. During
periods of average precipitation, only the upper layer of debris burned because the lower layer remained damp and fire resistant. Indians allowed

13. Silver, *New Face on the Countryside*, 18, 60–3; Stephen J. Pyne, *Fire in America: A Cultural History of Wildland and Rural Fire* (Princeton: Princeton University Press, 1982), 74, 83;
Cowdrey, *This Land, This South*, 14; Thomas Hansbrough, "Human Behavior and Forest Fires,"
in *Southern Forests and Southern People*, ed. Thomas Hansbrough (Baton Rouge: Louisiana
State University Press, 1963), 22–3; Buckner, "Prehistory of the Southern Forest," 20; M. Williams, *Americans and Their Forests*, 43; Greene, "Forest That Fire Made," 3; Forbes, *Timber
Growing*, 25.

such fires, which offered no threat to their life or property, to burn until they reached water courses or were put out by rain. These fires rarely harmed hardwoods and other pine species which occupied the swampy terrain that seldom played host to fires. But when areas that had escaped fire for a number of years finally did burn, considerable damage occurred, especially if the flames began spreading through the treetops. Because Indian burning was primarily localized and not all areas of the forest received even burning, such occasions were not uncommon. Lush undergrowth and a thick layer of debris could fuel a conflagration, which, if started during a period of summer drought when the entire forest floor was dry, could consume everything in its path. Such hot fires were especially damaging during the spring and summer seasons, when wood cells grew, and in dense stands of young trees. The vast differences in forest fire frequency and characteristics created different vegetation environments. Intense fires during dry periods could eliminate trees altogether, creating open fields with dense shrub growth on their periphery, while areas that experienced frequent low-burning fires became savannas with widely spaced trees, little undergrowth, and lush grasses.[14]

Indians, therefore, "made an indelible impact on the forest" through burning, historical geographer Michael Williams explains. "Far from being incapable of modifying his environment, the Indian created it, gradually replacing dense forest with thinner forest, thinner forest with grassland, and changing the composition of the standing forest." As the native population declined with the arrival of Europeans, cultural pressure on the environment relaxed and reduced the need for frequent burning. But European settlers quickly adopted and continued the Indian patterns, a practice that lasted for centuries and for a time enabled the longleaf to retain its dominance over the coastal plain.[15]

In addition to its ability to endure fire, other features of the longleaf favored its growth in the southeastern coastal plain. The tree thrives in poor, dry soil. With the exception of river flood plains, where longleafs rarely prospered, the soil of the southeastern coastal plain is relatively infertile. Southern topsoils are old, having endured the leaching effects of rain much longer than northern topsoils. They have also experienced more the process that reduces soil to a mixture of clay and aluminum hydroxides and iron hydrox-

14. Pyne, *Fire in America*, 35; Buckner, "Prehistory of the Southern Forest," 21; Silver, *New Face on the Countryside*, 18, 60; Greene, "Forest That Fire Made," 3; Forbes, *Timber Growing*, 25; M. Williams, *Americans and Their Forests*, 43; Cowdrey, *This Land, This South*, 14.

15. M. Williams, *Americans and Their Forests*, 43–4, 49; Buckner, "Prehistory of the Southern Forest," 22; Hansbrough, "Human Behavior," 23; Cowdrey, *This Land, This South*, 15.

ides. In such soils the soluble nutrients from organic decomposition are carried into the subsoil, beyond the reach of many plants' root structures. But
the longleaf's taproot, which penetrates well into the ground, enables it to
survive in such soils where the growth of other trees would be slow. Its long
taproot also helps the longleaf withstand severe weather conditions. During
dry periods it can access water deep down, and in high winds the taproot
acts as an anchor to prevent it from blowing over.[16]

Despite its ability to withstand harsh conditions—fire, poor soil, low precipitation, and high winds—the longleaf is not invincible. When the seedling
first emerges, ants may attack it, biting out the tenderest parts. Only after
the formation of needles does their threat end. Also, more than any other
pine species the longleaf is susceptible to brown-spot needle blight, a disease
that strikes seedlings that dead grass and rough have covered. Since young
longleafs can spend up to ten years as seedlings, they are easy targets for
needle blight. As its name suggests, the disease causes brown spots to form
on the needles. In severe cases, the young pine is defoliated and dies. Once
the young trees are two feet high, however, they are less susceptible to such
a damaging attack. Another enemy of the longleaf pine, feral hogs, were
especially destructive. These hogs, which savored the longleafs' energy-
packed taproots and terminal buds, could destroy scores of seedlings a day.
Introduced by the Spanish, hogs had little effect on existing forests because
they posed no threat to mature trees, but in later years, wild hogs became a
significant cause of the longleaf's inability to reproduce itself.[17]

Because of their abundance of longleaf pine, southern colonists, especially those in the Carolinas, were well situated to manufacture naval stores.
From the 1700s to the 1720s, most Carolina naval stores came from the region between the Cape Fear River and Charleston, South Carolina. In his
1709 account of travels through Carolina, John Lawson observed that "as for
Pitch and Tar, none of the Plantations are comparable for offering the vast
Quantities of Naval Stores, as this Place does." Planters in the colony took
advantage of their ability to make tar and pitch on a large scale. They possessed not only significant holdings of longleaf pine forest, but numerous
slaves, whom they set to building and burning tar kilns. After the bounty
made naval stores an attractive export product, some planters bought even
more slaves on credit to cash in on the trade's increased profitability. They

16. Cowdrey, *This Land, This South,* 2; Silver, *New Face on the Countryside,* 18; Forbes,
Timber Growing, 8–9.

17. F. C. Craighead, "Insects That Attack Southern Pines," 9, Cary Collection; Greene,
"Forest That Fire Made," 3; Weaver and Anderson, *Manual of Southern Forestry,* 286; Jack Tem-
ple Kirby, *Poquosin: A Study of Rural Landscape and Society* (Chapel Hill: University of North
Carolina Press, 1995), 205–6.

operated on a grand scale, employing their large slave labor forces in thousands of acres of pine forest. Between 1705 and 1718, Carolina exported 134,212 barrels of tar and pitch, and until the 1720s, naval stores export tonnage exceeded that of any other product.[18]

The sparsely settled Cape Fear Valley produced only small quantities of tar, pitch, and turpentine until the 1720s, when settlers began spreading up the river. Like their counterparts farther south, many naval stores producers in the Cape Fear Valley owned abundant land in the longleaf belt and controlled slave labor forces of considerable size. The Cape Fear and its tributaries provided makers of tar and other naval stores products with an extensive water transportation system. The first part of the journey was usually overland. Laborers drove a stick through each barrel of naval stores and left both ends protruding so it could serve as an axle. A draft animal drew the barrel, which rolled on its own hoops, to a landing, where workers sawed both ends of the stick off leaving it in the barrel. Then rafts took barrels of naval stores to points where they could be collected for export aboard larger vessels. The port at Brunswick, laid out in 1727 on the west bank of the Cape Fear River, handled most of the region's early naval stores exports. A rival port, Newton, planned in 1733 and incorporated as Wilmington in 1739, gradually drew commerce from Brunswick until, by the Revolution, Wilmington enjoyed the most active trade.[19]

Slaves typically labored at tar making during the winter and at crop cultivation and limited turpentine production during the warmer months. During the winter slaves built tar kilns, first gathering pine lightwood, then splitting it to the thickness of a man's leg, and finally building and firing kilns to extract the tar. They made earthen kilns by digging shallow pits as large as twenty-four feet in diameter. The floors of these pits sloped toward the center, from which a gutter led to the perimeter and extended outward anywhere from two to ten feet, providing a means of channeling tar from the kiln. Workers placed two- to three-foot-long pieces of split pine wood

18. Norman Hawley, "Naval Stores: America's First Widespread Forest Industry," *Southern Lumberman* (December 15, 1966): 163; John Lawson, *A New Voyage to Carolina* (1709; reprint, Chapel Hill: University of North Carolina Press, 1967), 11; Williams, "English Mercantilism," 176; Lawrence Lee, *The Lower Cape Fear in Colonial Days* (Chapel Hill: University of North Carolina Press, 1965), 59–60, 97, 151; Hautala, "European and American Tar," 76; Wood, *Black Majority*, 55, 110.

19. Lee, *Lower Cape Fear*, 97, 151–2; Harry Roy Merrens, *Colonial North Carolina in the Eighteenth Century* (Chapel Hill: University of North Carolina, 1964), 89–90, 106; William S. Powell, *North Carolina through Four Centuries* (Chapel Hill: University of North Carolina Press, 1989), 83; Crittenden, *Commerce of North Carolina*, 42, 57; Thomas J. Schoenbaum, *Islands, Capes, and Sounds: The North Carolina Coast* (Winston-Salem, N.C.: John F. Blair, 1982), 225, 227.

into these pits. The wood pile extended up and out over the sides of the pit until it formed what English traveler J. F. D. Smyth described as a "circular pyramid," that often reached from twenty-five to thirty feet in diameter and was ten to twelve feet high. Slaves covered the structure with earth and clay, sometimes mixed with pine straw, so that only an opening at the top was left. The kiln was then fired through this top vent, often around sundown. After a day of burning, the tar began to flow, falling first to the bottom of the kiln, then sliding to the center, and running out through the gutter, and finally collecting in a trough from which workers dipped it into barrels. Once the top wood was ignited and the combustion had begun to penetrate downward, workers covered the top hole and made vents in the walls. Slaves manning the burning kiln, it was reported in *American Husbandry,* "temper the heat as they think proper, by thrusting a stick through the earth, and letting the air in at as many places as they find necessary." If the kiln burned too fast, black smoke arose, indicating that the tar was burning before it reached the bottom. A hard wind from one direction could build up the fire on one side, requiring a worker to climb to the top of the kiln and stomp hard to seal the vents and smother the blaze. Building a tar kiln was not strenuous work but did require limited technical skill. Monitoring a kiln only meant keeping a constant eye on the flow of tar and the amount of smoke. But the job did require patience. A typical kiln that produced from 100 to 130 barrels of tar could take eight to nine days to burn completely. While the kiln burned, tar makers probably lived in brush lean-tos and did their own cooking as did those laborers who continued this occupation in the nineteenth century. Although neither stimulating nor exhausting work, firing a tar kiln could be hazardous. Workers who fell into them while sealing vents could be burned to death. Those who were injured were often miles from help. One observer found that in accidents with the kilns, "*Negroes* have been very much burnt or scalded."[20]

Although probably not as hazardous as tar production, work in turpentine manufacturing required special training. John Brickell's *Natural History*

20. Harry J. Carman, ed., *American Husbandry* (Port Washington, N.Y.: Kennikat Press, 1939), 244–5; Williams, "English Mercantilism," 180; John Brickell, *The Natural History of North-Carolina* (1737; reprint, New York: Johnson Reprint, 1969), 265–6; Snow, "Naval Stores in Colonial Virginia," 78; John Macleod, "The Tar and Turpentine Business in North Carolina," *Monthly Journal of Agriculture* 2 (July 1846): 17–8; Michaux, *North American Sylva,* 114; "Journal of a French Traveler in the Colonies," *American Historical Review* 26 (July 1921): 734; John Ferdinand Dalziel Smyth, *A Tour in the United States of America* (1784; reprint, New York: Arno Press, 1968), 95–7; William Tryon to Sewallis Shirley, 26 July 1765, *The Correspondence of William Tryon and Other Selected Papers,* vol. 1, ed. William S. Powell (Raleigh: Division of Archives and History, Department of Cultural Resources, 1980), 139.

of North-Carolina, published in 1737, describes slaves laboring to produce tur-
pentine. "The Planters," he writes, "make their Servants or *Negroes* cut large
Cavities on each side of the *Pitch-Pine* Tree (which they term *Boxing of the
Tree*) wherein the *Turpentine* runs, and the *Negroes* with Ladles take it out
and put it into Barrels." In 1765 a Frenchman traveling through North Carolina also noted that slaves worked in tar and pitch production and "that one
Negroe will tend 3000 [boxes], which will rendr about 100 Barls. terpentin."
Producers distilled little of the raw turpentine their slaves collected, "few
giving themselves to the trouble." The refining process required not only
considerable skill, but also the construction of large iron stills, which necessitated considerable capital outlay.[21]

Delighted by the increased export volume of colonial naval stores produced largely by these slave laborers, Britain was, nevertheless, greatly dis-
appointed with the products' quality. British buyers, as a rule, complained
about the condition of many colonial goods; they claimed, for example, that
colonial flour was too old and course, tobacco dark and sour, timber poorly
dried, linseed light in weight, and beeswax dirty in color. But naval stores,
particularly tar, appear to have been of especially poor quality. Consumers
grumbled that manufacturers added foreign matter—dirt, sticks, water,
grass—to barreled tar to increase its weight. Trash also accidentally mixed
with tar as it drained from earthen, woodland kilns. Ship builders and captains reported that the poor-quality, or "hot," tar "burned" the rigging, but
modern scholars disagree on the nature of the harm. Some maintain that
the inferior tar's acidity damaged the ropes. Timothy Silver explains that
"the high temperatures of the kilns led to the accumulation of wood acids
in the tar. When applied to the ship's rigging, those acids sometimes weakened or 'burned' the very ropes the tar was supposed to protect." Others
believe the complaints referred to how the hot temperature of melted tar
actually caught the ropes on fire. Before workers applied tar, it had to be
heated until its consistency was thin enough for it to penetrate into the rope
fiber. Colonial tar, the argument goes, was so thick and the temperature at
which it reached viscosity so high, that it literally burned the rope upon
application. "So by calling tar hot," Mikko Airaksinen writes, "the dockyard
workers actually meant it was too thick." Finally, tar often sat for long periods on wharves, where, unprotected from the hot sun, its temperature could
rise to degrees that permitted it to melt and ooze from cracks in poorly constructed barrels. Many barrels shipped from the colonies were reportedly
made of green timber. Although the cooper may have fashioned a tight bar-

21. Brickell, *Natural History of North-Carolina,* 265, 267; "Journal of a French Traveler,"
733.

rel at his shop, as the staves dried they contracted, opening cracks between them.[22]

As with tar, British consumers also complained about the quality of colonial pitch and turpentine. Buyers claimed that colonists processed their pitch only halfway, thus increasing its volume but rendering it useless. Colonial pitch was also reputed to contain dirt, rocks, and debris, a result of having been processed in earthen pits. Naturalist William Bartram, who toured the southeast in the 1770s, described the primitive method that led to the adulteration. He explained that "when they design to make pitch, they dig large holes in the ground, near the tar kiln, which they line with a thick coat of good clay, into which they conduct a sufficient quantity of tar, and set it on fire, suffering it to flame and evaporate a length of time sufficient to convert it into pitch, and when cool, lade it into barrels, and so on until they have consumed all the tar, or made a sufficient quantity of pitch for their purpose." Producers were also accused of packing pitch, like tar, into weak barrels that leaked. Turpentine quality received similar complaints. British buyers claimed that colonial turpentine, most of it shipped as raw gum, contained an abundance of wood chips, water, and other foreign matter. The barrels in which the colonists shipped it were so inferior and prone to leakage, the British said, that some originally packed with three hundred pounds of turpentine could arrive in Britain weighing only a few pounds.[23]

Three factors contributed to the low quality of American naval stores. First, the producers' economic situation—abundant timber and scarce labor—demanded that they extract the quickest return from their land with the least possible labor and capital expenditures. Producers, therefore, avoided the labor-intensive Baltic practice of barking and felling the trees from which to secure wood to build kilns, which produced high-quality "green tar," and instead instructed their slaves to gather dead pine wood in the forest. A second and related reason for poor-quality colonial tar, especially among less wealthy producers, was the practice of collecting dead wood from ungranted lands. No law forbade the scavenging of fallen limbs from unowned property, but to bark a tree and then later cut it down, as the Baltic method required, constituted trespassing. Third, American tar makers did not always choose shortcuts but simply did not know proper techniques.

22. Hautala, "European and American Tar," 58; Snow, "Naval Stores in Colonial Virginia," 88; Crittenden, *Commerce of North Carolina,* 58; Silver, *New Face on the Countryside,* 127; Airaksinen, "Tar Production," 121.

23. Crittenden, *Commerce of North Carolina,* 58; William Bartram, *Travels through North and South Carolina, Georgia, East and West Florida, the Cherokee Country, the Extensive Territories of the Muscogulges or Creek Confederacy, and the Country of the Choctaws,* in *William Bartram: Travels and Other Writings* (New York: Library of America, 1996), 339.

Since Britain had produced almost no naval stores for many decades before North American colonization, English settlers possessed little practical knowledge of tar making. Neither did their slaves. Whereas Africans arrived in America with an understanding of rice production, knowledge South Carolina planters quickly put to use, Africans had no prior experience with naval stores. Neither slaves nor producers knew the best wood to use and, as North Carolina governor Gabriel Johnston suspected, fired kilns to such high temperatures that all of the wood's juices came out with the tar.[24]

Enterprising colonists attempted to evade criticism of their tar by making pitch from it and marketing that product instead. Good pitch could be produced from even the poorest-quality tar, but pitch did not bring the profits that tar did. One barrel of pitch required two barrels of tar, thus reducing the quantity of marketable goods by half. Since the bounties for tar and pitch were the same, four pounds per ton, producers lost half of the potential profits by making pitch. From the colonists' perspective, however, receiving one-half payment for their pitch was better than receiving nothing for the tar that the navy rejected as substandard. Another advantage of pitch was that its shipping costs were half that of tar. Shipping firms favored hauling pitch over tar because tar had a tendency to leak from its barrels and ruin other merchandise during the voyage. This export pattern did not serve the purpose England had intended for the bounty because Britain's shipyards needed more tar than they did pitch. Furthermore, colonial pitch production contradicted the mercantilist economic policy. England, not the colonies, was supposed to refine goods.[25]

The British navy expressed disgust at the colonists' shift toward pitch production, the excessive expense of the bounty program, and the poor-quality tar they received at high cost. Between 1705 and 1724, the navy paid a yearly average of £18,703 for colonial naval stores. In years of active production the cost ran considerably higher—£27,410 in 1716 and £52,011 in 1718. Many British administrators advocated an end to the bounty system, favoring acquisition of naval stores supplies from the troublesome Baltic suppliers. Despite opposition, Parliament finally succeeded in renewing the bounty act in 1713 for eleven more years in anticipation that American tar quality would improve. By the early 1720s, however, standards had still not risen and prospects for the act's renewal at the end of 1724 appeared bleak. With the ap-

24. Martin, "American Gum Naval Stores Industry," 62; Cox et al., *This Well-Wooded Land*, 17; Snow, "Naval Stores in Colonial Virginia," 83; Lee, *Lower Cape Fear*, 53; Hautala, "European and American Tar," 58.

25. Airaksinen, "Tar Production," 123; Hautala, "European and American Tar," 64–8; Snow, "Naval Stores in Colonial Virginia," 92.

proaching bounty renewal threatened by mounting criticism, Parliament passed an act in 1722, to take effect on September 29, 1724, that would exclude from the bounty program any tar not made by the Swedish method. Some colonial producers fought unsuccessfully for the act's repeal. Others attempted the required method, but, unfamiliar with the technique, barked all the way around the trunk, essentially girdling it, and causing the tree's death. In the end, Parliament's effort to force a change in procedure succeeded no better than earlier colonial attempts. Little more green tar found its way to England, and the navy continued to complain. The act's greatest effect was to reduce naval stores production in areas with high labor costs—the northern colonies and South Carolina—and to push it into areas settled by poorer colonists, including the region surrounding North Carolina's Albemarle Sound.[26]

Throughout 1724, representatives of the tar issue's two sides refused to compromise, and on January 1, 1725, the bounty expired. Over the next few years, colonial naval stores exports to England dropped nearly 60 percent, from 81,003 barrels in 1725 to 66,667 barrels in 1726 to 34,277 barrels in 1727. The colonies simply could not compete with the Baltic states' lower production and shipping costs. The higher labor and shipping costs made a barrel of colonial tar seven and one-half shillings more expensive to produce and transport than a barrel of Finnish tar. The bounty had provided a payment of ten shillings per barrel, a payment that more than compensated for the colonists' disadvantage. With the act's disappearance, Russia and Sweden, who offered a better product at a cheaper price, resumed their exports to Britain. All was not well under the new situation, however. In the absence of competition from the English colonies, Sweden raised its prices. In addition, the English shipping business suffered with the colonial naval stores industry's decline, since British vessels lost the extra business that the naval stores bounty had generated. In part to end the shipping depression, Parliament restored the bounty in 1729.[27]

The new act subsidized colonial naval stores, but on terms more acceptable to the navy than those of the previous program. Tar made using the Swedish method received four pounds per ton, but the act reduced payment for common tar to two pounds four shillings per ton, and the payment for pitch to one pound per ton. Furthermore, only the lowest-quality tar, the

26. Williams, "English Mercantilism," 181, 183; Hautala, "European and American Tar," 48, 61; Snow, "Naval Stores in Colonial Virginia," 83; Martin, "American Gum Naval Stores Industry," 53.

27. Williams, "English Mercantilism," 175, 179, 184; Herndon, "Naval Stores in Colonial Georgia," 427; Snow, "Naval Stores in Colonial Virginia," 86; Hautala, "European and American Tar," 46, 48.

last half to emerge from the kiln, could be made into pitch. One pound ten shillings was paid for every ton of turpentine. In sum, the new act attempted to tailor production to England's needs. It encouraged higher-quality tar, reduced the reward for making common tar, and made pitch production a practice of last resort with only the worst tar. For the remainder of the colonial period Parliament unfailingly renewed the bounty act, once in 1742, again in 1750, and for the last time in 1758.[28]

The colonial naval stores industry quickly rebounded. England received 33,062 barrels from the colonies in 1730, 47,541 in 1731, and 70,428 in 1732. But these exports did not come as heavily from South Carolina as they had before the bounty act's lapse at the end of 1724. First, in the southern portion of South Carolina, the Yamasee War of 1715 had already disrupted naval stores production. Second, many producers in the colony had purchased slaves on credit to take advantage of the high naval stores prices resulting from the bounty. When the subsidies stopped, these indebted slave masters faced ruin unless they could find another way to put their slaves to profitable employment. South Carolina thus reduced naval stores manufacturing and turned its slaves' energy toward increased rice production. The cultivation of rice continued after 1729 because at the same time Parliament revived the naval stores subsidy, it also repealed restrictions on the rice trade. Third, indigo offered yet another alternative to naval stores, especially after 1748, when Parliament granted a subsidy of six pence per pound on indigo shipped directly to England. The naval stores bounty act's premium of four pounds per ton for green tar could not compete with these more profitable uses for slave labor. While tar and pitch production in South Carolina never ended entirely as a result of these circumstances, that colony's tar exports dropped in both relative and absolute figures and remained low for the remainder of the colonial period. By the first half of the 1760s, exports of tar, pitch, and turpentine from Charleston had dropped almost 65 percent from the first half of the 1730s. "South Carolinians," one historian explains, "believed that they had better things to do."[29]

28. Williams, "English Mercantilism," 184; Snow, "Naval Stores in Colonial Virginia," 86–7; A. K. Thurmond, Jr., "The Early American Naval Stores Industry," 6, Olustee Experiment Station Files, Georgia Agrirama, Tifton, Ga.; Hautala, "European and American Tar," 44.

29. Williams, "English Mercantilism," 176, 181; Robert M. Weir, *Colonial South Carolina: A History* (Millwood, N.Y.: KTO Press, 1983), 108, 145, 149–50; Lee, *Lower Cape Fear,* 97; Hautala, "European and American Tar," 79–81, 163; Henry Laurens to James Cowles, 22 July 1755, *The Papers of Henry Laurens,* ed. Philip M. Hamer et al. (Columbia: University of South Carolina Press, 1968), 1:297, and Henry Laurens to Henry Bright, 12 November 1763, 4:44; United States Department of Commerce, *Historical Statistics of the United States, Colonial Times to 1970,* bicentennial ed. (Washington, D.C.: U.S. Dept. of Commerce, 1975), 2:1194.

Yet North Carolina's naval stores exports, as a whole, increased during the late colonial era. The industry continued in the Cape Fear Valley and spread northward into the counties surrounding the Albemarle Sound. Only a sparse population of settlers inhabited the Albemarle area by 1730. The region's small farmers and backwoodsmen owned few slaves and contributed little to the colony's staple export trade except limited amounts of tobacco. Living among the longleaf pines, however, they could use their own labor to make and burn tar kilns and tap trees for raw turpentine. The renewed bounty on naval stores made production of these commodities profitable for Albemarle settlers, who heretofore had made only limited quantities. Because northeastern North Carolinians lacked the capital resources to invest in large slave labor forces and huge timber tracts, they manufactured naval stores on a small, part-time level, performing most of the work themselves, and often using timber they did not own.[30]

Not only did naval stores producers in the Albemarle region lack the financial means to develop large operations, they faced the challenge of transporting their goods to the open sea. The Albemarle region possessed no significant watercourses, such as the Cape Fear River, which could connect it to a port facility accessible to oceangoing ships. Exasperated ship captains had to ply its smallish rivers, picking up barrels of naval stores from the many small landings that dotted the banks. Even the largest Albemarle port, Edenton, could be reached from the Atlantic only with considerable time and difficulty.[31] In the 1780s Johann David Schoepf, a German traveling through the confederation, described this challenge:

> The road which ships must take coming in from the sea by the navigable and best channels is as much as 180 miles long, although the town [Edenton] itself is not more than 35–40 miles from the sea in a direct line. There would be a shorter passage if the Roanoke and other inlets were navigable for vessels even of a moderate tonnage. Coming in, vessels must first pass the Occacock Bar, where at high tide there is no more than 13 ft. water; and then there lies in the way another bank, 2–3 miles wide, called the Swash, consisting of firm sand, and at the highest tide giving a depth of only 9 ft. Ships, therefore, often

30. Hautala, "European and American Tar," 82; W. W. Ashe, *The Forests, Forest Lands, and Forest Products of Eastern North Carolina* (Raleigh: North Carolina Geological Survey, 1894), 18; Lefler and Newsome, *North Carolina*, 90, 113; W. Neil Franklin, "Agriculture in Colonial North Carolina," *North Carolina Historical Review* 3 (October 1926): 553–4; Hugh Williamson to John Jay, 14 January 1784, *The John Gray Blount Papers*, vol. 1, ed. Alice Barnwell Keith (Raleigh: State Department of Archives and History, 1952), 150.

31. Merrens, *Colonial North Carolina*, 91, 106.

take 8–12 days entering and clearing the Sound, at times must wait months for a favorable opportunity, and then are subject to the very inconvenience of lading and unlading at a distance from the town by means of lighters. And when at last a ship is freighted and past all obstacles, shortly after getting into the ocean the Gulf Stream must be contended with, which in this latitude approaches very near the main-land.[32]

Given shipping difficulties from their own state, some North Carolina producers near the Virginia border preferred to transport their naval stores overland to Norfolk. The volume of this traffic reached such a high level that Virginia, which remained an unimportant tar-producing colony itself, generated revenue from North Carolina naval stores by charging a duty of eighteen pence on each barrel of pitch and twelve pence on each barrel of tar that left the colony.[33]

Difficult market access also influenced North Carolina's economy by discouraging commercial lumber operations from developing in the Albemarle region as they had along the Cape Fear River. "It is found much more profitable," the author of American Husbandry explained, "to apply the timber they cut down to this use [turpentine] than to saw it or export it in any kind of lumber; and the tar &c. being far more valuable in proportion to bulk, is a circumstance of great importance in a country that does not abound with good ports." Moreover, the expensive mill equipment was well beyond the means of the relatively poor Albemarle settlers.[34]

From the mid-eighteenth century to the Revolution, the naval stores industry spread into the Washington and New Bern areas, and slowly migrated up the Tar and Neuse Rivers. In 1811, local historian Jeremy Battle explained that settlers from around the Albemarle region introduced naval stores production in Edgecombe County, through which the Tar River flowed. "The natives of this county . . . would have starved," he argued, "had they been possessed of no other means of subsistence. Emigrants from Virginia and the northeastern Counties of this State, settled on these barren lands, and converted the pines into meat, bread and money." Naval stores production grew increasingly important in the area west of the Pamlico Sound, which by the end of the eighteenth century represented the heart of North American naval stores manufacturing. In the Albemarle region production gradu-

32. Johann David Schoepf, Travels in the Confederation (1788; reprint, New York: Burt Franklin, 1968), 111–2.

33. Ashe, Forests, Forest Lands, and Forest Products, 18; Snow, "Naval Stores in Colonial Virginia," 91–2.

34. Merrens, Colonial North Carolina, 99; Carman, American Husbandry, 245.

ally declined so that by the end of the period it produced little naval stores. Virginia naval stores production, only a small part of that colony's economy, also declined. In 1743, England received approximately 8,000 barrels of tar and pitch out of the 10,000 made in Virginia. But from October 1764 to October 1765 only 470 left the upper James River area.[35]

Like the upper Albemarle area and Virginia, other regions of North America produced limited quantities of naval stores but failed to sustain an important and lasting industry. During Georgia's trustee period, which lasted from 1732 until 1753, its officials considered sending representatives to North Carolina to learn the trade. Nothing came of the plan, however, and it was not until later in the decade that the colony began shipping such products. By then the colony's ban on slavery had been lifted, and Georgians, like South Carolinians, found rice and indigo cultivation to be the most profitable employment for their slaves. Georgia consequently exported only small quantities of naval stores; their manufacture was confined to coastal areas and lands adjacent to the major rivers. From 1755 to 1775, Georgia exported a yearly average of only 220 barrels of tar, 149 barrels of pitch, and 44 barrels of turpentine.[36]

Florida and Louisiana, both colonial possessions of various European countries until the nineteenth century, experienced considerable difficulty with their respective naval stores trades. At the turn of the eighteenth century, the time when Britain experienced its most urgent need for a colonial naval stores supplier, Spain was also seeking a source. In a memorial to the king of Spain, probably written in 1700, the curate rector of St. Augustine reported that not only did Florida possess "a diversity of woods" suitable for masts, posts, and yards, but already "a very good pitch and tar necessary for the careening of the frigates and vessels of your majesty and the rest of the vessels of the presidio is made in the land." He admitted that the products were not as good as those available in Europe, "because the master is not very expert in the science and thus it is a little thick." Transporting the Florida naval stores to Cuba for the readying of ships, the rector believed, could save the crown the cost of shipping them from Europe. Spain did not take swift action in this matter; by the 1730s administrators were still attempting to implement the policy. In 1757, however, another governor developed an

35. Battle quoted in P. Perry, "Naval Stores Industry in the Ante-Bellum South, 1789–1861," 232; Ashe, *Forests, Forest Lands, and Forest Products*, 18; Snow, "Naval Stores in Colonial Virginia," 92–3.

36. Herndon, "Naval Stores in Colonial Georgia," 428, 430; Betty Wood, *Slavery in Colonial Georgia* (Athens: University of Georgia Press, 1984), 65; Cox et al., *This Well-Wooded Land*, 18; Herndon, "Naval Stores in Colonial Georgia," 428–31; I. James Pikl, *A History of Georgia Forestry* (Athens: Bureau of Business and Economic Research, University of Georgia, 1966), 4.

independent naval stores operation and, with the king's endorsement, shipped his goods to Havana. Further evidence of Spanish Florida tar and pitch production comes from William Bartram's report on his travels through America in the 1770s. While walking near Mobile Bay, then part of West Florida, he observed "three vast iron pots or kettles, each of many hundred gallons contents." He was informed that "they were for the purpose of boiling tar to pitch, there being vast forests of Pine trees in the vicinity of this place." Although the Spanish were most interested in tar and pitch, chipped faces discovered in the mid-twentieth century deep in the hearts of old Florida pines indicate that before 1750 turpentine production had also begun.[37]

French administrators in colonial Louisiana also struggled to stimulate naval stores production. In the early eighteenth century, Governor Bienville recommended that France offer subsidies, transportation, and a guarantee to purchase tar, pitch, and turpentine as well as import slaves to make them. Some production started. Bienville reported in 1734 that three or four tar works operated across Lake Pontchartrain from New Orleans. When the French crown cut the price it paid for naval stores by half, however, production slowed. As in the English colonies, higher returns from alternative staples drew efforts away from naval stores. Tobacco and indigo cultivation increasingly consumed the energy of slave laborers, as these products replaced naval stores in the hulls of merchant ships. In fact, the merchants' preference for products other than naval stores was so great that, despite offering advances to shippers for carrying naval stores, the colonial government found cargo space inadequate. Naval stores stock thus began overcrowding warehouses. Through the 1740s the importance of naval stores further declined as shipments of indigo, rice, cotton, timber, and pelts rose. Under Spanish rule, which lasted in Louisiana from the 1760s to the beginning of the nineteenth century, demand for the colony's tar and pitch rose slightly. However, it appears that no turpentine production developed. With only moderately successful efforts at developing naval stores production in Georgia, Florida, and Louisiana, North Carolina remained the manufacturing center of tar, pitch, and turpentine in North America.[38]

37. John H. Hann, "Translation of Alonso De Leturiondo's Memorial to the King of Spain," *Florida Archaeology*, n.s., 2 (1996): 195–6; Robert S. Blount, *Spirits of Turpentine: A History of Florida Naval Stores, 1528 to 1950* (Tallahassee: Florida Agricultural Museum, 1993), 8; Bartram, *Travels*, 339; Florida Writers' Project, "The Story of Naval Stores . . . ," *Florida Highways* 11 (May 1943): 12.

38. Jack D. L. Holmes, "Naval Stores in Colonial Louisiana and the Floridas," *Louisiana Studies* 7 (winter 1968): 295–301; Bernard Romans, *A Concise Natural History of East and West Florida* (Gainesville: University of Florida Press, 1962), 150; C. C. Robin, *Voyage to Louisiana* (New Orleans: Pelican, 1966), 29.

By the 1760s the focus of colonial naval stores production was located in North Carolina's Pamlico Sound and the Cape Fear River areas. The region's poor soil could not support extensive agriculture, but its expansive pine forests offered its residents a means of support. A traveler in the 1780s described the region as "a wide extended dead flat, covered in a thousand places with stagnated water." But, he continued, "this land that appears, and actually is, totally barren and altogether useless and unfit for any kind of culture, yields more profit to the occupiers, from the smallest capital imaginable, than can well be conceived. . . . This prodigious profit is derived from making tar, which is one of the most estimable staples of North Carolina." Another observer, surprised to find so few "plantations scattered about in these woods at various distances, 3–6 miles, and often as much as 10–15–20 miles apart," reported that rather than staple agriculture "it is the forest which supplies the present inhabitants of North Carolina not merely an occupation and a support, but the means as well of an easier life and often considerable estates." A Mr. Rutherfurd, for example, had "a vast number of Negroes employed" at a fine plantation called Hunthill. According to a Scottish woman who visited Rutherfurd in the mid-1770s, "the woods around him are immense and he has a vast piece of water, which by a creek communicates with the river, by which he sends down all the lumber, tar and pitch."[39]

Not only did counties between the Pamlico Sound and the Cape Fear River have a higher concentration of longleaf pines than the Albemarle area, its forests were closer to more accessible port facilities. The ports of Beaufort, Brunswick, and Wilmington all offered easier access to the open sea than did Edenton and together handled approximately 75 percent of the total naval stores exports from North Carolina and the majority of naval stores exports from North America. Yet despite the importance of these two ports in the naval stores trade, their overall size and total export volume paled in comparison to others such as Charleston and the northern ports. A Frenchman traveling through Beaufort in 1765 could not have been less enthusiastic about the town. He reported it was "a Small village not above 12 houses, the inhabitants seem miserable, they are very lasy and Indolent, they live mostly on fish and oisters, which they have here in great plenty." As for the harbor, "Non but small vessels Can come here there being but 13 feet water on the bar at low water. the tide does not rise above 4 feet. the little trade that is Caryed on here Consists in terpentine. tar and pich."[40]

39. Smyth, *Tour in the United States*, 94–5; Schoepf, *Travels in the Confederation*, 103; Evangeline Walker Andrews, ed., *Journal of a Lady of Quality* (New Haven: Yale University Press, 1922), 184.

40. Merrens, *Colonial North Carolina*, 88–9; "Journal of a French Traveler," 773.

North Carolina made naval stores, especially tar, its specialty. In 1768 England imported 135,000 barrels of tar, pitch, and turpentine from her colonies, around 60 percent from North Carolina. Colonists no longer tried to compensate for poor-quality tar by making it into pitch. By the late colonial period the percentage of pitch as part of naval stores export had dropped dramatically, down to only 7 percent by 1771. Although tar dominated naval stores shipments, turpentine nevertheless represented a significant commodity of North Carolina. Most often it was shipped in its raw form. Moreover, naval stores represented the colony's number one export. Although the export of all goods from six other colonies—Massachusetts, Virginia, Pennsylvania, New York, Maryland, and South Carolina—exceeded North Carolina's, North Carolina exported 70 percent of tar from the North American colonies, more than 50 percent of the turpentine, and 20 percent of the pitch. Wilmington saw the most overall trade activity of any of North Carolina's ports, handling a total tonnage of 8,500, and shipping the largest volume of naval stores.[41]

Despite North Carolina's success with its naval stores trade, the export of substandard and adulterated products persisted and continued to worry colonial officials. In a 1735 letter to North Carolina's Governor Johnston, a group of concerned gentlemen requested that he suggest to "the Assembly that some proper regulations might be enacted as rules for making Tar throughout the Province and a proper person or persons appointed to inspect the several kilns that penalties might be inflicted on such of them who transgress the said rules." They feared that "if the Tar of your Province should be brought into disrepute by the burning quality of it none of it will be exported from thence and that Manufacture will be quite lost to those of your Province who now maintain themselves thereby." In 1751 the colonial assembly passed a law regulating exports from the Cape Fear River, later applied to all ports, that provided for inspection of goods before shipment to ensure that they conformed to quality, weight, and packaging standards. Only marketable casks, each bearing the producer's initials, were to be exported. Each county court was responsible for appointing inspectors for its own jurisdiction, but because county judges were sometimes naval stores producers themselves, the inspectors' integrity rarely rose above suspicion.[42]

41. Williams, "English Mercantilism," 176, 185; Merrens, *Colonial North Carolina,* 86; Hautala, "European and American Tar," 69, 79, 85; Crittenden, *Commerce of North Carolina,* 41–51, 54, 70–73.

42. Fitz Walker et al. to Governor Johnson, 12 September 1735, *The Colonial Records of North Carolina,* vol. 4, ed. William L. Saunders (Raleigh: P. M. Hale, 1886), 16; Lee, *Lower Cape Fear,* 153; Crittenden, *Commerce of North Carolina,* 57; The Memorial of Messrs. Bridgen & Waller and Hindley & Needham Merchants Trading to North Carolina and Import-

Colonial administrators also attempted to deal with the problem of unscrupulous producers who made naval stores from trees on land they did not own. As early as 1717, Virginia passed a law stating that anyone manufacturing naval stores from material taken from crown lands for which they had no intention to patent and pay quitrents would be guilty of trespass. The problem arose in North Carolina as well, especially after 1730, when small producers, who owned little land, began production in the Albemarle area. In 1738 Henry McCulloh complained to the Board of Trade in London that "it has been a practice of long standing in the Colony [North Carolina] for people to Box pine trees for Turpentine and burn light wood for Pitch and Tarr without taking out Pattents." McCulloh requested that the board support the governor in his effort to collect quitrent on this property. As late as 1772 North Carolina governor Josiah Martin issued a proclamation addressing a similar problem. According to the governor, unprincipled colonists "have made frequent practice of entering Tracts of Land in the Secretarys Office and immediately set down on the same—carried off the timber and burnt the lightwood without further prosecuting their claim to a patent for the said Land."[43]

The American Revolution created volatility in colonial naval stores trade and production, but Britain possibly suffered more than the United States. As early as August 1774 the first North Carolina Provincial Congress, which was called to elect delegates to the Continental Congress, drew up a set of resolutions criticizing British colonial policies. One resolve threatened "That unless American Grievances are redressed before the first day of October 1775, We will not after that day directly or indirectly export Tobacco, Pitch, Tar, Turpentine, or any other articles whatsoever, to Great Britain, nor will we sell any such articles as we think can be exported to Great Britain." When bounty payment to the colonies ended with declared independence in 1776, North Carolinians, free from the navigation acts that had restricted colonial trade, found markets for their products in other countries and colonies. It appears that tar remained profitable, each laborer, according to one report, generating "from one hundred pounds, to two hundred pounds sterling, and upwards, annually." Britain, however, suffered a naval stores shortage. American tar and pitch exports to Britain dropped from 87,152 barrels

ers of Naval Stores to the Earl of Hillsborough, 31 March 1770, *The Colonial Records of North Carolina*, vol. 8, ed. William Saunders (Raleigh: Josephus Daniels, 1890), 189.

43. Snow, "Naval Stores in Colonial Virginia," 82; Merrens, *Colonial North Carolina,* 89; Henry McCullah to Secretary of Board of Trade, January 1738, *Colonial Records of North Carolina*, vol. 4, ed. Saunders, 284–5; Proclamation from Governor Martin, "American Gum Naval Stores Industry," to King George III, 26 May 1772, *The Colonial Records of North Carolina*, vol. 9, ed. William L. Saunders (Raleigh: Josephus Daniels, 1890), 294–5.

in 1774 to 78,358 in 1775, and then to 4,823 in 1776, and finally to 216 in 1777. The British navy was forced to obtain its badly needed supplies from the sources it had tried to free itself from decades earlier, Scandinavia and Russia. The rise in naval stores imports from Sweden, Russia, and Denmark corresponded with the falling of colonial trade.[44]

Britain attempted to secure at least a portion of its badly needed naval stores from Florida, which it had taken possession of in 1763 as part of the agreement ending the Seven Years' War. Despite Britain's early efforts to encourage naval stores production and population growth in its new colony, by 1776 only approximately three thousand settlers lived in Florida, and they made tar and pitch in but small quantities. During the American Revolution, however, loyalists from Georgia and South Carolina seeking political asylum and economic opportunity flooded into Florida. Between the war's outbreak and 1784, Florida's population grew to 17,000. As it rose, so did naval stores production. Florida made just 190 barrels of tar in 1776, but in one year output jumped to 2,241 barrels of tar and 417 barrels of pitch, and in 1778 it increased to 8,100 and 1,980 barrels, respectively. By 1783, the last year of British rule in Florida, the colony made 20,000 barrels of tar and turpentine, the production centered in the vicinity of the St. Marys, Nassau, and especially the St. Johns Rivers. An active turpentine trade also developed over these years. In a pine forest four miles north of St. Augustine, one producer used slaves to harvest turpentine from 25,000 trees. Another producer, John Imrie, made turpentine on 450 acres along Moultre Creek in northeastern Florida. But in 1783 Florida returned to Spain as part of the Treaty of Paris, and Britain lost this last colonial supplier. Spanish administrators did little to encourage the new naval stores industry's continuation, and by 1787 only three tar and pitch producers remained.[45]

Following the Revolution, North Carolina continued its dominant role in American naval stores production and export, despite the absence of a bounty. Manufacturing recovered steadily. In 1785 North Carolina exported

44. "Resolutions of the First Provincial Congress, August 27, 1774," quoted in Hugh Talmage Lefler, ed., *North Carolina History Told by Contemporaries* (Chapel Hill: University of North Carolina Press, 1948), 97; Smyth, *Tour in the United States,* 95; Gamble, "Early History," 22; Thurmond, "Early American Naval Stores," 6; Hautala, "European and American Tar," 105–7; Alexander Gillion to Henry Laurens, 16 November 1778, *Papers of Henry Laurens,* ed. Hamer et al., 14:502, and Henry Laurens to Babut & Co., 5 August 1776, *Papers of Henry Laurens,* 11:217.

45. Holmes, "Naval Stores," 304–5; *Historic Properties Survey of St. Johns County* (St. Augustine, Fla.: Historic St. Augustine Preservation Board, 1985), 23, 25; Romans, *Concise Natural History,* 149–50; Blount, *Spirits of Turpentine,* 12, 14; Stanley C. Bond, Jr., "The Development of the Naval Stores Industry in St. Johns County, Florida," *Florida Anthropologist* 40 (September 1987): 195.

56,000 barrels of naval stores, less than half the 128,000 barrels exported in 1768. By 1788 exports rose to 95,000 barrels. Tar remained the principal naval stores export product, followed by turpentine, pitch, and rosin. As the quantity of production resumed, so did poor quality.[46]

The industry's revival, however, was accompanied by some production and marketing changes. An increase in naval stores shipments through Port Roanoke and a decline through the state's more southerly ports indicated a northward shift in the products' manufacture toward the Albemarle area. Although the port at Brunswick saw its total export tonnage increase, its naval stores exports actually declined, while Port Roanoke's naval stores shipments almost doubled. At the same time, tobacco shipments from Brunswick and Beaufort increased over sixteen times from the late 1760s, while Port Roanoke, which had led in tobacco export, dropped to third place; Brunswick took the lead and Bath came in second. In another change, the northern states replaced Great Britain as the principal buyer of North Carolina naval stores. The revival of American shipping, especially in New England, led to this increased domestic consumption. But despite the changes, by 1800 North Carolina remained firmly established as the principal American naval stores producer and would continue to live up to its designation as the "Tar Heel State" for most of the nineteenth century.[47]

North Carolina achieved this distinction not solely because it possessed abundant longleaf pine trees, for expansive stands of the species grew in other southern colonies, but because North Carolinians lacked any other staple they could produce profitably. England's bounty, which compensated for the prohibitively high shipping costs from America, was required to stimulate colonial naval stores manufacturing. South Carolina manufactured tar, pitch, and turpentine until the bounty ended and changes in trade policies made rice and later indigo viable substitutes with even better returns. As Georgia's economy developed in the mid-eighteenth century, settlers there also preferred rice and indigo to naval stores. The same proved true in Florida and Louisiana. In North Carolina, however, tar, pitch, turpentine, and other forest products did not face competition from other staples. Except for tobacco, which grew well in the fertile eastern river bottom lands, and rice, which could be cultivated in limited sections of the coastal region near Wilmington, North Carolina lacked any other profitable export commodity. Even though naval stores did not bring the returns that rice and indigo pro-

46. Crittenden, *Commerce of North Carolina*, 160; Franklin B. Hough, *Report upon Forestry*, vol. 2 (Washington, D.C.: Government Printing Office, 1880), 333; Hugh Williamson, *The History of North Carolina* (Philadelphia: Thomas Dobson, 1812), 213–4.

47. Hautala, "European and American Tar," 121, 123.

vided other colonies, the bounty, which continued uninterrupted from 1729 until the Revolution, made profits from them adequate enough to attract the attention of both large and small producers. Although North Carolinians were able to produce lumber from their pine forests, scarcity of water power for sawmills and the difficulty and high cost of transporting lumber made tar and pitch relatively more profitable. Also, naval stores manufacturing, especially tar making, which could be performed at any time of the year, provided small farmers with a means to supplement their income. With no competing export commodity, limited transportation opportunities, and seasonal flexibility in the production, "tar-making conditions," as one scholar has explained, "were at their best in the Carolinas, especially in North Carolina."[48]

48. Airaksinen, "Tar Production," 121.

CHAPTER 2

TURPENTINE BOOM

DURING THE ANTEBELLUM PERIOD, turpentine developed into the most heavily demanded naval stores product, and its rapid production increase drove the industry, which remained centered in North Carolina, to impressive heights. New uses and a growing need for turpentine following the American Revolution brought prices high enough to make gum and spirit production an appealing alternative to cotton cultivation for the southeastern North Carolina counties, whose poor soils prevented extensive plantation agriculture. Such high returns attracted the attention of the state's planter class by the 1830s. With access to capital resources and the control of large, slave labor forces, these market-sensitive entrepreneurs invested in thousands of acres of previously undesirable pineland, constructed their own distilleries, and began production on a grand scale. At the same time, a transportation revolution in North Carolina facilitated turpentine's expansion into areas previously too remote to permit profitable manufacture. However, the rapid increase in turpentine manufacture taxed North Carolina's poorly organized marketing system. By the antebellum period's end, efforts were under way to organize better the system for selling naval stores.

During the first decades of the 1800s the variety of applications for rosin, tar, and turpentine grew. Rosin became widely used in making soap. It was painted on coarse surfaces to make them smooth and applied to posts to prevent rotting. Cuts on domestic animals that received a coat of tar stood less chance of infection, and the feet of cattle painted with tar were less likely to be injured by dampness or abrasion. Some farmers coated their grain seeds with tar to discourage hungry birds. At the beginning of the

nineteenth century, however, the greatest demand for naval stores continued to come from shipyards, and tar remained the most important naval
stores commodity. Turpentine production, however, increased rapidly, making turpentine the second most produced of naval stores products, ahead of
pitch. Turpentine served as a thinner for oil-based paint. Its use for this purpose increased until, by 1855, it was estimated that the paint industry consumed 112,000 gallons of it a day. Spirits also served as flea repellent and as
a waterproofing agent for cloth. It could even be used to wash clothes, particularly to remove grease spots. Popular belief held that turpentine possessed a multitude of curative properties, especially as a treatment for
respiratory disease and as a powerful purgative. So powerful was the effect
of turpentine perceived to be against cholera, diphtheria, whooping cough,
and hay fever that merely living in a pine forest was thought to provide some
protection. Patients with worms, hemorrhages, and severe gas might receive
turpentine rectally. Turpentine was even applied to both male and female
genitalia to treat gonorrhea and sores. But taken in too large a dose, turpentine could have dangerous consequences. Alex MacRae of Washington,
North Carolina, warned his brother Donald to "watch carefully the effects
of the vermifuge [medicine to expel parasites] + Spts. Turpt. . . . When
given too often or for too long a time results badly." MacRae recounted that
he "was once rendered blind + stupid as a goose for 24 hours for taking too
much" turpentine.[1]

In the 1830s the discovery of two new uses for turpentine further boosted
its production. The rubber industry, which was expanding during that decade, began using turpentine as a solvent. More importantly, turpentine became a main ingredient in a popular lamp fuel. During the 1830s Americans
experimented with alternatives to tallow-dipped candles and sperm whale
oil. Early efforts to burn turpentine as a substitute failed because it gave off
a strong odor and had a tendency to smoke. Attempts at burning turpentine-

1. Ashe, *Forests, Forest Lands, and Forest Products*, 74–5; Kirby, *Poquosin*, 30–1; Michaux,
North American Sylva, 112, 114; P. Perry, "Naval Stores Industry in the Ante-Bellum South,
1789–1861," 49; Gamble, "Early History," 23; G. Terry Sharrer, "Naval Stores, 1781–1881," in
Material Culture of the Wooden Age, ed. Brooke Hindle (Tarrytown, N.Y.: Sleepy Hollow Press,
1981), 252; "The Southern Pine Forest—Turpentine," *De Bow's Review* 18 (February 1855):
190–1; Hautala, "European and American Tar," 114–5; Francis Peyre Porcher, "Uses of Rosin
and Turpentine in Old Plantation Days," in *Naval Stores: History, Production, Distribution, and
Consumption*, ed. Thomas Gamble (Savannah: Review Publishing and Printing, 1921), 29–30;
John S. Haller, Jr., "Samson of the Terebinthinates: Medical History of Turpentine," *Southern
Medical Journal* 77 (June 1984): 752–3; Franklin B. Hough, *Report upon Forestry*, vol. 1 (Washington, D.C.: Government Printing Office, 1878), 138; Crittenden, *Commerce of North Carolina*,
160; Alex MacRae, Jr., to D. MacRae, 27 August 1863, Hugh MacRae Papers, Special Collections Library, Duke University.

based mixtures met with similar failure. The first widely used lighting alternative consequently was not turpentine but lard oil. Introduced in 1841, this fast-burning fuel gave off satisfactory light; however, in cold weather it hardened and became useless. Soon afterwards, a mixture of alcohol and turpentine, popularly known as camphene, camphine, teveline, and palmetto oil, appeared for general use and gradually replaced lard oil. Not only did camphene give off more light without ever flaring up, but also it was cheaper and burned longer. In February 1847, B. Murphy and Company, manufacturer of camphene lamps in Philadelphia, claimed of the lamps that for "*half the money* they will give *double the light* of any Oil or Lard Lamp yet invented." Camphene sold for about 40¢ per gallon. It soon became the most popular illuminant in America and burned in homes, businesses, hotels, public buildings, and aboard some trains. However, camphene had to be handled with great care. When used correctly this oil provided safe, effective lighting, but serious accidents sometimes occurred from carelessness with this volatile and flammable fluid. By the 1850s the annual deaths from accidents involving camphene lamps exceeded those from steamboat explosions and railroad accidents combined. In response to consumer concerns, a safer lamp soon appeared. Newell's Patent Safety Lamps kept the burning wick away from the vapor, thus reducing the risk of explosion. Also introduced was the safety can and filler which allowed for refilling of the lamp while it continued to burn.[2]

As camphene lamps grew popular and the resulting increased demand for turpentine raised its price, more North Carolinians began harvesting raw turpentine. The first burst of production began in the area between the Tar and Cape Fear Rivers, especially the Washington and New Bern areas, where the inhabitants were already familiar with the methods of turpentining. In the late 1830s, the quest for more suitable pineland led to the opening of turpentine operations on the west and south sides of the Cape Fear River. By 1840, when Edmund Ruffin traveled through the Cape Fear Basin, turpentining was "the almost sole business of the thinly settled population of the pine lands." Throughout the 1840s the industry moved up the Cape Fear toward the northwest into Cumberland and Harnett Counties and to the south, spreading into South Carolina. In 1844 one Henry Harrison cut the

---

2. By the mid-1850s, the rubber industry annually consumed 4,650 casks containing a total of 187,000 gallons of spirits. P. Perry, "Naval Stores Industry in the Ante-Bellum South, 1789–1861," 203–14; "Latest Improvement in the Camphene Lamp," *Wilmington Journal* (hereinafter WJ), 26 February 1847; "Camphine! Camphine!!" WJ, 2 March 1849; M. Williams, *Americans and Their Forests*, 158; "Camphine Lamps," *Wilmington Chronicle*, 21 December 1842; "The Southern Pine Forest—Turpentine," 191; "Death from Camphine Gas," WJ, 12 October 1849.

first boxes near the town of Manchester in Harnett County and shipped the gum to Fayetteville for distilling. Harrison's turpentine was probably handled by Thomas Lutterlaw, who that same year opened the first distillery in Fayetteville.[3]

Producers such as Harrison suffered from early industry growing pains. Becoming effective in May 1845, the repeal of British duties on turpentine made exports to England increase and American prices climb. Speculation followed. A New York firm attempted to corner the market, causing prices to rise from $2.30 per barrel to $3.00 to more than $5.00. Attracted by these outrageously high prices, reported the *Wilmington Journal*, "many of our citizens have withdrawn their labor and capital from their wonted channels, and have embarked them in making Turpentine." In the meantime, "lands and negroes have been both purchased and hired at high prices, in the anticipation that the product of the pine would continue to command such a price as would amply repay any outlay." However, the bubble soon burst and prices tumbled to $2.00 per barrel for crude gum and to 35¢ for a gallon of spirits. Producers were urged to hold their current crop off the market until the large supplies at New York, Liverpool, and London had diminished and the price recovered. The strategy apparently worked. By the fall of 1845 prices steadied at around $3.50 per barrel of raw turpentine and production resumed its expansion.[4]

By 1847 North Carolinians made an estimated 800,000 barrels of turpentine, valued at between $1,700,000 and $2,000,000. And around "four or five thousand laborers are engaged in making it, and perhaps three times as many more human beings are supported mainly from the proceeds of its first sale." *De Bow's Review* guessed that "there is no one article produced in this country by the same number of laborers, which contributes so much to the commerce and prosperity of the country as the article of turpentine." Stability and renewed profit potential was followed by further expansion. By 1850, turpentine production had become established in the upper reaches of the Cape Fear and Deep Rivers; and Cumberland County, especially its seat, Fayetteville, became the inland center of the trade.[5]

3. Edmund Ruffin, "Notes of a Steam Journey," *Farmer's Register* 8 (30 April 1840): 250; Ashe, *Forests, Forest Lands, and Forest Products*, 75; Percival Perry, "The Naval Stores Industry in the Old South, 1790–1860," *North Carolina Forestry History Series* 1 (April 1967): 8; P. Perry, "Naval Stores Industry in the Old South, 1790–1860," *Journal of Southern History*, 516; Hough, *Report upon Forestry*, 138.

4. P. Perry, "The Naval Stores Industry in the Old South, 1790–1860," *Journal of Southern History*, 517; "Naval Stores," *WJ*, 15 May 1846; "New York Market," *WJ*, 20 November 1846.

5. "Naval Stores"; "North Carolina, Its Resources, Manufactures, Etc.," *De Bow's Review* 4 (October 1847): 257; Ashe, *Forests, Forest Lands, and Forest Products*, 75–7; P. Perry, "Naval

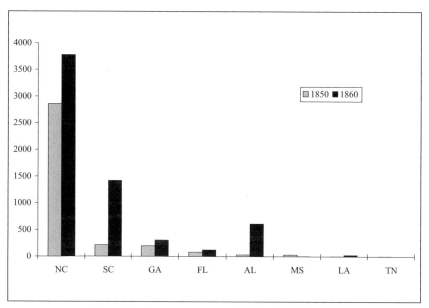

FIGURE 2.1. Number of hands employed in naval stores production, southeast United States, 1850 and 1860. Based on data from United States Department of the Interior, *Abstract of the Statistics of Manufactures, According to the Returns of the Seventh Census* (Washington, D.C.: Department of the Interior, 1850), 116; and United States Department of the Interior, *Manufactures of the United States in 1860* (Washington, D.C.: Department of the Interior, 1865), 2–14, 57–82, 168–204, 285–94, 420–38, 552–79.

A shift to planter control of production accompanied the turpentine industry's migration into the Cape Fear region. Since the late 1720s, small and middle-sized farmers had manufactured a significant portion of naval stores; as the industry expanded along the Cape Fear in the 1840s and continued its dramatic growth into the 1850s, men with capital and large numbers of slaves entered the production on a grand scale. Although these businessmen may not have participated in a classic market relationship with their bound labor, they, like other slaveholders, certainly engaged in a market exchange of this product to which they shifted to benefit from its increasingly profitable trade. The large producers included James R. Grist, who worked timber in Brunswick and Columbus Counties with over 100 slaves; James Metts, whose 65 slaves harvested turpentine in both North and South Carolina; John A. Avirett, whose 125 slaves were primarily employed in turpentine on

Stores Industry in the Old South, 1790–1860," *North Carolina Forestry History Series,* 8; P. Perry, "Naval Stores Industry in the Old South, 1790–1860," *Journal of Southern History,* 519.

his huge estate in Onslow County; and Daniel L. Russell, who with 25,000 acres in Brunswick County and 150 slaves, was one of the largest producers in the state. In many cases these large operators were the sons of Washington, North Carolina, area planters who could work their slave labor forces more profitably in the region's virgin timber than on its poor soils. As large turpentiners took control of more and more production in the 1840s and 1850s, evidence suggests, the size of the operation tripled. A sample of newspaper advertisements for the sale of operations reveals that while the average business in the 1840s consisted of around 25,000 boxes, by the 1850s the typical operation made use of 85,000 boxes.[6]

The increased prosperity and rise in land values that the turpentine boom brought seemed a blessing for North Carolinians living in the southeastern portion of the state where soil was incapable of sustaining commercial cotton agriculture. Edmund Ruffin, the South's leading agricultural reformer, like other observers, was struck by the poor, sandy soil of the southeastern pine region. He found the level land broken only by slight depressions of swampy areas where loblolly pine grew. "But whether dry or wet," he proclaimed, "all these pine lands, and the shallow 'bays' intersecting them are very poor . . . and will continue worthless for tillage." Frederick Law Olmsted understood that North Carolina dominated the South's naval stores production "because, in it, cotton is rather less productive than in the others, in an average of years." He observed that "in the region in which the true turpentine-trees grow, indeed, there is no soil suitable for growing cotton;

6. James Oakes, *Slavery and Freedom: An Interpretation of the Old South* (New York: Alfred A. Knopf, 1990), 54; William Dusinberre, *Them Dark Days: Slavery in the American Rice Swamps* (Athens: University of Georgia Press, 2000), 6, 24, 136, 289, 298, 300; P. Perry, "Naval Stores Industry in the Old South, 1790–1860," *Journal of Southern History*, 516; P. Perry, "Naval Stores Industry in the Ante-Bellum South, 1789–1861," 150–1; "Land for Sale on Cape Fear River," *Wilmington Chronicle*, 10 November 1841; "Lands for Sale," *WJ*, 27 June 1845; "Real Estate for Sale," *WJ*, 4 July 1845; "Plantation for Sale," *WJ*, 24 April 1846; "Valuable Turpentine Land for Sale," *WJ*, 20 November 1846; "Valuable Real Estate," *WJ*, 26 February 1847; "Valuable Lands for Sale," *WJ*, 22 December 1848; "Lands for Sale," *WJ*, 29 December 1848; "Valuable Farming and Turpentine Lands for Sale," *WJ*, 2 March 1849; "Valuable Land for Sale," *WJ*, 11 May 1849; "For Sale," *WJ*, 10 August 1849; "Notice.—A Valuable Plantation for Sale," *WJ*, 23 November 1849; "Valuable Plantation for Sale," *WJ*, 23 November 1849; "Land for Sale," *WJ*, 19 July 1850; "A Great Bargain," *WJ*, 4 October 1850; "Land and Negroes for Sale," *WJ*, 4 July 1851; "10,000 Acres of Land for Sale," *WJ*, 21 November 1851; "For Sale," *WJ*, 29 October 1852; "Valuable Cape Fear Plantation for Sale," *WJ*, 24 June 1853; "Valuable Real Estate for Sale," *WJ*, 4 November 1853; "Valuable Real Estate for Sale," *WJ*, 10 March 1854; "Land for Sale," *WJ*, 13 October 1854; "A Valuable Tract of Land for Sale," *WJ*, 4 January 1856; "Turpentine Land for Sale," *WJ*, 21 March 1856; "For Sale, Valuable Turpentine and Farming Lands in Bladen County," *WJ*, 21 March 1856; "Turpentine Lands in Florida for Sale," *WJ*, 21 March 1856; "A Turpentine Farm for Sale or Rent," *WJ*, 29 August 1856.

and it is only in the swampy parts, or on the borders of streams flowing through it, that there is any attempt at agriculture." A Bladen County resident commented that "in the pine region tracts owned by individuals unfit for cultivation, high prices of turpentine has added much to their value."[7]

For those few North Carolinians capable of profitably cultivating cotton, naval stores actually offered a better alternative in many years. At the same time turpentine prices rose during the 1830s and 1840s, cotton prices fell. The Panic of 1837 badly hurt the cotton market; the 1836 price of 13.3¢ per pound by 1839 had dropped to 7.9¢ and reached a low of 5.5¢ in 1844. With cotton prices generally depressed during the 1840s, one observer commented that "compared to other labor," turpentine "has, for the last ten years, been deemed the most profitable of all." In 1846 the *Fayetteville Observer* reported that the turpentine region of North Carolina "has never, to our knowledge, been in so prosperous a condition as at present. Lands have risen, one, two, or three hundred per cent, and labor is so profitable that the country is full of money to make investigations." It described "a gentlemen [sic] who had gone to Wilmington to sell his turpentine, in pocketing $1900, remarked that sum was the produce of the labor of four hands."[8]

Cotton prices recovered by the early 1850 and demonstrated remarkable stability. But turpentine prices also remained relatively constant and continued to rival cotton profits. Dugall McMillan of Wilmington maintained that the profit margin for turpentine was very good. It was "better by far than cotton raising," he reported, and "many cotton planters are going into it." Prices remained steady, he believed, because the demand expanded with the growing number of producers. The average hand, it was estimated in 1850, could make 150 barrels of dip and 50 of scrape. With the former selling at $2.50 per barrel and the latter at $1.25 a barrel, a producer could realize a gross profit of $437.50. Subtracting $137.50 in expenses ($60 for 200 barrels, $50 for shipping to market, and $27.50 in commission to the factorage house), the turpentiner could make $300 per hand. With cotton selling at 9¢ per pound, a planter could make only $200 per hand. Even with prices running around $2.31 for dip and $1.50 for scrape in 1852, the naval stores industry continued to attract producers. That year William Underhill of Wake County reported that "turpentine is all that is talk a bout nearby.

7. Ruffin, "Notes of a Steam Journey," 246; Frederick Law Olmsted, *A Journey in the Seaboard Slave States* (New York: Dix and Edwards, 1856), 338; J. Wright to Thomas D. McDowell, 9 December 1858, Thomas David Smith McDowell Papers, Southern Historical Collection, University of North Carolina at Chapel Hill.

8. Cooper and Terrill, *American South,* 192; "The Manufacture of Turpentine in the South," *De Bow's Review* 8 (May 1850): 455; "Product of Turpentine at the South," *De Bow's Review* 11 (September 1851): 305; "The Turpentine Region," *Tarboro Press,* 11 February 1846.

it[s price] has been very high this year." Naval stores prices soared in 1853. On the Wilmington market, dip sold for $3.90 to $4.00 per barrel, scrape for $2.10 to $2.30 and spirits at 63¢ to 65¢ per gallon. At these prices, the *Fayetteville Observer* reported, "the Naval Stores men of the state (and their name is legion,) are coining money out of the pine trees."[9]

In the mid-1850s turpentine continued to distract producers away from cotton. Turpentiner Benjamin Williams, explained his wife in 1854, did "not like to remove any of his hands from his turpentine land, the income from that being much larger than from the plantation." In 1855 *De Bow's Review* reported that "no business makes better returns for common labor, take one year with another, not even the culture of cotton and tobacco, especially when the amount of capital employed is taken into consideration." The same article claimed that a prime turpentine laborer could gather $600 or $700 worth of turpentine in a year. After deducting the costs of barrels, hauling, provisions, the overseer's wage, and other expenses, $200 per hand was a moderate return.[10]

With the increase in turpentine harvesting, the number of distilleries in port towns grew. In 1818 the first turpentine still in Wilmington began operating. In 1845 the *Tarboro Press* reported that Wilmington had nine turpentine distilling operations, with a total of thirty stills and a combined daily capacity of five hundred barrels of resin and four thousand casks of spirits. The largest distillery operated seven stills, while the smallest ran but two. Between September 1845 and March 1846 Wilmington added three new distilleries, bringing the city's number of stills to thirty-seven, with three more under construction. When completed, all the city's stills were thought to consume 1,500 barrels of crude turpentine a day and produce 200 barrels of spirits. A traveler visiting Wilmington in 1846 reported that "there are to be seen here twenty turpentine distilleries, most of them lately set up and all doing a very profitable business." So impressed was he with such activity in the port town that he proclaimed it North Carolina's commercial capital. Washington experienced a similar increase in distilleries. In 1842, three dis-

9. Cooper and Terrill, *American South,* 192; Dugall McMillan to *Southern Cultivator,* 14 April 1846, *Southern Cultivator* 4 (November 1846): 172–3; "Manufacture of Turpentine in the South," 455; "Review of the Newbern Market," *New Bern (N.C.) Newbernian,* 6 January 1852; W. M. Underhill to Brother and Sister, 20 December 1852, Ransom Lee Papers, Special Collections Library, Duke University; "High Prices," *Fayetteville Observer,* 1 February 1853.

10. Sarah F. Williams to Parents, 17 March 1854, Sarah Hicks Williams Papers, Southern Historical Collection, University of North Carolina at Chapel Hill; "Turpentine: Hints for Those about to Engage in Its Manufacture," *De Bow's Review* 19 (October 1855): 488; D. W. Kyle to John Buford, 29 March 1856, John Buford Papers, Special Collections Library, Duke University; G. W. Perry, *A Treatise on Turpentine Farming* (New Bern, N.C.: Muse and Davis, 1859), 87.

tilleries that together consumed up to two hundred barrels a day were operating in that town. Within four years, Washington, where naval stores
represented nearly 75 percent of the value of all products leaving port, had
seven turpentine distilleries in operation, and another was under construction. Between these seven operations there were fifteen stills which, when
all running at their peak capacity, required six hundred barrels of crude gum
a day. Distilleries consisted of one or more stills and their shelters. In 1849
one typical operation, located one-half mile north of Wilmington, had four
stills, capable of running one hundred barrels of gum a day; a large spirit
house, where distilled turpentine was stored to protect the casks from the
heat of the sun; a large glue house, where empty spirit casks were prepared
by coating their interior with hot glue; "a large Negro house," where the
slave workers slept; and a wharf.[11]

The increase in local distilling brought an end to the earlier practice of
shipping crude turpentine to the North and England for distillation. By 1844
50 percent of the crude gum distilled in the United States was distilled in
North Carolina, the result of the growing number of stills operating in the
state. Raw turpentine processing thus grew into an important segment of
the North Carolina economy. In 1847, the industry supported statewide 150
stills with an average cost of $1,500. One observer explained that "the cost
of distilling is very great, and when we reckon the cost of transportation,
the profits of distillers, of ship owners, commission merchants, and the
venders of the article abroad, it will be seen that the capital and labor employed is not only immense, but the numbers who are supported by the manufacture and sale of the article is astonishing."[12]

A temporary price drop in late 1846 and 1847 necessitated a reduction in
shipping costs to maximize profits and spurred a movement away from central distillation in the port cities and toward more inland locations, nearer
the source of production. Copper stills, introduced in the industry in 1834
and much like those used in the scotch whiskey industry, made this transition possible. They were much lighter than the large iron ones used in port
cities and could be transported. Because stills cost between $1,500 and
$2,000, only the largest producers could afford to erect their own. Wealthy
businessmen also constructed inland custom distilleries to take advantage of

11. "Steam Mills and Turpentine Distilleries," *Tarboro Press,* January 25, 1845; P. Perry,
"Naval Stores Industry in the Ante-Bellum South, 1789–1861," 243, 249; Sharrer, "Naval
Stores," 254; McMillan to *Southern Cultivator,* 172; "Trade of Washington," *Tarboro Press,* 21
January 1846; "Distillery for Sale," *Wilmington Chronicle,* 24 January 1849.

12. P. Perry, "Naval Stores Industry in the Old South, 1790–1860," *Journal of Southern
History,* 516; Martin, "American Gum Naval Stores Industry," 77; "North Carolina, Its Resources, Manufactures, Etc.," 258.

the spreading production. In 1854 Jonathan Worth, who would become the state's governor during Presidential Reconstruction, and his son operated a still in the extreme western part of Harnett County. Some Wilmington distillers brought their services closer to their clients. In 1848 W. O. Jeffreys of Wilmington advertised that he was constructing two new stills at Sarecta in Duplin County. With large producers and custom distillers investing in inland stills, a new economic sector developed. For example, where in 1844 Cumberland County had only one distillery, by 1852 thirty-two distilleries operated. They represented a combined capital investment of $75,000, required $300,000 of operating capital, and yielded an annual income of $348,000. And new distilleries were always being constructed, causing a rapid shifting in naval stores trading practices. By 1855, for example, about half of the spirits shipped from Washington had been distilled inland. As a result, port distilleries handled a decreasing percentage of the industry's gum processing, and the amount of spirits shipped from the United States rose over that of crude gum. Wilmington exported 145 times as many barrels of crude turpentine as casks of spirits in 1837; by 1848 only seven times as many gum barrels as spirit casks came through the port, and by the mid-1850s their numbers were about even. Washington experienced a similar pattern. In 1848, *Scientific American* reported that "twenty years ago, there was more spirits of turpentine distilled in Europe than in the United States, but the tide has now turned and Europe gets turpentine from America." By this time, North Carolina was unquestionably the most important turpentine producer not only in the United States but also in the world, far exceeding Finland and Russia, which continued to specialize in tar. In 1860, North Carolina produced 96.7 percent of the naval stores made in the United States. The total value of crude and distilled turpentine produced that year, $5,311,420, represented a more than 200 percent rise from ten years earlier.[13]

With naval stores promising high returns, not only did businessmen erect

13. Ashe, *Forests, Forest Lands, and Forest Products*, 76–7; "To Turpentine Makers in Duplin," *WJ*, 12 May 1848; Martha Green Hayes, "General History of the Turpentine Industry," 53, Georgia Agrirama, Tifton, Ga.; Nollie Hickman, *Mississippi Harvest: Lumbering in the Longleaf Pine Belt, 1840–1915* (University: University of Mississippi, 1962), 126; P. Perry, "Naval Stores Industry in the Ante-Bellum South, 1789–1861," 59, 258–9; P. Perry, "Naval Stores Industry in the Old South, 1790–1860," *Journal of Southern History*, 518; Richard C. Cook, "Naval Stores: The Forgotten Industry in Tar Heel State," *Naval Stores Review* 77 (July 1967): 8; "Turpentine Business in North Carolina and Georgia," *Commercial Review of the South and West* 5 (April 1848): 364; Hautala, "European and American Tar," 115; U.S. Dept. of Interior, *Abstract of the Statistics of Manufactures, According to the Returns of the Seventh Census* (Washington, D.C.: Department of the Interior, 1858), 116; U.S. Dept. of Interior, *Manufactures of the United States in 1860*, 438.

stills in North Carolina's port communities and pine forests but sections of the piney woods experienced a population increase, as hopeful producers rushed into the area. Fayetteville and Cumberland County, for example, saw solid economic and population growth, each related to the turpentine industry's prosperity. Between 1840 and 1850 Cumberland's white population increased from 15,284 to 20,160, a rise of 34 percent. However, the slave population rose 75 percent, from 4,285 to 7,217. The *Fayetteville Observer* explained in 1853 that "the population of this county has increased about 1000 since the first of the present month—about 300 whites and 700 slaves having come here from other parts of the State to engage in the turpentine business." Area boosters looked forward to the increased business this production would bring, since "grain, provisions, and other necessities of life, would be in demand."[14]

One result of the rise in manufacturing activity was a rapid increase in labor costs. Although the slave population rose, it was apparently not enough to keep up with demand. The Fayetteville *North Carolinian* reported that "Negroes hired on New Year's day for prices higher by 25 to 33 per cent than last year—first rate men bringing from 100 to 135 dollars." The paper attributed the higher prices to, among other projects such as area transportation improvements, "the increasing production of turpentine in the surrounding country." Olmsted found that in the early 1850s "wages of ordinary practiced turpentine hands (slaves) are about $120 a year, with board, clothing, etc., as usual." A few years later owners could hire them out for between $150 and $175 annually. The rising cost of hiring turpentine slaves in the 1840s and 1850s is illustrated by the prices charged by the Francis Harper heirs of New Bern, who hired out slaves to turpentine producers. In 1849 they received $56.50 for "Amas" and $49.50 for "Haywood." In 1852 Amas and Haywood were each rented for $125, and by 1853 Amas's hiring price had risen to $175 and in 1854 to $215. This increase corresponds with a 1853 *Fayetteville Observer* report indicating that the annual cost of hiring a good naval stores laborer was $150 to $175. By 1860 turpentine workers were hired for as much as $250, with especially skilled slaves costing even more to rent.[15]

14. P. Perry, "Naval Stores Industry in the Ante-Bellum South, 1789–1861," 258–9; "The Tide Turned," *Fayetteville Observer,* 25 January 1853.

15. P. Perry, "Naval Stores Industry in the Ante-Bellum South, 1789–1861," 42, 258; Olmsted, *Journey in the Seaboard Slave States,* 346; W. M. Underhill to Brother and Sister, 20 December 1852, Lee Papers; "High Prices"; Slave Hiring Agreements, 1849, 1852, 1854, 1854, Francis Harper Papers, Special Collections Library, Duke University; Alfred Smith to James R. Grist, 11 January 1853, "List of *Negroes* belonging to *Mr. John W. Grist* and Worked by *Grist + Strikney* during the year of 1861," 1860, James Redding Grist Papers, Special Collections Library, Duke University.

Producers could rent not only slaves, but turpentine boxes as well. The rental price depended on the boxes' age and their distance from transportation. In 1854 landowner C. W. Smith received $181.32 for the rent of 17,435 boxes for four years. The price amounted to $26.00 per year for 10,000 boxes. However, some rental agreements were made for only one year. For the turpentine season of 1846–47 William D. Rodman rented his turpentine boxes to Mabum Minifield and Allison Whitly but found new renters for the next season. In cases of a turnover in renters, it was common for the gum in the boxes to be reserved for the previous year's renter until time for the new renter to commence chipping. Rental agreements usually contained other stipulations. When a producer rented turpentine boxes belonging to the estate of A. B. Mattick for 1860, he was required to post notes of security before working the boxes and had to agree to maintain a split rail fence on the premises. For this lease, the renter had use of a house on the land, its outbuildings, and the orchard.[16]

As naval stores prices rose and created such a demand for previously unwanted pineland that owners could actually rent it, more areas went into production. Convenient access to a still or market, however, determined whether or not even thick stands of virgin pine were worked for turpentine. Olmsted noted that "it is yet thought a harder venture to start the business where more than thirty miles wagoning is required to bring the spirits of turpentine to a railroad or navigable water." Pine forests on the periphery of transportation systems were often so isolated they could not be profitably worked at all or could, at most, be worked for only the most valuable gum.

Some producers could only profitably harvest gum, not scrape (hardened gum attached to the tree's face), or work the tree for only a few years. While traveling through North Carolina Olmsted observed trees at a prohibitively far distance from the market that had never been scraped. In such cases scrape, which contained about half the spirits of gum and was therefore less valuable, was not worth the expense of the labor to collect it and the transportation to get it to market. But at the time of his journey, he added, "the price of turpentine being now much higher than usual, many of the small proprietors are this year scraping their trees, that have not scraped before." Edmund Ruffin explained that in the case of scrape, which "is sold at half the price of the fluid turpentine[,] . . . the expense of land-carriage is a suffi-

16. P. Perry, "Naval Stores Industry in the Ante-Bellum South, 1789–1861," 44; John F. Minifield to William R. Rodman, 30 October 1847, William Blount Rodman Papers, North Carolina State Archives; "The Condition of renting farm land + Turpentine Boxes belonging to the estate A. B. Matttick dec.," 28 December 1859, William Basden Papers, Special Collections Library, Duke University.

cient bar to the production of so heavy and low-priced products, where the distance is considerable." Other times when prices were not as high, pine trees located some distance from transportation were worked only three or four years and then abandoned for new areas. The greatest profits came during the first year's harvest, which yielded virgin turpentine and number one rosin, the finest quality of these respective products. Second- and third-year harvests were also profitable. But as the distance that the gum had to flow down the face to the box increased with each season, the more the gum deteriorated from greater exposure to the sun, and the less valuable it became.[17]

The copper still helped producers push "into the depths of the forest" and affected the turpentine industry much like the gin had cotton production. Distilling in the vicinity of gum harvesting permitted turpentining to be done further from transportation routes near to which the industry had previously been confined. Naval stores products were bulky relative to their value. With on-site stills, producers were no longer burdened by the trouble and expense of hauling the heavy barrels of raw turpentine to port. Turpentine manufacturers were advised to locate their operations as nearby a still as possible. Producers could also save by shipping just the lighter and more valuable spirits and transporting rosin only when its price was high enough to bring a profit. Rosin prices reached these high levels only occasionally. At distilleries located near rivers, producers saved just the first- and second-quality rosin while the poorer qualities were run off and wasted. One distillery, by the mid-1850s, had accumulated an estimated $15,000 worth of rosin, which was simply drained out of the still and left at the site because the freight prices were too high to justify shipping it to market.[18]

As with stills, transportation improvements—opened rivers, plank roads, steamboats, and railroads—also facilitated the naval stores industry's expansion by regularizing shipping and reducing transportation costs. Commercial traffic on the Cape Fear River faced a considerable challenge. Although steamboats came into general use nationally in the 1830s, through the next

17. Olmsted, *Journey in the Seaboard Slave States*, 339, 343; Thomas D. S. McDowell to Sir, 16 January 1843, McDowell Papers; Ruffin, "Notes of a Steam Journey," 250; P. Perry, "Naval Stores Industry in the Ante-Bellum South, 1789–1861," 45; G. W. Perry, *Treatise on Turpentine Farming*, 78.

18. Olmsted, *Journey in the Seaboard Slave States*, 339, 345; "Turpentine Business in North Carolina and Georgia," 364; P. Perry, "Naval Stores Industry in the Old South, 1790–1860," *Journal of Southern History*, 514; Kenneth B. Pomeroy and James G. Yoho, *North Carolina Lands: Ownership, Use, and Management of Forest and Related Lands* (Washington, D.C.: American Forestry Association, 1964), 14; Ashe, *Forests, Forest Lands, and Forest Products*, 76; "The Southern Pine Forest—Turpentine," 190.

decade most naval stores traffic continued to move by raft and pole boat, with each carrying anywhere from twenty to three hundred barrels. The Cape Fear was commonly too low for steamboat navigation during the summer, and during many weeks even rafts were prevented from making the journey. Often, naval stores had to wait at landings until winter rains brought the river to a passable level. Wilmington's port's activity depended on the Cape Fear's water level. Its market was busiest after heavy rains when the valley's creek and river levels rose high enough for inland producers to launch their rafts, weighted with naval stores, lumber, and other commodities.[19]

In the 1850s, the Cape Fear and Deep River Navigation Company, supported by innovative Wilmington interests concerned with increasing the port's activity, set about making the Cape Fear River navigable as far north as Chatham County. Initiated to provide access to coal beds in Chatham County, the resulting improvements consisted of a series of dams and locks. Because this newly navigable stretch of river passed through the longleaf belt, it provided cheap transportation for an area that had previously been effectively cut off from the coastal market. Enterprising men constructed stills at the landings that dotted the newly open stretch of the Cape Fear, permitting the naval stores industry to extend into the far western reaches of North Carolina's longleaf pine belt.[20]

By the 1850s, new light-draft steamers were able to navigate the Cape Fear's low water level during the summer months and helped make naval stores marketing a year-round activity. Steamboats could carry from three hundred to five hundred barrels of naval stores, but most often the products were transported aboard large flats, called lighters. Pulled behind steamboats, the lighters could carry from 300 to 1,100 barrels, depending on their size and the depth of the river. Introduction of riverboats and navigation improvements gave Wilmington an advantage over New Bern and Washington. The Tar and Neuse Rivers that serviced the latter port communities were too shallow and sluggish to allow steam navigation, forcing producers to continue using carts, wagons, and flatboats to transport their commodities to market.[21]

19. Thomas Gamble, "Pages from Wilmington's Story as America's First Great Naval Stores Port," in Naval Stores: History, Production, Distribution and Consumption, ed. Thomas Gamble (Savannah: Review Publishing and Printing, 1921), 31–2; P. Perry, "Naval Stores Industry in the Ante-Bellum South, 1789–1861," 85–7, 89–90, 99–100; "Wilmington Market," WJ, 18 April 1845, 16 May 1845, 8 August 1845, 19 December 1845, and 17 April 1846.

20. P. Perry, "Naval Stores Industry in the Ante-Bellum South, 1789–1861," 97.

21. Gamble, "Pages from Wilmington's Story," 32; P. Perry, "Naval Stores Industry in the Ante-Bellum South, 1789–1861," 85–7, 89–90, 99–100; Frederick Law Olmsted, The Cotton Kingdom (1861; reprint, New York: Modern Library, 1984), 150.

Just as navigation improvements and steamboats facilitated water transportation, plank roads, which radiated from Fayetteville into the pine forests, provided better overland transportation. These roadways were constructed of heart pine planks, cut nine to sixteen inches wide, at least eight feet long, and three to four inches thick, laid at a ninety-degree angle over heavy sills which rested on a graded roadbed. Ditches and culverts provided adequate drainage to keep them dry. With these roads producers could haul their naval stores during any type of weather, even the rainiest periods, when work in the forest slowed and time was best spent transporting their goods to market. The first road built was the Fayetteville and Western, also known as the "Appian Way of North Carolina." Incorporated in 1849, completed in 1854, and reputed to be the longest plank road ever constructed, it extended for 129 miles from Fayetteville, toward the northwest, to the Moravian settlement of Bethania in Forsyth County. Its success as a toll road, especially from naval stores traffic, led to the construction of other such roads radiating from Fayetteville. One ran from Fayetteville through the western section of Cumberland County. Another, which was supposed to connect Fayetteville with Raleigh by passing through Harnett and into Wake County, never was completed. However, the finished portion provided access to areas of the pine forest that before had been too remote for profitable turpentine production.[22]

Plank roads facilitated the naval stores industry's spread into inland forests and funneled a considerable portion of the new production toward Fayetteville. In 1852 the *Fayetteville Observer* reported "that within the last three years the lands along the line of the Fayetteville and Western Plank Road in this country, . . . *have risen in value far more than the cost of that road through the country.*" Land prices rose because "the country, for sixty miles, has been thrown open to the production of various articles which previously could not be brought to market. We may instance [sic] Turpentine which is too heavy for transportation long distances over bad roads. But upon the Plank Road a number of Distilleries have been put up, and one is now going up *sixty miles* from this place." Plank roads made Fayetteville the center of wagon trade for the state and the inland seat for the handling of naval stores and distillation of crude gum. Most of the products collected at Fayetteville were shipped down the Cape Fear to Wilmington for export. However,

22. Lefler, ed., *North Carolina History Told by Contemporaries,* 229; P. Perry, "Naval Stores Industry in the Old South, 1790–1860," *Journal of Southern History,* 514, 519–20; Ashe, *Forests, Forest Lands, and Forest Products,* 77; Powell, *North Carolina through Four Centuries,* 305; P. Perry, "Naval Stores Industry in the Ante-Bellum South, 1789–1861," 116, 118; "The Tide Turned."

wooden roads, also referred to as "farmers' railroads," deteriorated rapidly, making their maintenance difficult and expensive. Not only did they fall into disrepair but also the cost of moving goods on them was relatively expensive, like all overland transportation, although not as costly as over dirt roads.[23]

In the end, roads of iron worked the most lasting impact on the naval stores industry's growth. In 1833 farsighted citizens of Wilmington, who believed correctly that their future prosperity depended on rail transportation, subscribed $400,000 for the Wilmington and Raleigh Railroad, which they chartered the following year. When Raleigh, which lacked Wilmington's enthusiasm for the project, failed to raise its share of the capital, the projected route shifted northward to the Roanoke River. In 1836 the charter was revised, and in 1837 construction began on the Wilmington and Weldon Railroad. By 1838 the line was already operating out of Wilmington along the right bank of the Cape Fear River for a distance of sixty-four miles. Upon completion in April 1840, the Wilmington and Weldon was 161.5 miles long, the longest railroad in the world. It cut northward through the heart of the longleaf pine forest, crossing the regions that had historically relied on the Tar and Neuse Rivers for transportation. As a result, much of the naval stores trade that had once flowed toward Washington and New Bern now rolled toward Wilmington, especially since railroads reportedly gave turpentine shipping priority. Though cotton bales sometimes sat beside the tracks for two or three weeks before they were loaded, naval stores rarely had to wait as long.[24]

Wilmington sought to continue its hold on the naval stores trade in the 1850s by constructing other rail lines that would terminate at its port. The Wilmington to Manchester Railroad, completed in 1853, extended 158 miles through the pine forest of Columbus County to Manchester, South Carolina. By opening the forest in the southeastern tip of North Carolina and northeastern South Carolina, it helped develop the naval stores industry in these regions. In 1850 De Bow's Review reported that "the route contemplated for the Wilmington and Manchester railroad runs through the center of it [the pine forest]; and in anticipation of the success of this enterprise, lands

23. P. Perry, "Naval Stores Industry in the Ante-Bellum South, 1789–1861," 116, 118; "The Tide Turned"; P. Perry, "Naval Stores Industry in the Old South, 1790–1860," Journal of Southern History, 514, 519–20; Ashe, Forests, Forest Lands, and Forest Products, 77; Powell, North Carolina through Four Centuries, 305.

24. P. Perry, "The Naval Stores Industry in the Old South, 1790–1860," Journal of Southern History, 519–21; Ashe, Forests, Forest Lands, and Forest Products, 77; Ruffin, "Notes of a Steam Journey," 243; P. Perry, "Naval Stores Industry in the Ante-Bellum South, 1789–1861," 110.

which once brought no more than ten to twenty cents per acre, have risen to $1 and $1.50."[25]

The next major North Carolina railroad project, although it did not run to Wilmington, was nevertheless designed to protect that town's shipping volume. Fearful that a proposed line from Danville, Virginia, through Charlotte, North Carolina, and on to Columbia, South Carolina, would take trade away from North Carolina's ports, particularly Wilmington, W. S. Ashe, a Democratic congressman from New Hanover County, introduced a bill in the North Carolina General Assembly in 1849 chartering the North Carolina Railroad Company. The state subscribed two million of the three million dollars needed for the project. Completed in 1856, the new rail line ran for 223 miles, from Goldsboro, North Carolina, through Hillsborough, Greensboro, Salisbury, and ended in Charlotte. Its eastern leg provided more access to the western reaches of the pine barrens.

Wilmington sponsored yet another railroad in 1855. The Wilmington, Charlotte, Rutherfordton Railroad was projected to run westward from Wilmington, through Bladen, Robeson, and Richmond Counties. By the eve of the Civil War, however, the line was completed only a few miles beyond Lumberton, a distance of eighty miles. It nevertheless opened up the pine forests of the region south of the Cape Fear River and permitted turpentine production in that area until the Civil War interrupted it. As historian Percival Perry has observed, "improved transportation and the expansion of the naval stores industry in North Carolina went hand in hand, and each greatly influenced the other."[26]

These transportation improvements—clearing the Cape Fear River, steamboats, plank roads, and railroads—raised Wilmington's prominence in the naval stores trade. Producers preferred to send turpentine to Wilmington by railroad rather than by boat to Washington. The railroad offered a more reliable and regular means of transportation to a more established market where prices were higher because of lower shipping costs to northern ports. But while the railroad linked Wilmington to previously inaccessible longleaf pine stands, it also made outside markets, particularly those of

25. Powell, *North Carolina through Four Centuries*, 285–9; P. Perry, "Naval Stores Industry in the Old South, 1790–1860," *Journal of Southern History*, 519–21; "Manufacture of Turpentine in the South," 451; Ashe, *Forests, Forest Lands, and Forest Products*, 77.

26. Powell, *North Carolina through Four Centuries*, 285–9; P. Perry, "Naval Stores Industry in the Old South, 1790–1860," *Journal of Southern History*, 514, 519–21; Ashe, *Forests, Forest Lands, and Forest Products*, 77; Allen W. Trelease, *The North Carolina Railroad, 1849–1871, and the Modernization of North Carolina* (Chapel Hill: University of North Carolina Press, 1991), 105, 264.

the North, accessible to the individual producers. Consequently a portion of the new turpentine production in the Cape Fear region bypassed Wilmington and traveled directly to inland distributors. However, the railroad channeled a larger portion of this new production to Wilmington, which became the trading center of North Carolina naval stores, eclipsing both New Bern and Washington. In 1837 Wilmington had exported but 81,872 barrels of naval stores. By 1855 it handled 698,780 barrels and in 1860 777,691 barrels. In the mid-1850s, a British traveler explained that "nearly the whole trade of the town is derived from the produce of the pine forests. The Wharves display immense quantities of pitch and resin barrels, and stills for the manufacture of turpentine are numerous. Pitch and turpentine afford an export trade of nearly one million sterling." This trade helped make Wilmington's population the fastest growing of any town in North Carolina. By 1860 Wilmington's population, the largest of any town in the state, had grown to 9,552, doubling in size since 1840. New Bern had 5,432 residents, and Fayetteville, which remained an important inland naval stores market but was bypassed by all the main railroad arteries, had 4,790. Yet by most standards, Wilmington remained a small town. In 1860, over one million people lived in New York, 565,000 in Philadelphia, and 169,000 in New Orleans. One visitor to Wilmington in 1855 found that "the houses are chiefly built of wood, and a little plot of garden ground surrounds the best of them. There is only one street paved, and the others are no better than the loose sand can make them. The numbers of mean negro huts, in some parts, are by no means a pleasing feature of the place."[27]

As Wilmington began to dominate the antebellum naval stores trade, the process of marketing these products developed into a more standardized practice. Turpentine producers had a choice of ways to sell their product. One means, popular among small farmers, was to sell raw turpentine to a distillery owner. "Those collecting but a small quantity [of turpentine]," Olmsted observed, sell to large producers who own stills "or to custom distilleries, owned by those who make distilling alone their business." Small producers in areas where turpentine was of little importance and located a considerable distance from a distillery could sell their few barrels of gum to large planters who marketed it themselves. For example, in the 1850s, Wil-

27. P. Perry, "Naval Stores Industry in the Old South, 1790–1860," *Journal of Southern History*, 519–21; P. Perry, "Naval Stores Industry in the Ante-Bellum South, 1789–1861," 257; Powell, *North Carolina through Four Centuries*, 285–9; "Manufacture of Turpentine in the South," 451; Ashe, *Forests, Forest Lands, and Forest Products*, 77; Cook, "Naval Stores," 8; Robert Russell, *North America: Its Agriculture and Climate* (Edinburgh: Adam and Charles Black, 1857), 158; Guion Griffis Johnson, *Ante-Bellum North Carolina: A Social History* (Chapel Hill: University of North Carolina Press, 1937), 117.

liam R. Smith, a planter from Halifax County, North Carolina, handled small quantities of locally produced gum. Smith maintained accounts for producers whose turpentine he purchased and offered them either cash or such supplies as coffee, pork, corn, bacon, and turpentining tools. Other small producers, who could get their gum or spirits to market, sold them to speculators who bought naval stores on commission for northern firms. Speculators commonly worked on a small scale because they lacked wharf accommodations and worked only during the busiest time of the marketing season. Tar shipments into Wilmington peaked from January to May and turpentine from June to April, but the latter was present in its greatest quantity from November 20 to February 1. If a producer rafted his own turpentine to the market, he might serve as his own agent, finding a buyer and making the sale while the barrels remained on the raft. By custom, the buyer purchased the whole raft as landed. The buyer subtracted the cost of handling, inspection, and cooperage, a charge of from ten cents to fourteen cents per barrel. If the producer could not accompany his product, it was not uncommon before the mid-1840s for an inspector to serve as his agent for the sale. However, this arrangement proved unsatisfactory to many turpentiners. In 1843 forty producers maintained "that great dissatisfaction exists among turpentine makers with regard to the mode of inspecting that article in the town of Wilmington, the way in which it is disposed of, and the manner generally of conducting the business connected with its sale, leading to the belief that they are not fairly dealt with." They requested a change in either the inspection laws or the manner of selling. When the practice of inspectors serving as agents ended in 1844, some inspectors quit their posts and became agents.[28]

Most producers, however, especially the large ones, employed the services of a commission and forwarding merchant, or factor, who, upon the naval stores' arrival in port, saw that they were unloaded, inspected, and sold. In the 1840s distillers and factors competed for gum. The stiff competition gave producers such an advantage that they often had the option of contracting their product in advance, which guaranteed them the highest market price at time of delivery and saved them the commission fee. As the amount of individual inland distilling increased and the volume of distillation in Wilmington waned in the later 1840s and 1850s, competition loos-

28. Olmsted, *Journey in the Seaboard Slave States*, 343; William R. Smith Memorandum Book, 1852–1853, Special Collections Library, Duke University; P. Perry, "Naval Stores Industry in the Ante-Bellum South, 1789–1861," 148–9, 152; Gamble, "Pages from Wilmington's Story," 31–2; "To Turpentine Makers," *Wilmington Chronicle,* 27 December 1843; "To Turpentine Makers," *WJ,* 21 September 1844; "Notice," *WJ,* 30 May 1845.

ened and the business for factors grew. Most large producers chose to sell their naval stores through factors because factors proved adept at marketing their commodity to the producers' best advantage and offered a variety of other helpful services. Factors were reputed to have had the best knowledge of the naval stores trade. And they provided prompt sale of naval stores and avoided speculation unless directed to do so by their client. They also advanced capital to producers whose wealth was tied up in slaves and pineland. Unlike banks, which were few in the region and did not lend on the security of pine timber tracts or still facilities because of their temporary and transient nature, factors supplied the necessary operating capital. If an account went unsettled, they would simply extend the balance to the next year; they rarely called in debts. Finally, the factor defended the producer against any complaint from the buyer.[29]

Factors were not unique to naval stores marketing. Historian Harold Woodman explains that factorage houses served as the most common means by which antebellum southern planters marketed their cotton crop. The factor bought, sold, received, and forwarded goods, for which he received a commission. The 2.5 percent commission that both cotton and turpentine factors received for their services was a carryover from the standard used by London factors who handled American tobacco sales in the seventeenth and eighteenth centuries. As the producers' representative in the market, factors possessed the skill, experience, and information sources to make the proper judgments in their clients' best interest. Because the factor had to be an expert on market fluctuations, crop size, and quality, not to mention the producer's needs as well, he most often specialized in only one commodity. However, it was not uncommon for factors dealing in turpentine also to trade timber and lumber. Factors also ensured that producers received their needed supplies. If they did not actually stock what was needed, they acquired it from elsewhere, paid the bill, and charged the producer's account. Factors usually extended a line of credit. Producers who required funds typically turned to their factor rather than to banks, although ultimately it was a bank that supplied the credit. Planters could only draw a note on the bank with the factor's endorsement. Woodman explains that "this, of course, changed the whole nature of the loan: banks were lending not on the security of a plantation, slaves, or cotton but on the liquid assets of a city merchant. In a word, by adding his endorsement to the planter's note, the factor

29. P. Perry, "Naval Stores Industry in the Ante-Bellum South, 1789–1861," 148–9, 152, 157–8; Hayes, "General History," 98.

was guaranteeing the payment of the note at maturity." Woodman empha-
sizes that the factor, far from holding producers in debt peonage, provided
an essential service in the South's plantation economy. Not only did they
bring capital into the region, but also with their knowledge of price and
market conditions, they were the most effective brokers to sell commodities
and, with their connections in port towns, to keep the inland producers supplied with goods. But, as with cotton, the real locus of power in financing,
marketing, and pricing of naval stores was not found in the southern port
cities where factors and shipping firms handled these commodities, but in
New York and Liverpool, where trading firms monitored the world supply
and set prices.[30]

As with cotton, the cost of marketing turpentine—which included, on
top of the 2.5 percent factor's commission, cost for freight, drayage, inspection, storage, cooperating, and insurance—consumed more than a small portion of the product's gross value. Turpentine shipped through R. W. Brown
and Son, a Wilmington factor, serves as an example of the expenses involved
in marketing naval stores. In October 1835 the firm shipped seventy-seven
barrels of raw turpentine aboard the *Regulus* from Wilmington to New York.
In addition to the freight cost, handling charges included $1.54 to land the
shipment when it first arrived in Wilmington, $2.34 to transport the barrels
around the dock, 60¢ to deliver the barrels to the schooner for the trip to
New York, and 20¢ to load them aboard the ship. To inspect the shipment
cost $2.20, and to repair either deficient or damaged barrels cost $3.04. The
fee for storage at the wharf was 76¢. The commission paid to the factor for
handling the shipment was 5 percent, $13.79, double the usual fee. Total cost
of marketing the turpentine shipment amounted to $24.47, a little more
than 9 percent of the shipment's gross value of $267.51. This is similar to
the cost of marketing cotton: 6 to 10 percent of the gross proceeds.[31]

Marketing naval stores could not only be costly, but confusing as well.
Until naval stores developed into a big business within its borders, North
Carolina neglected to create a uniform marketing code for these products.
For most of the antebellum period there existed only chance consistency in
production standards and weight among the several ports that handled naval

30. Harold Woodman, *King Cotton and His Retainers: Financing and Marketing the Cotton
Crop of the South, 1800–1925* (Lexington: University Press of Kentucky, 1968; reprint, Colum-
bia: University of South Carolina Press, 1990), 6, 14, 22, 26, 32, 39, 41, 49, 114–6, 130, 174–5;
"Agency for the Sale of Timber, Lumber, and Naval Stores," *WJ*, 5 January 1849; "Notice,"
Wilmington Chronicle, 1 June 1849.

31. Shipping Receipt, 17 October 1835, Oliver H. Jones Papers, Special Collections Library,
Duke University; Woodman, *King Cotton*, 177.

stores in the state. Inspectors employed relatively arbitrary standards in their duties because the legislature provided only vague guidelines. They examined barrels to determine how free the product was of dirt, wood chips, bark, straw, leaves, and water. They also decided if the raw turpentine was "hard" or "soft," hard being the scrape removed from the face and soft the gooey resin dipped out of the box. The standards for soft and hard gum were well established. However, barrels containing a mixture of hard and soft turpentine were more difficult to grade. Typically, hard turpentine sold for half the price of soft, so unscrupulous producers mixed soft and hard gum in hopes that the mixture could be sold as soft. In such cases inspectors had few guidelines by which to judge the quality, a situation that often led to disputes between buyers and sellers. Inspectors also checked to see that barrels were branded with the producer's initials. Inspections were valid only for twenty days before export. If the barrels sat for longer, they had to be reinspected to determine if exposure to the sun's heat had damaged the material or made it more viscous, causing it to leak from the barrels. Contributing to the marketing confusion until the late 1840s was the inconsistency in the size of North Carolina's turpentine barrels. The barrels used at Washington and New Bern weighed 280 pounds gross, but those shipped through Wilmington weighed 320 pounds gross. Because Washington and New Bern had first handled the bulk of the turpentine trade, the New York market had established their 280-pound barrel as the standard trade weight. After a chaotic period of dual barrel sizes and price scales, the Wilmington dealers, in 1849, finally submitted and accepted the smaller barrel.[32]

Despite early confusion regarding marketing, during the antebellum era, naval stores production, especially turpentine manufacturing, grew into a large-scale business dominated by a wealthy class of entrepreneurial producers who required the services of factorage houses to financially sustain their businesses as well as consistent quality standards to ensure their products' marketability. In the late eighteenth and early nineteenth centuries naval stores production languished as a marginally profitable business which no state, save North Carolina, wanted. Prevented by its poor soils from participating in the cotton boom that other southern states enjoyed, North Carolina's economic development stagnated through the 1830s, earning it the unfortunate distinction as the "Rip Van Winkle State." But as demand for turpentine outstripped that for tar and its price persisted at relatively high levels, spirits developed, in a sense, into a substitute for cotton which attracted the attention of some of the state's wealthier men. Their ability to

32. P. Perry, "Naval Stores Industry in the Ante-Bellum South, 1789–1861," 161–7, 171–3, 179, 190–3, 198–9; "Notice to Dealers in Turpentine & Tar," WJ, 25 June 1847.

construct their own stills, coupled with transportation improvements, permitted the industry to expand into previously inaccessible areas of southeastern North Carolina. As the resulting flow of naval stores through the state's ports, especially Wilmington, increased, factors handled the marketing of these products manufactured largely by slave laborers, but also by poor whites and yeomen.

CHAPTER 3

LIFE AND LABOR IN THE PINE FORESTS

SOUTHERNERS—POOR WHITES, small piney woods farmers, and slaves—who occupied the antebellum pine forest and labored in some capacity in the turpentine industry all lived an existence different from that of most southerners engaged in agriculture. Poor whites, who lived a relatively isolated and subsistence-based existence in the pine barrens, either harvested small quantities of gum, which they sold for finished goods or food, or worked on an irregular basis for larger producers. Other, more middle class whites worked on a somewhat larger and more regular schedule to produce turpentine for the market, sometimes with the help of several slaves. Unlike the piney woods whites, however, large naval stores operators often did not reside in areas quite so isolated, but rather close by small population centers or at least near major transportation routes. They lived lives more similar to large plantation owners than other southern whites who produced on a smaller scale with their own labor. Because big producers came to dominate the antebellum industry, slaves performed the vast majority of labor. For these unfree laborers, the expansion of naval stores manufacturing after 1830, the various procedures involved in harvesting turpentine, the size and location of the turpentine forests, and the ways that these three factors affected slave-management practices created a distinct "work and . . . manner of life." In fact, turpentine slaves perhaps endured harsher working and living conditions than bondsmen on a typical agricultural plantation.[1]

Poor whites who lived in the southern pine forest often engaged in tur-

1. William J. Parham to James R. Grist, 1 May 1854, Grist Papers.

pentining in some way, whether producing small quantities on their own or laboring for a large producer. Unfortunately little is known of the smaller-scale producers. Illiterate for the most part, they left scant written record. It is known, however, that the few white dwellers of the piney woods lived in near isolation. The longleaf pine prefers light, sandy soil and clay subsoil. These soil conditions could not sustain staple agriculture and, consequently, caused most settlers to bypass the pine barrens. Mid-nineteenth-century travelers commented on the dearth of inhabitants in the region. When reporter David Hunter Strother (pen name Porte Crayon) turned from the main road to explore the North Carolina countryside, he could not "resist the feeling of loneliness that creeps over one on entering these silent forests, or to repress a sentiment of superstitious dread as you glance through the somber many-columned aisles, stretching away on every side in interminable perspective." Frederick Law Olmsted described the road which he traveled upon in the same region as "a narrow opening through a forest of long-leafed pine." The pine branches, fully tipped with needles, formed a dense canopy that shaded the forest. "In ten miles," he claimed, "I passed half a dozen cabins, one or two small clearings, in which corn had been planted, and one turpentine distillery, with a dozen sheds and cabins clustered about it." Still another traveler reported that one could journey for a day anywhere in the region between Wilmington and Raleigh and not pass more than one or two houses. Signs of life and development, however, reportedly increased as one approached the Wilmington and Weldon Railroad corridor. Yet even there William C. Corsan, an Englishman touring the Confederacy in 1862, found the countryside along the railroad "depressing": "Low swampy levels, intersected with turbid streams," he explained, "were followed by long stretches of poor, sandy, monotonous country, covered with pitch pines, and destitute apparently of inhabitants."[2]

Despite Corsan's failure to find human settlement, a sparse population of poor whites occupied the unwanted clay bottomlands and sand hills of the piney woods South. Across the South, from the Carolinas through the Gulf South, they either lived in an empty log cabin with the owner's consent or constructed a log hut on a plot upon which they squatted. The infertile land was of such low financial value that poor white families could, with little

2. P. Perry, "Naval Stores Industry in the Ante-Bellum South, 1789–1861," vi; Rupert B. Vance, *Human Geography of the South: A Study in Regional Resources and Human Adequacy* (Chapel Hill: University of North Carolina Press, 1935), 112; Thomas D. Clark, *The Greening of the South: The Recovery of Land and Forest* (Lexington: University Press of Kentucky, 1984), 15; Crayon, "North Carolina Illustrated," 746; Olmsted, *Journey in the Seaboard Slave States*, 326; McMillan to *Southern Cultivator*, 14 April 1846, 122; W. C. Corsan, *Two Months in the Confederate States* (Baton Rouge: Louisiana State University Press, 1996), 68.

harassment, find small tracts on which to live. Here they worked small gardens plots and did occasional odd jobs on the few neighboring plantations. They commonly furnished their simple houses with just a few chairs, a bench, one or two beds, a corner cupboard, an oven, and a skillet and frying pan. Yards typically included a well with a cypress bucket, fodder stacks consisting of corn leaves held above the ground by tall poles, three well-protected sweet potato hills, and empty gourds used for martin houses. Most yards had fruit trees or a scuppernong grapevine. Corn, sweet potatoes, peas, and collards grew in gardens; hogs foraged for themselves in the forest. Poor whites supplemented their diet with such game as they could shoot in the forest—wild hogs, deer, wild turkey, squirrel, raccoon, and opossum.[3]

Despite their ability to gather food from the forest, "common whites did not . . . live in a purely subsistence economy in which they never bought or sold anything," as historian Bill Cecil-Fronsman argues. Bradley Bond agrees. He finds that piney woods people did not live in complete isolation or by self-sufficiency, but participated in the market economy. Most used the market to acquire finished goods and probably to supplement the little grain they grew. To acquire the money for what they needed to buy, small farmers produced crops for market or engaged in home manufacturing. In the piney woods, turpentine production often provided a family of small means the only staple they could produce from the sandy pineland. Despite little capital, the father and older boys were able to cut boxes and chip while the wife, girls, and younger boys dipped. Such a family operation could turn a profit—even if it had to rent the boxes, buy the barrels, and pay to have the product hauled to the market or to a larger operator who would buy the gum. Edmund Ruffin observed that white families living in the piney woods relied almost solely on tar and turpentine for a marketable product.[4]

Piney woods folk not only produced naval stores themselves but worked

3. Johnson, *Ante-Bellum North Carolina,* 69, 72; Grady McWhiney, "Crackers and Cavaliers: Shared Courage," in *Plain Folk of the South Revisited,* ed. Samuel C. Hyde, Jr. (Baton Rouge: Louisiana State University Press, 1997), 190; Grady McWhiney, "Antebellum Piney Woods Culture: Continuity over Time and Place," in *Mississippi's Piney Woods: A Human Perspective,* ed. Noel Park (Jackson: University Press of Mississippi), 47; Paul H. Buck, "The Poor Whites of the Ante-Bellum South," *American Historical Review* 31 (October 1925): 43, 45; Crayon, "North Carolina Illustrated," 746–7; Olmsted, *Journey in the Seaboard Slave States,* 348–50.

4. Bill Cecil-Fronsman, *Common Whites: Class and Culture in Antebellum North Carolina* (Lexington: University Press of Kentucky, 1992), 10, 100, 102; Bradley G. Bond, "Herders, Farmers, and Markets on the Inner Frontier: The Mississippi Piney Woods, 1850–1860," in *Plain Folk of the South Revisited,* ed. Samuel C. Hyde, Jr. (Baton Rouge: Louisiana State University Press, 1997), 81, 86; "Turpentine: Hints for Those about to Engage in Its Manufacture," 488; Johnson, *Ante-Bellum North Carolina,* 486; Ruffin, "Notes of a Steam Journey," 246, 250.

for large operators as well. At Onslow County's Richlands Plantation, for example, poor white families aided with fire prevention. With insurance impossible to obtain for such a combustible business as turpentine manufacturing, the only protection from the destruction caused by fire was for piney woods whites to police the forest and extinguish any flame as soon as possible. Log cabins in which the families lived dotted the expansive forest of twenty thousand acres. Families lived rent-free and could cultivate as much land as they chose, which was rarely more than a garden. Typically the women worked their plot and raised young children while the older children gathered wild berries and the men hunted and fished. In return, these families rendered several services to the plantation, most importantly guarding against fire. Whenever fire broke out, it was the families' responsibility to extinguish it. If flames got out of control, they were to blow horns to summon the other families in the forest to assist. Their secondary task was to tend the plantation's livestock, which grazed loose in the forest. Once a week they provided salt to the cattle herd, and each night they drove the sheep into a pen for protection from predators. The white families also cared for the plantation's bees and gathered the honey for the big house. When the plantation's roads required repairs, they performed the work. To earn cash they sold their game, poultry, and berries to the plantation. James Avirett reported that these poor whites kept to themselves. "They never mingle with the more thrifty white people," he explained, "while the negroes on the estate look down upon them, calling them, most disdainfully, 'poor white trash.'"[5]

Small, independent farmers and turpentiners occupied a slightly higher status in piney woods white society, but as Cecil-Fronsman explains, "the line between poor whites and their more prosperous yeoman neighbors was never rigid." Many small producers lived in cabins, although these were better constructed than those belonging to the poorer whites. Some inhabited frame dwellings. Their houses had no glass windows, but did contain more abundant furniture than those of the poorest classes; their yards included a vegetable garden with collards. These small piney woods farmers also owned a few dogs, more hogs, and raised more corn than the poor whites, but cultivated very little in way of staple crops. Their property holdings, which in some cases could be surprisingly considerable, consisted mainly of slaves. One small naval stores producer, for example, worked three slaves, at least one he hired. Because of his farm's poor soil he grew only a little cotton,

5. James Battle Avirett, *The Old Plantation: How We Lived in Great House and Cabin before the War* (New York: F. Tennyson Neely, 1901), 70–1.

just enough for his family to make cloth for their own clothes, and instead concentrated on turpentine.[6]

Large, specialized operators, whose numbers grew sharply during the three decades after 1830, produced far more turpentine than did yeoman farmers. For example, James Avirett's father, John Avirett of Richlands Plantation, raised tobacco, rice, sorghum, cotton, wheat, oats, rye, and corn, as well as several hundred head of hogs and sheep, but his thirty-thousand-barrel-a-year turpentine operation consumed the largest portion of Richlands' labor. The plantation's twenty-two thousand acres of pine forest provided enough boxes to keep busy 125 slaves, 2 turpentine distilleries, and several cooperage shops. John Avirett, born in 1797 and descended from German Huguenots who settled in the area in the 1740s, had become prominent enough by 1791 to host George Washington during his southern tour. As a powerful planter, John Avirett served a term in the state senate and nearly twenty years as Onslow County's sheriff. In his forties when turpentine demand swelled, he used the industry to make his short-lived fortune. His expansive operation lay on the stage road fifty-eight miles north of Wilmington and forty-two miles south of New Bern. An avenue of elms, 1,200 feet long and 40 feet wide lead to his impressive home, which rested on five-foot-high brick pillars. A piazza extended around his three-story residence, whose large windows opened to the floor. The outbuildings included a kitchen, which was connected to the house by the piazza, three smokehouses, a flour house, a cotton house, and a large storage house. Located to the rear of these buildings were the chicken coops that John Avirett's son James explained were "well fenced in, secure from the egg-sucking cur of the negro quarter, as well as from mink or weasel at night." Near the poultry yard was a one-acre vegetable garden and a weaving room where slaves wove the cotton and woolen cloth used on the plantation. Beyond the quarters was the Richlands gin house, with shed rooms built around it where carpenters worked. Down the hill from it stood a storage building for groceries and wagons and a corral for the 150 horses and mules used on the estate.[7]

James R. Grist was another representative large producer, who, like Avirett, lived in relative grand style for the area. While Strother was traveling through North Carolina in 1857 the only object that caught his eye in Washington was the Grist residence, located "at the end of the main street, with

6. Cecil-Fronsman, *Common Whites*, 17; Olmsted, *Journey in the Seaboard Slave States*, 350; R. Russell, *North America*, 160–1.

7. Avirett, *Old Plantation*, 22–5, 36–41, 51–4, 64–6 (quotation on page 40); David S. Cecelski, "The Rise and Fall of the Rich Lands," *Coastwatch* (January–February 1997): 22; David S. Cecelski, "Oldest Living Confederate Chaplain Tells All? Or, James B. Avirett and the Rise and Fall of the Rich Lands," *Southern Cultures* 3 (winter 1997): 10.

beautifully-improved grounds." In the early 1850s, Grist entered the turpentine business with his father in Beaufort County but later moved to areas near the Cape Fear River and South Carolina. Grist became a wealthy and influential businessman in eastern North Carolina. For example, he assisted the Banks brothers' steamboat company by endorsing their loans and using his influence to convince a Wilmington factorage house to use the Bankses' boats to carry its goods. Out of gratitude, the Bankses in 1854 named their new steamer the *James R. Grist.*[8]

The experiences of Sarah Hicks Williams offers insight into the lives of women married to large turpentine producers, such as Grist and Avirett. Sarah Hicks of New Hartford, New York, had known Benjamin Williams for five years when he first proposed marriage in 1850. Although she was certain of his affection for her, she disliked two characteristics about him—"his owning of slaves" and his "not being a professed Christian." However, when Williams renewed his proposal three years later, Sarah, for unknown reasons, agreed to overlook these qualities and accepted. An ambitious North Carolina doctor, Williams had served in the state legislature, invested in both forest and cleared land, and operated a turpentine operation about seven miles from his Greene County residence. After moving to her new home in the North Carolina pine barrens during the fall of 1853, Sarah was struck by the region's isolation and lack of development. During a twenty-mile journey from her home to the town of Wilson, she did not "think we passed over a half dozen houses. The road on both sides was bounded by woods, mostly pine, and the trees are much taller and larger than ours" in New York. She was also surprised to find that North Carolinians "live more heartily" than northerners, always serving two or three different kinds of meats for breakfast and dinner. Although the portions were more plentiful than those issued to the slaves, Sarah's diet, which included regular servings of corn bread, biscuits, and sweet potatoes, resembled that of the bondsmen who labored at her husband's turpentine operation. But while the slaves probably received salted hog meat, the Williamses enjoyed fresh pork prepared in traditional Carolina fashion. "Red pepper," she observed, "is much used to flavor meat with the famous 'barbarcue' of the South and which I believe they esteem above all dishes is roasted pig dressed with red pepper and vinegar." The Williamses also ate peaches and apples when they were in season. Sarah occupied her time attending church, receiving visitors or visiting in others' homes, and helping with housework and even with management of the plantation. She shared the doctor's two-story wood frame

8. Crayon, "North Carolina Illustrated," 750; P. Perry, "Naval Stores Industry in the Ante-Bellum South, 1789–1861," 95, 523.

house with her mother-in-law, who acted as mistress of the home. Sarah had her own room, furnished with her belongings, in which she could read and write in privacy. When not engaged with church or visits, she assisted the doctor's mother in sewing clothes for the slaves who worked about the plantation. Sarah explained that although many plantations "keep a seamstress to do this, . . . Mother Williams has always done it herself with the assistance of her daughters when they were home." They did not, however, sew for slaves who labored at the distant turpentine operation. Sarah persisted in her opposition to slavery, but admitted that she found "no unkind treatment of the servants, indeed I think that they are treated with more familiarity than many northern servants." The slaves' consistent presence "in the parlor + in your room, + all over" unnerved her.

After a couple of years in North Carolina, Sarah gained more responsibility for her home and the plantation, especially when her husband was absent on his frequent trips to tend to his turpentine operation. During his absences, "I see to his business," she explained in 1855. "I am up before sunrise to give out the keys, he told me how to order, + sometimes I steal Mother's thunder I watch, and see what her hands are doing + then I order ours as if I knew it all." She played an increased role in the plantation's management when she moved with her husband to south Georgia in the late 1850s. By 1859 her responsibilities had become so great that she complained, "my mind is so filled" with the care of the slaves. She was in charge of "sixteen here [Carleton County], + five up in Ware Co + over thirty getting Turpentine though these latter do not come to me for clothes, or food, still they call this their home + several of them always are here Sundays." She also tended sick slaves who labored at the house as well as those who worked for the turpentine operation several miles away. In October 1860 she was not only tending to her sick cook, but "Jim was sent home from the still half sick, so now I have two to take care of."[9]

A foundation of slave laborers like Jim supported the turpentine boom of the 1830s, '40s, and '50s. More than anything else, the longleaf pine's seasonal growth cycle shaped their work schedule. In large trees the center dark-colored wood, the heartwood, is physiologically dead. Its cells no longer function and it does not grow. Sapwood, a younger and lighter-colored wood, surrounds the heartwood and facilitates the movement of nutrients and water between the roots and the needles. A thin layer of cells called the cambium surrounds the sapwood, which is in turn encased in a layer of inner bark called the phloem. Trees grow each year by the division of cam-

9. Sarah F. Hicks to Parents, 7 March, 10 October, 17 November, 10 December 1853, 22 May 1855, 25 March 1859, and 21 October 1860, Williams Papers.

bium cells which create a layer of new wood called the xylem. All pine trees contain resin ducts, tiny tubes that run horizontally and vertically, creating a network in the sapwood that extends from the inner layer of bark to a depth of one inch or more into the tree. When the tree reaches maturity, these passages become lined with a tissue, the epithelium, from which resin is secreted. The resin serves as a protective outer coating in case the bark is damaged and falls away from the tree. In such instances resin oozes from the ducts over the wound to create a shield that diseases and insects are unable to penetrate and thereby provides time for the bark and cambium layer to heal. Resin is not sap. The epithelium cells manufacture resin only when required to protect the tree; it does not circulate through the tree as sap, a water-based solution that does. Resin ducts are particularly large and abundant in longleaf pines. Moreover, the gum of this species does not harden as rapidly when exposed to air and water and flows more freely over the wood than in most other southern pines. The longleaf's resinous quality was widely recognized in early America. Naturalist F. André Michaux reported that its "resinous matter, which is abundant, is more uniformly distributed than in the other species."[10]

When beginning a turpentine operation, producers attempted to identify pine acreage that they believed would yield the most abundant resin. Turpentiner G. W. Perry recommended that turpentiners concentrate their efforts on healthy, straight trees with large tops. In 1855 turpentine producers in Alabama were informed that thick stands would not produce as much turpentine as those with trees more sparsely placed and therefore free to grow with less competition. Another producer agreed that "the best trees are young, thriving, on pretty good soil, of quick growth, having the most sap-wood. If found on low, level, or moist lands, they will yield all the better. Dry seasons are unfavorable for a large crop of turpentine, and, of course, trees on lands that suffer easily from drouth are least profitable for market."

---

10. Donnie D. Bellamy, "Slavery in Microcosm: Onslow County, North Carolina," *Journal of Negro History* 62 (October 1977): 343; Weaver and Anderson, *Manual of Southern Forestry*, 33, 35; A. J. Panshin et al., *Forest Products: Their Sources, Production, and Utilization* (New York: McGraw-Hill, 1962), 439–40; Karl Peteraschak, "The Further Development of the Technique of Turpentining Pines," 4, Cary Collection; Nelson Courtlandt Brown, *Forest Products: The Harvesting, Processing, and Marketing of Materials Other Than Lumber, Including the Principal Derivatives, Extractives, and Incidental Products in the United States and Canada* (New York: John Wiley and Sons, 1950), 183–4; M. D. Mobley and Robert N. Haskins, *Forestry in the South* (Atlanta: Turner E. Smith, 1956), 230; Eloise Gerry, "The Production of Crude 'Gum' by the Pine Tree," in *Naval Stores: History, Production, Distribution and Consumption*, ed. Thomas Gamble (Savannah: Review Publishing and Printing, 1921), 152; Peter Koch, *Utilization of the Southern Pines* (Washington, D.C.: United States Department of Agriculture Forest Service, 1972), 1476; Michaux, *North American Sylva*, 108.

Other observers also commented on the importance of soil quality. Perry explained that the sandy and gravelly land was the best for making turpentine. He argued that poor, moist soil grew less resinous trees that would fill the boxes only slowly. And he was sure that mountainous or hilly land would never make much turpentine.[11]

Once producers had selected a likely forest, beginning in November and ending around the first of March, slave laborers performed the first and most important procedure, boxing. Using a special ax with an elongated head, workers cut a hole, or box, as it was called, eight to fifteen inches wide and three to four inches deep, at the base of a pine tree trunk. The length of the box gradually increased, as the upper edge was cut away to freshen the wound and maintain the flow of gum. The boxes were cut down at an angle and could hold one to two quarts of raw turpentine. Laborers had to use care when cutting boxes. First they decided the number of boxes to cut into the pine, which depended on the tree's size. Pines less than one foot in diameter could not support a box as readily as larger trees could. If smaller ones were to be tapped, they could have only one small box; a full quart-size box would cause the tree to fall or to decay prematurely. In no case were workers to allow the box to extend deep into the tree's heart. Larger trees could support larger boxes, and trees of great size could support multiple boxes, usually around three. In such cases the ideal placement of the boxes was side by side with four inches of bark between them, with a third or more of the tree's face left uncut for circulation of sap between the needles and the roots. Some producers, instead of cutting all the possible boxes at one time, worked only one side of the tree for five or six years, then back-boxed the opposite side when the yield of the old boxes diminished.[12]

Second, workers had to adapt boxing methods to their employer's particular specifications. Some producers preferred the boxes cut at the swell of the root so they would remain safely away from the heart. Other producers found boxes cut as high as eighteen inches from the ground more beneficial. Although increasing the risk that the heart of the tree might be cut, putting the box farther off the ground ensured against rain washing into it.

11. G. W. Perry, *Treatise on Turpentine Farming*, 18, 84, 94, 134, 154; "Turpentine Product of the South," *De Bow's Review* 18 (January 1855): 61. "Turpentine: Hints for Those about to Engage in Its Manufacture," 486.

12. "The Pine Forests of the South," *De Bow's Review: After the War Series* 3 (February 1867): 196; Ruffin, "Notes of a Steam Journey," 250; "Manufacture of Turpentine in the South," 454; "Turpentine: Hints for Those about to Engage in Its Manufacture," 486; Johnson, *Ante-Bellum North Carolina*, 487; "Production of Turpentine in Alabama," *De Bow's Review* 7 (December 1849): 560–1; "Product of Turpentine at the South," 303; "Turpentine Product of the South," 61; MacLeod, "Tar and Turpentine Business," 14; Description of turpentining, John McLean Harrington Papers, Special Collections Library, Duke University.

Finally, the position of the box also depended on the configuration of the tree. If a tree leaned, the best location for the box was on the side opposite the direction of the lean. Not only did this side generally have the most prominent root, but it was also the only position that guaranteed that a sufficient amount of raw turpentine would reach the box. If a box was located anywhere else on such a tree, the gum would fall outside the box in increasing amounts as the scarred face moved up the trunk with every harvest season. When the shape of the tree permitted, producers found that placing boxes on the north side was beneficial. This location protected gum in the box from evaporation caused by the sun's heat and ensured a higher grade of gum, which would produce more spirits.[13]

Boxing required not only care but strength, skill, and experience. Strong men could be trained to become adequate boxers in several days, and the amount of work performed by box cutters varied with the skill of the worker and the demands of the operator and overseer. Producers agreed that new hands could not cut as many boxes as experienced ones and that driving them to do so would result in low-quality boxes and inadequate yield from the orchard. Men planning to enter the business were advised that "beginners will not cut at first more than 50 boxes a day, and there is nothing gained by tasking them too high, until they have got well used to the proper shape and size of boxes." Producers valued slaves skilled at boxing. In 1851 Grist's manager reported that he was "cutting boxes with all of the best hands + giting timber + distilling with the ballans I have a good many green hands + they ar hard to learn to cut boxes." White managers accepted the idea that "Negroes are generally expert with the axe." An experienced laborer was expected to cut 75 to 80 boxes a day or 450 to 500 a week. However, exceptional workers could cut 90 to 100 a day. On one operation the best boxers reportedly cut 125 a day. The number of boxes cut in a day also depended on the number of daylight hours. As days grew longer, workers were usually expected to cut more boxes. The size of the pines and their distance from each other also determined the hand's task. Because larger trees could support more than one box, laborers could spend more time cutting and less time walking from tree to tree. The distance of the trees from one another also influenced walking time. If trees grew far apart, workers spent a larger portion of their time walking to them. On average an acre contained about 100 boxes.[14]

13. "Manufacture of Turpentine in the South," 452–3; "Turpentine: Hints for Those about to Engage in Its Manufacture," 486; A. W. Schorger and H. S. Betts, *The Naval Stores Industry* (Washington, D.C.: United States Department of Agriculture, 1915), 16.

14. "Pine Forests of the South," 196; Ruffin, "Notes of a Steam Journey," 250; "Manufacture of Turpentine in the South," 454; "Turpentine: Hints for Those about to Engage in Its Manufacture," 486; Johnson, *Ante-Bellum North Carolina*, 487; "Production of Turpentine in

After the boxes were cut they had to be cornered. Usually performed around the first of March with an ordinary ax, cornering involved removing a one-inch triangular chip from the top two corners of the box. Each corner could usually be cut with two strokes. One gash rose diagonally from the apex of the box and the other rose perpendicularly from the corner of the box. The ax cuts had to be precise, because the angle of the corners guided the gum into the box. While some producers calculated that workers should corner 500 to 600 boxes a day, others reckoned the task at 600 to 800 boxes.[15]

Once they had been cornered, the boxes began to fill with gum and had to be dipped. The number of dippings per season varied from four to seven, with more dipping performed during the tree's first two years of harvesting than in later ones. The process required a dipper, an instrument with a spade-shaped blade and a handle. The harvester collected gum by thrusting the dipper into one end of the box, pushing it to the bottom, and bringing it up to the opposite side—all in one quick motion. The sticky contents of the box adhered to the flat surface of the dipper. As laborers dipped each box, they carried the gum to one of two buckets. The buckets usually held eight gallons and had bases wider than their tops, making them less likely to spill. A strip of hoop-iron attached to the edge of the bucket served as a scraper that cleaned the gum off the dipper. When the first bucket was full, a slave carried it to a forty-gallon barrel, turned it upside down, and left it to drain while filling the second bucket. When the second was full, it took the place of the first. Although dipping was a light task requiring little physical strength, it was a dirty operation that smeared the workers' hands and clothing with gum.[16]

Many factors influenced the number of boxes that could be dipped and consequently the amount of gum that could be harvested. Weather conditions, for one, affected the dipping frequency. Temperature influenced the raw turpentine's consistency and thus the ease and speed with which it

---

Alabama," 560–1; "Product of Turpentine at the South," 303; Benjamin Grist to Allen Grist, 21 January 1851, Grist Papers; MacLeod, "Tar and Turpentine Business," 14; "Production of Turpentine in Alabama," 561; "Manufacture of Turpentine in the South," 452; Avirett, *Old Plantation*, 67; Percival Perry, interview by author, 9 April 1991, notes in author's possession, Wake Forest University, Winston-Salem, N.C.

15. MacLeod, "Tar and Turpentine Business," 14; Schorger and Betts, *Naval Stores Industry*, 16; "Product of Turpentine at the South," 303; "Turpentine: Hints for Those about to Engage in Its Manufacture," 486.

16. "Turpentine: Hints for Those about to Engage in Its Manufacture," 486–7; "Production of Turpentine in Alabama," 561; Ruffin, "Notes of a Steam Journey," 250; "Product of Turpentine at the South," 303–4; MacLeod, "Tar and Turpentine Business," 14; "Pine Forests of the South," 197; Schorger and Betts, *Naval Stores Industry*, 17; Avirett, *Old Plantation*, 68.

could be dipped. In hot weather it had a viscous quality, but when the thermometer dropped it stiffened. G. W. Perry explained that "by the continuance of cool weather, the dipper will be hard to get down in the box, and if the turpentine be left therein, it will remain stiff until the return of warm weather in the following spring." Dry weather also affected gum yield. The manager of the Grist operation observed that "all of work is going on well but it is too dry for the pines to run well." Wet weather too slowed dipping. One producer explained that "an early or backward spring or fall, long drouths, during which the tree almost stops running, or heavy driving rains which fill the boxes with water and float out the turpentine, all have their effect on the number of drippings [sic], which depends otherwise on the frequency and care with which chipping is done." Perry recommended that in bad weather, the forest workers be put to such indoor tasks as assisting the coopers hoop barrels. When it rained continuously one March day in 1856, the coopers at G. I. Germond's turpentine operation in the region of south Georgia and north Florida continued to work in their shop, but the other hands were put to shelling seed corn. Finally, the dippers' task depended on the age of the boxes. Because newer boxes produced more gum than older ones, more time was required for emptying the buckets and fewer boxes could be dipped. Workers could manage dipping 10,000 to 12,000 older boxes and perhaps as few as 8,000 new ones a week.[17]

Because some stands produced more gum than others, thus creating a potential situation in which the hardest workers could actually bring in less gum, Perry advocated not tasking dippers by the barrel but by the number of boxes they attended. The quantity of barrels dipped in a day was not necessarily an indication of a slave's effort. In March 1856 G. I. Germond observed that his "boxes are not filling well," consequently the seven hands who had been dipping "could not get their task." In fact the amount of gum collected by individual dippers could vary significantly. In 1855 fifteen slaves labored for one week dipping boxes and collected an average of 44.5 barrels of gum. Two collected as much as 48 barrels, and one collected only 32 barrels. Like boxing, the size of the task varied with the individual producer. Some expected workers to fill from 4 to 7 barrels with raw turpentine a day.

17. G. W. Perry, *Treatise on Turpentine Farming*, 32, 88, 116–7, 123; Benjamin Grist to James R. Grist, 17 July 1860, Grist Papers; "Turpentine: Hints for Those about to Engage in Its Manufacture," 487; Gilbert Isaac Germond, Work Journal, 18 March 1856, Department of Special Collections, George A. Smathers Libraries, University of Florida; "Pine Forests of the South," 197; Johnson, *Ante-Bellum North Carolina*, 488; William Kauffman Scarborough, ed., *The Diary of Edmund Ruffin*, vol. 1 (Baton Rouge: Louisiana State University, 1972), 52; MacLeod, "Tar and Turpentine Business," 14–5; McMillan to *Southern Cultivator*, 172; Michaux, *North American Sylva*, 141.

Truly exceptional dippers could fill 10. Of turpentiners who tasked by the box, some found 1,800 boxes a day sufficient, others apparently tasked their laborers as high as 3,000.[18]

Once gathered, producers strove to get their resin, especially the highest-quality and most valuable gum, to distilleries quickly before it deteriorated. Every year a tree was worked, the dip became thicker and darker, moving from a light cream color toward an orange. Virgin dip, gum harvested from new boxes, possessed a thin, oily, transparent quality and produced the best rosin. Since virgin dip was much more valuable than gum harvested from older boxes, it was important for hands to keep it separate and best to get it to market quickly. Spirits evaporated rapidly from the gum, especially in hot, dry weather, and soft gum was the most susceptible to the effects of heat. It was recommended that "as fast as they are filled the dip barrels should be hauled to the still and emptied into it." One strong hand with a wagon and two mules could haul the turpentine dipped by ten hands for an average of three miles and also be able to supply the workers with provisions and empty barrels. Hauling in wet weather could be difficult, especially down the muddy cart paths that wound through the pine forest. An overseer managing an Alabama operation reported that "the ground is so wet we cannot run the wagon to any advantage hence I stop."[19]

A pine would bleed only as long as its wound was fresh. Within seven or eight days the gum crystallized at the opening of the wounded resin ducts, and so fresh wounds were required about once a week in warm weather, less often during cooler periods. Chipping, as this operation was called, was done with a hack or shave, a circular piece of iron with a sharp lower edge and a two-foot handle. It involved cutting the bark away just above the box and extending the cut to the corners or outer edges of the box. Each new chip, located just above the last one, extended the face upwards after each task. With each stroke, the chipper cut a gash through the bark and into the sapwood. The chip was commonly one inch broad, causing the face in some cases to rise two feet each year; the oldest orchards contained trees with

18. G. W. Perry, *Treatise on Turpentine Farming*, 116–7; Germond, Work Journal, March 1856; Michaux, *North American Sylva*, 141; M. Jones to James R. Grist, 30 October 1855, Grist Papers; "Pine Forests of the South," 197; Johnson, *Ante-Bellum North Carolina*, 488; Scarborough, ed., *Diary of Edmund Ruffin*, 52; MacLeod, "Tar and Turpentine Business," 14–5; "Turpentine: Hints for Those about to Engage in Its Manufacture," 487; McMillan to *Southern Cultivator*, 172.

19. "Product of Turpentine at the South," 304; G. W. Perry, *Treatise on Turpentine Farming*, 110, 124; Description of turpentining, Harrington Papers; "Manufacture of Turpentine in the South," 453; "Turpentine: Hints for Those about to Engage in Its Manufacture," 487; Thomas F. Strikney to Allen and James R. Grist, 26 February 1861, Grist Papers.

faces extending up twelve to fifteen feet. When the face reached shoulder height, workers switched to using a puller, a long-handled tool with a metal scraper on the end, which allowed them to reach high. Producers sought well-trained workers for the task, since the skill of the chippers determined how many years an orchard could be harvested. If the gashes were too deep, the tree's life was shortened; if the cut was too broad, the face would soon rise out of reach and the tree could no longer be harvested. Moreover, producers required that this difficult task be executed with considerable speed. Although some operators calculated that chipping 800 to 1,000 faces a day for average laborers and 1,200 to 1,500 for better workers was standard, others found that 12,000 to 17,000 faces a week were possible for the average chipper. A few extraordinary laborers were reported to have chipped 20,000 faces a week. In the most sophisticated operations hands specialized in either dipping or chipping. It was recommended that "the dipping should be done by hands employed for the purpose, and the hackers should continue their work without changing the proper interval between the hackings of each tree." It was also suggested that chipping be "done by the strongest and most expert hands, these should be kept at it regularly through the season, while women or inferior hands can dip very well." Four to six chippings were required to fill a box with turpentine.[20]

The season's last chipping occurred in mid-October and the last dipping around the first of November. After this, scraping began. Scrape was gum that had hardened to the face, lost much of its spirits in evaporation, and was therefore only half as valuable as liquid gum. It was important to remove the scrape promptly before high winds caused the pine to sway so violently that the hardened turpentine fell off. Workers used a small blade attached to a long handle to dislodge scrape from the face. They then gathered it in a specially designed box that measured about two and one-half feet square and was open at the top and one end. The tree supported the bottom of the opened end, and the closed end sat on two constructed legs or sometimes wheels. When collecting scrape, laborers would drag or roll these boxes through the forest, lean the open end against the tree, just below the face,

20. Brown, *Forest Products*, 184; Description of turpentining, Harrington Papers; V. L. Harper and Lenthall Wyman, *Variations in Naval-Stores Yields Associated with Weather and Specific Days between Chippings* (Washington, D.C.: United States Department of Agriculture, 1936), 10, 15; Ruffin, "Notes of a Steam Journey," 250–1; "Product of Turpentine at the South," 304; "Manufacture of Turpentine in the South," 453–4; Hickman, *Mississippi Harvest*, 123–4; "Turpentine: Hints for Those about to Engage in Its Manufacture," 487; MacLeod, "Tar and Turpentine Business," 15; Olmsted, *Journey in the Seaboard Slave States*, 342; Avirett, *Old Plantation*, 67–8; Schorger and Betts, *Naval Stores Industry*, 17; G. W. Perry, *Treatise on Turpentine Farming*, 78; "The Pine Forests of the South," 197.

and pull the scrape down into them. Each box held 100 to 150 pounds of scrape. After the boxes were full of scrape, their contents was transferred into resin barrels, pounded in, and hauled to the still. Scrape collecting was usually completed during December or January.[21]

When the boxes stopped filling and the scrape had been collected, the turpentine laborers' work was still not finished. If new pine forests were to be opened for the next season, the strongest and most skilled laborers began cutting boxes immediately. The laborers who were not boxing cleared grass, pine straw, and tree limbs from the bases of trees and burned the debris. Still others collected the timber needed to make the barrels for the next season. At one operation a tar kiln was fired in mid-December when the turpentine work was almost completed. In 1851, De Bow's Review reported that, "like the engagements of a farm-hand, in always finding something needful to be done in every day of the year, and something that should not be neglected; so with the turpentine hand, the whole year has its various demands upon him in their proper season, so that there is no time to spare from his turpentine crop." But if the turpentine production was part of the operation of a traditional agricultural plantation, some laborers were used for work unrelated to turpentine. A sample of operations listed for sale in the 1840s and 1850s indicates that fewer than half included any cropland. Of those that did, there was an average of just over 240 acres which could potentially be cultivated. The most common crops grown included corn, peas, potatoes, oats, and wheat. Few operations produced any cotton. Joining the field hands at such operations, turpentine laborers sometimes opened ditches, cleared new ground, trimmed hedgerows, mended fences, and repaired roads. On February 27, 1856, for example, turpentiner G. I. Germond had three slaves—Dick, Moses, and Adam—getting timber for a pig pen. The next day his slaves cleared a field for planting and burned off another tract. The day after that they burned over one more area. James Battle Avirett, whose father owned Richlands Plantation, wrote that only "by joining these two industries, the [turpentine] orchards and the plantation," could the plantation be maintained.[22]

21. MacLeod, "Tar and Turpentine Business," 15; "Manufacture of Turpentine in the South," 453; "Product of Turpentine at the South," 304–5; Ruffin, "Notes of a Steam Journey," 250–1; Schorger and Betts, Naval Stores Industry, 18; G. W. Perry, Treatise on Turpentine Farming, 109.

22. Benjamin Grist to Allen Grist, 21 January 1851, Grist Papers; "Turpentine: Hints for Those about to Engage in Its Manufacture," 488; John Carr to Sir, 15 December 1858, McDowell Papers; "Product of Turpentine at the South," 305; McMillan to Southern Cultivator, 172; "Land for Sale on Cape Fear River," Wilmington Chronicle, 10 November 1841; "Lands for Sale," WJ, 27 June 1845; "Real Estate for Sale," WJ, 4 July 1845; "Plantation for Sale," WJ, 24 April

Certainly, distillers, who were the most skilled turpentine workers, were too busy for such tasks. To ensure a high-quality product, they distilled the gum and scrape as quickly as possible. Distilleries were often two-story structures. A wood or occasionally an oil furnace sat at ground level, and a copper still rested above it on the second floor. These facilities were located near streams, which provided water to cool the condensing tube, or worm— the long, coiled tube in which the spirits of turpentine were transformed into a liquid. Although these stills ranged in capacity from five to thirty barrels, most had between a ten- and twenty-barrel capacity. To charge or fill them, workers brought barrels of gum to the second floor, often by rolling them up a ramp, and the distiller removed the head of the still and dumped in the gum. He then replaced the head and connected it to the condensing tube. When everything was ready, he fired the furnace. The distilling process generally lasted two or two and one-half hours. The frequency with which a still was fired depended on the volume of gum coming from the woods. At the peak of the dipping season the operator of the Grist Alabama operation had "to run my still three times a day to keep up."[23]

Because of the primitive nature of mid-nineteenth-century distilling technology, still operators faced significant challenges in successfully processing a charge of gum. Distillers first needed to bring the still temperature to a

1846; "Valuable Turpentine Land for Sale," WJ, 20 November 1846; "Valuable Real Estate," WJ, 26 February 1847; "Valuable Lands for Sale," WJ, 22 December 1848; "Lands for Sale," WJ, 29 December 1848; "Valuable Farming and Turpentine Lands for Sale," WJ, 2 March 1849; "Valuable Land for Sale," WJ, 11 May 1849; "For Sale," WJ, 10 August 1849; "Notice.—A Valuable Plantation for Sale," WJ, 23 November, 1849; "Valuable Plantation for Sale," WJ, 23 November 1849; "Land for Sale," WJ, 19 July 1850; "A Great Bargain," WJ, 4 October 1850; "Land and Negroes for Sale," WJ, 4 July 1851; "10,000 Acres of Land for Sale," WJ, 21 November 1851; "For Sale," WJ, 29 October 1852; "Valuable Cape Fear Plantation for Sale," WJ, 24 June 1853; "Valuable Real Estate for Sale," WJ, 4 November 1853; "Valuable Real Estate for Sale," WJ, 10 March 1854; "Land for Sale," Wilmington Journal 13 October 1854; "A Valuable Tract of Land for Sale," WJ, 4 January 1856; "Turpentine Land for Sale," WJ, 21 March 1856; "For Sale, Valuable Turpentine and Farming Lands in Bladen County," WJ, 21 March 1856; "Turpentine Lands in Florida for Sale," WJ, 21 March 1856; "A Turpentine Farm for Sale or Rent," WJ, 29 August 1856; Germond, Work Journal, 27, 28, and 29 February 1856; Avirett, Old Plantation, 68–9.

23. Olmsted, Journey in the Seaboard Slave States, 344; "Pine Forests of the South," 197; "Production of Turpentine in Alabama," 561. Although Tatum is describing experiences at a pine woods distillery in the early twentieth century, the still was the same as those used in the antebellum era. Fitzhugh Lee Tatum, interview by Ruth L. Stokes, 19 October 1974, transcript, p. 1, Southern Oral History Program, Southern Historical Collection, University of North Carolina at Chapel Hill; Panshin et al., Forest Products, 453; Schorger and Betts, Naval Stores Industry, 29; A. David King III, interview by author, 14 June 1996, notes in author's possession, Georgia Agrirama, Tifton, Ga.; Benjamin Grist to James R. Grist, 7 July 1860, Grist Papers.

steady, gradual rise to ensure that the gum heated evenly and distilled thoroughly. Heating the kettle too quickly would result in the bottom becoming excessively hot and burning the gum. When adding wood, distillers needed to know the direction of the temperature in the kettle. When heating the still distillers also needed to consider the quality of the gum that they were about to distill, since different grades of gum distilled at slightly different temperatures. Higher grades required less heat than lower ones; scrape required the hottest temperatures. Moreover, because antebellum producers had not learned to add water, which would have aided the distilling process, still operators had to cope with serious difficulties. In the absence of water, raw turpentine, which is 75 percent rosin and 25 percent spirits, does not boil until it reaches around 363°F. However, rosin begins to decompose when it reaches 392°F, coloring the spirits yellow and thus lowering the quality. Therefore, the distiller had a margin of error of only 29°F. Making his task even more challenging was the property of gum that causes its temperature to rise rapidly as it distills. Only rarely, then, was more than a portion of the turpentine distilled before the rosin began to decompose. If the temperature fluctuated too far, disastrous consequences could threaten life and property. In cases when the fire grew too low, the distilling mass began to cool, trapping the spirit vapor within the rosin and causing the volume in the still to increase, boil over, and create a danger of fire. If the still temperature rose too quickly, causing the vapor in the still to grow too abundant, a similar situation could occur. Because the temperature of the rosin was critical in the process, distillers needed to know exactly when to extinguish the furnace. Since stills had no gauges, however, workers had to rely on other methods to monitor the progress of the gum. They could collect the distilled emissions from the worm in a clear drinking glass and then examine the proportion of water and turpentine. Gum releases water as it distills, and the longer the still ran, the more water it emitted. Or the distiller could place his ear against the lower end of the worm to listen to the gum boiling. An experienced worker could determine from the sound what stage the gum had reached.

The distillation of gum resulted in two products: rosin and spirits of turpentine. Crude turpentine yielded from six to eight gallons of spirits per barrel of gum, depending on how soon it was distilled and its purity. Five gallons of gum generally yielded one gallon of spirits. During distillation a mixture of 90 to 95 percent spirits of turpentine and 5 to 10 percent water flowed from the worm into a fifty-gallon barrel. Because turpentine is lighter than water, it floated to the top, where it could run off into another barrel or be dipped off. Rosin remained in the still. When the distilling of a charge was completed, the rosin was drained from the still through a gate at the bottom. It flowed through a series of screens, which filtered out wood chips, dirt, and other foreign matter, and into a cooling vat. If the hot liquid rosin did not cool and become less viscous before it was put into barrels, considerable loss could occur through leakage. When ready it was dipped into barrels for shipment.

Workers who could perform the complicated distilling process were scarce and expensive. A white distiller earned between $500 and $600 a year, and a hired slave distiller cost more than a less-skilled turpentine worker. Evidence suggests that whites usually served as head distillers, although their assistants were likely to be skilled slaves. At a fifteen-barrel still, Olmsted found "one white man and one negro employed under the oversight of the owner." As the naval stores industry grew during the 1840s and 1850s, distillers became harder to find, and producers advertised for their services. Some operators even attempted to train their own slaves to operate a still.[24]

The great volume of naval stores refined at stills required a large number of barrels for use as shipping containers. As a general rule, every fifth man in a naval stores operation worked as a cooper. Unlike distillers, most coopers in the turpentine industry were slaves. Constant demand made them among the more expensive turpentine laborers. As early as the 1780s, Johann Schoepf found that "A cooper, indispensable in pitch and tar making, cost his purchaser 250 Pd., and his 15-year old boy, bred to the same work, fetched 150 Pd." In the mid-1850s the cost of hiring slave coopers ran from $1.50 to $2.00 a day. They labored all year. They constructed barrels during harvest season, some reportedly singing as they worked: during the off-season they collected timber for the next year's staves. Since rosin hardened once it cooled, making it highly unlikely to leak, cheaply made barrels with loose pine staves could suffice for this product. Because craftsmanship was not important, a cooper could make eight to ten rosin barrels in a day. Raw turpentine barrels, though, were somewhat more carefully constructed. With a forty-gallon capacity, these barrels were made from good pine staves and fastened with six light iron hoops. Spirits of turpentine barrels, however, were built with the greatest precision. Usually holding forty to forty-

24. King, interview; Schorger and Betts, *Naval Stores Industry*, 12–4, 30–1; Panshin et al., *Forest Products*, 453; Robson Dunwody, "Proper Methods of Distilling and Handling in the Production of Turpentine and Rosin," in *Naval Stores: History, Production, Distribution and Consumption*, ed. Thomas Gamble (Savannah: Review Publishing and Printing, 1921), 128; Tatum, interview, 1, 4; Hickman, *Mississippi Harvest*, 126; Olmsted, *Journey in the Seaboard Slave States*, 345–6; "Production of Turpentine in Alabama," 561; P. Perry, "Naval Stores Industry in the Ante-Bellum South, 1789–1861," 45; "Notice," *New Bern (N.C.) Newbernian*, 6 January 1852.

five gallons, they were made of well-seasoned white oak staves and were tightly looped with strong iron hoops. To protect against leakage, the interior of these barrels was given a coat of glue, and the exterior was thickly varnished or painted. While ordinary coopers could be trusted to make rosin and gum barrels, only expert coopers made spirit barrels, which normally required half a day to assemble. During the 1840s and 1850s, some producers began importing spirit barrels from the North. Commonly these casks were secondhand barrels that had been used to transport naval stores to New York or Boston and were returned for resale in lots of five to six hundred.[25]

Coopering was by no means a unique occupation to the naval stores industry, but boxing, chipping, dipping, and scraping were, and producers had to adapt slave-management techniques to accommodate the characteristics of these special tasks. Under slavery, two distinct methods of labor management developed: the task system and the gang system. Under the latter, plantation owners gave a gang of slaves an allotment of work that they were expected to complete as a group. This system worked best in the open fields, where the overseer had a clear view of workers' performance. Where slaves could not be closely supervised, producers preferred the task system. Under it, individual slaves worked at an allotted job. Each slave could set the pace, taking as little or as much time as necessary to complete the assignment, as long as it was performed to the producer's satisfaction.[26]

Because dipping, chipping, and boxing required workers to fan out in all directions through the expansive pine forests, producers found that the task system worked best for harvesting turpentine. Many of the pine forests were large and isolated. *De Bow's Review* described "a suitable place for operations" as one "where one or two thousand acres of proper pines lie in an unbroken body, convenient to water transportation." The pinelands at Richlands Plantation covered twenty-two thousand acres. To organize the tasks in such an expansive work environment, producers marked off turpentine orchards in grids of continuous blocks. They created these blocks, or "crops," by blazing a line of trees and further dividing each crop with rows

25. J. I. McRea to Thomas S. D. McDowell, 16 September 1850, J. W. Wheeler to Thomas S. D. McDowell, 12 July 1853, and Thomas S. D. McDowell Account with H. H. Robinson, October 1855 entries, McDowell Papers; Schoepf, *Travels in the Confederation*, 148; Olmsted, *Journey in the Seaboard Slave States*, 340; "Turpentine: Hints for Those about to Engage in Its Manufacture," 488; P. Perry, "Naval Stores Industry in the Ante-Bellum South, 1789–1861," 45, 79; "Pine Forests of the South," 197–8; "Production of Turpentine in Alabama," 561; MacLeod, "Tar and Turpentine Business," 16; Avirett, *Old Plantation*, 65; James to Grist, 23 August 1853, Grist Papers; Shipping receipt, 30 June 1859, William H. Turlington Papers, Special Collections Library, Duke University.

26. Kenneth M. Stampp, *The Peculiar Institution: Slavery in the Ante-Bellum South* (New York: Vintage Books, 1989), 54–5.

of stakes placed at fifty-yard intervals, cutting the forest into half-acre squares. Tasks consisted of ten thousand boxes, or roughly one hundred acres. Without such a division, reportedly, "the overseer of several hands cannot possibly inspect their work with any accuracy, nor can the hands, however faithful, avoid skipping a great many boxes in *cornering, dipping, and chipping.*"[27]

With their workers organized under the task system, producers feared that the arrangement would undermine slave discipline and dependence in the isolated forest. Some operators worried that unless they were carefully watched, their chippers would cut only the obvious trees around the perimeter of their allotment and would neglect those in the center that were more difficult to detect.[28] A producer who explained that "watchful care will be necessary in attending to the hands, or the cunning old negroes will frequently neglect to chip the pines regularly," believed that the work was best monitored by "looking on the surface for the chip which has lately fallen, as that will retain its new color long enough to enable you to discover whether the tree has been recently chipped or not." Turpentiners were also concerned that "streaks on the face would be made too short, the chip too shallow, or trees chipped only on one side, the side the producer or overseer would see when they passed." *De Bow's Review* warned producers that "it is important . . . to see that the hands perform their task properly, and not allow them to mislead you, as they will frequently do, by saying they perform their task, without half doing so." Operators were also advised that "in task work like this [turpentine], constant watchfulness will be necessary to insure faithful execution of the work." After inspections, G. W. Perry advised that good hands should not be confronted about trees that they may have missed for it would shame them. He believed that producers should instead mark the missed trees so slaves would not "lose confidence in their owners, and fail frequently to do their duty, when they would not have done so otherwise." Perry also recommended that producers not show excessive anger over poor work or too much gratification for improvement. "This treatment," he explained, "keeps them in their proper places; and as they perceive, by your daily conduct, that things pass over and are settled at the same

27. "Pine Forests of the South," 196; Avirett, *Old Plantation,* 64; Hickman, *Mississippi Harvest,* 122; "Turpentine: Hints for Those about to Engage in Its Manufacture," 486–7; Johnson, *Ante-Bellum North Carolina,* 487; Bellamy, "Slavery in Microcosm," 344; "Product of Turpentine at the South," 303; Adam Hodgson, *Remarks during a Journey through North America in the Years 1819, 1820, and 1821 in a Series of Letters* (New York: Samuel Whiting, 1823), 112; Scarborough, ed., *Diary of Edmund Ruffin,* 52; Russell, *North America,* 159.

28. Johnson, *Ante-Bellum North Carolina,* 487; Hickman, *Mississippi Harvest,* 124–5; Peter Kolchin, *American Slavery, 1619–1877* (New York: Hill and Wang, 1993), 32.

time, a confidence is engrafted in the negro toward his owner. Masters may rely upon it that hands will work better from firm conviction than any other way."[29]

The task system also aided owners and overseers in organizing their labor force into multi-unit work groups. Because the harvest season for turpentine was limited to the warmer months when the tree produced resin, none of the directly related operations—chipping, dipping, scraping, and distilling—could wait until the slower season. Therefore, in the more active periods different hands performed whatever tasks were required on a given day. In October 1855 a Grist overseer had "ten hands dipping turpentine + four hands getting timber, five hands at the still, six hands coopering, one hand cutting wood, one heading rosin + four hands helping." But by November the overseer had altered the tasks. He had "five hands scrapping . . . + ten hands dipping, six hands getting timber, seven hands at the cooper shop, five hands at the still, one hand cutting wood, [and] three wagoning." By assigning tasks to the forest hands, such potentially chaotic arrangements were better organized.[30]

In most agricultural situations slaves preferred the task system to gang labor, for it afforded a relative degree of autonomy. Laborers could work at their own pace and enjoy free time if their job was completed early. Although their work was inspected, they escaped the persistent driving that gang laborers endured. Despite their preferences, agricultural slaves most commonly worked in gangs. They remained under the constant surveillance of a driver or overseer, who kept them working at a brisk pace. All laborers, no matter how well or fast they worked, continued their labor until all workers in the gang were discharged in the evening. They had no way of earning incentive payment for hard work or free time for work completed early. Nor did gang labor offer any opportunity for laborers to develop self-reliance or to exercise control over their work schedules; every workday was the same as the one before.[31]

Many turpentine producers believed that their slaves preferred task work in the forest over gang labor in agriculture. One remarked, "no set of hands have ever been known to willingly leave it and go back to cotton." Olmsted found "the negroes employed in this branch of industry . . . to be unusually

29. G. W. Perry, *Treatise on Turpentine Farming*, 75, 114–5, 118; "Manufacture of Turpentine in the South," 453; "Pine Forests of the South," 196.

30. Olmsted, *Journey in the Seaboard Slave States*, 346; M. Jones to James R. Grist, 24 October 1855, and M. Jones to James R. Grist, 5 November 1855, Grist Papers.

31. Kolchin, *American Slavery*, 31–2; Stampp, *Peculiar Institution*, 54–6; Charles Joyner, *Down by the Riverside: A South Carolina Slave Community* (Urbana: University of Illinois Press, 1984), 43.

intelligent and cheerful." Accepting these claims, Percival Perry writes that "once trained in turpentine operations, blacks preferred turpentining to other forms of farm labor because it was based on the task system and they were somewhat more independent in their work." He also finds that "turpentine plantation slaves worked as part of a production team, yet at an individual task, rather than in gang labor. This may have contributed to a sense of independence, responsibility, and greater contentment." While Perry accurately describes labor under the task system, his conclusion that this made work in the turpentine forest more pleasant than agricultural labor is questionable. Both the task and gang systems had advantages and disadvantages, but in the long run the type of work and amount of labor expected of turpentine slaves greatly affected the relative difficulty of tasks. Moreover, Perry fails to consider important factors related to the isolation of the camps—the realities of work that significantly shaped the lives of slaves.[32]

Although turpentine workers perhaps did not endure the same drudgery as did gang laborers, the task system, as used by naval stores producers, denied the slave laborers community. On rice plantations the task system facilitated close contact among bondsmen. Slaves who received allotted rows to hoe in cotton fields worked closely with other slaves, as did those laboring in adjoining rice patches. However, in the turpentine forests, workers encountered a different situation. Because producers marked their tasks in half-acre squares, and boxers, dippers, and chippers were assigned several tasks, laborers were placed at considerable distances from one another and lacked social interaction to break the monotony of their work.[33]

For many turpentine laborers, loneliness did not end with their workday. Producers, taking advantage of mid-nineteenth-century transportation improvements, purchased virgin forests and moved their stills, overseers, slaves, and equipment into isolated camps. The camps were commonly so far away from agricultural plantations that men in the labor force had no regular contact with their families and, for the most part, no female companionship. Only a few women and children worked in the antebellum naval stores industry because, except for dipping, the tasks demanded consider-

32. "Turpentine Making," *Soil of the South* 5 (December 1855), 357–8, quoted in P. Perry, "Naval Stores Industry in the Ante-Bellum South, 1789–1861," 39; Olmsted, *Journey in the Seaboard Slave States*, 348; Charles Reagan Wilson and William Ferris, eds. *Encyclopedia of Southern Culture* (Chapel Hill: University of North Carolina Press, 1989), s.v. "naval stores"; Randall M. Miller and John David Smith, eds., *Dictionary of Afro-American Slavery* (New York: Greenwood Press, 1988), s.v. "naval stores industry."

33. Eugene D. Genovese, *Roll, Jordan, Roll: The World the Slaves Made* (New York: Vintage Books, 1976), 324; Joyner, *Down by the Riverside*, 43, 59.

able strength; therefore, men dominated the labor force. At Benjamin Williams's operation in southeast Georgia, for example, the slave women and children stayed at his home, where his wife was in charge. Men were deprived of the emotional support of their relatives and friends. Some turpentine slaves, however, took measures to alleviate their loneliness. At the Williams Georgia operation, it was reported that without permission or passes to leave, "some of our turpentine hands will work all day + then walk eight or ten miles to dance all night."[34]

Producers commonly used labor incentives to stimulate lonely and unhappy workers to greater productivity and to encourage them to work during their own time, a practice also employed by rice planters. Incentives came as cash rewards for completing more than their assigned tasks and as time off for finishing tasks early. Because such tasks as boxing and chipping were vitally important and overseers had difficulty closely monitoring each hand's work, incentives helped to ensure that slaves performed work properly. In 1854 Williams was so pleased with his workers that he paid some of them as much as fifty dollars during the season. In the winter of 1856, eleven slaves at one operation in the vicinity of south Georgia and north Florida earned an average of $8.23 for extra work cutting boxes. The most made was $19.20 and the least was $1.69. At Richlands Plantation, laborers could earn from 40¢ to 60¢ by continuing their work on Saturdays. To encourage speed, tasks were designed to allow a free day (usually Saturday) in the work week. James B. Avirett explained that laborers "must be stimulated to their best work . . . by so regulating their work that a portion of each week is their own to do as they please with."[35]

Turpentine producers, like virtually all slave masters, also employed punishments, especially the whip. Slaves received beatings for not working fast enough, for failure to complete tasks, for complaining, and simply because their master arbitrarily decided to punish them. G. W. Perry found that his turpentine slaves "required whipping every time after dipping when chipping was commenced." As a solution to poor work, he considered whether the slave "knows how to course pines well or not, and whether his tool is in

---

34. "Pine Forests of the South," 197; Johnson, *Ante-Bellum North Carolina*, 488; Account Book, 1846–1849, Daniel W. Jordan Papers, Special Collections Library, Duke University; McMillan to *Southern Cultivator*, 172; Sarah Hicks Williams to Parents, 11 March 1860 and 25 March 1859, Williams Papers; Genovese, *Roll, Jordan, Roll*, 324.

35. Kolchin, *American Slavery*, 31–2; Joyner, *Down by the Riverside*, 50–1; Genovese, *Roll, Jordan, Roll*, 314; Robert S. Starobin, *Industrial Slavery in the Old South* (New York: Oxford University Press, 1970), 100–2; Hickman, *Mississippi Harvest*, 124; Miller and Smith, *Dictionary of Afro-American Slavery*, 521; Sarah Hicks Williams to Parents, 20 December 1854, Williams Papers; Avirett, *Old Plantation*, 68, 70; Germond, Work Journal, 16 February 1856.

good order or not, and thrash[ed] him accordingly." In May 1856 G. I. Germond punished one slave for allowing his horse to get away and then lying about it. That same month he found three slaves had been negligent with their hacking, and each received forty lashes. But Germond, like other slaveholders, did not always resort to the whip to punish his slaves. When he discovered that one hand had not properly attended to his task of trees, he "told him that I had no confidence in his Honesty + that I should watch him very close + if I detected any such thing in him again that I would Punish him (or any other one for a similar offense) by not allowing to Work at task work any more for the year." In March 1856 he "Brought Lymons home with hands tied behind him + locked him up in the Smokehouse till night to punish him for going to Mr. Simpsons without a pass on Saturday."[36]

Observations by economist Stefano Fenoaltea help explain why the turpentine industry's form of labor organization and combination of incentives and punishments took the shape that they did. He explains that in managing slave labor, pain and reward incentives were best used in various combinations for different types of work. Pain incentives were the most effective at generating greater worker effort but did not promote carefulness. For labor-intensive activities where brute effort, not precision, was important, as in breaking rocks, slaves most often worked in gangs and were punished with physical pain if they failed to work fast or hard enough. Because the threat of pain produces high anxiety levels, it does not facilitate carefulness. Not only did anxiety impair the slaves' ability to work carefully, but threats could generate ill-feeling among the slaves and lead to intentional carelessness. Rewards, which tended to cause a reduction in work effort and productivity, however, also led to labor with greater care. Slaves who worked by reward incentives, Fenoaltea continues, were more typically self-supervised and less likely to work as part of a gang. In this case, by allowing the slaves to retain a portion of their production they could be made to work with less supervision. Fenoaltea maintains that masters typically used a combination of pain and reward incentives. They adjusted the levels of each until the maximum benefit for the specific job was reached. Fenoaltea also argues that slavery was most likely used in occupations where the working conditions were unpleasant and free workers would require a high percentage of the product produced in order to voluntarily perform the labor.[37]

36. Thomas D. S. McDowell Account with R. H. Riualdi, 2 June 1860 entry, McDowell Papers; G. W. Perry, *Treatise on Turpentine Farming*, 98, 114; Germond, Work Journal, 10 March 1856 and 15 March 1856.

37. Stefano Fenoaltea, "Slavery and Supervision in Comparative Perspective: A Model," *Journal of Economic History* 44 (September 1984): 636–40, 644–8, 655.

The difficult work involved in turpentining, carried out in the isolation of the southern piney woods, required slaves to perform reliable and adequate work away from supervision as constant as that allowed in agriculture. Workers spread out across the forests could not be continuously monitored. Yet as far as owners were concerned, the slave workers absolutely had to carry out tasks with precision. If the boxes were improperly cut the turpentine harvest for those trees was permanently ruined. Poor chipping would at least diminish the turpentine yield and at worst kill the trees. Incentives such as time off and small cash payments were therefore required to ensure that the work these slaves were forced to perform was done well. Yet physical punishments, such as the whip, were also needed to force the slaves to perform the long hours of such backbreaking work as boxing and chipping.

As with expansive agricultural plantations, large turpentine operations relied on overseers or foremen to be as watchful as possible. Usually referred to as "woodsriders," these men rode through the forest on horseback inspecting each worker's task. Given the distance of each laborer from other workers, a single overseer could supervise no more than twelve slaves. Producers sought overseers familiar with turpentine production. One North Carolina turpentiner desired "some competent person who thoroughly understands the business, to over see hands in getting Turpentine." In 1850 a producer near Wilmington sought "a Man of sober, industrious habits, an experienced farmer, with some knowledge of the Turpentine business." As was often the case with overseers for slaves involved in agricultural production, those for turpentine commonly did not meet the producers' expectations. James Avirett complained about the overseers at his plantation, Richlands. He described them as low-class whites who could not be relied upon to run the turpentine operation well and who by their third year acted as if they owned the enterprise themselves. Avirett consequently relied also on black drivers. Because the overseers' success was usually measured by the amount produced under their supervision and not by the health of the slaves under their care, they usually drove the hands hard. In August 1854 an overseer employed by James R. Grist reported: "I shall dow all in my power to make all I can for I am Working for my self as well as for Grist + Daves for my work has to be my recommendation in the State sow it is to my interest to make all I can." Another letter reports that "I am driving a head + doing all I can to get as much done [of] the turpentine as feasible."[38]

38. Sandra Jo Forney, "Kin to Kant: Naval Stores Production Was a Major Industry of the Nineteenth Century," *Women in Natural Resources*, n.s. 1, vol. 9 (1987): 17; "Pine Forests of the South," 196; "Notice," *New Bern (N.C.) Newbernian*, 6 January 1852; "Overseer Wanted," *WJ*, 30 August 1850, 1; Avirett, *Old Plantation*, 117–8; R. M. Wadsworth to James R. Grist, 11 August 1854, and Benjamin Grist to James R. Grist, 21 October 1855, Grist Papers.

This fast-paced driving was especially true in the case of hired slaves, a large percentage of whom worked in the naval stores industry. As larger producers entered the business, adequate labor for the piney woods operations became a constant concern. Correspondence between members of the Grist family and their overseers is filled with frequent complaints that "we bearly have enough to work the business." Producers could either hire slaves or use their own, and many chose to do both. In 1859, for example, Ben Williams employed "about thirty or thirty-five hands besides his own." Hired slaves were vital to the Grist operation, which in 1851 worked thirty-five slaves belonging to six different owners. Hiring slaves not only aided established producers such as Grist and Williams, but enabled men of moderate means to enter the expanding turpentine business by freeing them from making heavy initial investments in slave laborers. It was common for producers who were starting in the business to purchase or rent several hundred to a thousand acres and hire slave laborers. After a few years they could make enough money to buy slaves and possibly a still. The ability to hire slaves strengthened the "peculiar institution" by increasing small slaveholders' and nonslaveholders' dependence on the labor of bondsmen. At least one producer, however, discouraged using hired slaves, "for they will invariably put more mean tricks into the heads of your own negroes than they ever knew before."[39]

While the hired slaves' labor was highly valued, their welfare was only of temporary interest to their employers and overseers. Because the slaves' time was the commodity purchased and the value and overall well-being of the slaves was of financial concern only to their owners, employers generally sought to extract as much work as possible from hired slaves and gave little attention to their welfare. This meant that their work hours were long and their shelter, clothing, and provisions lean. Moreover, the use of hired slaves in an isolated setting, combined with the environment of the turpentine forest and the migratory nature of the industry, created living conditions for the naval stores slaves that were comparably worse than those of bondsmen in agriculture. Given their isolation, turpentine operations were often hidden from travelers and were seldom visited by anyone but the owner of the

39. James R. Grist to Father, 4 February 1851, and Benjamin Grist to Allen Grist, 21 January 1851, Grist Papers; Sarah Hicks Williams to Parents, 7 November 1859, Williams Papers; Kolchin, *American Slavery*, 109–10; Stampp, *Peculiar Institution*, 71; Starobin, *Industrial Slavery*, 12, 129–30, 135, 138; Rosser Howard Taylor, *Slaveholding in North Carolina: An Economic View* (Chapel Hill: University of North Carolina Press, 1926), 38–40; P. Perry, "Naval Stores Industry in the Ante-Bellum South, 1789–1861," 42; G. W. Perry, *Treatise on Turpentine Farming*, 120.

operation. With no witnesses to their treatment of laborers, naval stores producers experienced little outside pressure to provide properly for them.[40]

The owners of slaves hired to turpentine producers expressed concern for their hands' safety and health. One irate owner from Wake Forest wrote that his slaves, John and Albert, had run away because they were overworked and underfed. It was his "expectation that those who hire them will see that they are taken proper care of in every respect. The plan of giving up the management of hands entirely to overseers who have no feeling, is to my mind most shocking." The owner asked that Grist "deal leniently with the runaways, as they are first of my negroes which have left you, and I feel confident—there was some improper oppression which drove them to it." He requested a report on the condition of his other slaves in Grist's hire. When one slave owner hired his laborers out to a turpentine operation only to learn that they got so sick they were unable to work, he became "very much displeased with the business + is anxious to take them home."[41]

One facet of the turpentine slaves' poor living conditions was housing. In the decades before the Civil War the quality of plantation slave quarters ranged from relatively roomy cottages with brick or stone fireplaces and glazed windows to one-room log cabins with dirt floors and chimneys crudely fashioned of clay and sticks. Housing for turpentine laborers was probably even worse than the latter. Plantation quarters were built for extended use (as long as the plantation operated), but turpentine operations, which were in a forest and usually distant from the plantation, lasted for no more than ten years. Therefore housing was intended to be temporary, and was often little more than sheds. In similarly transitory operations such as fishing, shingle, and lumber camps, the quarters were only crude lean-tos. Ruffin described the living quarters of shingle-getters in the Dismal Swamp as "houses, or shanties . . . barely wide enough for five or six men to lie in, closely packed side by side—their heads to the back wall, and their feet stretched to the open front, close by a fire kept up through the night. The roof is sloping, to shed the rain, and where highest, not above four feet from the floor." Cabins built to house turpentine workers in the early 1900s, reported to be much like those inhabited by enslaved turpentine laborers, "were one room huts, made of pine poles and possessing neither floors, doors, nor windows."[42]

40. Stampp, *Peculiar Institution*, 82–4, 185; Kolchin, *American Slavery*, 109–10.

41. L. F. N. to James R. Grist, 18 August 1853, and Thomas F. Strikney to Allen and James R. Grist, 26 February 1861, Grist Papers.

42. John Michael Vlash, *Back of the Big House: The Architecture of Plantation Slavery* (Chapel Hill: University of North Carolina Press, 1993), 153–65; Kolchin, *American Slavery*, 114; Robert William Fogel and Stanley L. Engerman, *Time on the Cross: The Economics of American Negro Slavery* (Boston: Little, Brown, 1974), 115–6; Stampp, *Peculiar Institution*, 294; Staro-

Some producers provided for religious services in these crude quarters. In 1855 Germond "attended services at the Negro quarters at 11 O'clock[.] I read from the 12 chapter of Matthew + tried to explain its contents as best I could." At Williams's Greene County, North Carolina, operation the slaves "can go to Church (Preaching, as they say) on the Sabbath. . . . On Sundays they dress up and many of them look very nice." A distance of six miles from the producer's home, the church was "a rough framed building in the midst of woods. With a large congregation consisting of about equal numbers of white + black." Meetings were held twice a month and led by uneducated preachers.[43]

Despite Williams's slaves appearing "very nice" on Sundays, turpentine hands appear to have been generally poorly clothed, even by slavery standards. Each adult male plantation slave commonly received four shirts, four pairs of pants, and one or two pairs of shoes each year. Every several years they were issued a hat and blanket. Some turpentiners followed a similar pattern. Each year Avirett provided his slaves with three suits of clothing, three pairs of shoes, two blankets, one wool hat, one straw hat, and wool and cotton from which the slave women made socks and stockings. However, naval stores producers did not always use this distribution pattern, especially not for the slaves they hired. Owners tried to ensure that their slaves received proper clothing by including instructions in their contracts. The Francis Harper heirs required that whoever hired their slaves had "to furnish the males Three Suits Cloths one to be of woolen, one pr. shoes, and two if worked in Turpentine one pr. of stockings + one Hat + blanket. . . . All to be new and well made." But these instructions were not always followed. An angry slave owner wrote to the turpentine producer who had hired his slaves, "My Negroes told me they had not got all their clothing, their hats Blankets & c." One turpentine producer in Fayetteville presented his slaves with clothes only when he identified individual needs, a policy that caused clothing to be unevenly distributed. For example, in 1849, one slave, Bill, received two pairs of pants, two shirts, a pair of shoes, and a blanket. An-

bin, *Industrial Slavery*, 60; Porte Crayon, "The Dismal Swamp," *Harper's New Monthly Magazine* 8 (September 1856): 451; Joyner, *Down by the Riverside*, 120; Edmund Ruffin, "Observations Made during an Excursion to the Dismal Swamp," *Farmer's Register* 4 (January 1837): 518. While the cabins described were built for laborers in the Mississippi turpentine forests, they serve to illustrate the most likely conditions of housing for slaves in the North Carolina operations. Hickman, *Mississippi Harvest*, 147, 152; Forney, "Kin to Kant," 17. The housing arrangement at Avirett's Richlands Plantation was atypical of turpentine operations. The cabins were of relatively high quality and situated in close proximity to the master's house. Avirett, *Old Plantation*, 58–9.

43. Germond, Work Journal, 30 January 1855; Sarah Hicks Williams to Parents, 10 October and 22 October 1853, Williams Papers.

other, Obey, received two pairs of pants, two shirts, a pair of shoes, and a coat. But in that year Lewis was given only one pair of pants. G. W. Perry complained that his turpentine slaves would make it known when it was time for their clothing allowance or when their clothes and shoes had given out. He reported that he "had them to walk by me, and let the old shoes drop off their feet, so that I should notice it, and at other times to complain that their feet were badly cut up, for want of shoes." When one slave persisted in demonstrating how his worn-out shoes would easily drop off his feet, Perry "let him repeat it until I felt satisfied that he knew I noticed it: I then had him whipped, without telling him the cause, and whether he understood it or not, he never tried a repetition of the maneuver." Slave clothes were usually made of "Negro Cloth." Manufactured primarily in northern mills, this cloth was durable and sturdy but uncomfortably rough. Plantation mistresses often sewed their slaves' clothes, but larger and more organized operations employed slave women for this task. In some cases the slaves made their own clothes. Evidence suggests that clothes for turpentine workers were made at the forest camps. On Ben Williams's Georgia plantation the white women made clothes for the agricultural laborers but not for the turpentine workers. James Grist shipped cloth directly to one of his turpentine operations in Columbus County, North Carolina, where it apparently was to be cut and sewn into clothing at the site.[44]

Holidays, especially Christmas, were important to slaves. Masters customarily gave them at least one or two days off and sometimes a week or more. Many masters allowed their slaves to have a feast, and some gave them small presents. But hired slaves, who worked some distance from their homes, and workers such as turpentine slaves, who labored in camps many miles from their master's house, were often not allowed to return home on special occasions. One slave owner wrote to the turpentine producer who had hired his slaves, "I am quite willing . . . that they should remain with you during the Christmas holidays. It can do them no good to come home . . . and . . . their stay will be so short, that they cannot expect to enjoy

44. Avirett, *Old Plantation*, 58–9; Kolchin, *American Slavery*, 114; Fogel and Engerman, *Time on the Cross*, 116–7; Starobin, *Industrial Slavery*, 54–7; Contract to Hire Slaves, 2 January 1849, Harper Papers; Miller and Smith, *Dictionary of Afro-American Slavery*, 521; "Clothing for Negroes, Delivered," 1849, in Task Book, 1849–1851, Tillinghast Family Papers, Special Collections Library, Duke University; G. W. Perry, *Treatise on Turpentine Farming*, 120; "Production of Turpentine in Alabama," 561; M. Jones to James R. Grist, 5 November 1860, Benjamin Grist to James R. Grist, 21 October 1855, and "List of *Negroes* belonging to *Mr John W. Grist* Worked by *Grist + Strikney* during the year of *1860*," Grist Papers; Stampp, *Peculiar Institution*, 290–1; Genovese, *Roll, Jordan, Roll*, 551; Sarah Hicks Williams to Parents, 10 December 1853 and 25 March 1859, Williams Papers.

themselves much." However, evidence suggests that producers permitted limited holiday celebrations in the camps. For Christmas 1860 the slaves in one turpentine camp received "2 hogs + a barrel of Flower + potatoes so they can have a dinner." The overseer promised to "due my best to keep the negros all strat [straight] + satisfied[.] I hope that they will behave well."[45]

This Christmas dinner menu differed little from the provisions issued to turpentine slaves every other day of the year—cornmeal flour, salt pork, and often potatoes. On some small operations, producers worked in the forest with their slaves and also engaged in agriculture. A few larger operators attempted both farming and turpentining, but most often they gave more attention to turpentine and agriculture was only to supply the turpentine operations. It appears that the Grist operation produced its corn and some of its pork. Free-range hogs, which the train frequently hit, supplied a portion of the pork. Another operator raised potatoes as well as hogs. But although some turpentine producers tried to provide corn and bacon for their own needs, operators typically purchased provisions for their workforce. Olmsted observed that "few turpentine-farmers raise as much maize as they need for their own family; and those who carry on the [turpentine] business most largely and systematically, frequently purchase all the food of their hands. Maize and bacon are, therefore, very largely imported into North Carolina." He found that "the farmer in the forest, makes nothing for sale but turpentine, and, when he cultivates the land, his only crop is maize." Plantations, where food was more often produced, afforded hungry slaves greater opportunity to raid smokehouses, chicken coops, orchards, dairies, gardens, and cornfields. Turpentine workers found stealing food more difficult. When these supplies arrived at camps, usually by boat or railroad, they were locked in storehouses. But naval stores laborers did have one advantage over plantation slaves, who during their free time, commonly hunted and fished to supplement their diet. Because they worked in the forest, turpentine slaves had more opportunity to catch wild animals and collect edible herbs. Squirrels, possums, raccoons, rabbits, and turtles were plentiful in the turpentine orchards and occasionally supplemented the workers' diet. In exceptional cases slaves raised some of their own food. Behind their cabins at Richlands plantation the slaves maintained chicken yards, pig pens, and garden plots in which they grew cabbage, corn, and peas. James Avirett ex-

45. Kolchin, *American Slavery*, 115–6; Stampp, *Peculiar Institution*, 365; Genovese, *Roll, Jordan, Roll*, 573. According to Sarah Williams in Georgia, the slaves who worked in the distant turpentine orchards still considered their master's plantation their home. Sarah Hicks Williams to Parents, 25 March 1859, Williams Papers; Starobin, *Industrial Slavery*, 95; Benjamin Grist to James R. Grist, 25 December 1860, Grist Papers.

plained that slaves worked these plots "On Saturday afternoon or by moon-light . . . instead of going coon hunting." They could either sell their produce in New Bern or to the plantation. Another unusual source of provisions for Richlands slaves was from a small store that a slave named Philip ran from his cabin. He traded in such basic goods as coffee, tea, sugar, cheese, cakes, peanuts, and home brewed beer. The slaves paid with the money they earned for extra work and often with raccoon, rabbit, and squirrel pelts.[46]

Drinking water, unlike wild game, was often scarce in the forests. Where clear, flowing streams ran through the pines, workers had little difficulty obtaining water; but often there were no such streams. Many workers justi-fiably feared drinking from the murky, slow-moving swamps that they com-monly found in the woods. Instead, they carried a hollow reed straw that they used to suck the water collected in turpentine boxes after rains. But during particularly dry seasons, rainwater was not available. In the summer of 1860, for example, Alabama experienced a dry spell. At the Grist opera-tion near Mobile it was necessary "to keep Dave hauling water with the carte all the time in the woods to the hands." Although it was difficult for workers to obtain adequate water during periods of little rain, the water they drew from the boxes, when able, was probably unhealthy to drink. Evidence sug-gests that laborers suffered from digestive problems possibly caused by in-gestion of turpentine. Avirett reasoned that the water from the resin boxes was safe, "impregnated as it is with the turpentine," because it "reaches . . . his [the slave's] liver and keeps him healthy." Avirett's assertion is doubtful. Turpentine is a local irritant and a central neural depressant that is easily absorbed from the gastrointestinal tract. Its ingestion probably induced flux, a form of dysentery reportedly common among turpentine workers, which was characterized by abdominal pain, inflammation of the intestine, and fre-quent stools. However, because the lethal dose of turpentine for adults is four to six ounces, ingestion through the drinking water was rarely if ever fatal.[47]

46. Taylor, *Slaveholding in North Carolina*, 39; James R. Grist to Father, 4 February 1851, M. Jones to James R. Grist, 5 November 1855, 5 November 1860, and 12 November 1860, Grist Papers; Germond, Work Journal, 24 January and 18 February 1856; Olmsted, *Journey in the Seaboard Slave States*, 338; Avirett, *Old Plantation*, 48, 63–65, 87; P. Perry, "Naval Stores Indus-try in the Ante-Bellum South, 1789–1861," 42; Starobin, *Industrial Slavery*, 51; Kolchin, *Ameri-can Slavery*, 113; Stampp, *Peculiar Institution*, 282; Genovese, *Roll, Jordan, Roll*, 486–8, 599–606; Hickman, *Mississippi Harvest*, 150; Fogel and Engerman, *Time on the Cross*, 110–1; Julia Floyd Smith, *Slavery and Rice Culture in Low Country Georgia, 1750–1860* (Knoxville: Uni-versity of Tennessee Press, 1985), 114–8.

47. Benjamin Grist to James R. Grist, 17 July 1860, Grist Papers; Hickman, *Mississippi Harvest*, 150–1; Avirett, *Old Plantation*, 69; Bellamy, "Slavery in Microcosm," 344; P. Perry, "Naval Stores Industry in the Ante-Bellum South, 1789–1861," 39; Robert E. Gosselin et al., *Clinical Toxicology of Commercial Products*, 4th ed. (Baltimore: Williams and Wilkins, 1976),

Laborers came into contact with turpentine in other ways. When laboring in the forests, workers' "hands and clothing become smeared with the gum." Raw gum is extremely sticky and difficult to clean off clothes and skin. While traveling through North Carolina in 1856, for example, D. W. Kyle reported that he "*got turpentine all over me.*" Unable to clean it off, he had to throw away his suit and buy a new one. While its adhesion to workers' clothing was only a nuisance, its contact with their skin could cause dermatitis. Treatment of this skin irritation is ineffective until the offending agent is removed. Laborers who found themselves afflicted during the harvest season had to wait until November at the earliest for a cure.[48]

Fumes were another problem, especially around the still, which emitted a pungent turpentine smell. Even workers handling barrels in the pine forest were exposed to spirit vapors. A twentieth-century reporter explained that "it's like nothing you've ever smelled before. Sweet, spicy, raw. Something like sassafras tea but magnified to a degree that almost clears your sinuses." Fitzhugh Lee Tatum recounted that a still in Bladen County "smelled awful turpentiney!" "After you'd inhale it a while you could feel it all down in your throat." While no direct evidence from before the twentieth century indicates physical harm from such exposure, more recent medical research indicates otherwise. Twentieth-century workers have been found to develop occupational asthma when exposed to such high concentrations of these fumes, which are readily absorbed through the respiratory tract. Some have shown neurological damage and intellectual impairment. Moreover, laboratory tests reveal a higher mortality rate among the progeny of rats exposed to turpentine fumes. With these discoveries, strict regulations of such solvents are recommended to prevent tissue lesions in workers and to protect pregnant women.[49]

---

s.v. "turpentine"; *Dorland's Illustrated Medical Dictionary*, 25th ed. (Philadelphia: W. B. Saunders, 1974), s.v. "dermatitis" and "flux"; Sarah Hicks Williams to Parents, 11 March 1860, Williams Papers.

48. "Pine Forests of the South," 197; D. W. Kyle to John Buford, 29 March 1856, Buford Papers; Michael G. Carraway, telephone interview by author, 6 April 1991, Museum of the Cape Fear, Fayetteville, N.C.; Perry interview; *Industrial Toxicology*, 3d ed. (Acton, Mass.: Publishing Sciences Group, 1974), s.v. "wood dust"; David N. Holvey, ed., *The Merck Manual of Diagnosis and Therapy*, 12th ed. (Rahway, N.J.: Merck, Sharp, and Dohne Research Laboratories, 1972), s.v. "contact dermatitis"; Gosselin et al., *Clinical Toxicology*, 315.

49. Carraway, interview; Tatum, interview, 5; Thomas F. Strikney to Allen and James R. Grist, 26 February 1861, Grist Papers; Kathy Hawk, "Turpentine: An Ancient Technology Almost Tapped Out in St. Johns County," *St. Augustine Ancient City Beacon*, 25 June 1982, 1; M. S. Hendy, B. E. Beattie, and P. S. Burge, "Occupational Asthma Due to an Emulsified Oil Mist," *British Journal of Industrial Medicine* 42 (January 1985): 54; Per Gregersen et al., "Neurotoxic Effects of Organic Solvents in Exposed Workers: An Occupational, Neuropsychological, and

Another hazard to slaves was the explosive nature of stills and their flammable contents. Given the difficulty of regulating these crude devices, distillers could not always determine the pressure generated by the evaporating spirits of turpentine. Therefore, explosions and fires were common and could kill or seriously injure anyone close by.[50]

Turpentine slaves reportedly complained of "headache, pain in the eyes, arms and legs, their knees hurting them, pain in the back, stiff neck, feet and hands feeling dead, pain across the breast, and a severe griping in the bowels." All these ailments are easily explained as the result of either fume exposure, overwork, or turpentine ingestion through the water. However, G. W. Perry recommended that producers not listen to complaints, initially, "just tell them it is a busy time, and you will not allow any such sickness, and that will be sufficient." He believed that if a slave was actually ill the producer could tell easily enough and should give the slave the proper medicine and see that he takes it. Turpentine laborers often sought to cure themselves of maladies by relying on medicines made from forest products. A tea made from the leaves of the yellowtop plant treated flux. The leaves of the dollarleaf plant were supposed to remedy dysentery, and those from the boneset plant relieved vomiting. Butterfly weed was thought to cure diarrhea, while sufferers of rashes, burns, and other skin ailments drank smartwood tea. Black snakeroot tea remedied fever.[51]

In some cases overseers reluctantly permitted sick or injured slaves to return to their owner's home plantation for care and rest or the attention of a doctor. In 1860 one sick slave at the Williams Georgia operation was sent to Williams's residence, where his wife looked after him. After "boy Moses," who worked at a Grist operation, had suffered from sores in his throat for several weeks, his overseer wrote, "though I regret very much to have him off the place[,] . . . I would suggest to let him go back to the doctor at once . . . as he is not fit to work in turpentine." Moses stayed with the doctor for several months, during which time he drove the doctor's buggy. In return for Moses' service to the doctor, Grist received $25 a month and was not charged for the slave's medical care. In October 1855, five slaves laboring for Grist got sick and were allowed to miss work. Five years later, one slave working for Grist in Cumberland County missed work because of a cold, and another, Ruffin, was allowed to rest from his work for a week. When a hand

Neurological Investigation," *American Journal of Industrial Medicine* 5 (1984): 214; Joaquin Garcia-Estrada, Antonio Rodriguez-Segura, and Pedro Garzon, "Cerebral Cortex and Body Growth Development of Progeny of Rats Exposed to Thinner and Turpentine Inhalation," *General Pharmacology* 19 (1988): 470; Gosselin et al., *Clinical Toxicology*, 315.

50. Starobin, *Industrial Slavery*, 43; Avirett, *Old Plantation*, 70.

51. G. W. Perry, *Treatise on Turpentine Farming*, 120; Hickman, *Mississippi Harvest*, 150–1.

was kicked in the face by a mule and badly cut, he also rested a week and received care from the doctor. A doctor made regular visits to one of Grist's North Carolina operations. Between October 13, 1853, and July 29, 1854, a Dr. P. D. Mott saw thirty-eight slave patients at a total cost of $59.50. When the owner of slaves hired by Grist learned that one had died and another was down with fever, he requested that Grist spare no expense for the welfare and comfort of his other slaves who remained at work for Grist. Also, the owner wrote, "allow me kindly to request you to adhere strictly to the Doctors instructions relative to the administration of stimulants and food. For any thing furnished extra you shale be paid."[52]

The wilderness nature of the turpentine forests contributed further to harsh working conditions. Wild animals, poisonous snakes, malarial mosquitoes, ticks, and chiggers found in the pine woods could make turpentine production a miserable, and sometimes hazardous, occupation. The heat and humidity of the southeastern coastal plain added to the difficulties. In 1854 turpentine laborers fainted in the forest from these extreme conditions. Moreover, workers could easily lose their direction in the expansive pine forests. In 1859 a hand in a Georgia operation became lost in the woods and wandered for nearly six days before finding his way home. Despite a week of nursing care, he died of fever brought on by hunger and exposure. In another instance, a hired slave, Willis, who worked for Grist, drowned and another slave, Jack, almost drowned when they tried to remove turpentine casks from a remote platform near a swollen river. In such cases, the isolation and loneliness of the turpentine forests, combined with heavy work demands, poor housing, inadequate clothing and food, and unhealthy and dangerous labor conditions, made the slaves' already difficult work and manner of life unbearable. It is no wonder that the turpentine industry had the reputation for having "ruined more hands than anything else in this country."[53]

Some slaves resisted these terrible conditions. According to Edmund Ruffin, producers believed the fires that occasionally roared through the pine forests were "committed by the negroes who would have to attend the trees,

52. Sarah Hicks Williams to Parents, 21 October 1860, Williams Papers; Thomas F. Strikney to Allen and James R. Grist, 26 February 1861, M. Jones to James R. Grist, 30 October 1855, 12 November 1860, and 16 December 1860, P. D. Mott to James R. Grist, Bill for doctor's visits, 13 October 1853, and S. B. Carraway to John L. Wright, 10 October 1854, Grist Papers; Sarah Hicks Williams to Parents, 21 October 1860, Williams Papers.

53. Starobin, *Industrial Slavery*, 42; Clark, *Greening of the South*, 22; James R. Grist to Father, 17 September 1852, and R. M. Wadsworth to James R. Grist, 11 August 1854, Grist Papers; Sarah Hicks Williams to Parents, 25 March 1859, Williams Papers; G. W. Perry, *Treatise on Turpentine Farming*, 116.

to collect turpentine, which labor they dislike very much, because it is solitary." Further evidence of the discontent comes from the stories of runaway turpentine slaves. Although it is impossible to determine the frequency of escapes, evidence of slaves fleeing the James R. Grist operations suggests such acts were not uncommon. In all cases these slaves cited harsh living and working situations as their reason for flight. Two hired slaves, John and Albert, ran away in 1853 because they were "over worked and not well fed." John reached Greenville, North Carolina, "in a most exhausted condition," but Albert lost his way. Their owner blamed their harsh treatment for their escape. That same year a turpentine cooper ran away when he and his partner were whipped for working too slowly.[54]

The most dramatic story of escaped turpentine slaves involved two brothers, Ned and Colin, who were purchased from their owner in Sussex County, Virginia, by a slave trader in Richmond. When James Grist bought them, "they were sent off into the pine woods to make turpentine." But they "could not stand the work and the life before them and ran away" in 1854. While they were fleeing across a bridge near Fayetteville, someone shot at them and probably wounded Colin. The two slaves then ran in different directions and became separated. Colin reached Greenville and worked on the Seaboard Railroad until eventually caught by a search party later that year. Ned reached the home of a planter, William Parham, who was a neighbor of his former master in Sussex County and lived not far from Ned's wife and child. When Ned reached Parham, he was very sick, and Parham nursed him back to health. While Ned recovered, Parham wrote to Grist, informing him of Ned's location and condition. According to Parham's letter, Ned vehemently disliked the work in the turpentine forest. Parham reported that "the work and the manner of life in making turpentine he cannot stand, it is hard work and would kill him by piecemeal, and he had rather be killed at once."[55]

Historians have offered two interpretations of the lives of industrial slaves such as Ned and Colin. Ronald L. Lewis, who examined slave labor in the coal and iron industry in Virginia and Maryland, and Charles B. Dew, who studied slaves in the iron foundries in Virginia, question whether industrial slavery was "the most brutal phase of the regime." Lewis shows how industrial slaves challenged their masters' authority and consequently improved their quality of life by negotiating extra rations, gaining more autonomy, and receiving payment for work performed beyond their normal tasks.

54. Scarborough, ed., *Diary of Edmund Ruffin*, 52; L. F. N. to James R. Grist, 18 August 1853, and James to Grist, 23 August 1853, Grist Papers.

55. William F. Parham to James R. Grist, 1 May 1854, 14 November 1854, and 20 November 1854, Grist Papers.

Similarly, Dew's work, especially his *Bond of Iron,* demonstrates that in iron manufacturing the slaves' skill and determination, combined with southern iron producers' desire to maintain an appeased, and thus more reliable, labor force, created a middle ground in which those in bondage could exercise some control over their working conditions, family affairs, and livelihoods. Lewis and Dew convincingly substantiate their conclusions regarding iron manufacturing and coal mining; these findings may be valid for cotton mills, salt works, and the chemical industry as well. But they do not hold entirely true for the naval stores industry, an enterprise that operated in isolated forests and was perhaps less "industrial" than iron manufacturing.[56]

The experiences of naval stores laborers conform more to Robert S. Starobin's generalized description of industrial slavery. Industrial slaves, he argues, were men, although a few women and children also labored in such enterprises. The majority of industrial slaves lived not in large cities but in rural areas, small towns, or on plantations. In most cases their employer owned them; only one-fifth were hired. But in extractive industries, such as turpentine making, an integrated workforce of owned and hired slaves and even a few white laborers became common. Like agricultural slaves, industrial slaves were commonly managed by overseers or drivers, not by their owners or employers. However, Starobin writes that "working conditions were usually worse than those for laborers engaged in southern farming, since industrial development often demanded longer and harder working days than did plantation agriculture." Starobin argues that "the tendency to drive industrial slaves to the utmost, and to feed, clothe, and shelter them at subsistence levels, as well as the inadequate medical knowledge of the time, contributed to a tragic incidence of disease and fatality in virtually all industrial occupations." "The rigors of bondage and the hazardous nature of southern industries," Starobin concludes, revealed that the conditions experienced by industrial slaves differed from those of plantation laborers.[57]

"The work and the manner of life in making turpentine" was much like that of other industrial slavery occupations. Industrial slaves tended to labor

56. Ronald L. Lewis, *Coal Iron and Slaves: Industrial Slavery in Maryland and Virginia, 1715–1865* (Westport, Conn.: Greenwood Press, 1979), 8; Charles B. Dew, *Bond of Iron: Master and Slave at Buffalo Forge* (New York: W. W. Norton, 1994); see also Charles B. Dew, "David Ross and the Oxford Iron Works: A Study of Industrial Slavery in the Early Nineteenth-Century South," *William and Mary Quarterly,* 3rd ser., 31 (April 1974): 189–224; Charles B. Dew, "Disciplining Slave Ironworkers in the Antebellum South: Coercion, Conciliation, and Accommodation," *American Historical Review* 79 (April 1974): 393–418; Charles B. Dew, "Sam Williams, Forgeman: The Life of an Industrial Slave in the Old South," in *Region, Race, and Reconstruction: Essays in Honor of C. Vann Woodward,* ed. J. Morgan Kousser and James M. McPherson (New York: Oxford University Press, 1982), 199–239.

57. Starobin, *Industrial Slavery,* 11–2, 36, 37, 63, 138.

for absentee producers, were worked excessively hard by overseers, and received food, clothing, and shelter inferior to what was given agricultural laborers. Environmental factors played a major role in the harsh conditions of turpentine making. As geographically isolated and expansive enterprises, turpentine orchards possessed spatial attributes considerably different from those of open agricultural fields. Given the size of the pine forests and the methods of harvesting resin, producers could not permit workers to labor in groups. Instead, they instructed their slaves to spread widely throughout the forest and labor at individually assigned tasks. Since tasks were clearly marked, overseers could effectively monitor and evaluate each worker's performance. Although slaves generally preferred task work because of the relative degree of autonomy it offered, in the naval stores industry this independence was accompanied by solitude. The work location denied social interaction that would have broken the monotony of the job. Such loneliness did not end with the workday. The camps were commonly so far away from agricultural plantations that the male-dominated labor force was prevented from regular interaction with their families and largely denied female companionship. Because few visitors journeyed to the isolated camps, production operators and overseers received little social incentive to care properly for their slave laborers, especially for the many hired bondsmen. This lack of supervision contributed to relatively poor housing and food provisions for laborers. The natural setting of the turpentine orchards also accounted for these conditions. Most owners found it unfeasible to raise food at the campsites. Instead, food was hauled into the forests by producers who tended to keep rations at a subsistence level. Unlike many plantation slaves, turpentine laborers lacked the opportunity to supplement their diets with food raided from local smokehouses, chicken coops, and cornfields and gathered from their own garden plots. However, because they labored in the forest, workers possessed more of an opportunity to hunt wild animals and collect edible herbs. The migratory nature of the industry discouraged producers from constructing substantial cabins to house their workers. Instead, laborers could take refuge only in crude shed-like lean-tos that could be easily dismantled, moved, and reconstructed. The unique attributes of the naval stores industry created conditions that inevitably led to misery and discontent among the slaves, who, after the first decades of the nineteenth century, made up most of the industry's workforce.

The isolation of the pine forest also influenced the lives of its white inhabitants. In the remote forest, poor landless whites found plots where they could squat, construct a cabin, and cultivate a small garden with a minimum of harassment. They also harvested small quantities of gum for themselves to trade or worked on an irregular basis for larger producers. Small farmers likewise lived in the piney woods and cultivated a few crops and barrels of turpentine for the market, sometimes with the help of several slave laborers. The output of these smaller producers, however, paled in comparison to that of the larger operators, who made thousands of barrels of turpentine annually. For such naval stores men as Avirett, Williams, and Grist, the experience of managing a large-scale operation with scores of slaves and several overseers differed only moderately from that of plantation owners. However, the bondsmen, whose labor created the turpentine men's wealth, were not the only victims of the industry.

CHAPTER 4

SUICIDAL HARVEST ON THE MOVE

BY THE 1850s, production intensity had stressed North Carolina's longleaf pine forests so greatly that few stands remained. After ten years of gum harvesting, a large percentage of turpentined trees succumbed to reduced vitality, weakened trunk structure, insect infestation, and disease. When gone, the longleaf failed to reproduce itself, and a different vegetation replaced the once nearly solid pine growth. As they witnessed their eastern pine forests' disappearance, some North Carolinians turned against the turpentine industry despite its continued profitability. Beginning with the state's older naval stores region, producers increasingly switched to staple cotton production, which the introduction of new fertilizers made possible. Not all turpentine producers, however, so willfully abandoned their business. Those who refused to make the switch to agriculture moved with their slave labor forces to other southern states and continued the destructive harvesting practices that had driven them out of North Carolina.

By the beginning of the 1840s the damage to the turpentine forests was becoming clear. Fourteen miles outside of Plymouth, North Carolina, on his way to New Bern, Edmund Ruffin observed that the pine trees were "deformed by being skinned for extracting turpentine." Closer to Wilmington he recognized that "where vicinity to market, or cheapness of carriage, permits this business to be in full operation, it cannot last long, as the long leaf pines will be destroyed and will not be renewed." In 1843, William Cullen Bryant, the New York City editor and poet traveling from Richmond, was astonished at the number of boxes in North Carolina pines. "This is the work of destruction," he reported, "it strips acre after acre of the noble trees, and, if it goes on, the time is not far distant when the long-leaved pine will be-come nearly extinct in this region." In 1855, yet another observer reported that "from Rocky Mount to Wilmington (with now and then an exception to the rule) the country presents the appearance of a dreary desolate pine barren waste." And by 1860, the industry was in decline in areas where the boom had begun in the 1830s, with the pines around Washington, North Carolina, nearly exhausted and those up the Neuse River from New Bern only slightly more plentiful.[1]

Boxes were responsible for much of the damage to trees. Producers in-structed their laborers to cut boxes in the swell of the pine's most prominent root. With the box there, more gum could be collected from trees that leaned. Placed elsewhere and gum began dripping outside the box as the face grew higher and extended over the base. Also, laborers preferred to cut boxes here because they could be made with the greatest of ease and in the least time. But because boxes were usually cut seven inches deep into the root, they could seriously interfere with the flow of sap. In larger roots, which represented a substantial portion of the pine's root system, the box caused the greatest injury to the tree. Although precise mortality statistics were unknown in the antebellum years, in 1909 forester A. L. Brower esti-mated that 7 percent of boxed trees died from reduced vitality before a stand was worked to its fullest potential. Boxes also weakened the stability of the pines, making them more susceptible to wind. Larger trees were not as vul-nerable to strong gusts, but in smaller pines if more than one box was cut into the base they were sometimes nearly severed. Brower reported that a hurricane or strong windstorm could down 90 percent of boxed timber, whereas only 30 percent of round timber would fall. Boxes also collected rainwater. In stands where gum harvesting continued, this was not of con-siderable consequence, for not only did the continuous gum flow provide the wood with some protection from the moisture, but in dipping the gum out of the box most of the water was removed as well. Standing rainwater, however, could be especially damaging in abandoned turpentine orchards where the wood's continuous contact with moisture encouraged fungus growth and subsequent decay. Another problem was the occasional practice of trying to deter fire by filling old boxes with dirt at the conclusion of a forests' use. The dirt, which acted like a sponge, held water that might other-wise have evaporated in the box, hastening decay.[2]

1. Ashe, *Forests, Forest Lands, and Forest Products,* 18, 76; Ruffin, "Notes of a Steam Jour-ney," 245, 250, 253; Bryant, quoted in Kirby, *Poquosin,* 32–3; unidentified farmer, quoted in P. Perry, "Naval Stores Industry in the Ante-Bellum South, 1789–1861," 10; Cook, "Naval Stores," 9; M. Williams, *Americans and Their Forests,* 160.

2. Asa L. Brower and John O. La Fontisee, "Report of the Investigation on the Naval Stores Industry and Statistics of the Production of Turpentine and Rosin for the Seasons of

Fire, often intentionally set by the turpentiners themselves, posed a particularly dangerous threat to boxed trees. Stephen Pyne explains that "perhaps nowhere in the country were Indian burning practices more thoroughly adopted and maintained than in the piney woods, in the sand hills, and on the sandy soils where rice or cotton plantations failed to penetrate." Like the Indians, white settlers and turpentiners used burning to reduce fuel as a means of preventing conflagrations, to open the choked woods for easier passage, to encourage more abundant grazing grasses, and to reduce pests. Despite efforts by turpentiners to guard against the damaging effects of fires on their forests, accidental tree burning was all too frequent. Edmund Ruffin observed that although producers took care to control their burning, "they cannot always command the progress of the fires; and from that, or other less carefully made fires, great havoc is often made among the boxed trees." Olmsted found that burning in round timber rarely harmed the trees. In such forests the fire "burns slowly, and with little flame, and the living trees, the bark of which is not very inflammable, are seldom injured." Where the trees had been boxed, however, great harm could result. "The chips lie about it, these take fire, and burn with more flame; so that frequently the turpentine in the box, and on the scarified wood above it, also takes fire."[3]

Such fires either greatly reduced the tree's productivity or, as was often the case, killed it. Turpentine producer G. W. Perry of Craven County explained that "in cases where pines are much burned by the fire, they will never make as much turpentine afterward; it makes the wood dry and tough, kills many of them, and finally renders them useless for turpentine, or so much so that will never run enough to pay." Ruffin noted in 1840 that "without other cause or decay or destruction, the trees will live and yield well until the sides can be shaved no higher. But the spreading of accidental fires seldom fails to kill the tree earlier. For the entire face of the cutting being encrusted with turpentine, and the wood below being converted to solid lightwood, no trees can be more inflammable; and the fire burns so deeply in, as to kill the strips of living bark by heat, or to weaken the trunk so much that it yields to, and is prostrated by, the next storm." While on another trip through North Carolina in the late 1850s, Ruffin attended a tea at which the

---

1907–8 and 1908–9," 17–21, Cary Collection; Schorger and Betts, *Naval Stores Industry,* 26; Charles H. Herty, *A New Method of Turpentine Orcharding* (Washington, D.C.: United States Department of Agriculture Bureau of Forestry, 1903), 12–3.

   3. Pyne, *Fire in America,* 144–6, 149; Ruffin, "Notes of a Steam Journey," 250; Olmsted, *Journey in the Seaboard Slave States,* 341.

talk was "of much recent destruction of the long-leaf pine trees, 'boxed' to collect turpentine, in this neighborhood, by firing the woods."[4]

Fires in abandoned turpentine forests caused the most damage. Such stands were highly flammable after three to five years of sitting unattended. With no one to rake around their bases or burn off the yearly collection of debris, trees here often sat surrounded by a thick mass of pine straw, limbs, resinous chips, and pools of gum. Moreover, the turpentined pines, their faces covered with hardened gum and their boxes and bases coated with resin, were extremely flammable. A fire, started either by lightning, an arsonist, or human carelessness, easily ignited the box and climbed up the face. When it did, the dried gum of the face often melted and ran down into the box, increasing the fires' intensity. If such fires did not destroy the tree, they at least burned away much of the fresh growth of new wood around the box and face, thus slowing the pine's recovery from turpentining.[5]

Fires that did not kill longleafs could weaken them, making them susceptible to other problems. One ailment that plagued turpentined longleaf pines was a condition known as dry face, in which resin soaked the inner bark and wood. Pines with this affliction experienced a permanent cessation of gum flow from all or part of the face. In severe cases, lesions formed above and beside the dry area and resin oozed through the bark. Fire contributed to dry face when it burned the gum on the face, killing the living tissue above the face. Poor chipping practices could also exacerbate the problem. Cutting a face wider than half of the tree's circumference, chipping too deeply into the wood, or working two or more faces on the same tree could weaken the pine by taxing its capability to produce gum and thus lower its vitality. Also, as producer G. W. Perry warned, "if they chipped immediately after burning, the turpentine which is brought down by the fire will run out and leave the grain of the wood open, which will fill them full of dry faces, and occasion the death of many which would have lived had they not been chipped."[6]

Drought, however, was probably the most significant factor in weakening pines and making them susceptible to dry face. In the longleaf belt the soil possesses relatively low water-retaining capability, making the region

---

4. G. W. Perry, *Treatise on Turpentine Farming*, 16–7; Ruffin, "Notes of a Steam Journey," 250; Scarborough, ed., *Diary of Edmund Ruffin*, 52.

5. Johnson, *Ante-Bellum North Carolina*, 486; Herty, *New Method of Turpentine Orcharding*, 13; Brower and La Fontisee, "Report of the Investigation on the Naval Stores Industry," 20–1.

6. C. S. Schopmeyer and Otis C. Maloy, *Dry Face of Naval Stores Pines*, Forest Pest Leaflet 51 (Washington D.C.: United States Department of Agriculture, 1960), 1–3; R. P. True, "Dry Face of Turpentine Pines," *Forest Farmer* 8 (August 1949): 6, 14; G. W. Perry, *Treatise on Turpentine Farming*, 17, 28.

acutely susceptible to periodic precipitation declines. During the average growing season, June through August, nearly all precipitation is lost through evaporation or transpiration. The quantity of available water is not affected by long-term carry-over. The sandy soils can hold sufficient moisture to sustain vegetation growth for only a few weeks during this season. Thus the moisture level of the soil constantly fluctuates with precipitation. During the summer, dry spells stressed turpentined trees' vitality, increasing their susceptibility to dry face. If left standing, dry-faced pines commonly became the host to various species of fungi and with time frequently yielded to strong wind. Weakened pines were also susceptible to another menace, insect infestation.[7]

Because wood-boring insects are attracted to the wounded areas of trees, turpentine faces, especially on weakened pines, were particularly vulnerable to attack. Ips beetles are the most common pine bark beetle and probably killed more turpentine pines than the other bark beetles combined. Infested trees are commonly scattered throughout the forest, but with favorable breeding conditions the ips beetle can kill trees in groups. The beetles are especially attracted to chipped and fire-scarred trees. Because there actually are three different varieties, each with its own preference for part of the tree, they can attack a pine from its crown to the base of its trunk. Hundreds of beetles attack at the same time. They become active when the weather turns warm in the spring, boring through the bark until they reach the wood. As it bores, the beetle lays eggs spaced about one-sixteenth inch apart along each side of the tunnel. The cream-colored worms which hatch from these eggs bore their own tunnel out from the beetle's tunnel. They hatch in such numbers that in feeding on the cambium layer they essentially girdle the tree. When the larvae stop feeding after a few weeks, they rest and metamorphose into adult beetles. They then burrow out of the tree in search of other trees in which to start the cycle again. During the summer when breeding conditions are at their best, a new brood is produced about every four to six weeks. Each tree that they attack and kill produces enough beetles to attack at least five more. As the ips beetles breed though the spring and summer, their numbers, by fall, grow enormous. If the winter is mild and dry, the adults remain alive and active, causing considerable tree deaths by late spring, and by the next fall the damage may be severe. Normal winter temperatures, however, considerably reduce the ips population, and in cases

7. John C. Hoyt, *Droughts of 1930–1934* (Washington, D.C.: United States Department of the Interior, 1936), 15–6; Schopmeyer and Maloy, *Dry Face*, 3–5; True, "Dry Face of Turpentine Pines," 6; Lenthall Wyman, *Experiments in Naval Stores Practice* (Washington, D.C.: United States Department of Agriculture, 1932), 10.

where drought is associated with the infestation, soaking rains usually stop their activity.[8]

Another insect, turpentine borers, take advantage of fire-scarred and dry-faced pines as well. They rarely attack healthy trees. These grayish brown and $1\frac{1}{4}$-inch-long beetles lay their eggs only on trees where wood has been exposed by a scar or wound. When the whitish gray grubs with broad flat heads emerge from these eggs, they tunnel into the inner wood, often riddling it. This activity can continue within the tree for three years or more, filling it with hollow galleries, thus weakening the tree's stability and making it susceptible to wind. After about three and a half years the life cycle is complete and the adult beetles emerge from the trees in the spring.[9]

The black turpentine beetle also takes advantage of longleafs stressed by turpentining. The dark brown or black one-quarter- to one-third-inch-long beetles prefer freshly cut stumps but also invade weakened as well as apparently healthy trees. The most severe infestations occur in slash and loblolly pines, but because it is attracted to fresh resin and scorched bark, longleafs that had been overworked through excessive turpentining offered an acceptable home. The black turpentine beetle's habits are different from those of any other bark beetle. It rarely attacks above the tree's bottom six feet and usually only the bottom two feet. The adult beetles bore through the outer bark and stop when they reach the soft phloem. There they lay eggs. When the eggs hatch, ten to fourteen days later, the creamy white one-third-inch-long grubs begin to feed in groups, side-by-side, on the cambium, working their way from the egg gallery. They eventually eat out an irregular fan-shaped patch that may grow to become twelve inches across. Where several broods occur at approximately the same height on the trunk, the larvae can actually girdle the tree.

The black turpentine beetle kills more slowly than other bark beetles. Usually only a few beetles attack each tree, making their buildup to outbreak proportions slow. After the beetle attacks the trunk, it quickly moves against

8. William H. Bennett, Charles W. Chellman, and William R. Holt, *Insect Enemies of Southern Pines* (Washington, D.C.: United States Department of Agriculture, Southern Forest Experiment Station, 1958), 7–9; R. J. Kowal, *Ips Beetles Are Killing Pines: What Shall We Do about It?* Research Notes (Asheville, N.C.: United States Department of Agriculture, Forest Service, Southeastern Forest Experiment Station, 1955), 1; R. J. Kowal and Harry Russell, *Beetles in Your Pines? How Good Cutting Practices and Management Stop Beetles from Killing Your Timber* (Asheville, N.C.: United States Department of Agriculture, Forest Service, Southeastern Forest Experiment Station, 1958), 3–4; Ralph W. Clements, *Manual: Modern Gum Naval Stores Methods* (Asheville, N.C.: United States Department of Agriculture, Forest Service, Southeastern Forest Experiment Station, 1960), 29.

9. F. C. Craighead, "Insects That Attack Southern Pines," 2, Cary Collection; Bennett, Chellman, and Holt, *Insect Enemies*, 16.

the lateral root. If the root's infestation becomes severe, it can hasten the tree's death. When they attack forests disturbed by fire, logging, or wind, the beetle seldom persists at high levels of population for more than one or two years. But in stands boxed for turpentine, the activity could continue for three to five years. Intensely worked trees in dense stretches were particularly susceptible to their attack.[10]

A variety of other insects made the weakened turpentine trees their home for breeding as well. The southern pine sawyer, a large, gray, mottled beetle with very long feelers, lays eggs in small oval pits which it gnaws in the bark. The eggs hatch and the larvae bore into the bark and through to the sapwood, on which they feed. The larvae remain beneath the bark for about twenty days, during which time they cause complete destruction of the wood. The pitch moth has a similar breeding pattern. This small moth lays eggs along the edge of faces, and when the eggs hatch, the larvae bore into the tissue. Although frequently abundant, they rarely cause serious injury. However, in association with other insect infestations, they can contribute to the trees' death. Damage from all these insects could be considerable, even if they did not directly kill the trees. Moreover, the fungi that often accompanied them could cause considerable decay of the wood above the face.[11]

It is difficult to know precisely which insects plagued the mid-nineteenth-century North Carolina turpentine forest. Twentieth-century entomology and forestry research, however, provide clues as to what probably happened. Yet historians can only speculate because the contemporary observers' limited knowledge of insects resulted in vague descriptions. In his *Treatise on Turpentine Farming,* for example, G. W. Perry identifies a "black bug" as one such invading beetle. That he is describing some form of bark beetle is clear, but the insect that he discusses has attributes of turpentine borers, black turpentine beetles, and ips beetles. He explains that this black bug laid eggs from which emerged a "cutting worm" that fed on the sapwood. He goes on to create such descriptive terminology for the creature as

10. Bennett, Chellman, and Holt, *Insect Enemies,* 10–2; R. H. Smith and R. E. Lee III, *Black Turpentine Beetle,* Forest Pest Leaflet 12 (Washington, D.C.: United States Department of Agriculture, 1972), 1–6; Richard H. Smith, *Benzene Hexachloride Controls Black Turpentine Beetle,* 1–2, reprint from *Southern Lumberman,* 15 December 1954, copy in Olustee Experiment Station Files, Georgia Agrirama, Tifton, Ga.; R. H. Smith, *A Control for the Black Turpentine Beetle in South Georgia and North Florida,* Research Notes (Asheville, N.C.: United States Department of Agriculture, Forest Service, Southeastern Forest Experiment Station, 1955), 1; Clements, *Manual,* 28; Kowal and Russell, *Beetles in Your Pines,* 7–8.

11. Schopmeyer and Maloy, *Dry Face,* 1; Craighead, "Insects That Attack Southern Pines," 4–5.

"Ramming worm, Laboring worm, or Forward-moving worm." Presumably this "worm" is the larval stage of the black bug, but Perry treats it as another species of insect. He also identified a "black worm," apparently the larva of another beetle that he believed "is caused by a black fly laying its eggs on the edge of a scar," and a "straw worm," which lived in the boughs of the tree on the green straw. Perry admits that he is "not able to give the origin of this insect, but have no doubt, from the time of its appearance, that it is produced by some large fly."[12]

An example of the devastation that insects could cause in turpentined forests occurred in the late 1840s. In 1848 both boxed and round pines in the eastern half of North Carolina began mysteriously and rapidly dying in large numbers. The greatest damage appears to have occurred below the Cape Fear, especially in Brunswick County. One timber owner there reportedly lost 130,000 trees. Another owner's loss was estimated at an astonishing 750,000 pines. Symptoms of the blight also appeared in several counties to the north. That summer a traveler on the road from New Bern to Kinston and Waynesboro, a now vanished community then located probably near Goldsboro, reported seeing tracts of pine either dead or dying. The death of so many trees threatened the entire region's economy. Newspapers speculated about the cause of the tree deaths. The *Mobile Herald* attributed the blight to atmospheric conditions. The *Tarboro Press* thought it was caused by a bug which laid its eggs in the tops of pines. These bugs, the paper theorized, were attracted to the smoke of burning rosin which turpentine stills emitted, a theory that seemed logical to some because the decline of the pine forests came on the heels of the increased number of small, backwoods stills.

When in July the pines around Wake Forest College, then located just north of Raleigh, began to succumb, Professor John D. White's investigations found that two kinds of small bugs were the culprit. White observed that these beetles entered the bark by boring a small hole and tunneling between the inner bark and sapwood. The beetles' small size, their ability to kill the trees quickly, and White's claim to have identified two different varieties, seem to point toward ips beetles as the cause. The problem apparently began in early 1848, when eastern North Carolina enjoyed a mild winter, which allowed the beetle to continue breeding. By the spring and summer of that year their numbers were huge, and they began killing pines en masse. These insects multiplied into the spring of 1849 until the area suffered a freak snowstorm. On April 14 the temperature dipped, and the next day sleet began falling. Within five or six hours the precipitation turned to snow,

---

12. G. W. Perry, *Treatise on Turpentine Farming*, 103–7.

which continued to fall into the night. Before daybreak the weather cleared, and the next day the sun melted the snow, but the brief storm stopped the attack by reducing the number of adults and larvae. Still, for the year that the insect's numbers had increased unchecked, tremendous tree loss resulted, and as turpentining continued into the twentieth century, infestations would reoccur with similarly disastrous consequences.[13]

The changing nature of turpentine production from a small-scale business dominated by casual producers who also dabbled in agriculture to one controlled by large and highly specialized operators likely accelerated forest devastation, brought on by reduced tree vitality, structural weakening, dry face, and insects. When a turpentine operation was a small part of a larger farming enterprise, producers probably used more care to extend the life and efficiency of the forest so that it would not wear out more quickly than the agricultural land. Turpentiners who operated on a grand scale and focused almost exclusively on gum and spirit production had less incentive to prolong their use of the pines and ran more exploitative operations. The increasing number of such producers in the 1840s and 1850s meant more widespread forest degradation. As the practice of leasing became more common, it too led to greater inefficiency and waste. Because operators paid for the number of boxes, not the amount produced, they tried to maximize their yields by making frequent and deep chippings.[14]

As the longleaf stands died from the effects of turpentining, they failed to replace themselves. In 1840 Ruffin found that the pines around Wilmington had vanished. Although in this particular case the clearing was probably owing to a demand for timber for fences, houses, and firewood, rather than turpentining, the result gave an early indication of how removal of the longleaf pines could transform the region's vegetation. The longleaf pines were not replaced by a second growth of more longleaf, but rather by what Ruffin described as an "almost unmixed growth of thickly set dwarfish 'scrub' oaks which rarely rose higher than six feet." In other areas further inland, Ruffin found a second growth of shortleaf pine, but no longleaf. "The other kinds of pines are not worth working for the purpose [turpentine]." In the more western reaches of the pine belt, John MacLeod of Johnson County observed that "where pines are destroyed by blasts, hurricanes, or turpentining, a growth of oak, hickory, etc. arises in their stead, not a solitary instance of the longleaf." Olmsted questioned whether there ever would be a revived growth of longleaf given its slow growth and its apparent inability to repro-

---

13. P. Perry, "Naval Stores Industry in the Ante-Bellum South, 1789–1861," 261–70.
14. Ibid., 46; Martin, "American Gum Naval Stores Industry," 98–9.

duce itself. He reported that "when the original long-leafed pine has been destroyed, and the ground cultivated a few years, and then 'turned out,' a bastard variety springs up, which grows with rapidity, but is of no value for turpentine, and of but little for timber."[15]

Longleaf pines failed to come back for two reasons, one of which contemporary observers understood. Hogs, Ruffin believed, were the primary reason for the slow-growing longleaf's inability to reproduce itself. Hogs eagerly devoured the pine's large cones, allowing few seeds to sprout into seedlings. For those seeds that did escape and germinate, hogs posed a continued threat. Ruffin reported that "of the few that do sprout, scarcely any of the young trees survive the after attacks of the hogs, which root up the young trees, to eat the roots, even when the trees are several years old. Hogs ranging in the woods are quite fond of the tender roots, and the bark of the roots of older trees, and live on this food principally in the winter and spring, after the pine seeds are consumed." G. W. Perry likewise blamed hogs for eating the bark off the roots of saplings. Second, and apparently unrecognized by observers of the day, the absence of regular low-burning fires contributed to the longleaf's failed reemergence. As unwanted and neglected property, old and dying turpentine forests received little if any management such as yearly undergrowth firing, a practice that had originally created and sustained the southern longleaf forest by killing off competing species. Without fire, loblolly and shortleaf pines quickly shaded out any longleaf seedlings fortunate enough to escape the ravenous hogs. When abandoned turpentine forests burned by accident, the fires blazed so intensely they killed off all vegetation, including the young longleafs.[16]

In the wake of longleaf pine forest depletion, operators faced three options: make no changes and face inevitable ruin, switch to agricultural production, or move southward in search of fresh stands. The rise and decline of the Richlands Plantation turpentine business typifies the consequence of the first response. Although turpentine was probably produced on the tract in Onslow County as early as the eighteenth century, it did not become the plantation's focus until John Avirett undertook it on a large scale in the 1840s. As turpentine prices climbed, so did Avirett's output and profits, until his annual income eventually reached $60,000. But Avirett failed to diversify his business, focusing his slaves' energy on the plantation's pineland and doing little to develop his agricultural operation. By the early 1850s the busi-

15. Ruffin, "Notes of a Steam Journey," 245, 250; Clark, *Greening of the South,* 143; Mac-Leod, "Tar and Turpentine Business," 13; Olmsted, *Journey in the Seaboard Slave States,* 346–7.

16. Ruffin, "Notes of a Steam Journey," 250; G. W. Perry, *Treatise on Turpentine Farming,* 27.

ness's exploitative harvesting practices began to take their toll on the Richlands forests. In 1850 Avirett first advertised the sale of the entire operation,
even the 125 slaves who labored to make his naval stores, in North Carolina
newspapers. He found no buyers, however, and in 1857 Richlands failed, its
pine forest destroyed. Deeply in debt, Avirett at last sold off all his property,
including his distillery and even the family graveyard. By 1860 he was living
in Goldsboro, where he died in 1863, allegedly in either a poorhouse or an
insane asylum. His son James, who was born at Richlands in 1835 and was
raised in the big house, received no inheritance with which to continue the
family legacy. He became an Episcopal priest and served as chaplain under
Stonewall Jackson's chief cavalry officer. In his memoir of his youth at Richlands he postulated that "It would have been far better for the landed estates
of the South if the timber, especially the hardwood, had been more carefully
guarded and economized."[17]

Many more operators looked to agriculture. As turpentining's destruction
of the North Carolina longleaf pine stands proceeded and it became more
obvious that the industry could continue in the state only for a limited time,
many North Carolinians began to condemn turpentine production and emphasized the need to raise cotton instead. Whereas the area's poor soils had
earlier discouraged staple crop production, the introduction of lime, manure, superphosphate, and guano fertilizers during the mid-nineteenth century made the shift to cotton cultivation feasible. Edgecombe and Pitt
Counties, where turpentine production had persisted since the early part of
the century, led the move toward cotton just as the naval stores industry was
moving into counties farther south. In Edgecombe County in the early 1850s
cotton began to replace turpentine, a trend that continued into the late
1850s. The *North Carolina Planter* encouraged it with its report that
"throughout the entire region hitherto devoted to the production of turpentine, cotton may be cultivated at great advantage. Even our sandy lands,
aided by compost and other manures, produce it finely, and will give to
planters a better remunerating crop than turpentine has ever done." In 1853,
one commentator, in a discussion on Edgecombe's shift to cotton, called
turpentining "*that great curse* to our state" which had seduced farmers with
the promise of great profits but proved "to be only a temporary resource."
"When this resource failed," the writer continued, "they then, through necessity, turned their attention to the cultivation of their farms and began to
look around to discover the advantages which were in their midst, but hith-

17. Avirett, *Old Plantation*, 26, 29, 69; Cecelski, "Rise and Fall of the Rich Lands," 22–4;
"Valuable Real Estate for Sale," *WJ*, 16 August 1850; Cecelski, "Oldest Living Confederate
Chaplain," 21.

erto unobserved." In Pitt County, the *North Carolina Planter* reported in 1860 that "cotton is manic here; larger plantations devoting most of their time and attention to it." Planters believed that their crop that year would be larger than ever before.[18]

Southeastern North Carolinians also began to question their heavy reliance on turpentine production, but because the vast longleaf stands were slower to disappear than the sparser ones in the more northern counties, residents there were slow to make the shift to cotton planting. As early as 1848 a Duplin County farmer complained that farmers of that area placed too much emphasis on turpentining and not enough on agriculture. Because the strongest hands were used in turpentine production, he explained, farms had fallen into disrepair and producers had to buy corn and pork because they no longer supplied their own food staples. Three years later the *Fayetteville North Carolinian* asked if "it were not better for our farmers in this neighborhood to turn their attention to raising stock and making corn, and not devote so much time to getting turpentine." Whereas in earlier years Fayetteville had supplied Wilmington with corn and pork, now these supplies moved in the opposite direction, through the port at Wilmington and into the Cape Fear Valley. Since the turpentine industry's expansion, the area's importation of corn and bacon had quadrupled. In 1853 a Beaufort County farmer advocated a shift to agriculture where the turpentine industry was in decline. He explained that "our means of transportation have greatly increased, but the resources that have been operated upon chiefly— namely: Naval Stores—are becoming very limited and used up, while those of agriculture and horticulture, the ones mostly to be relied on, have not been developed." The *Wilmington Journal* agreed, arguing that "it is a great mistake that when once the turpentine falls we must fall too. It may be the best thing for us when staple agriculture is substituted for a dependence upon the products of the forest."[19]

Little advancement in southeastern North Carolina agriculture resulted from this admonition, however, and by the late 1850s area agricultural organizations took up the cause. In November 1858, William A. Allen addressed the Duplin Agricultural Society on that county's need to concentrate on agriculture. He was "fully persuaded that if there never had been a barrel of

18. P. Perry, "Naval Stores Industry in the Old South, 1790–1860," *Journal of Southern History,* 509; Richard C. Sheridan, "Chemical Fertilizers in Southern Agriculture," *Agricultural History* 53 (January 1979): 308–9; P. Perry, "Naval Stores Industry in the Ante-Bellum South, 1789–1861," 286, 287; "Cotton Growing in the Old North State," *North-Carolina Planter* 3 (August 1860): 263.

19. P. Perry, "Naval Stores Industry in the Ante-Bellum South, 1789–1861," 10, 255–6, 278, 291.

turpentine made in the county, the people would have been better off, and the county would to-day have been recognized . . . as perhaps the richest agricultural county in North Carolina." The editor of the *Wilmington Journal,* who was in the audience, agreed with Allen that the Cape Fear counties required "the devotion of a larger degree of attention to the cultivation of the soil, and a less reliance upon mere products of the forest—naval stores and lumber—since agriculture is reliable, progressive, self-sustaining, while the other business which had at one time usurped its place is necessarily exhausting and inevitably tends to work itself out." In Onslow County, where agriculture was of only moderate importance, a group of farmers in 1859 organized an agricultural society, hoping "to create a spirit of improve-ment among the farmers . . . and that better crops may be made thereby." The organizers aspired for Onslow to become more of a farming county. That it was not, they believed, was because "we make Naval Stores exten-sively, thereby neglecting the more important of all the farming interest by omitting to properly fertilize and improve the soil." That same year a Bruns-wick County farmer believed that the area had reached a crossroads. "This county heretofore has been almost exclusively engaged in getting timber, lumber, and Naval stores for market," he explained, "but now, all the choice timbered [*sic*] and lumber making growth within reach of market, is gone, turpentine trees worked up, and our citizens must either move off to a fresh country or turn their attention to agriculture." Yet despite such encourage-ment, cotton cultivation increased only slightly in the southeastern counties. Although North Carolina's cotton crop grew larger over the course of the 1850s, most of the production came from the northeastern and central east-ern counties, while excitement over turpentine continued in those to the southeast. In 1859, in fact, naval stores exports from Wilmington reached their highest level ever.[20]

Where some turpentine producers gradually turned to cotton cultivation, others looked for new pine stands in which to continue their enterprise. Evidence suggests that manufacturers who were diversified, producing both turpentine and agricultural products, were more likely to make the switch to cotton. Slightly less than half of turpentine operations appear to have in-cluded as much as two hundred acres of farmable land. Although most such cultivated plots grew mostly grain crops in the 1840s and 1850s, fertilizer

20. P. Perry, "Naval Stores Industry in the Ante-Bellum South, 1789–1861," 288, 291–2; "Organizing an Agricultural Society in Onslow County," *North-Carolina Planter* 2 (October 1859): 311; "Cotton Crop in North Carolina," *North-Carolina Planter* 3 (October 1860): 320; Sam Bowers Hilliard, *Atlas of Antebellum Southern Agriculture* (Baton Rouge: Louisiana State University Press, 1984), 71.

applications could have enabled cotton production on them by the 1850s, providing turpentiners, whose exhausted forests yielded small returns, with an alternative staple commodity. However, large producers, whose financial dedication to naval stores prevented flexibility, typically chose to move south, demonstrating the same relative disregard for community and the land as the plantation cotton farmers who, between the 1830s and 1850s, moved from their exhausted fields in the East to the black belt and Lower Mississippi Valley. One observer of the naval stores industry has argued that "turpentine represented the extensive and exhausting practices that had long characterized use of southern land. Like tobacco in Virginia in the seventeenth century and indigo in South Carolina during the eighteenth century, turpentining stood for the maximum exploitation of land and labor in the short run."[21]

North Carolina producers who wished to remain in the business began buying virgin pine forests in states to the south and moving their slaves, who were already familiar with turpentining practices, there to begin production. In fact, North Carolinians were responsible for much of the industry's antebellum growth in other southern states. Immigrant producers possessed the experience in this unique industry that the natives of other pine-rich states lacked. Indeed, one Wilmington man doubted that anyone without practical experience could make a success of turpentining. He advised that if "you have any idea of going into the business, you had better employ a young man from North Carolina to superintend for you the first year; at least one accustomed to the business, who can put your hands in the way of making, coopering, &c."[22]

A state-by-state analysis reveals that South Carolina, Georgia, and Alabama attracted the most North Carolina turpentine producers, though Florida, Louisiana, and Mississippi lured a few, too. As early as 1840, production began to increase in South Carolina, largely as a result of North Carolina producers drifting across the border in search of fresh pineland. The early naval stores activity in South Carolina essentially represented an extension of that in North Carolina, the product being made by North Carolinians, who marketed it mainly through Wilmington, especially after completion of the Manchester Railroad. Agricultural journals of the day assured them of the South Carolina pines' productivity. An 1846 *Monthly Journal of Agriculture* article reported that "very recently several enterprising individuals have engaged in this business in South Carolina." The writer was confident that

21. Sharrer, "Naval Stores," 260.

22. P. Perry, "Naval Stores Industry in the Ante-Bellum South, 1789–1861," 276; McMillan to *Southern Cultivator*, 172.

turpentine "will add considerably to the other resources of the State." He promised consumers and potential producers that pines of South Carolina differed in no way from those found in North Carolina and yielded resin in equal abundance. *De Bow's Review* agreed, reporting that "travelers through the middle and lower districts of the State, agree in pronouncing the pine forests of these sections as well adapted as those of North Carolina for the manufacture of turpentine." Such claims apparently convinced some North Carolinians. While traveling through South Carolina in the 1850s, Olmsted found that North Carolinians had been working turpentined trees there for several years. Shortly after the Civil War, northern correspondent Whitelaw Reid, too, reported that "turpentine growers have for many years been abandoning" North Carolina's depleted forests "for the more productive forests of upper South Carolina."[23]

From the late 1840s to 1860, South Carolina's naval stores industry grew steadily. By 1848 Charleston had a turpentine distillery with a one-hundred-barrel-per-day capacity, and plans were under way to expand the facility. Around this time, Robert I. Hyslop moved from North Carolina to South Carolina and began teaching people in the Barnwell District how to make turpentine. In 1849 one producer whom he had instructed reportedly netted $398.84 with the help of just one hand. Another man, in Ridgeville, South Carolina, about thirty-five miles northwest of Charleston, made $3,000 from the work of forty hands, who together dipped five thousand barrels of turpentine. At the time, turpentine prices were relatively low, at $2 per barrel. By at least the early 1850s one S. T. Cooper operated a large, thirteen-crop operation along Black Mingo Creek in the Georgetown, South Carolina, area. The increasing production activity drove up land prices in some areas of South Carolina. "In the vicinity of Orangeburg," *De Bow's Review* reported in 1850, "the range is from $1.50 to $5 [per acre]. Many of the neighboring planters have embarked in the business, and at present it is difficult to obtain suitable locations." However, affordable pineland was still available in

23. Martin, "American Gum Naval Stores Industry," 74; P. Perry, "Naval Stores Industry in the Old South, 1790–1860," *Journal of Southern History*, 522; Jeffrey R. Dobson and Roy Doyon, "Expansion of the Pine Oleoresin Industry in Georgia: 1842 to Ca. 1900," *West Georgia College Studies in the Social Sciences* 18 (June 1979): 44; United States Department of State, *Compendium of the Enumeration of the Inhabitants and Statistics of the United States, . . . Sixth Census* (Washington D.C.: Department of State, 1841), 194; "Manufacture of Turpentine in the South," 454; "Notes on the Long-Leafed Pine," *Monthly Journal of Agriculture* 2 (July 1846): 12–3; "Manufacture of Turpentine in the South," 451; P. Perry, "Naval Stores Industry in the Ante-Bellum South, 1789–1861," 277; Whitelaw Reid, *After the War: A Tour of the Southern States, 1865–1866* (New York: Harper and Row, 1965), 28.

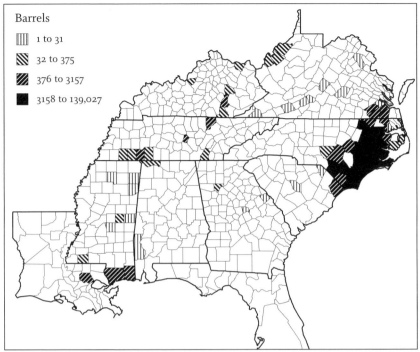

FIGURE 4.1. Tar, pitch, turpentine, and rosin production by county in the southeastern United States, 1840. Based on data from United States Department of State, *Compendium of the Enumeration of the Inhabitants and Statistics of the United States as Obtained at the Department of State, From the Returns of the Sixth Census, 1840* (Washington, D.C.: 1841), 158, 170, 182, 194, 206, 218, 230, 242, 254, 266, 338.

other areas. Near Summerville, a village twenty-two miles northwest of Charleston, pineland had sold for as low as seventy-five cents to a dollar and in a couple of instances fifty cents per acre. In the lower part of Barnwell, Colleton, and Charleston Districts, good land sold for from fifty cents to two dollars per acre. The Edisto River ran through the region, providing water transportation to the coast. Also, the South Carolina Railroad traversed the area, crossing the Edisto at Branchville in what is today Orangeburg County. By 1855, a distillery operated at Reevesville, beside the South Carolina Railroad, fifty-two miles northwest of Charleston. At that time 150,000 to 180,000 boxes were worked in the area. As North Carolinians took advantage of their southern neighbors' pinelands, South Carolina's naval stores industry grew at a fierce pace during the 1850s. The number of turpentine operations more than doubled, from forty in 1850 to ninety-five in 1860.

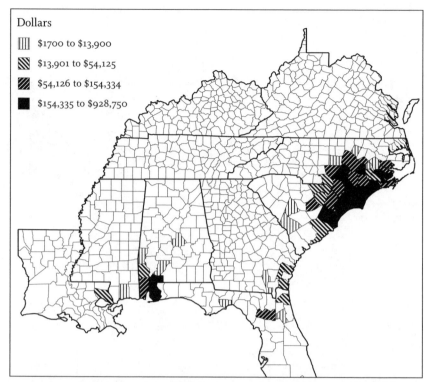

Dollars

|||| $1700 to $13,900

\\\\ $13,901 to $54,125

//// $54,126 to $154,334

■ $154,335 to $928,750

FIGURE 4.2. Value of crude and distilled turpentine by county in the southeastern United States, 1860. Based on data from United States Department of the Interior, *Manufactures of the United States in 1860* (Washington, D.C.: 1865), 2–14, 57–82, 168–204, 285–94, 552–79.

Even more dramatic, the capital invested in these businesses jumped fourteen times; the number of hands grew six times, from 220 to 1,359; and the product value increased 450 percent, from $235,836 to $1,076,725.[24]

In the late 1840s and early 1850s, turpentining also began along the Savannah and Altamaha Rivers in Georgia. The first producers appear to have been mostly young, single, native Georgians who began operation on a modest scale. In 1850, fourteen producers manufactured turpentine in Georgia with the aid of a total of 202 laborers. Of the eight producers that historians Jeffrey R. Dobson and Roy Doyon identified in the 1850 census, five were

24. P. Perry, "Naval Stores Industry in the Ante-Bellum South, 1789–1861," 273–4; "Great Yield of Turpentine," *Wilmington Chronicle,* 9 May 1849; "Manufacture of Turpentine in the South," 452, 454; "A Turpentine Farm for Sale or Rent," *WJ,* 29 August 1856; "Notice," *WJ,* 21 March 1856; U.S. Dept. of Interior, *Abstract of the Statistics of Manufactures,* 116; U.S. Dept. of Interior, *Manufactures of the United States in 1860,* 559.

slaveholders, with combined holdings of fifty-six male slaves. They contributed to Georgia's estimated production of 28,000 barrels of turpentine that year. At the same time, Savannah boasted a large distillery, and throughout the state there were ten such facilities either erected or ordered, and seven to eight new producers were thought to have entered the business. *De Bow's Review* reported that "if its production goes on increasing, for a few years longer, as rapidly as during the last year or two past, it will not take long to transfer the general head quarters of the turpentine trade from North Carolina to Georgia." However, despite these increases and the claims made by boosters, in 1850 Georgia's turpentine industry was of relatively little significance, contributing only $55,000 to the state's $7,000,000 gross manufacturing product.[25]

Yet conditions were right for the industry's expansion during the 1850s, mainly due to Georgia's abundant pinelands. Hundreds of thousands of the finest longleaf pine acreage remained available. As one 1849 advertisement explained, in Georgia "companies engaged in the Lumber and Turpentine business will, upon examination, find the above Lands *much* more favorably located than any in the [other] Southern States, being in such large bodies and accessible to market by navigable streams." The tracts were enormous. Ten thousand acres were offered in Camden County, 87,000 acres in Ware County, and a contiguous tract of 72,000 acres in Wayne County. An 18,000-acre pine tract on the Satilla River in Ware County promised to "be sold cheap" in 1850. Moreover, by the late 1850s demand for Georgia pine and improved access to it made the lands of southeastern Georgia particularly marketable. The Georgia Land Agency of Macon began selling off parcels of 150,000 acres which it owned in the Satilla River basin. The land company had received the titles from the state in 1850, a period when, except for transportation on the river, there was no access to the region and very little was even known about it. During the 1850s, however, railroad lines that extended into the region from Brunswick and Savannah improved access.[26]

During the decade, North Carolina producers moved to the region. One Richard Cogdall left North Carolina because the pines there were exhausted and established a new turpentine operation on the Altamaha River, ten miles

25. P. Perry, "Naval Stores Industry in the Old South, 1790–1860," *Journal of Southern History*, 522; Dobson and Doyon, "Expansion of the Pine Oleoresin Industry," 45, 47; U.S. Dept. of Interior, *Abstract of the Statistics of Manufactures*, 116; "Turpentine Business in Georgia," *De Bow's Southern and Western Review* 9 (July 1850): 118–9.

26. "To Lumber and Turpentine Companies," *WJ*, 7 September 1849; "18,000 Acres Turpentine Land for Sale," *WJ*, 28 June 1850; James R. Butts, *150,000 Acres Yellow Pine Timber, Turpentine and Cotton Lands* (Macon: Georgia Land Agency, 1858), 1–3.

above the town of Davis. He was one of five or six North Carolinians to have purchased land in the area and begun operations. The combined harvest of these producers was expected to yield 10,000 to 12,000 barrels. As producers such as Cogdall steadily expanded into Georgia between 1850 and 1860, the industry grew. The combined capital of naval stores producers rose from $110,000 to about $200,000 in 1860, and although the census indicates that the number of operations decreased from fourteen to thirteen, the number of workers rose from 202 to 307, indicating the operations were growing larger in size. The product value, however, experienced a remarkable rise. It appears that high productivity and a concentration on distilled spirits over raw gum caused the value of manufactured turpentine to jump over 400 percent from $55,068 to $236,111. Yet despite the turpentine industry's advancements, by 1860 Georgia's Wiregrass region remained sparsely populated and relatively undeveloped.[27]

Dr. Benjamin Williams, a producer from Greene County, North Carolina, illustrates the naval stores manufacturer's process of moving from the older turpentine region and establishing himself in Georgia where he could take advantage of the abundant pine forests. In January 1855, in preparation for his planned move, Williams began selling off his North Carolina property. As the turpentine season for that year concluded in November, he hurried to complete the harvest and begin the relocation with his wife, Sarah, to Charlton County, Georgia, located in the extreme southeastern corner of the state and covered largely by the Okefenokee Swamp. By November 1858 his new Georgia operation, which he apparently owned with a partner, was going well. With relief Sarah reported that "*we are now out of* debt, + in the Turpentine business[. T]hey are able to pay for their land, their still, their wagons + mules + the hire of their hands, + have about ($3000) three thousand to divide." Not only that, but Williams had purchased some land in Ware County, the county adjacent to Charlton, and possibly part of the tract offered by the Georgia Land Agency. This 490-acre parcel, which cost $1,000, slightly more than $2 per acre, reportedly contained beautiful pine trees and was conveniently located by the Albany and Gulf Railroad, which passed through one corner of it. Moreover, because it appeared healthier and was relatively convenient to Savannah (about a four- or five-hour ride away), it promised to make a more appealing home than theirs at Burnt

27. W. H. Turlington to A. J. Turlington, 11 December 1853, A. J. Turlington Papers, Special Collections Library, Duke University; P. Perry, "Naval Stores Industry in the Ante-Bellum South, 1789–1861," 277; Dobson and Doyon, "Expansion of the Pine Oleoresin Industry," 47; U.S. Dept. of Interior, *Abstract of the Statistics of Manufactures*, 116; U.S. Dept. of Interior, *Manufactures of the United States in 1860*, 82; Mark V. Wetherington, *The New South Comes to Wiregrass Georgia, 1860–1910* (Knoxville: University of Tennessee Press, 1994), 28–30.

Fort in Charlton County. By September 1859, Williams had also purchased property at St. Johns Bluff, Florida. Here there were "about six thousand young fruit trees of different kinds, which have been carefully selected from the best nurseries, and a good dwelling house, which cost $5000.00 when built twenty years since." He desired to live there if it were not so distant from his concerns in Georgia.

Williams was by this time selling timber along with producing turpentine, and he continued to plan a move to Ware County. Not only was transportation better there, but he believed the fresh trees yielded gum capable of making high-grade rosin. He hoped to divest himself of the Charlton County operation, which he anticipated he could sell for more than it cost him when he began it two years earlier, an indication of the heightening interest in naval stores in the area. Within a month and a half, Williams found a prime tract of 3,000 acres in Ware County on the Satilla River. The Albany and Gulf Railroad ran through it, just as it did the 490-acre parcel he purchased the year before, and the nearest depot and post office were only two and a half miles away. He planned to erect a still beside the railroad and already had a distiller, overseer, and between thirty and thirty-five slaves ready to dispatch to the location. By January, Williams had forty-five hands, who came from Virginia, North Carolina, and Georgia, at work in Ware County, and he and his partner, a Mr. Becker, were working thirty-five hands at the old operation in Charlton County, which he had not yet sold. Later that winter, Williams oversaw the construction of his still in Ware County and set out four or five hundred fruit trees that he ordered from a nursery in Savannah. In late May the new Ware County operation produced turpentine and the still was up and running. Williams also began shipping timber from the area to New York. As the turpentine harvesting season continued in the fall of 1860, Williams rushed to complete the house in Ware County that he had been planning for some years. He had just recently sold his Charlton County place, and his wife busily packed their belongings for the household's move. By early December the Williamses were finally residing in Ware County. Ben's patient wife reported that they were "living in the kitchen and the house is going up slowly, but I had rather wait longer & have it more convenient." The acquisitive doctor had recently purchased yet more land, five hundred acres, at the point where the Savannah, Albany, and Gulf Railroad and the Brunswick and Florida Railroad intersected. His wife explained that "he considers it a good investment." "You see," she wrote her parents, "the Dr believes in negroes + pine land." Benjamin Williams's case shows how some producers, determined to remain in the turpentine business, were willing to sell their entire North Carolina holdings and begin anew, often with a partner, hundreds of miles away in another state. As with Williams, it was not uncommon for turpentiners to purchase different parcels of land scattered across several counties, usually near a transportation source, run separate operations on them, or to enter a related business such as timber cutting.[28]

Whereas producers such as Williams relocated to Georgia, others moved to Alabama. Turpentining probably began in that state in the late 1840s, most likely in the Mobile vicinity. One Colonel R. D. Jones of Clarke County, located due north of Mobile and serviced by the Alabama River on its east side and the Tombigbee on its west, reportedly began experimenting with turpentine in 1847. The area offered not only high-quality pineland but excellent river access to the port at Mobile. A North Carolina producer interested in starting an operation there received a very favorable report from Mobile that "there is *plenty* plenty of Pine Land in the whole South [of Alabama] as well Adapted to the making of Turp as the finest sections are in the Old North State and as far as I can judge it can be got to market equally as cheap as the charges are at present on the Will Rroad [Wilmington Railroad]." The writer believed that "the freights on the River are very low + from here to N York not 'on an average' over 20 pr ct higher from Wilmington." In 1849 an article in the *Mobile Planter* argued that an operator could start with twelve hands and net $4,857 a year; within three years, after reinvesting his earnings, he could increase production and make $18,920 with thirty-eight hands. For a planter to make the same profit, cotton would have to sell at 25¢ per pound; it then brought somewhere between 11¢ and 12¢.[29]

In December 1854 turpentine producers met in Mobile to discuss ways to encourage the industry. A report offered at the meeting made the possibly exaggerated claim that Alabama yielded 1,060,000 gallons of turpentine and 130,000 barrels of rosin worth $750,000. Two million dollars was invested in its production. At the same convention a Mr. Price estimated "that with the same rates of increase for the next five years, it will amount to the sum of many millions of dollars, provided the inducements and encouragement can be afforded." Price assured his fellow conventioneers of the favorable profits "of naval stores over that of cotton." "The region's forest resources," he explained, remained "uncultivated, and utterly worthless in a pecuniary

28. Sarah Hicks Williams to Parents, 21 January 1855, 26 November 1855, 16 January 1858, 23 November 1858, 7 November 1859, 18 January 1860, 11 March 1860, 21 October 1860, and 6 December 1860, Benjamin F. Williams to Samuel Hicks, 25 September 1859 and 31 May 1860, Williams Papers.

29. S. H. Gaines to Grist, 23 March 1854, Grist Papers; "The Southern Pine Forest—Turpentine," *De Bow's Review*, 18 (February 1855): 188; P. Perry, "Naval-Stores Industry in the Old South, 1790–1860," *Journal of Southern History*, 523; "Production of Turpentine in Alabama," *De Bow's Review* 7 (December 1849): 560–2.

point of view, both to the general government and the State." The convening producers were justifiably excited about their industry's prospects. Between 1850 and 1860, the number of turpentine-making establishments grew from four to thirty-seven. The rise in the number of laborers and production value indicate that the average size of operations doubled. In 1850, thirty-three workers labored in turpentine. By 1860, that number had risen to 614, an increase of more than 1,800 percent. The value of turpentine produced jumped thirty-six times, from $17,800 to over $642,000.[30]

James R. Grist's turpentine operation well represents the industry's spread from North Carolina into Alabama. Grist first entered the turpentine business with his father in the older turpentine region of Beaufort County, North Carolina. When the demand for turpentine grew, he purchased six thousand acres of pineland in Brunswick County, south of the Cape Fear River. When he had exploited that tract, he relocated up the Cape Fear, but with the completion of the Wilmington to Manchester Railroad in 1853, he once again moved south of the river, to a place in Columbus County. However, by the mid-1850s the unexploited pine tracts which had brought Grist his fortune had grown increasingly limited; he was forced to search elsewhere for pine acreage to maintain his business. In 1854 he received a favorable report on the opportunities for turpentine in Alabama, and four years later he sent his cousin Benjamin Grist, who had managed one of his North Carolina operations, to open a new operation on the Fish River in the Mobile Bay area. With the labor of around one hundred slaves, the Alabama operation in the 1859–60 season yielded 26,337 barrels of crude turpentine, from which was distilled 3,020 barrels of spirits and 15,118 barrels of rosin, producing gross revenues of more than $70,000.[31]

Other southern states experienced only a limited growth in production. Although the Florida turpentine industry reemerged at about the same time that it increased in Georgia, Florida attracted few large producers like Williams or Grist. In 1847 seventy barrels of turpentine produced in northeastern Florida reached Jacksonville for export. It was believed to be the first to be collected in Florida since it had become part of the United States in 1819. One year later, thirty pounds of Florida tar were shipped to the Savannah market. By 1851, as the *Wilmington Journal* reported, it was "no longer a matter of doubt that Turpentine can be profitably made in this section of coun-

30. "Southern Pine Forest—Turpentine," 188–91; U.S. Dept. of Interior, *Abstract of the Statistics of Manufactures*, 116; U.S. Dept. of Interior, *Manufactures of the United States in 1860*, 14.

31. P. Perry, "Naval Stores Industry in the Ante-Bellum South, 1789–1861," 95; P. Perry, "Naval Stores Industry in the Old South, 1790–1860," *Journal of Southern History*, 523.

try, as there are already a number of persons largely and successfully engaged in the business." Yet production did not gain the momentum that industry boosters hoped. One complained that Florida "is exporting considerable lumber and turpentine; but where one is engaged in either of these branches of business, there should be at least twenty." Florida possessed not only an abundance of good pine timber, but easy access to the coast. In order to increase turpentine and rosin production, *De Bow's Review* argued that "we need only look to an accession of laborers in this productive field, for it to become a most valuable and important resource of the state." More workers, however, were difficult to come by in the sparsely populated and underdeveloped state. But despite this obstacle, timber and turpentine did grow in importance in the region, stimulated by cheap and abundant pineland. For example, in 1851 an attractive 12,000-acre tract reportedly "peculiarly adapted to the Turpentine business, being covered with a thick growth of pine, and having a River front of more than five miles" came up for sale on the St. Johns River. Throughout the 1850s prices for such land remained relatively low, selling for between $1 and $1.25 per acre, and attracted production. Although only five concerns operated in both 1850 and 1860, over the decade their average capitalization grew from $5,600 to $28,200. The total number of laborers also increased roughly 50 percent, from 82 to 127, and production value jumped nearly three and a half times, from $29,671 to $100,676.[32]

In Mississippi and Louisiana the industry developed even more slowly than in Florida. Peter Hammond, for whom Hammond, Louisiana, was named, began producing naval stores soon after arriving in the state from his native Sweden around 1820. He purchased land from the government in the piney woods region of present-day Hammond for a few cents an acre. The tar, pitch, and turpentine that he made had to be hauled to Springfield, Louisiana, a town about five miles southwest of Hammond with river access to Lake Maurepas, and from there it was shipped to New Orleans. Although he reportedly prospered from his naval stores operation, few producers joined Hammond. Both the 1850 and 1860 censuses list only one Louisiana turpentiner. Mississippi attracted but a few more. In 1842, Fairfax Washington, a North Carolina naval stores operator, tapped trees in Mississippi, and

32. P. Perry, "Naval Stores Industry in the Ante-Bellum South, 1789–1861," 273; "12,000 Acres of Turpentine Land for Sale," *WJ*, 10 January 1851; "Florida," *De Bow's Southern and Western Review* 10 (April 1851): 411–2; *Historic Properties Survey of St. Johns County*, 31; "12,000 Acres of Turpentine Land for Sale"; Felix Livingston to Alex MacRae, 21 January 1850 and 5 September 1859, MacRae Papers; "Turpentine Lands in Florida for Sale," *WJ*, 21 March 1856; U.S. Dept. of Interior, *Abstract of the Statistics of Manufactures*, 116; U.S. Dept. of Interior, *Manufactures of the United States in 1860*, 60.

by late in the decade several distilleries operated along the Gulf coast area. One relatively large facility was built a few miles above the mouth of the Pearl River by Nathaniel Mitchell in 1847. By 1850 naval stores were produced in all three of Mississippi's coastal counties. But between 1850 and 1860 the number of operations actually dropped from five to just one. Correspondingly, the number of laborers fell from thirty-three to four and the product value tumbled from $19,680 to $1,700. Few North Carolina producers, it appears, were willing to move the distance to either Mississippi or Louisiana where they would have to compete with the lumbering industry, whose importance was growing in the region during the years before the Civil War, for capital and timber resources.[33]

By the mid-nineteenth century, the North Carolina naval stores industry began to suffer from a problem inherent in production practices, the widespread destruction of the pine forest. Boxing and chipping seriously weakened the trees' bases and left them vulnerable to decay and dry face. Fire badly scorched the flammable faces and boxes, especially in abandoned stands where hardened gum coated the old wounds and flammable debris carpeted the forest floor. Pines, weakened in these various ways, were left susceptible to insects which invaded the tree's bark and sapwood, nibbling at the live wood until too little was left to support the tree. As North Carolina's longleaf pines yielded to these destructive forces, a cessation of regular burning in abandoned tracts prevented a regeneration of this once expansive forest. As the pines disappeared, many North Carolinians turned against the turpentine industry and switched to agricultural production, which new fertilizers made possible in the eastern counties' sandy and infertile land. Other producers, determined to continue in the business, purchased fresh pine tracts in South Carolina, Georgia, and Alabama and to a limited extent in Florida, Louisiana, and Mississippi. To these new locations such men as Benjamin Williams and James R. Grist moved their slaves and continued the same destructive harvesting practices that had forced them from North Carolina.

33. Isabel Nelson Lovel, "Hammond, Louisiana, and Its Swedish Founder," *Swedish Pioneer Historical Quarterly*, n.s., 4 (1967): 221–2; U.S. Dept. of Interior, *Abstract of the Statistics of Manufactures*, 116; U.S. Dept. of Interior, *Manufactures of the United States in 1860*, 203, 294; Hickman, *Mississippi Harvest*, 127–9.

CHAPTER 5

INDUSTRY CHALLENGES, OLD AND NEW

FOLLOWING THE CIVIL WAR, in the late nineteenth and early twentieth centuries, the naval stores industry at once experienced the persistence of old, established characteristics and new, disruptive changes. Production began a steady recovery after the Civil War as operators attempted to take advantage of high prices in the late 1860s and 1870s. With the industry's revival, North Carolina operators continued their southward movement in search of unexploited timber stands in Georgia and Florida. Producers migrated southward so rapidly in fact that by 1900 the industry was firmly centered in the Deep South states, with North Carolina and South Carolina responsible for only a small fraction of the county's naval stores production. Unlike their predecessors in the antebellum years when forest lands were plentiful, late-nineteenth-century producers had to compete for timber with large, well-financed lumber companies to the extent that by the first decades of the twentieth century the naval stores industry faced a serious timber resource crisis. As stands grew increasingly scarce, and consequently more expensive, labor and supply costs also rose, reducing the industry's profitability. At the same time, producers had to adjust to a change in market demand that drove rosin prices above those for spirits. During these difficult years the gum naval stores operators experienced growing competition from foreign producers, most notably the French, whose superior methods became the envy of American producers. The development of a revolutionary new way of manufacturing turpentine by well-capitalized, heavy industry at home intruded on their market as well. Along with profitability declines, a change in market emphasis, and new challenges for market share, the factorage system, which by the late nineteenth century had virtually disappeared in cotton production, developed an even firmer grip over the naval stores trade than ever before. All of these developments created a difficult business environment for naval stores producers during the first three decades of the twentieth century.

The Civil War temporarily devastated the turpentine industry and interrupted its southward movement out of North Carolina. Even before the first shots were fired, prewar political conflict took its toll on the business by upsetting commodity markets. A week and a half after Lincoln's election, concern over the South's ability to sell and export its goods sent prices in the region's coastal markets tumbling. In mid-November 1860 a New Orleans factor reported to James R. Grist "the past week has been a remarkably bad one for trade of all kinds, the principal cause of which is to be found in the late Presidential election and its effects upon the South." Naval store prices fell to such low levels that at least some factors, unable to believe prices could sink lower, encouraged producers to hold their barrels off the market as long as possible in anticipation of improvement. Moreover, the fear of bank failures, compounded by the lingering effects of the Panic of 1857, forced lenders severely to rein in their loans. To make matters worse, in late February 1861 the cost of marketing naval stores rose when the Confederate Congress passed an export tax on such goods as cotton, tobacco, tar, pitch, turpentine, and rosin.[1]

As war loomed, turpentine producers threw their full support behind the Confederacy. Grist's partner in Alabama desired that "the good old north state take a bold *stand?* put her shoulders to *the* (or rather) Our Wheel (Southern Confederated) + let the miserable *fanatics* see we cannot be *run* over." A producer in Georgetown County, South Carolina, who also believed North Carolina should join the Deep South states in secession, wondered in March 1861 if the three crops of boxes his slaves were then cutting would ever pay off. "The affares of the Country," he wrote, "are such, that every kind of business depends so far as success is concerned, upon the great + very important dicision waiting to be made by the U.S. + the Confederate States." Even Sarah Williams, the wife of Georgia turpentine producer Benjamin Williams and a transplanted Yankee, felt "the Spirit of 76" and prepared to aid the Confederate cause. Two weeks after the firing on Fort Sumter, she was busy knitting and sewing clothes. "Before we shall buy of

1. Marxhall J. Smith and Company to Allen and James R. Grist, 17 November 1860, Thomas F. Strikney to Allen and James R. Grist, 26 February 1861, Grist Papers; Douglas B. Ball, *Financial Failure and Confederate Defeat* (Urbana: University of Illinois Press, 1991), 207–8.

Black Republicans," she proclaimed, "we shale go barefooted and wear homespun." The Williamses and their neighbors began planting more food crops than usual and "if necessary we shall take hands out of turpentine in order to insure a good crop."[2]

Once the political conflict became a military one, prices at southern ports sunk to their lowest level ever. No rosin sold, and the few barrels of spirits that moved went at depressed prices, which brought no profit to the producer. On the New York market, in contrast, prices soared for the same reason that they fell in the South. Ever-growing fear that southern commodities could not leave the region set prices for such goods as naval stores at a premium, especially after Lincoln ordered a blockade of southern ports on April 19, 1861. Gum rose to between $4.50 and $5.00 per barrel and spirits climbed to 75¢ to 80¢ per gallon. If, given these prices, southern producers could locate a ship heading north, it was to their advantage to pay freight prices as high as five times the normal amount to get their naval stores to northern ports. The blockade and restrictions on vessels in northern ports sailing south, which was firmly in place by the end of 1861, also prevented turpentiners from receiving such needed supplies as pork and spirit barrels.[3]

Transportation interruptions and poor market conditions were not the only contributors to the industry's wartime difficulties. Neglected turpentine boxes lost much of their productive capacity, and in some areas whole orchards burned. Problems were aggravated when, in their search for supplies of desperately needed metal, the Confederate army seized the copper stills. Moreover, the railroad system's destruction left operators with no means of transporting their products. In many cases turpentine that had been harvested before the war simply sat unattended in its barrels. While traveling by train through southeastern North Carolina during the war, an Englishman observed that "at every stopping place, this valuable staple [gum] was piled in thousands on thousands of barrels, apparently belonging to, or cared for by nobody, hoops off, staves loose, and the resin melted by the hot sun into enormous masses, and plainly left to take care of itself until the war is over." A few producers, however, went to great lengths to pre-

2. Thomas F. Strikney to Allen and James R. Grist, 26 February 1861, Grist Papers; C. C. Mercer to Brother, 9 March 1861, Mercer Family Papers, Southern Historical Collection, University of North Carolina at Chapel Hill; Sarah Hicks Williams to Parents, 28 April 1861, Williams Papers.

3. Marxhall J. Smith and Company to Allen and James R. Grist, 27 April 1861, April 30, 1861, New York Commodity Price Listing, 4 May 1861, R. M. Blackwell and Company to Allen and James R. Grist, 2 May 1861, and R. M. Blackwell and Company to Allen and James R. Grist, 30 April 1861 and 24 May 1861, Grist Papers; P. Perry, "Naval Stores Industry in the Old South, 1790–1860," *Journal of Southern History*, 525.

serve their gum. When Simon Temple from the Starke, Florida, area heard that northern troops were approaching, he ran his stored resin through a trough into a cypress pond to hide it. When the threat had passed, he and his laborers recovered it. Unsatisfied with merely protecting their commodity, some stubborn southerners continued efforts to market their naval stores throughout the war. In 1864 M. J. Parker of Washington, North Carolina, made efforts to get turpentine to Philadelphia, and Joseph V. Smedly searched for a low-cost means to ship his rosin. Despite such endeavors, by 1865 the disruption in trade, the loss of stills, and especially the emancipation of the slaves, whose labor had produced the turpentine, had effectively brought the southern naval stores industry to a halt. By the spring of 1865 the southern forests formerly boxed for turpentine lay in unsalvageable ruin, and the region's naval stores exports had dwindled to nearly nothing.[4]

Nevertheless, during the next five years, the industry began an impressive recovery. Market conditions made a return to naval stores production an attractive opportunity for many southerners. The United States' rapid industrialization during and after the war expanded the demand for naval stores at the same time that the South was unable to provide the supply. The prices of naval stores products therefore reached record highs. In mid-January 1866, spirits of turpentine sold on the New York market for an astonishing $1 to $1.03 per gallon, crude turpentine for $7.50 to $8.50 per 280-pound barrel, high-grade rosin for $15 to $16 per barrel, and even common rosin sold for around $6 a barrel. In the 1850s, producers had rejoiced when spirit prices temporarily soared to 63¢ or 65¢ per gallon and gum to $3.90 to $4 per barrel.[5]

As early as March 1866 signs of renewed production appeared. That month a *New York Tribune* correspondent traveling on the Charleston and Manchester Railroad "saw vast numbers of barrels of turpentine and rosin,

4. P. Perry, "Naval Stores Industry in the Old South, 1790–1860," *Journal of Southern History,* 525; William McKee Evans, *Ballots and Fence Rails: Reconstruction on the Lower Cape Fear* (Chapel Hill: University of North Carolina Press, 1966), 36; "Pine Forests of the South," 197; Corsan, *Two Months in the Confederate States,* 69; Zonira Hunter Tolles, *Shadows on the Sand: A History of the Land and the People in the Vicinity of Melrose, Florida* (Gainesville: Storter Printing, 1976), 183; M. L. Parker to C. Schrack and Company, 26 April 1864, C. Schrack and Company Papers, Special Collections Library, Duke University; Joseph V. Smedley to Wife, 10 July 1864 and 25 August 1864, Joseph V. Smedley Papers, Special Collections Library, Duke University.

5. Campbell, Unkrich, and Blanchard, *Naval Stores Industry,* 10; "The Quotation for Naval Stores Today," 16 January 1866, Wooten and Taylor Company Papers, Special Collections Library, Duke University; "High Prices," *Fayetteville Observer,* 1 February 1853; Ashe, *Forests, Forest Lands, and Forest Products,* 76; Robert Somers, *The Southern States since the War, 1870–71* (1871; reprint, University: University of Alabama Press, 1965), 33.

both in its crude and prepared state." North Carolina exported 57,000 casks of turpentine in 1866, 89,000 in 1867, 96,000 in 1868, and 120,000 in 1869. Rosin exports rose steadily as well. Yankees, along with southerners, took advantage of the high prices. While digging on a riverbank in New Bern, some northern soldiers struck the hardened rosin that the town distilleries had discarded over the previous decades. The group reportedly made thousands of dollars by quietly mining the rosin and shipping it to the North. Another northerner assembled and burned a tar kiln on an occupied North Carolina plantation while the owner was locked in the Craven County jail. With high prices spurring a revival of manufacturing, the South's production had, by 1870, returned to one-half the value of the naval stores made in 1860.[6]

The large number of producers who rushed into the industry competed so fiercely for land and labor that they drove up production costs. During the winter boxing season of 1866, the first in which turpentiners had to rely upon paid labor, the demand for box cutters drove up wages until, by January and February, they received $40 per month plus rations. The pay scale for different jobs reflected the difficulty of the work and the lack of skilled hands to perform the tasks. For the whole 1866 turpentine season, boxers and chippers received wages of around $40 per month, coopers around $60 per month. Distillers got the same as a coopers, teamsters received $40, and dippers took in little more than $27 per month. Most hands did not work all year, however; only the boxers and chippers did. The dippers worked for seven months and the other workers for eight months, from April to November. Boxers and chippers received around $480 for the year. Even working for just over half a year, dippers, who were the lowest-paid workers, earned at least $189. With the new paid labor force, wages were estimated to consume 52 percent of an operation's annual operating expenses.[7]

As with labor, the price of leasing timber for turpentining appears to have risen above that of the antebellum period. In 1870 James H. Aycock of Richmond County, North Carolina, leased 200,000 boxes for $1,400, a cost of

6. "Wilmington—Business—The Turpentine Trade—How Turpentine Is Obtained—The Pine Trees—Pitch and Tar—Speculations in Lumber," *New York Tribune,* 17 March 1866; Somers, *Southern States since the War,* 33; Reid, *After the War,* 30; M. H. Baker to D. W. Bell, 5 March 1866, J. H. Hunter to George Henderson, 8 December 1911, and H. A. Marshall to George Henderson, 21 December 1911, George Holland Collection, North Carolina State Archives; U.S. Dept. of Interior, *Manufactures of the United States in 1860,* 2–14, 57–82, 168–204, 285–94, 420–38, 552–79; United States Department of the Interior, Census Office, *The Statistics of the Wealth and Industry of the United States, Ninth Census, 1870* (Washington, D.C.: 1872), 627.

7. "Pine Forests of the South," 197–8; List of *Negroes* belonging to *Mr John W. Grist* Worked by *Grist + Strikney* during the year of *1860,* Grist Papers.

$7 per thousand, an almost 63 percent increase over what another North Carolina producer paid per one thousand boxes in 1854. The same prewar arrangements between lessee and lessor continued, however. As with typical antebellum leases, producers after the war agreed to cause no unnecessary damage to the trees and only cut as much timber as they needed for the barrels, fuel, and buildings required to carry on their business. They had the right to remove any stills and fixtures they constructed on the property. It also appears that producers only paid for the productive boxes and according to how much gum the boxes yielded. This meant that for each year the boxes were worked, their leasing rate dropped. An innovation, working turpentine tracts on shares, appeared in the 1870s as a means to confront high production costs. Like undercapitalized southern farmers, small turpentine producers could finance their business by offering a portion of their product to the property owner as rent.[8]

As the industry recovered, production methods remained essentially unchanged, except for slight advancements in distilling. The addition of water during the distilling process allowed turpentine distillation at a temperature of only 302°F, which not only increased the yield and quality of the turpentine, but also provided a fine, light-colored rosin. However, whereas the addition of water allowed for the production of a somewhat higher grade of spirits and rosin, distillers continued to face the challenges of regulating stills by the most primitive of methods.[9]

But where the distillation of gum improved slightly, gum harvesting changed none at all. Producers continued to instruct their laborers to cut multiple boxes in the pine's bases and to chip the faces wide and deep. Conservation was not a consideration; producers worked one tract until it was exhausted and then moved on to the next. The tools and equipment also remained the same. Boxing axes, hacks, pullers, dippers, scrapers, and stills were neither improved nor replaced. This lack of advancement was not an unusual characteristic of southern industry. The South did not develop an

8. John Avery Gere Carson to H. C. Harwood, 8 May 1897, John Avery Gere Carson Papers, Manuscripts Collection, Georgia Historical Society, Savannah, Ga.; W. W. Nettles to J. W. M. Nettles, 28 August 1869, Probate Record 1511, Darlington County Historical Commission, Darlington, S.C.; P. Perry, "Naval Stores Industry in the Ante-Bellum South, 1789–1861," 44; Leases for turpentine boxes, 25 November 1869, 16 January 1871, and 14 January 1873, Dorothy Fremont Grant Collection, North Carolina State Archives; Lease between William Knight and George S. Cole, 22 January 1873, Aaron Ashley Flowers Seawell Papers, Southern Historical Collection, University of North Carolina at Chapel Hill; W. J. Wikeson to F. G. Smith, 24 September 1870, McDowell Papers; Testimony regarding working boxes on shares, 30 May 1883, Sessions 805, Darlington County Historical Commission.

9. Schorger and Betts, *Naval Stores Industry*, 12–4, 21–8; Charles Mohr, *Timber Pines of the Southern United States* (Washington, D.C.: United States Department of Agriculture, 1897), 70.

indigenous base of mechanics and engineers who could develop the technology required by the region. "It was a 'country' that was not large enough or strong enough or cohesively organized enough to have its own technology, its own industrial standards, specifications, techniques," Gavin Wright maintains. Because the naval stores industry was almost completely southern-owned and operated and had not existed outside the region since the colonial era, the methods remained stagnant.[10]

Like the traditional harvesting techniques, the folk practice of burning the forest also continued. Each spring piney woods people fired the woods to kill pests and vermin, drive out game, and encourage grass growth. One witness reported that when fires were set, "huge clouds of smoke would rise skyward and, depending on the wind direction, would come over our neighborhood for days." As during the antebellum period, southerners raked the pine straw and debris from the trees' base so that fire would not damage them. However, when these fires got out of control, they not only destroyed seeds and seedlings but injured the older trees as well.[11]

The antebellum migration pattern resumed following the war, as producers continued their use of harvesting methods that killed the longleaf pine in their home state and then sought out the fresh pines readily available to their south. By 1860, the pines around Washington, North Carolina, were nearly exhausted, and those up the Neuse River from New Bern were only slightly more plentiful. During the 1880s the latter region's stands were consumed. To understand fully the potential environmental devastation caused by the turpentine industry, argued a late-nineteenth-century observer, "it is only necessary to examine the condition of the Pine-forests in eastern North Carolina, where the turpentine industry was first established and has thus been longest practiced." In 1893, only 55,876 acres of round longleaf pine remained, less than 10 percent of the area covered by abandoned turpentined trees, down from the four to five million acres that grew in the state when turpentining first began to boom around 1840, and about the same number of trees put into turpentine production on a yearly basis during the industry's heyday. In response to the timber decline, North Carolina turpen-

10. In the cases of lumber and textile manufacture, both of which employed the most up-to-date equipment, the technology was developed outside the South. "The Changing Situation in the Naval Stores Field," address to members of the Georgia Forestry Association, American Turpentine Farmers Association Papers, Georgia Agrirama, Tifton, Ga.; Gavin Wright, *Old South, New South,* 60–1, 157, 173.

11. T. D. Clark, *Greening of the South,* 7, 9; Erwin Duke Stephens, "Longleaf Pine Country," 26 September 1984, Erwin Duke Stephens Papers, Special Collections Library, Duke University; S. G. Thigpen, *A Boy in Rural Mississippi and Other Stories* (Picayune, Miss.: S. G. Thigpen, 1966), 181; Stephens, "Longleaf Pine Country."

tiners either purchased or leased timberlands in the still heavily forested states to their south, typically forming partnerships with friends or relatives to start their businesses.[12]

The railroad's expansion through the southeastern pine belt after the Civil War and the accessibility of large and inexpensive tracts of mature longleaf pine permitted the naval stores industry to resume its trek. Following the war, southern state governments under the control of both Democrats and Republicans facilitated railroad construction as a means to economic growth. In fact, from the end of Reconstruction to the turn of the century, southern railroad construction consistently outpaced that in the rest of the nation. Railroad construction through the pine region began in the 1870s and made impressive gains during the 1880s.[13]

Construction was especially robust in Georgia. By the 1880s that state's Wiregrass region, with dense stands of longleaf pines, could be crossed by rail in less than a day. The journey previously required a week. One line, the Savannah, Florida, and Western Railroad, began in Savannah and ran for 237 miles across South Georgia to Bainbridge in the extreme southwestern corner of the state. One branch from this main line ran from Thomasville for 58 miles north to Albany, another ran from DuPont southward for 48 miles to Live Oak, Florida, and a third branch stretched for 74 miles from Waycross to Jacksonville, Florida. A second major line, the Macon and Brunswick Railroad, ran from Brunswick, on Georgia's southern coast, for 189 miles to Macon, with a 10-mile branch from Cochran in Bleckley County across the Ocmulgee River to Hawkinsville in Pulaski County. (A booklet published in 1881 to promote settlement in Georgia claimed that between then and 1876 the lumber and naval stores businesses had more than dou-

12. Ashe, *Forests, Forest Lands, and Forest Products,* 42–4, 51–2, 76, 86, 89; Cook, "Naval Stores," 9; M. Williams, *Americans and Their Forests,* 160; C. G. Pringle, "Waste in the Turpentine Industry," *Garden and Forest,* 4 (4 February 1891): 50; Jane Twitty Shelton, *Pines and Pioneers: A History of Lowndes County, Georgia, 1825–1900* (Atlanta: Cherokee, 1976), 184, 198–9; Wallace Leigh Harris, *History of Pulaski and Bleckley Counties, Georgia, 1808–1956* (Macon: J. W. Burke, 1957), 574–7, 582–7, 589–91; *Biographical Souvenir of the States of Georgia and Florida* (Chicago: F. A. Battey, 1889), 127–8; Karen Harvey, "Maguire Born into Turpentine Family: Industry Once Had Major Impact on County," *Compass,* 26 April 1990, pp. 8–9; Elliott Maguire, interview, Oral History Collection, Research Library, St. Augustine Historical Society, St. Augustine; Elliott Maguire, interview by author, St. Augustine, 5 June 1996; William T. Kennedy et al., eds., *History of Lake County, Florida* (1929; reprint, Tavares, Fla.: Lake County Historical Society, 1988), 101; Hickman, *Mississippi Harvest,* 131–2; J. A. G. Carson to J. P. Williams, 11 September 1888, Carson Papers; K. Hayrus to Thomas David Smith McDowell, 20 November 1871, 8 January 1872, and 6 May 1872, McDowell Papers.

13. Ayers, *Promise of the New South,* 9; E. W. Carswell, *Holmesteading: The History of Holmes County Florida* (Tallahassee: Rose Printing, 1986), 141–2.

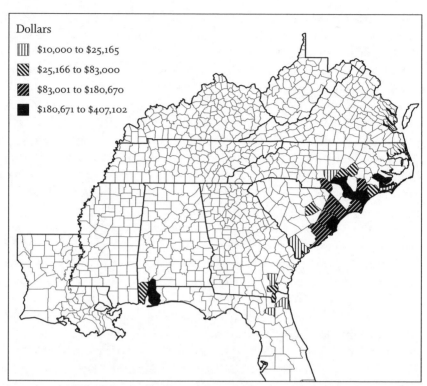

FIGURE 5.1. Value of tar and turpentine by county in the southeastern United States, 1870. Based on data from *The Statistics of the Wealth and Industry of the United States, Ninth Census, 1870* (Washington, D.C.: 1872), 493–4, 505–8, 537–8, 554–6, 568–9, 627, 637–8, 645–8, 669–70, 674–8, 685, 709–10, 732–5.

bled along this line.) Another spur to Rome was completed in the early 1880s. A third major line also began in Brunswick and ran 171 miles virtually parallel to the Savannah, Florida, and Western Railroad and terminated in Albany. During the decade the line was extended westward to Selma, Alabama. In 1889 a fourth line covering the 153 miles from Macon to Valdosta opened. All these new rail lines opened the Georgia pine forest to market access. Encouraged by the accessibility that the new lines provided, naval stores operators moved into areas previously too landlocked to be profitably worked.[14]

14. Jack N. Averitt, *Georgia's Coastal Plain* (New York: Lewis Historical, 1964), 2:540; Joseph Tillman and C. P. Goodyear, *Southern Georgia: A Pamphlet* (Savannah, Ga.: Savannah Times Steam Printing House, 1881), 5–6, 38; Shelton, *Pines and Pioneers,* 182; Wetherington, *New South Comes to Wiregrass Georgia,* 73; Dobson and Doyon, "Expansion of the Pine Oleoresin Industry," 49.

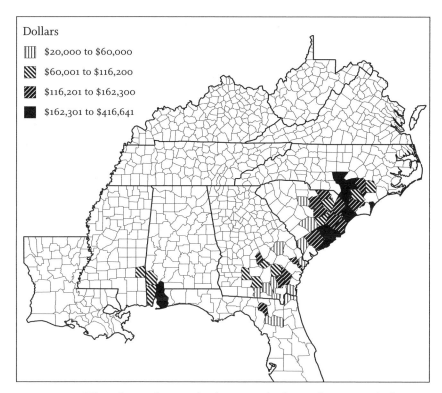

FIGURE 5.2. Value of tar and turpentine by county in the southeastern United States, 1880. Based on data from United States Department of the Interior, Census Office, *Report on the Manufactures of the United States at the Tenth Census (June 1, 1880)* (Washington, D.C.: 1883), 88–9, 103–6, 140–5, 159–61, 173–4, 193–4, 206–10, 277–8, 317–9, 353–5.

By 1890 Georgia's railroad network reached every county in the piney woods. That same year the state had 228 naval stores operators who employed nearly 10,000 workers, whose labor produced tar and turpentine valued at $4,000,000. Ten years later, the number of producers had more than doubled to 524, the workforce had nearly doubled to over 19,000, and capital investment had risen by more than 500 percent to $3,800,000, reflecting the growing cost of production, and the products' value had doubled to more than $8,000,000. Of the 39 counties engaged in this business by 1900, all had railroad service.[15]

15. Dobson and Doyon, "Expansion of the Pine Oleoresin Industry," 53; United States Department of the Interior, Census Office, *Report on Manufacturing Industries in the United States at the Eleventh Census: 1890*, part 1 (Washington, D.C.: Department of the Interior, 1895), 308–9; U.S. Dept. of Commerce and Labor, *Manufactures, 1905*, part 3, p. 650.

Florida developed its rail network more slowly than did Georgia. By the early 1870s Florida's railways, the state's commissioner of land and immigration explained, were "grand in design, but yet very partially complete." The state's extensive coastline made railroads less important for transportation. Roughly half of Florida's counties possessed a shoreline, and rivers ran through a considerable portion of its pine forest. In many areas served by rivers and large streams, waterways offered a cheaper if slower and less reliable means than trains of moving naval stores to port cities. In 1873 only two rail lines served the state, one from Fernandina, located just north of Jacksonville, to Cedar Key in the Gulf of Mexico, about fifty miles southwest of Gainesville. Another railroad ran from Jacksonville through the panhandle's northern-tier counties to the Choctawhatchee River. At Live Oak in Suwannee County the line connected with the Georgia Railroad. Both Florida lines provided improved access to the pine forests, and by 1873 only lumber exceeded turpentine as Florida's most valuable product. Cotton ranked third.[16]

The major growth in Florida's railroad network came in the 1880s and gave a boost to both the naval stores and timber industries. The state possessed only 518 miles of railways at the beginning of the decade; five years later it had 1,654 miles and, by 1890, 2,489 miles. This far-flung rail system facilitated the naval stores industry's explosive growth in the state during the 1890s. In that decade the number of establishments jumped more than twenty-four-fold, from 15 to 366, the number of workers leaped by thirty-one times, from 484 to 15,073, and the value of tar and turpentine production increased more than thirty-four times, from $191,859 to $6,469,605.[17]

Continued railroad construction in the early twentieth century helped ultimately make Florida the largest turpentine-producing state. Also, the increasing miles of hard-surface roads provided access to very remote forests during this period and were reportedly cheaper to haul on than railroads. By the early 1910s naval stores production was the most important industry in Florida, with 529 establishments representing a combined capital investment of $14,376,088. The 21,262 laborers it employed earned a total of

16. D. Eagan, *The Florida Settler; Or, Immigrants' Guide: A Complete Manual of Information Concerning the Climate, Soil, Products, and Resources of the State* (Tallahassee: Floridian, 1873), 11, 14, 22–8; Wetherington, *New South Comes to Wiregrass Georgia*, 63–4.

17. C. R. Clark, *Florida Trade Tokens* (St. Petersburg: Great Outdoors, 1980), 1; Carswell, *Holmesteading*, 141–2, 249; E. A. Ziegler, A. R. Spillers, and C. H. Coulter, *Financial Aspects of Growing Southern Pine, Washington County, Florida* (Tallahassee: Florida Forest Service, 1931), 13; Kennedy et al., eds., *History of Lake County, Florida*, 25; U.S. Dept. of Interior, *Report on Manufacturing Industries*, part 1, pp. 308–9; U.S. Dept. of Interior, *Manufactures, 1905*, part 3, p. 650.

$6,047,048. In comparison, there were 528 sawmills in Florida, representing $13,271,658 of investment capital. Their 13,083 wage earners made a total of $5,098,568. The only other areas of manufacturing that approached naval stores and sawmills were phosphate, kaolin, and fuller's earth mining and cigar manufacturing.[18]

As with Florida, railroads in Alabama encouraged production, especially after 1900. When first reported in 1850, Alabama turpentine production was valued at $17,800. By 1870 production was up to $280,203. Only three years later the Mobile market received about 20,000 casks of spirits, between 75,000 and 100,000 barrels of rosin, and 100 barrels of tar and pitch, together valued at around $750,000. In 1875, the state's value reached $1,200,000, but by 1883 production showed a slight decline to $1,109,760 because of dwindling timber supplies accessible by the transportation routes. Turn-of-the-century railroad development, however, made formerly isolated tracts more accessible. In 1902, for example, the completion of a rail line from Georgiana, Alabama, in the south-central heart of the state, to Graceville, Florida, in northern Holmes County—a distance of nearly one hundred miles—provided convenient transportation to the pine region that possessed no water access, and turpentine camps quickly developed along the route. Although Alabama naval stores production had long fluctuated, by 1908–09, the state ranked as the third largest naval stores producer.[19]

In Mississippi, where the naval stores industry was in its infancy in the 1850s, production recovered very slowly in the years immediately following the war. During the next decade, railroad construction and increased demand for naval stores led to the industry's growth. By the late 1870s operations had begun along the major transportation routes in Mississippi's southern counties near the Mobile and Ohio and the Louisville and Nashville Railroads and on the Pearl, Pascagoula, and Biloxi Rivers. In 1880 the state possessed 11 naval stores–producing establishments, which together employed 53 laborers who manufactured goods valued at $97,000. Some of these operations were established by former Alabama turpentiners who were

18. Draft of agreement with railroad builders, 1913, William C. Powell Papers, Special Collections Library, Duke University; Maguire, interview, St. Augustine Historical Society; George B. Tindall, *The Emergence of the New South, 1913–1945* (Baton Rouge: Louisiana State University Press, 1967), 256–7; Ziegler, Spillers, and Coulter, *Financial Aspects of Growing Southern Pine,* 18; Harvey, "Maguire Born into Turpentine Family," 9; Brower and La Fontisee, "Report of the Investigation on the Naval Stores Industry," 4, 34–6, 49, 54, 59; Ziegler, Spillers, and Coulter, *Financial Aspects of Growing Southern Pine,* 40; Campbell, Unkrich, and Blanchard, *Naval Stores Industry,* 21; *Twelfth Biennial Report of the Department of Agriculture of the State of Florida from the Years 1911 to 1912* (Tallahassee: T. J. Appleyard, n.d.), 428–9.

19. Brower and La Fontisee, "Report of the Investigation on the Naval Stores Industry," 54, 59, 33, 36–7, 51, 4; Carswell, *Holmesteading,* 105.

attracted by the fresh timber in Mississippi as their own became exhausted. In the late 1890s producers from the older naval stores regions to the East were also settling in Mississippi, which ultimately possessed, on average, one small distillery for every five miles of rail line. During the 1890s, the number of producers rose 600 percent, from 24 to 145, and the number of laborers increased three and one half times, from 645 to 2,288. The value of the naval stores production rose nearly twice as fast, from $282,066 to $1,772,435, probably the result of an increase in distilled spirits over raw gum. But declining longleaf timber stands caused a rapid reduction in Mississippi naval stores activity after 1900. By 1909 nearly half of the Mississippi pines had been tapped, and by the late 1920s, the little Mississippi turpentine production that remained could be found only on small, usually scattered tracts.[20]

In eastern Louisiana, where the naval stores industry was essentially an extension of that in Mississippi, the longleaf forest and industry suffered the same fate. However, the southwestern Louisiana pine forest, separated from the east by the lowlands of the Mississippi valley, experienced surprising success. The timber was of exceptional quality and was jealously guarded by the few large concerns who owned it. By 1909, only twenty-five producers operated in Louisiana, most in the eastern pine forest, and but eight worked in Texas.[21]

As their tracks extended across the piney woods South, railroad companies actively encouraged naval stores producers to locate near their lines in order to add to their shipping volume. Railroads gladly built platforms by any still that located along its tracks, knowing that the facility's success would bring thousands of barrels of spirits and rosin for shipping. They also advertised the economic potential of the countryside that lay on either side of their tracks. In 1881, for example, the Savannah, Florida, and Western Railroad, the Brunswick and Albany Railroad, and the Macon and Brunswick

20. Turpentiners were also badly affected by a hurricane in 1906. J. M. Stauffer, "The Timber Resource of 'The Southwest Alabama Forest Empire,'" *Journal of the Alabama Academy of Science* 30 (January 1959): 57–8; Hickman, *Mississippi Harvest*, 129, 131; United States Department of the Interior, *The Statistics of the Wealth and Industry of the United States, Ninth Census* (Washington, D.C.: Department of the Interior, 1872): 494, 538; U.S. Dept. of Interior, *Report on the Manufactures*, 89, 141; U.S. Dept. of Interior, *Report on Manufacturing Industries*, part 1, pp. 308–9; U.S. Dept. of Commerce and Labor, *Manufactures, 1905*, part 3, p. 650; Hickman, *Mississippi Harvest*, 133, 135–7; Brower and La Fontisee, "Report of the Investigation on the Naval Stores Industry," 54, 59, 4, 36–7, 52; James L. McCorkle, Jr., "Mississippi from Neutrality to War (1914–1917)," *Journal of Mississippi History* 43 (May 1981): 92–4.

21. Brower and La Fontisee, "Report of the Investigation on the Naval Stores Industry," 5, 37–41, 53, 48–9, 54, 59; "Turpentine in Texas," *Houston Post*, 16 September 1903, clipping in Turpentine News Clipping File, Forest History Society, Durham, N.C.

Railroad published a pamphlet aimed at boosting the region by attracting travelers, farmers, and especially naval stores and lumber producers. The pamphlet reported that Pelham, a town in southwest Georgia, would "offer superior inducements to manufacturers of naval stores. Timber plentiful and convenient to line of railroad. Only one man engaged in the business here. Plenty of room for more. Hands are easily had that understand working the trees, such such [sic] as cutting boxes and hacking, etc." That Pelham was a distant 224 miles from Savannah meant the railroad would be paid substantially to haul the product to market.[22]

The expanding southern rail system which provided turpentine operators access to even such inland timber tracts as those around Pelham, Georgia, also opened the forests to a competing interest, the northern-owned national lumber industry, which moved into the region in the late nineteenth century and hastened naval stores manufacturing's southward movement. The lumbermen's migration into the South represented a continuation of their persistent movement around the country in search of fresh timber supplies. By 1860 the nation's lumber-production center had clearly passed from New England to New York, and cutting was already increasing in the Great Lakes region. At the same time, the vast southern pine forests lay relatively unexploited, except for those felled for local timber consumption and tapped for gum. Lackluster markets for southern pine, limited transportation routes through the longleaf pine belt, and a shortage of capital among southerners with which to buy large timber tracts and construct high-volume lumber mills prevented the widespread prewar exploitation of southern woodland. After the Civil War, the Southern Homestead Act of 1866 also slowed the expansion of large-scale lumber production in five states—Florida, Alabama, Mississippi, Louisiana, and Arkansas—for ten years. In an effort to make the act's benefits as widely available as possible, Congress limited public homestead grants to eighty acres. Although agents acting for big lumber companies filed a large number of the 67,427 homestead claims made from 1866 to 1876 fraudulently, the legislation did successfully curb the large-scale taking of public land.

By the mid-1870s, southern congressmen argued that the homestead restrictions unfairly limited their states' abilities to use their timber resources for economic development and in 1876 succeeded in pressuring Congress to revise the restrictive provision, thus allowing open land purchases of the 47.7 million acres of public land in the five affected southern states. Northern investors quickly rushed in. These "timber carpetbaggers," as forest his-

<hr />

22. "Turpentine Orchards," *Northern Lumberman,* 2 August 1896, clipping in Turpentine News Clipping File; Tillman and Goodyear, *Southern Georgia,* 27.

torian Thomas D. Clark calls them, came primarily from New York, Michigan, Indiana, Illinois, and Kansas. Their buying spree began slowly, totaling only 2,095 acres in 1877, 14,262 in 1878, and 16,836 in 1879. However, by 1880, sales reached 86,873 acres, and two years later increased to nearly ten times that. In 1883 sales topped one million, with much of the property selling for between $1 and $1.25 per acre. As large northern concerns gobbled up the best timberland, southern congressmen hurried to reverse the 1876 change to the act. But before the March 1889 renewal of federal land purchase restrictions, lumbermen pressed to take advantage of the liberal sales policies while they could and purchased a record 1,223,772 acres in 1888. Although some southern investors bought a number of these tracts, northern financiers and groups purchased the majority of the 5,692,259 acres sold between 1877 and 1888.[23]

Large tracts of state and privately held land could also be purchased cheaply. In 1872 a member of a family that controlled about 200,000 acres of Georgia property in the vicinity of the Brunswick and Albany Railroad reported that the pinelands in his state could "be bought very cheaply at an average of $1.00 to $2.00 p acre." In 1889, 9,015 acres in Coffee County sold for $3,000, or around 33¢ per acre. Florida sold an enormous tract of timberland to a New York lumber company for the bargain price of 10¢ per acre. By 1886, the price of privately held land in Florida sold for about the same as federal land. Even land located near a railroad line could sometimes be purchased for less than $2 per acre. As with the federally owned timberlands, large lumber companies purchased most of these tracts.[24]

The combination of southern railroad expansion, cheap timber, and well-

23. Jeffrey A. Drobney, *Lumbermen and Log Sawyers: Life, Labor, and Culture in the North Florida Timber Industry, 1830–1930* (Macon: Mercer University Press, 1997), 24, 36–42; M. Williams, *Americans and Their Forests*, 193–4; Jeffrey A. Drobney, "The Transformation of Work in the North Florida Timber Industry, 1890–1910," *Gulf Coast Historical Review* 10 (fall 1994): 97–8; T. D. Clark, *Greening of the South*, 15–6; Cowdrey, *This Land, This South*, 111–2. Over these ten years the number of federal acres sold in Alabama was 878,413, in Arkansas 628,744, in Florida 1,021,112, in Mississippi 1,296,775, and in Louisiana 1,867,215. R. J. Duhse, "Timber Pirates to Tree Farms," *North Florida Living* (March 1985): 44; C. L. Peek to Donald MacRae, 13 April 1886, MacRae Papers; Frank Bedingfield Vinson, "Conservation and the South, 1890–1920" (Ph.D. diss., University of Georgia, 1971), 101–2; Ayers, *Promise of the New South*, 124; C. Vann Woodward, *Origins of the New South, 1877–1913* (Baton Rouge: Louisiana State University Press, 1951), 116–7.

24. Henry C. Day to Judge Pierreporch, 29 February 1872, letter attached to a copy of James R. Butts, *150,000 Acres Yellow Pine Timber, Turpentine and Cotton Lands* (Macon: Georgia Land Agency, 1858) in Special Collections Division, University of Georgia Libraries, University of Georgia; Deed of Conveyance, 8 July 1889, Powell Papers; J. A. G. Carson to H. C. Harwood, 8 May 1897, Carson Papers; Kerrhners and Calder Brothers to Thomas David Smith McDowell, 6 February 1877, McDowell Papers; Tillman and Goodyear, *Southern Georgia*, 51–2.

financed northern investors in need of forest resources created a burgeoning lumber industry in the South. Southern lumber production grew steadily during the 1870s and 1880s and absolutely exploded by the 1890s. On the eve of the Civil War, southerners themselves cut only about half a billion board feet of longleaf pine a year. By 1870 southern lumber manufacturing had surpassed output on the eve of the Civil War. In 1875 production in the eight longleaf pine states reached one and a half billion board feet, and in 1880 that figure rose to two billion. Even with this increasing rise, the South in 1880 still contained twice as much pine timber as the rest of the nation. During the 1880s, as the large northern companies pushed rapidly into the region, not only did the size of the property holdings swell, but also the mills grew larger, and unlike the earlier small southern-owned mills which were periodically dismantled and moved to the timber, they remained in place while the logs were transported to them. Companies like the Georgia Land and Lumber Company, which controlled between 300,000 and 400,000 acres of choice pineland in the early 1880s, came to dominate production. With these larger companies in place, the South's lumber output grew exponentially. In 1870 the South produced 11 percent of the nation's lumber. By 1910 that amount had grown to 45 percent.[25]

The lumber industry's southward migration in the late nineteenth century pushed the turpentine industry ahead of it. The same desire for cheap accessible pineland that attracted northern lumbermen also interested turpentiners. The two businesses were not, however, viewed as compatible. Lumber companies and consumers incorrectly believed that turpentined timber made an inferior grade of lumber, so lumbermen and turpentiners did not use the same timber and competed with each other for tracts. Because the lumber producers usually had much better access to capital than did the turpentiners, they could squeeze the naval stores operators out of areas where timber stands became scarce. As Thomas D. Clark observes, lumbermen and turpentiners had the same relationship in the southern pine forest that cattlemen and sheep herders had on the western prairie. Declining available pine acreage, especially near transportation lines, caused timber costs to rise in the late 1890s. The cost of leasing turpentine tracts rose

25. W. G. Wahlenberg, *Longleaf Pine: Its Use, Ecology, Regeneration, Protection, Growth, and Management* (Washington, D.C.: Charles Lathrop Pack Forestry Foundation, 1946), 8; Drobney, *Lumbermen and Log Sawyers*, 25; Gavin Wright, *Old South, New South*, 161; T. D. Clark, *Greening of the South*, 15, 25, 157–60; Thomas F. Armstrong, "The Transformation of Work: Turpentine Workers in Coastal Georgia, 1865–1901," *Labor History* 25 (fall 1984): 519; M. Williams, *Americans and Their Forests*, 238; Ayers, *Promise of the New South*, 125; Cowdrey, *This Land, This South*, 113.

from $100 to $200 per crop (10,000 boxes) in 1896 to around $500 in 1899.[26]

Pressure on timber resources persisted into the first decades of the twentieth century, creating a chronic problem for turpentiners. From 1880 to 1920 lumber production in the South increased nearly ten times, from 1.6 billion board feet to 15.4 billion board feet. The First World War created an immense national demand for lumber, of which the South provided 37 percent. Turpentining also took its toll on timber stands and significantly contributed to the timber scarcity. By 1909, the turpentine industry was responsible for the loss of an estimated 37 billion board feet of southern timber. Georgia lost more than any other turpentine-producing state, 10 billion board feet. Thirteen billion disappeared from the Carolinas. Florida, where the industry had only recently expanded, lost 5 billion; Alabama, where the industry had continued steadily since the Civil War, saw a reduction of 6 billion; and Mississippi fell by 3 billion. In 1920 the United States secretary of agriculture reported to the Senate that "so pronounced is depletion of the timber upon which our naval stores industry depends for its supplies that it is commonly regarded as a dying industry in the United States." As timber supplies dwindled, a problem developed as lumber companies grew ever more hostile to the practice of leasing their jealously guarded pines to naval stores men before harvesting the trees or, as the practice was known, "turpentining ahead of the cut." Some lumber companies experimented with leasing but found turpentining too damaging to standing timber and suspended the practice. Others chose to work stands for turpentine themselves. In 1919 corporations employed 41 percent of the industry's wage earners, operated 47 percent of the distillery operations, and were responsible for the same portion of product output.[27]

An analysis of state naval stores production statistics reveals how rapidly the industry moved into the Deep South ahead of the timber scarcity. When naval stores production resumed following the Civil War, North Carolinians

26. Martin, "American Gum Naval Stores Industry," 94–5; T. D. Clark, *Greening of the South*, 23; "Turpentine Orchards."

27. "The First Forest," 1, Southern Forest Institute Papers, Special Collections Division, University of Georgia Libraries, University of Georgia; Brower and La Fontisee, "Report of the Investigation on the Naval Stores Industry," 27–9; Schorger and Betts, *Naval Stores Industry*, 40–1; Thomas Gamble, "Mining for Rosin in the Old North State," in *Naval Stores: History, Production, Distribution and Consumption*, ed. Thomas Gamble (Savannah: Review Publishing and Printing, 1921), 37; M. Williams, *Americans and Their Forests*, 238; T. D. Clark, *Greening of the South*, 26; Tindall, *Emergence of the New South*, 55–6; P. L. Buttrick, "Commercial Uses of Longleaf Pine," *American Forestry* 21 (spring 1915): 904; James H. Jones, interview by Roy R. White, 9 July 1959, pp. 1, 3–4, Oral History Interview, Forest History Society, Durham, N.C.; Maguire, interview by author.

held their dominant position in the business, operating more turpentining establishments with a higher product value than all other naval stores–producing states—South Carolina, Georgia, Florida, Alabama, and Mississippi—combined. By 1880, however, both the disappearance of the longleaf pine in the older turpentine areas of North Carolina and the spread of railroad lines in other states had pushed production southward. South Carolina, at this time, replaced North Carolina as the industry leader. Throughout the 1880s the naval stores industry continued its movement so that by 1890 Georgia led the business, North Carolina ranked second, and South Carolina, which only ten years earlier had ranked first, dropped to third place. Georgia maintained its leading position during the 1890s, nearly doubling its production value by the turn of the century. Florida, however, with an astonishing industry growth of nearly 3,400 percent from 1890 to 1900, ran a close second and within the next ten years overtook Georgia. Alabama, which experienced impressive growth similar to Florida's in 1890s, ranked third. Mississippi was fourth; North Carolina fifth; and South Carolina, which just twenty years earlier had led the industry, ranked second to last, ahead of only Louisiana, which for the first time since the war reported production.[28]

The naval stores industry's southward movement influenced activity at southern ports. Wilmington, North Carolina, had been North America's principal naval stores port from the colonial period to the late nineteenth century. As the industry pushed into South Carolina, Charleston rose in importance, but it never surpassed Wilmington's naval stores volume. As production continued to move southward, Savannah saw a surge in trade, and in 1882 its naval stores volume surpassed Wilmington's. By the 1896–97 production season, the port of Savannah handled 1.6 million barrels of naval stores, the largest volume ever to pass through any port in the industry's history. In 1900 the port's naval stores yards were said to contain barrels "almost as far as the eye could see."[29]

28. U.S. Dept. of Interior, *Statistics of the Wealth and Industry*, 494, 503, 508, 538, 556, 569; U.S. Dept. of Interior, *Report on the Manufactures*, 89, 103, 106, 141, 161, 174; U.S. Dept. of Interior, *Report on Manufacturing Industries*, part 1, pp. 308–9; U.S. Dept. of Commerce and Labor, *Manufactures, 1905*, part 3, p. 650.

29. Shelton, *Pines and Pioneers*, 184; Dwight Wilson, interview, Oral History Collection, Research Library, St. Augustine Historical Society, St. Augustine; Campbell, Unkrich, and Blanchard, *Naval Stores Industry*, 9, 13–4; Richard C. Davis, ed. *Encyclopedia of American Forest and Conservation History* (New York: Macmillan, 1983), s.v. "naval stores"; Thomas Gamble, "Charleston's Story as a Naval Stores Emporium," in *Naval Stores: History, Production, Distribution and Consumption*, ed. Thomas Gamble (Savannah: Review Publishing and Printing, 1921), 35–6; Pikl, *A History of Georgia Forestry* (Athens: Bureau of Business and Economic Research, University of Georgia, 1966), 8; Thomas Gamble, "Savannah as a Naval Stores Port, 1875–

Savannah's control of the pricing structure and standards for naval stores products tightened as increasing amounts of turpentine moved through the port. In 1874 the city's only daily paper began quoting rosin and turpentine prices. The next year naval stores traders established an informal association to maintain statistics on the trade and to post prices. When in 1882 Savannah became the busiest naval stores port in the world, the port's naval stores factors founded the Savannah Naval Stores Exchange to manage the enormous trade. The next year directors amended the charter to create the Savannah Board of Trade, which oversaw all the port's activity. Three factors and three brokers or exporters sat on the board's division that handled naval stores. Their duties included enforcing inspection regulations, setting standards of quality and grade, settling disputes among its members, promoting its members' interests, and expanding Savannah's trade facilities. Their most important job, however, was setting the daily price quotes. Each morning, from 1883 to 1950, Savannah's Board of Trade set the naval stores prices for the United States.[30]

In the absence of national naval stores standards, the Savannah Board of Trade made efforts in the 1890s to institute more uniform industry product regulations to replace the existing chaotic, state-by-state system that resulted in product inconsistency. In 1894 the Savannah Board of Trade established the Office of Supervisor to ensure naval stores standards. The requirements set by this office technically applied only to naval stores leaving the port of Savannah, but as the most important exporter of these products, Savannah's standards increasingly set the rule for the whole industry. When the federal government established its own standards in the 1920s it used Savannah's.[31]

The Florida naval stores industry's growth, like Georgia's, was reflected in the increased traffic of the state's ports. The port at Fernandina, just north of Jacksonville, handled the majority of Florida's early naval stores exports, but by the end of the nineteenth century, trade shifted to Jacksonville. It was Jacksonville's growing importance as a railroad center after 1880 that increasingly attracted trade. In 1905 Jacksonville surpassed Savannah as the

1920," in *Naval Stores: History, Production, Distribution and Consumption,* ed. Thomas Gamble (Savannah: Review Publishing and Printing, 1921), 61.

30. Thomas Purse, "How the Savannah Board of Trade Fixes Prices and Regulates the Trade," in *Naval Stores: History, Production, Distribution and Consumption,* ed. Thomas Gamble (Savannah: Review Publishing and Printing, 1921), 56; Gamble, "Savannah as a Naval Stores Port," 59–61; Davis, *Encyclopedia of American Forest,* 478–9; Pikl, *History of Georgia Forestry,* 8; Eldon Van Romaine, "Naval Stores, 1919–1939," *Naval Stores Review* 100 (July–August 1990): 10.

31. Hough, *Report upon Forestry,* 1:139–40; Purse, "How the Savannah Board of Trade Fixes Prices," 56; Gamble, "Savannah as a Naval Stores Port," 59–61; Davis, *Encyclopedia of American Forest,* 478–9; Pikl, *History of Georgia Forestry,* 8.

predominant naval stores exporting port. (The title reverted back to Savannah in 1923.) The Commanders Point Terminal Company operated the largest naval stores yard in the world on the city's waterfront. The yard possessed storage space for 200,000 barrels of rosin, covered space for 12,000 barrels of turpentine, and tank storage capacity for another 33,000 barrels of turpentine. Pensacola handled the export trade for Florida's western panhandle counties. The naval stores industry in this area received a boost when the L&N Railroad completed its Pensacola and Atlantic line across the panhandle in 1883, providing easy access to the port city. The town of Chipley in Washington County, located between Pensacola and Tallahassee, served as the interior's collection point for naval stores and achieved status as the world's largest inland shipping center for these products.[32]

As timber decline and lumber producers propelled the turpentine industry southward, North Carolinians and their descendants continued to dominate production. Migration from the Tar Heel State predated the Civil War. In 1860 over one-half of the eighteen producers in Georgia were either North Carolinians or their sons. By 1880, immigrants from the old turpentine region had taken greater control of Georgia's turpentine production; 73 percent of producers came from North Carolina. The newly transplanted turpentiners in Georgia shared many similarities with those still in North Carolina. Most were family men in their thirties and forties and many had other occupations, such as merchanting, factoring, and lumber cutting.[33]

An analysis of individual turpentine producers reveals that not only did the majority originate from the turpentine area of North Carolina, but many pioneered the development of a middle-class business community in the previously sparsely settled southern pine region. The Peacock brothers were such men. They helped introduce the naval stores industry in south-central

32. Brower and La Fontisee, "Report of the Investigation on the Naval Stores Industry," 64, 67; Ziegler, Spillers, and Coulter, *Financial Aspects of Growing Southern Pine*, 40; Campbell, Unkrich, and Blanchard, *Naval Stores Industry*, 14; William Thomas Cash, *The Story of Florida* (New York: American Historical Society, 1938), 1:798; "Would Preserve Pine Forests," *Atlanta Constitution*, 2 June 1901, clipping in Turpentine News Clipping File; George H. Baldwin, "Jacksonville as a Naval Stores Port and Market," in *Naval Stores: History, Production, Distribution, and Consumption*, ed. Thomas Gamble (Savannah: Review Publishing and Printing, 1921), 107–8; A. Stuart Campbell and Alvin Cassel, *The Foreign Trade of Florida* (Gainesville: University of Florida, 1935), 11, 28, 33, 41, 83; Pleasant Daniel Gold, *History of Duval County, Including Early History of East Florida* (St. Augustine: Record, 1929), 123–4, 126, 178, 184, 196; Cash, *Story of Florida*, 796–8; E. W. Carswell, "'Naval Stores' Industry Came to Northwest Florida in 1883," *Pensacola News-Journal* File, Pensacola Historical Resource Center, Pensacola.

33. Dobson and Doyon, "Expansion of the Pine Oleoresin Industry," 48; Wetherington, *New South Comes to Wiregrass Georgia*, 116–7; Campbell, Unkrich, and Blanchard, *Naval Stores Industry*, 10; Buttrick, "Commercial Uses of Longleaf Pine," 905.

Georgia, and their children became early members of the piney wood South's town-based middle class by opening factorage houses and banks and helping to found towns. Albert Peacock, one of the first North Carolinians to come to Georgia as a turpentiner, was born in 1826 in Wayne County. Peacock married Virginia O'Berry of Winfield, Virginia, in 1859, and soon afterward the couple moved to south Georgia. They first settled in Burnt Fort, near the present town of Folkston and the same area where Dr. Benjamin Williams, turpentiner from Greene County, North Carolina, settled a few years earlier. Here Peacock began operating one of the first turpentine distilleries in the state. Although he returned to North Carolina after the Civil War, Peacock moved back to Georgia in 1875 with his rapidly growing family. He began the second turpentine operation near the town of Eastman.[34]

Albert's brother Peter Lewis Peacock arrived in Georgia in 1873. He and another man purchased a large tract of forest land near Cochran, Georgia, where they began a turpentine operation. Peter excelled in the turpentine business, progressing from producer to factor with the establishment of the Peacock-Hunt Naval Stores Company in Savannah. Another Peacock brother joined Albert and Peter in Georgia in 1881, and although the brother does not appear to have entered the turpentine business, his son went to work for Peacock-Hunt.[35]

The other Peacock children joined the New South's growing middle class. Albert's son Zebulon Vance Peacock, born in 1873, attended college in Georgia before organizing the first bank in Baxley and the First National Bank of Cochran and serving as president of the First National Bank of Hawkinsville after the turn of the century. He won seats in the Georgia House of Representatives and the Senate and sat on the Hawkinsville board of education. Peter's daughter, Virginia Peacock, born in 1871 and Zebulon Vance Peacock's cousin, married John Harris, who became a partner in the family factorage business. Harris moved to Jacksonville, Florida, where he organized Flynn, Harris, Bullard Company, Naval Stores Factor, and served a director of the Atlantic National Bank of Jacksonville. Peter's son John attended the University of Virginia and graduated with honors from the Johns Hopkins University Medical School. Dr. Peacock returned to Cochran and served as the president of the First National Bank of Cochran and president of the Chamber of Commerce and was elected town mayor and to the school board.[36]

34. W. L. Harris, *History of Pulaski and Bleckley Counties*, 574–6.
35. Ibid., 582–5.
36. Ibid., 576–7, 586, 589–91.

Other turpentine producers also helped the region develop economically. North Carolinian Arthur T. Wiggs, born in Goldsboro in 1839, came to Pulaski County, Georgia, in the early 1870s. He settled first in the town of Chauncy before finally moving to the community of Dubois. There he began acquiring farm and turpentine lands and, with his partner J. W. Hunt, established the firm Hunt and Wiggs, which ran a turpentine still, cotton gin, and store. The Bush brothers of Bladen County, North Carolina, also sought the opportunities offered in south Georgia's growing economy. Owen Bush, born in 1841, and his brother Madison, born one year later, both served in the Confederate Army and entered into business for themselves afterwards. In 1876 Madison moved to Towns, Georgia, in Wheeler County, where he worked as a naval stores manufacturer and merchant. In 1878 his brother Owen moved to Chauncy, Georgia, about twenty miles from Towns, where he manufactured turpentine and entered general merchandising. In September 1883 he was elected the first mayor of Chauncy.[37]

Georgia, however, was not the final destination of all North Carolina transplants. By the late 1890s, producers in areas of both Georgia and South Carolina, where the pine forests were dwindling just as they had earlier in North Carolina, relocated to regions where both turpentining and logging were practiced less extensively and the pine forest was more plentiful. Elliott E. Edge, raised south of Fayetteville, tired of working for others in the declining North Carolina turpentine industry during the late nineteenth century and moved with his wife to Georgia to begin a business for himself. After only a short stay in Georgia he sought out the less exploited pine forests in Lake County, Florida, midway down the peninsula. There, in 1893, he formed Edge Mercantile Company, which included a turpentine business, a sawmill, and a citrus orchard. In another case, a Mr. Both and a Mr. Decker of Columbia, South Carolina, began a five- or six-thousand-acre operation near South Lake in Lake County in 1899. Others, like the Carr brothers, who settled in Bond, Mississippi, came from Georgia after the timber there grew scarce. The Carrs worked ten or eleven crops as long as the timber in the region lasted, and when leases were no longer available near Bond, they moved to a new area.[38]

The experience of Hervey Evans who, at the age of thirty-seven, moved from North Carolina to Florida, reveals much about the experiences of men who came south to enter the naval stores business. When Evans married

37. Ibid., 687; *Biographical Souvenir,* 127–8.

38. Harvey, "Maguire Born into Turpentine Family," 8–9; Maguire, interview, St. Augustine Historical Society; Maguire, interview by author; Kennedy et al., eds., *History of Lake County, Florida,* 101; Carswell, *Holmesteading,* 99; Hickman, *Mississippi Harvest,* 131–2.

businessman John McNair's daughter Martha, McNair brought Evans into his naval stores enterprise. In July 1899, after the wedding, Evans left North Carolina for Florida to oversee McNair's turpentine business in Fairfield, about fifteen miles south of Gainesville, and prepare for his new wife to join him. When Evans arrived he found the weather hotter and more debilitating than he was accustomed to in North Carolina. After more than a week in the state, he complained that Florida had more gnats, frogs, fleas, and mosquitoes as well. He was also surprised at how frequently it rained and how little business activity, other than turpentining, lumbering, and phosphate mining, took place. The large number of abandoned and dilapidated houses that dotted the countryside, no doubt the result of the transient nature of Florida's principal industries, amazed him. The region's population likewise failed to impress Evans. "All the people I have met are ignorant, indolent, and clever," he reported.[39]

His house did little to lift his spirits or arouse his wife's anticipation of joining her husband in Florida. The dwelling sat on a large treeless tract which provided a full view of the turpentine operation's still, commissary, and workers' quarters. Nine windows provided ventilation for the house's five small rooms and kitchen. Its three-foot-wide hallway probably failed to provide adequate cross breeze to cool a house that sat fully exposed to the sun. Not only was the structure likely hot, but it was also filled with vermin. Its sparse furnishings included two beds, a dining table, five chairs, a rocker, and mosquito nets. Hogs, chickens, and a cow provided meat, eggs, and milk. The well water was "awful," but Evans had a barrel of drinking water brought from Gainesville once a week and planned to begin having ice brought in as well. Barreled water and ice represented the few minor luxuries available in only portions of the Deep South's pine forests. As Evans's experience demonstrates, the turpentiners who moved into Georgia, Florida, Alabama, and Mississippi found themselves more isolated, their living conditions more primitive, and the climate less comfortable than what they were accustomed to in North Carolina. The relocation, for many, represented nothing short of a move to the frontier.[40]

For operators like Evans, Edge, and the Peacocks, who came South in the late nineteenth century, the early-twentieth-century business climate—high production costs, low profit margins, the intensified strength of factorage

39. "Inventory," 16, Hervey Evans to Mattie McNair, 5 June 1899, Hervey Evans to Mattie McNair Evans, 13 July 1899, 30 July 1899, and 16 August 1899, and Hervey Evans to Susan Murphy Evans, 22 July 1899, Patterson Papers.

40. Hervey Evans to Mattie McNair Evans, 21 July 1899 and 30 July 1899, and Hervey Evans to Augusta Evans Currie, 31 July 1899, Patterson Papers.

houses, and competition from foreign and domestic sources—proved enormously challenging. The lumber industry's tight control of remaining stands and its expansion into naval stores production presented difficulties by creating a timber scarcity that drove up both purchasing and leasing prices throughout the South. In the early 1900s, Georgia pinelands, which could have been purchased for from 50¢ to $1.50 several decades before, sold for between $4 and $8 and by the 1920s for between $50 and $100 or more an acre. Prices rose in Florida as well. In 1917, a large Florida timber owner offered 38,000 acres of timberland for $7.60 per acre. At these relatively high prices it was easier for producers to lease than purchase pine timber tracts; the number of acres owned by producers consequently dropped 20 percent between 1909 and 1914 while the number of leased acres grew nearly 18 percent. The cost of leasing, like that of purchasing timber, rose as supplies grew scarcer. Leases that cost from $100 to $200 per crop in 1896 increased to as much as $500 by 1899. Leasing costs continued to rise from the turn of the century into the 1920s. By then, prices reached the astonishing heights of between $1,000 and $2,000 per crop for a three-year lease. By the mid-1920s lease costs increased to $2,000 and even $2,500, and some crops in Georgia reportedly reached as high as $3,000 to $3,500.[41]

The greatest area of production cost increase during the World War I years, however, came from labor, which represented between 50 and 60 percent of manufacturing expense. As alternative employment opportunities at-

41. Martin, "American Gum Naval Stores Industry," 107, 143; Pikl, *History of Georgia Forestry,* 10; Michael D. Tegeder, "Prisoners of the Pines: Debt Peonage in the Southern Turpentine Industry, 1900–1930" (Ph.D. diss., University of Florida, 1996), 61; Hickman, *Mississippi Harvest,* 125; J. Arthur Johnston to W. C. Powell, 13 December 1817, and letter to the Germain Company, 17 May 1919, Powell Papers; R. D. Forbes and R. Y. Stuart, *Timber Growing and Logging and Turpentining Practices in the Southern Pine Region* (Washington, D.C.: United States Department of Agriculture, 1930), 69; Turpentine rent agreements between L. N. Dantzler Lumber Company and Union Naval Stores Company, 5 February 1901, 5 August 1901, and 11 July 1905, Dantzler Lumber Company Papers, Special Collections, Mitchell Memorial Library, Mississippi State University; Turpentine rent receipt to B. D. Clark, 16 March 1906, Belton Decatur Clark Papers, South Caroliniana Library, University of South Carolina; J. A. G. Carson, "The Increased Cost of Naval Stores Production," in *Naval Stores: History, Production, Distribution, and Consumption,* ed. Thomas Gamble (Savannah: Review Publishing and Printing, 1921), 73; Wyman, *Florida Naval Stores,* 9–11; Deed, Bill of Sale and Assignment of Leases, A. L. Marsh and Ruby Marsh to E. E. Edge and Leo Maguire, 16 July 1928, in possession of Maguire Land Corporation, St. Augustine; Charles H. Herty, "The Turpentine Industry in the Southern States," *Journal of the Franklin Institute* 181 (March 1916): 356; Sample mortgage agreement, 1929, Cary Collection; Campbell, Unkrich, and Blanchard, *Naval Stores Industry,* 88; Thomas Gamble, "The Production of Naval Stores in the United States," in *Naval Stores: History, Production, Distribution, and Consumption,* ed. Thomas Gamble (Savannah: Review Publishing and Printing, 1921), 81.

tracted blacks away from turpentine work, the cost of hiring skilled workers such as chippers, cup raisers, and distillers more than doubled, and in some cases tripled, while less-skilled workers saw their wages rise from 50 to 100 percent. Such high labor costs, combined with already expensive timber resources, drove many producers out of the business.[42]

The experience of the Leonard brothers reveals how some operators who entered the business around the turn of the century withstood the difficult years only by expanding their business interests into areas other than naval stores. In 1900 the three brothers, Samuel, Wade, and Henry, all in their twenties, left North Carolina. With Henry serving as manager of their company, H. C. Leonard and Brothers, they began buying property in Calhoun County, Florida. Backed by their factor, they purchased wholly or in partnership 33,000 acres, mostly timberland. Before the First World War their annual naval stores shipments reached approximately $100,000. Like other turpentine producers, however, the Leonards' business suffered with the beginning of war in Europe. The brothers attempted to hold rosin off the market, hoping for better prices in the near future. When prices failed to rise, they mortgaged two pieces of property with a combined value of $172,740 to meet their debts. They ultimately survived the industry's wartime downturn only by diversifying into other areas. By 1918 they ran six small mills producing cane syrup, which outsold their naval stores. The same year they also began a lumber business.[43]

As American turpentine producers such as the Leonards struggled to survive high production costs and resulting low profit margins, factors' control over production and marketing intensified. The naval stores factors' increased power represented a reversal of the development Harold Woodman describes in the cotton trade during the same years. The decline of the cotton factor after the Civil War constituted the continuation of a pattern already under way before the Civil War. Transportation improvements across the South during the 1850s made it possible for itinerant merchants to gather the cotton from individual growers in the inland crop-growing regions and to send it to market. The merchants' efforts made it easier for smaller growers to market their crops and gave large producers an opportunity to sell theirs more quickly than if they had waited for the bales to reach their factor in a port town and for the factor to find a buyer. Thus merchants gained control of cotton marketing at the factors' expense.[44]

42. "Division of Cost of Producing Naval Stores," 1–3, Cary Collection; Clifton Paisley, "Wade Leonard, Florida Naval Stores Operator," *Florida Historical Quarterly* 51 (April 1973): 390.

43. Paisley, "Wade Leonard," 381–5, 390–4, 398–400.

44. Woodman, *King Cotton*, 84–5, 95.

Although the role of the factor declined in cotton marketing, the naval stores industry's transient nature and different labor system required factors to continue serving as the financial and marketing agents for turpentine producers into the 1930s. First, whereas it was reasonable to assume that cotton production would continue in a local area, thus providing a stable business environment for merchants, the destructive turpentine-harvesting practices, which rendered the pines useless after several years, required that producers continually search out fresh stands. An operation might move a few miles or a few hundred miles. There was consequently very little reason for a merchant to believe that local turpentiners would remain his steady customers for longer than a few years and make good on any outstanding balances in the end. However, factors located in port cities could be relatively assured that turpentine producers, although located many miles inland and not necessarily working in the same area each year, would still use the rail lines to ship their product to the factor's location. Second, the industry's post-war labor arrangement, which approached and often reached debt peonage, left the largely black workforce dependent on the producers, not local merchants, for supplies. Whereas tenant farmers in cotton production required the services of the merchant, the turpentine worker did not. Third, many turpentiners had little to offer as collateral except their livestock and equipment. Merchants were not interested in securing loans with pineland that after a few years of turpentine work would be rendered virtually worthless. Moreover, turpentiners commonly worked leased tracts, which could not be used for collateral. For the same reason that merchants refused to finance producers, banks avoided them as well. Emancipation and the improvements in transportation that led to a shift in cotton marketing away from factors served to intensify the role of the factorage house in the production and marketing of naval stores.[45]

Because factorage houses had to take relatively unsecured risks with their clients, they kept a careful watch over each producer's activities and, through the late nineteenth and early twentieth centuries, increased their control over the industry. They sold producers all equipment and supplies, often on credit, and in many cases even leased them the timber tracts they worked. Factors also provided the advances that producers required to support themselves and cover operating costs during the winter season, when work continued but no gum was harvested. They stayed informed on labor, weather, market conditions—anything that could affect business—and remained in continuous contact with their clients regarding these matters. They advised producers on leasing and purchasing timber as well as on mat-

45. Campbell, Unkrich, and Blanchard, *Naval Stores Industry,* 13.

ters relating to their general business practices. Because the factors depended on their clients' success, they encouraged a good business environment and sound decisions. Although factors usually made a profit from each of their clients, losses occasionally occurred. It was common practice to roll balances over year after year, but when the factor sensed serious problems at an operation, he protected himself by taking possession of the leases or mortgage on the land, animals, and equipment. He then sought another producer to take over the operation.[46]

During the last three decades of the nineteenth century, producers and factors, dependent on each other for successful business, began efforts, not always jointly agreed upon, to improve the naval stores market. In 1874, a group of turpentiners met in Florence, South Carolina, to organize the Turpentine Manufacturing Association in an effort to coordinate business policies they hoped would improve the trade, which at the time was suffering from a recent economic depression. Like the Grange, which addressed farmers' needs, this association hoped to improve the lives of turpentine operators. According to the *Marion Star* they first complained that the world's markets were "copiously supplied" with turpentine. Second, the high cost of marketing and transporting their produce also cut into profits. Third, not only were the fees of factors, railroads, and shipping lines excessively high, they complained, but "the irregular manipulations of inspectors and weighers together with the impervious regulations of the Chamber of Commerce, do not comport with the constant decreasing price of produce." Finally, "the high rents, high labor and low prices for Turpentine are simply preposterous."[47]

At the same meeting, organizers unanimously elected officers and adopted several resolutions, including a promise to discharge all workers laboring on old and unprofitable boxes and any other unneeded workers. This measure probably represented an effort to raise market prices by reducing production. Members were to request rate reductions from transportation lines and commission merchants as well as relaxed regulation by chambers of commerce. Any producers in the southern states not represented at the meeting were to organize themselves into councils, elect officers, and report to the Florence association, which would furnish them with information and

---

46. Martin, "American Gum Naval Stores Industry," 256; Herbert L. Kayton, interview by Roy R. White, transcript, 7 October 1959, p. 4, Forest History Society, Durham, N.C.; Davis, *Encyclopedia of American Forest,* 475; John Avery Gere Carson to Savannah Branch, Southern Travelers' Association, 30 May 1891, Carson Papers; Campbell, Unkrich, and Blanchard, *Naval Stores Industry,* 13.

47. "Turpentine Manufacture," *Marion (S.C.) Star,* 15 July 1874 (copy at Darlington County Historical Commission).

instruction about the organization. Copies of the meeting proceedings were to be sent for publication to the Charleston and Wilmington papers and local papers in South Carolina.[48]

Most important, the association recommended that producers and factors work together, since their interests intertwined. Because of declining prices, producers were growing increasingly indebted, which not only jeopardized their own businesses but also threatened to bring the factors down with them. They recommended that producers put themselves in the factors' hands and appealed to "the factors, transportation lines, and the good sense of any party anywise [sic] connected with the turpentine business to do their utmost in restoring life to its wasting prosperity, in order to avert a pecuniary and commercial calamity to the whole country." The success of the organization is uncertain because nothing is heard about it again. Given the record of cooperative schemes, however, the organization probably dissolved quickly. Not only did the factors of the late nineteenth century period lack the size and coordination to effectively direct the market, but operators rarely adhered to their directives regarding production.[49]

When, in the late 1880s, factors themselves initiated efforts to influence prices by controlling production, they met with little more success than had the turpentine producers in the previous decade. For much of the 1880s turpentine prices remained relatively steady, between 30.75¢ and 34.5¢ per gallon, although they did dip as low as 28.75¢ in the 1884–85 season. Moreover, rosin prices fell so low that speculators, almost certain values could not drop further, were ordering thousands of barrels with the intention of unloading them when prices rose. In 1888 Savannah factors put out a circular asking producers to stop barreling their rosin. To the producers it was evident that in the long run they would benefit from the resulting rise in prices, but in the immediate future they would take a loss by discarding, rather than selling, their rosin, which would have brought in low returns but returns nonetheless. It is uncertain what role the factors' program played in influencing market prices, but rosin values did indeed rise. Between 1889 and 1892 prices increased to an average of 38.5¢, but dropped in 1893 with the depression of that year to around 27¢.[50]

With the economy still depressed in February 1894, Savannah factors tried a more direct approach to reduce production; they restricted capital

48. Ibid.

49. Ibid.; Cook, "Naval Stores," 9; Horance F. Rudisill, Director, Darlington County Historical Commission, to author, 3 June 1996, letter in author's files.

50. John Avery Gere Carson to J. P. Williams, 11 September 1888, and John Avery Gere Carson to Editor *Morning News*, 17 April 1893, Carson Papers.

advances to manufacturers. The factors feared that at the rate producers were cutting boxes that year, by mid-March there would be 10 percent more new boxes than the year before, resulting in a glutted market of virgin turpentine and high-grade rosin by late spring at a time when prices were already depressed from the panic of 1893. From the factors' perspective, production limits were necessary for two reasons: to prevent naval stores prices from sinking more, further reducing the value of their stock, and to help already-overdrawn producers avoid further credit problems. Producers, however, saw the factors' move as strangulation and hoped to compensate for the lower prices by increasing their production of high-grade turpentine and rosin by chopping new boxes. But despite the factors' efforts, turpentine production continued to increase and business remained unprofitable.[51]

Conditions became so desperate by the end of the decade that producers agreed to work with factors to reduce the number of boxes. As one factor explained, "the factors and operators realizing that they were fast using up their best asset (Virgin Pine Timber), without profit and without hope of replacing same, determined to bring about some united action that would put their business on a profitable basis once more." Their dramatic plan called for cutting only one-third the number of boxes that producers had cut the previous season, thus reducing the production of fine turpentine and rosin by 66 percent. By reducing the number of new boxes so dramatically, the plan was expected to cut overall turpentine production in 1897 by 20 percent. However, their cooperative plan failed, and prices dropped even lower than those of 1893.[52]

Whether initiated by producers, factors, or a cooperative effort by both, schemes to raise turpentine prices by reducing production commonly did not succeed. Similar plans in other industries often yielded the same outcome. In general, the formation of specialized business associations occurred most frequently among industries, such as turpentining, in which the individual producers were evenly matched in manufacturing capabilities. Turpentiners also displayed typical behavior in that their voluntary agreements to reduce output tended to collapse during periods of depression, when producers commonly tried to manufacture at full capacity to compensate for low prices. According to this fixed-cost theory, explains historian Naomi Lamoreaux, "prices might hover indefinitely at a level too low to enable firms to break even, but too high to compel them to shut down." Thus,

51. John Avery Gere Carson to F. W. B., 6 February 1894, Carson Papers; "Naval Stores History," *Naval Stores Review* 100 (March–April 1990): 7; Wahlenberg, *Longleaf Pine*, 18.

52. John Avery Gere Carson to Thomas Gamble, 8 May 1897, and John Avery Gere Carson to J. P. Williamson, 21 September 1896, Carson Papers; "Turpentine Orchards."

during the 1870s and especially the 1890s, when low naval stores prices drove small producers out of the business, medium- and large-sized operators either held steady or increased their production.[53]

Despite their failed efforts to raise prices in the late nineteenth century, the factors' overall control of the industry grew in the first part of the twentieth century, not only from individual producers' greater dependence on them, but from increased market control. Industry observers estimated that in the first decades of the twentieth century, between 70 and 90 percent of turpentiners used factors to finance their operations and market their products, indicating that the South's banking structure remained immature and that naval stores production continued as a relatively risky line of business.[54]

As in the late nineteenth century, during the first decades of the twentieth century factors sought to stabilize the industry in an effort to perpetuate their business. They periodically withheld advances to producers who intended to bring more faces into production during years of declining prices. This action helped prevent prices from falling further and limited producers to levels that allowed them to meet their financial obligations. The rise of a huge new factorage house further intensified the factors' power over producers. In 1902, four Florida and three Georgia factors merged to form the aptly named Consolidated Naval Stores Company, thus creating the largest naval stores trader in the United States, with offices in Savannah, Jacksonville, and Pensacola. Controlled by a Chicago banking firm, Consolidated possessed $1,950,000 of working capital and served over seven hundred operators who in all controlled a total of five million producing acres. By only the company's second year it handled 50 percent of the United States' naval stores manufacture. Over the next few years Consolidated established several other companies to serve producers, including Consolidated Grocery Company and Florida Export Company. Another subsidiary, Consolidated Land Company, bought timberland to ensure continued naval stores resources in the future. By 1922 it owned over 1.5 million acres of longleaf pine. To control the spiraling cost of spirit barrels, Consolidated purchased Florida Cooper-

53. Naomi R. Lamoreaux, *The Great Merger Movement in American Business, 1895–1904* (New York: Cambridge University Press, 1985), 25, 27, 45, 52; Joseph B. Hosmer, *Economic Aspects of the Naval Stores Industry* (Atlanta: Georgia School of Technology, 1948), 35.

54. Davis, *Encyclopedia of American Forest,* 476; "Turpentine Production for the Year Declined," 1; Brower and La Fontisee, "Report of the Investigation on the Naval Stores Industry," 5–6; Martin, "American Gum Naval Stores Industry," 107, 258–9; Campbell, Unkrich, and Blanchard, *Naval Stores Industry,* 25; Antwerp Naval Stores Company et al. to W. F. Hottsman, 20 October 1933, Cary Collection; Maguire, interview by author; I. F. Eldredge, interview by Roy R. White, 9 July 1959, p. 9, Austin Cary File, Forest History Society, Durham, N.C.; Wyman, *Florida Naval Stores,* 40.

age Company, thereby acquiring the ability to supply its clients with 390,000 casks annually. With the 1907 incorporation of the Florida Pine Company, Consolidated began working some of its pineland itself rather than leasing it to independent operators. Over the course of its history, close to forty subsidiaries belonged to Consolidated Naval Stores Company. As both a horizontally and vertically consolidated conglomerate, the business represented a desire to impose order and efficiency on a notoriously risky and unpredictable trade. It also demonstrated the ability of northern finance capital to create such a large business in the South, the majority of whose native investors lacked substantial resources.[55]

Producers held mixed feelings about their relationship with Consolidated and other factors. Factors advanced operating capital required to pay workers and sold producers all the supplies and equipment they needed. However, factors usually loaned money relatively freely. Each house feared losing clients to competing firms if they did not agree to finance them. The factor charged interest on all sums borrowed, in part to cover his own interest expenses. Factors had some operating capital of their own but needed to borrow a portion, typically about 40 percent, from some of the same banks that would not loan directly to turpentiners. Some operators believed that the factors were fair in their lending practices, at least more so than northern bankers, whom operators believed exploited them at every chance. Fellow southerners, producers assumed, would charge them more reasonable interest rates. Other producers believed factors exploited them by charging excessive prices for supplies, equipment, and interest on finance capital. Such turpentiners resented their dependence on the factors and the control over their operations that factors could exert if they disapproved of their management.

Factors usually secured loans to producers with mortgages on land, leases, and equipment and, to protect their interests, would take control of poorly run operations. When factors came into possession of such operations through foreclosures, they commonly went into partnerships with producers, who worked it for them. The factor retained 51 percent of the stock and the producer owned 49 percent. Producers often had to borrow from the factor to buy his 49 percent. In some instances, however, factors sold the operation to someone who could take over the debt. One producer, drawing an analogy between the operators' relationship with their black workers and

55. Brower and La Fontisee, "Report of the Investigation on the Naval Stores Industry," 50; Martin, "American Gum Naval Stores Industry," 134–6; Robert S. Blount, "Spirits in the Pines" (master's thesis, Florida State University, 1992), 83–7, 104–5, 118; Blount, *Spirits of Turpentine*, 31; Butler, *Treasures of the Longleaf Pines*, 164.

the producers' connection to their factor, explained that "we owned the niggers, and the factors owned us."[56]

At the same time that factors strengthened their grip on trade, *gum* naval stores producers faced growing competition from both domestic and foreign sources that offered a superior product. In the early twentieth century, producers continued to distill their gum in copper stills of the same design as those introduced in the 1830s. Technological innovations, however, slightly improved the regulation of the process and thus the quality of the finished product. Beginning in the late nineteenth century, the addition of water to the still at the beginning and during the distilling process enabled producers to extract more spirits and also resulted in both spirits and rosin of a somewhat higher quality than before. Along with the continued practice of adding water, the introduction of a still thermometer helped in regulating temperature. But even with the thermometer, distilling remained an art, and distillers continued to hold the highest status among turpentine workers.[57]

Operators found themselves threatened by new American *wood* naval stores manufacturers who used a radically different procedure to make similar and ultimately better products. The new method of destructive distillation, which resulted in a wide variety of products—tar, pitch, turpentine, pine oil, and charcoal—from pine stumps, was initially attempted in the early 1840s. However, the first partially successful plant was built in Wilmington, North Carolina, in 1872, but it and other late-nineteenth-century efforts at wood naval stores production only partially succeeded. Increases in naval stores prices around 1900 revived efforts to perfect the process. In 1907 Homer T. Yaryan, a chemist, made substantial advancements in the technique of extracting tar and turpentine from pine stumps at an experimental

56. Brower and La Fontisee, "Report of the Investigation on the Naval Stores Industry," 5–6; Martin, "American Gum Naval Stores Industry," 107, 256, 258–9; Campbell, Unkrich, and Blanchard, *Naval Stores Industry,* 25; Antwerp Naval Stores Company et al. to W. F. Hottsman, 20 October 1933, Cary Collection; Maguire, interview by author; Eldredge, interview, 9; Wyman, *Florida Naval Stores,* 40; William L. Jenkins, monthly statement of account with Peninsular Naval Stores Company, 11 December 1914, Peninsular Naval Stores Company v. Addie Jenkins, Inventory of receiver, January 21, 1915, Affidavit of B. W. Blount, 26 December 1914, Special Masters Report, 28 May 1915, and Consolidated Naval Stores Company v. J. A. Miller et al., 20 May 1918, St. Johns County Court Cases, St. Augustine Historical Society, St. Augustine; Gay Goodman Wright, "Turpentining: An Ethnohistorical Study of a Southern Industry and Way of Life" (master's thesis, University of Georgia, 1979), 76.

57. James Berthold Berry, *Farm Woodlands* (Yonkers-on-Hudson, N.Y.: World Book, 1923), 344; Dunwody, "Proper Methods of Distillation," 128; King, interview by author; Ostrom, "History of Gum Naval Stores Industry," 222; Gay Goodman Wright, "Turpentining," 106, 108; Hulda Summerall Baker, "Summerall Turpentine Still," Museum of Coastal History, St. Simons Island, Ga., 9–10.

plant in Michigan. Two years later a plant using the Yaryan design and financed by a wealthy Toledo stockbroker was completed in Gulfport, Mississippi. In 1912 a second such factory opened in Brunswick, Georgia.[58]

The destructive distillation method involved collecting wood from pine stumps, cutting it into smaller pieces, and placing it into retorts, where it was heated with hot gases to the point of charring. A system of iron pipes kept the heat uniform in the kiln and allowed the temperature to be controlled to within one degree Fahrenheit of that desired. Distillation of a charge required fifteen to twenty hours. By basis of weight, the process yielded 79 percent rosin, 9 percent turpentine, 8 percent pine oil, and 4 percent other chemicals. The rosin settled to the bottom of the retort, where it could either be drawn off, barreled, and sold without further treatment or be processed into separate products: creosote oils, acetic acid, and rosin oils. The vaporous extract was further refined into spirits. What remained in the kiln was charcoal.[59]

The wood naval stores industry got off to a very slow and, for its backers, disappointing start. It at first had to compete with gum naval stores producers, who manufactured a better product. The destructive distillation process produced only one relatively low grade of rosin and a substance known as pine oil. Not only was there no market for pine oil, but also gum rosin was superior in quality. However, improvements in wood naval stores production following the First World War allowed the industry to successfully compete with gum products. The well-financed plants turned to engineering, chemical, and market research to develop superior naval stores of a uniform quality. They studied their consumers' needs and created products aimed specifically at certain market sectors. This action enabled them to offer buyers the exact type of turpentine and rosin they required. Wood naval stores makers also provided their customers technical advice to enable them to use the products most effectively. In addition, they carefully advertised their

58. Richard C. Crosby, Jr., "Captains of the Naval Stores Industry," *Naval Stores Review* 91 (September–October 1981): 15–6; "Naval Stores History," 7–8; John Drew, "The Early Days of the Naval Stores Industry," *Naval Stores Review* (November–December 1981): 17; Martin, "American Gum Naval Stores Industry," 109–11; *Naval Stores Statistics, 1900–1954*, Statistical Bulletin No. 181 (Washington, D.C.: United States Department of Agriculture, 1956), 2; Janice Croft, "A Twin Success Story: Pensacola and Newport," Pensacola Historical Resource Center, Pensacola, 5, 7; Davis, *Encyclopedia of American Forest*, 477–8; Butler, *Treasures of the Longleaf Pines*, 93–5, 97.

59. Romaine, "Naval Stores," 11–2; *Naval Stores Statistics*, 2; Richard C. Cook, "Early Industry Accounts through 1920," *Naval Stores Review* 77 (August 1967): 7–8; "Destructive Distillation of Pine Used," *Gamble's International Naval Stores Year Book, 1930–31* (Savannah, Ga.: Thomas Gamble, 1930), 165–6.

wide variety of new naval stores. The struggling and unorganized gum indus-try lacked the resources to devote such energy to product development and marketing, and their market standards remained independent of the custom-ers' needs.[60]

As wood naval stores increased market share, more plants sprang up across the coastal areas of the South. After Yaryan's wood naval stores facili-ties went up in Gulfport and Brunswick in 1909 and 1911, the next two plants to be constructed became part of a large wood naval stores–producing operation which remains in existence today. Newport Turpentine and Rosin Company began as Armin A. Schlesinger's effort to provide his family's small Milwaukee paper company with a steady and reliable supply of rosin for paper size. In 1913 he completed a plant at Bay Minette, Alabama, to extract rosin from pine stumps. The plant was capable of processing seventy tons of stumps each day. With growing success, Schlesinger moved to expand his operation. A new plant, constructed in Pensacola where a deepwater harbor, plentiful supply of area stumps, and three railroads combined to provide an ideal location, was completed in 1916 and had over twice the production capacity of the Bay Minette facility. As Pensacola's first major industry, the plant employed approximately six hundred workers, the majority of them technical and managerial personnel brought from Milwaukee, where they had previous associations with Schlesinger.

Newport Company served as a leader in the wood naval stores industry's expansion. Demands for naval stores during the First World War kept both company plants working near maximum capacity, but an early 1920s reces-sion hurt sales. In response to the downturn, the Pensacola facility devel-oped extremely pale grades of rosin that could find buyers even in the poor market. With renewed vigor, Newport expanded again in the second half of the 1920s with the purchase of a wood naval stores plant in De Quincy, Louisiana, originally completed in 1922. Like the Pensacola plant, the one in De Quincy had a 150-ton capacity. Then in 1929 Newport helped organize Armstrong-Newport Corporation, which used the wood left over from the chemical extraction process to manufacture fiber insulation board and ceil-

60. Crosby, "Captains of the Naval Stores Industry," 15–6; "Naval Stores History," 7–8; Drew, "The Early Days of the Naval Stores Industry," 17; Martin, "American Gum Naval Stores Industry," 109–11, 184–5; *Naval Stores Statistics*, 2; Croft, "Twin Success Story," 5, 7; Davis, *Encyclopedia of American Forest*, 476–7; Butler, *Treasures of the Longleaf Pines*, 93–5, 97; "Naval Stores History We Never Knew 'Til Now," 4–5, Olustee Experiment Station Files, Georgia Agrirama, Tifton, Ga.; R. C. Palmer, "New Standard for Turpentines," Pine Institute of America report, p. 1, Turpentine News Clipping File, Forest History Society, Durham.

ing tile. After the 1920s other companies moved to Pensacola to operate in conjunction with Newport.[61]

Although Newport dominated the wood naval stores industry in the 1920s, other companies contributed to the expansion. In 1920 Hercules Powder Company purchased the Yaryan plants in both Gulfport and Brunswick, and one year later, the Continental Turpentine and Rosin Company began operations at a new facility in Laurel, Mississippi. By 1928 Dixie Pine Products Corporation of Hattiesburg, Mississippi, completed its conversion from a lumber mill to a wood naval stores facility.[62]

Despite its eventual success in claiming a market niche, the wood naval stores industry developed slowly. However, with high product quality and low prices, contemporary industry observers predicted a surge in the wood naval stores market share within the near future. The wood naval stores industry's greater attention to customer need, combined with the periodically low naval stores prices during the 1920s, allowed it to gain market share at the gum naval stores industry's expense. During market downturns, the lower production costs of wood naval stores manufacture enabled the plants to operate profitably and even expand where the relatively high operating costs of gum producers led to net losses in their industry. By 1930 wood turpentine made up 12.1 percent of the spirits market, and wood rosin constituted 18 percent of the rosin market. Throughout the 1930s the market gain for wood naval stores would become much greater.[63]

The development of the wood naval stores industry shows that despite nineteenth-century efforts by southerners to establish such methods, it was the support of innovators from outside the region that resulted in the initial successes. Although southerners attempted to produce naval stores products for wood as early as the 1840s, it was a professionally trained chemist, Yaryan, who first designed a viable facility in Michigan and then helped perfect the extraction method once an Ohio-based businessman backed the con-

61. "Naval Stores History We Never Knew," 4; Croft, "Twin Success Story," 4–7; John H. Appleyard Agency, "Draft . . . Newport Talk for Historical Society . . . April 19, 1984," Pensacola Historical Resource Center, Pensacola, 8; "Waste Stumps from Dixie Cut-over Land Become Hundreds of Products at Plant," 2 October 1949, *Pensacola News-Journal* File; Charlotte Wittwer, "Stumpwood to Resins—Oldest Pensacola Industry," *Pensacola News-Journal* File; "Naval Stores History," 8.

62. Gum turpentine producers also faced competition from a growing number of substitutes manufactured by the petroleum and coal tar industries. Crosby, "Captains of the Naval Stores Industry," 16; T. F. Dreyfus, "Old Stumps Yield New Wealth," *Illinois Central Magazine*, May 1931, 14; "Naval Stores History We Never Knew," 4.

63. *Naval Stores Statistics*, 2; Thomas Gamble, preface to *Naval Stores: History, Production, Distribution, and Consumption*, ed. Thomas Gamble (Savannah: Review Publishing and Printing, 1921); Martin, "American Gum Naval Stores Industry," 21, 185, 193–4.

struction of a plant in Mississippi. A Milwaukee family established the Newport company which broadened the industry's market share. Southerners lacked trained scientists and engineers capable of designing such plants and did not possess the financial resources required to properly construct the large and technically sophisticated facilities.

Along with the expanding wood naval stores industry introduced from outside the region, southern gum naval stores producers faced competition from a rising number of foreign manufacturers who seriously threatened their export trade. As the world's largest gum naval stores manufacturer, the United States produced far more than it consumed, requiring foreign markets to absorb over 50 percent of the supply. Because the industry relied so heavily on exports, the disruption in trade caused by the First World War was severely damaging. European exports were virtually halted, and naval stores deteriorated in their containers at American ports. During the 1920s United States exports rose as European consumption revived, but foreign trade never reached its prewar levels. By the mid-1920s the United States exported just over eleven million gallons of spirits, compared to over sixteen million during the 1907–08 season. Growing competition from foreign manufacturers explained why. During the 1920s Spain, Portugal, Greece, and the USSR began production. It was France, however, that developed as the United States' greatest naval stores competitor. In the first two decades of the twentieth century France experienced a rapid increase in naval stores exports despite considerable trade interruptions caused by World War I. By 1921, it exported naval stores to nearly all European nations and even to the United States, which bought France's light-grade rosin. Six years later, France manufactured 20 percent of the world's naval stores.[64]

Although France produced just a third as much as did the United States, its superior conservation methods were the envy of American observers. Not only did France maintain a vibrant and sustainable naval stores industry, but it did so on land that had once been barren sand dunes. At the beginning of the nineteenth century, the Landes area in the southeastern corner of France represented one of the poorest in the country. Centuries earlier, fire and neglect had destroyed the original forest and dunes blew up, encroaching inland between 2½ and 5 miles for a distance of 120 miles along the

64. Brower and La Fontisee, "Report of the Investigation on the Naval Stores Industry," 62–3, 66; Blount, Spirits of Turpentine, 26; Martin, "American Gum Naval Stores Industry," 188–9; George H. Priest, Jr., Naval Stores: Production, Consumption, and Distribution (Washington, D.C.: United States Department of Commerce, 1927), 12, 16–7, 19–20; "Turpentine Production for the Year Declined," 2; Romaine, "Naval Stores," 9; W. L. E. Barnett, "Preliminary Report for Naval Stores Commission," 23 August 1924, pp. 31–4, Cary Collection; J. F. Butler, "Production and Trade in Naval Stores in France," 20 July 1924, pp. 17–8, Cary Collection.

coast. In the early nineteenth century Napoleon began a program to bring back the forest. He had the dunes leveled and planted with tough grass and native pine trees. The maritime pine forest prospered and formed a protective barrier between the ocean and the agricultural land and mixed forest that grew in the better inland soil. The French government continued reclamation efforts so that, by 1865, the forest grew over most of the region. By the first decades of the twentieth century, this former barren, sandy wasteland constituted 10 percent of the forest area in France, its population had grown to 14,000, and it had become one of the country's most prosperous regions. The turpentine production area covered about 2,900 square miles, roughly the size of four moderate-sized counties in Georgia.[65]

Unlike American producers, the French followed a forest-use pattern that permitted them to continuously produce naval stores from the same stands. Operators cut only one face per tree, which they worked for five years. The pines then rested for three to five seasons before they were cupped again. By the beginning of the next cupping most of the previous faces had healed. This cycle could continue for up to eighty years. Then, once trees were designated for wholesale cutting, they were cupped in as many places as the trunk would permit and worked for four to five years before felled. Along with operating the most advanced gum naval stores industry in the world, the French took steps to ensure continued progress by establishing a research organization that focused exclusively on production and consumption technology. Their accomplishments amazed American producers and forestry researchers. Where France had created a highly successful naval stores industry from a once-barren sand region, the American South had accomplished the opposite, transforming a healthy pine forest into a near-worthless wasteland. Moreover, the southern United States possessed more environmental advantages—better soil, longer growing season, and more plentiful rain—than the Landes region, but was still outpaced.[66]

65. Barnett, "Preliminary Report for Naval Stores Commission," 2–3, 35; Theodore S. Woolsey, Jr., "Conservative Turpentining by the French," in Naval Stores: History, Production, Distribution, and Consumption, ed. Thomas Gamble (Savannah: Review Publishing and Printing, 1921), 176; J. F. Butler, "Production and Trade in Naval Stores in France," 1–3; Campbell, Unkrich, and Blanchard, Naval Stores Industry, 18; R. Zon, "Notes on French Turpentine Industry," 5 December 1918, pp. 1–3, files transferred from Olustee Experiment Station, Georgia Agrirama, Tifton, Ga.; Gamble, "Production of Naval Stores in the United States," 81.

66. "Good Naval Stores Practice" (Washington, D.C.: United States Department of Agriculture, 1927), 4; J. F. Butler, "Production and Trade in Naval Stores in France," 4–6, 16–7; "The Following Brief Description of the Management of the Government Owned Maritime Forests Is Given," Cary Collection; I. F. Eldredge, "How the French Turpentine System Looked to an American," in Naval Stores: History, Production, Distribution and Consumption, ed. Thomas Gamble (Savannah: Review Publishing and Printing, 1921), 169–70; Barnett, "Preliminary Re-

One bright spot shown through the gloomy industry climate; beginning in the first decade of the twentieth century and continuing thereafter, rosin prices rose, creating a market for what heretofore represented nothing more than a byproduct of distillation. Whereas rosin remained an important ingredient in soap as well as in the manufacture of paints, varnishes, and lacquer, its growing use in paper production represented a significant change. Since around 1820, rosin had been used as sizing to reduce paper's permeability by liquid. This use steadily grew until, by 1924, it became the most widespread application for rosin. Rosin was also used in the production of plastic compositions such as sealing wax and roofing cement, in making ointments, plasters, and emulsifying compounds, and in linoleum production, the last-mentioned providing a market for low-grade rosins. These new applications brought rapid change to the market. In 1908 the U.S. Forest Service made the startling announcement that "for the first time in the history of the naval stores industry, the production of rosin in the United States . . . led turpentine in value."[67]

The growing market demand for rosin led to the regular practice of rosin mining. During the antebellum era only the highest grades of rosin brought prices that justified the expense of marketing it. Distillers consequently disposed of most rosin by emptying it into a channel that led from the still to a stream, river, or lake, or by simply dumping it on the ground near the distillery. The practice of harvesting the discarded product began just after the Civil War, when a Union soldier in Sherman's army learned of a large rosin deposit near the town of Angier in Harnett County, North Carolina. The soldier returned two years later, bought the right to mine it, and profited from the venture until naval stores prices dropped with the resumption of southern production. As new uses for rosin grew in the late nineteenth century, mining revived. Miners first hacked rosin out of beds created where the content of stills had been repeatedly emptied on the ground. Using pick axes, laborers—most of them black—chopped the dried rosin into transportable chunks, which when melted possessed the same qualities as the day it had drained from the still. During the first two decades

port for Naval Stores Commission," 23–4, 35–6; Priest, *Naval Stores,* 14; "Annual Report of the Starke Branch for the Year 1929–30," 25 October 1930, p. 2, Cary Collection.

67. "Naval Stores History," 6; Romaine, "Naval Stores," 8, 11; Bureau of Chemistry, "The Principal Uses of Rosins and Spirits Turpentine," in *Naval Stores: History, Production, Distribution, and Consumption,* ed. Thomas Gamble (Savannah: Review Publishing and Printing, 1921), 99–100; Wyman, *Florida Naval Stores,* 42; Koch, *Utilization of the Southern Pines,* 1490, 1492; "Rosin Passes Turpentine in Naval Stores Value," Turpentine News Clipping File, Forest History Society, Durham, N.C.

of the twentieth century, miners probably recovered more than 100,000 barrels of the discarded rosin.[68]

One of the most ambitious mining projects began around 1920 at the old Avirett plantation, Richlands, which possessed one of the largest and most inaccessible rosin beds. Two brothers constructed a dam around the most rosin-rich portion of Lake Catherine, pumped the water out, removed the silt layer at the bottom, and began the laborious task of recovering the long-discarded product. The brothers melted the rosin in a vat at the old still site, ran it through a strainer and dipped it into barrels. Within less than a year, they had recovered 15,000 barrels of rosin and had yet to begin recovery of the main portion.[69]

The changes in market emphasis toward rosin aside, the naval stores industry recovered rapidly after the Civil War and resumed its antebellum patterns. The New South's railroad-building boom provided access to more and more previously isolated tracts of longleaf pine, just as had the antebellum transportation improvements in the Carolinas. The old harvesting process, which dated back to colonial times, persisted, and consequently the destruction of the turpentined timber stands continued as well. These practices and their effect on the forest perpetuated the industry's transient nature, forcing turpentiners to move, not only out of the Carolinas and into Georgia and Florida, but also throughout the pine forests of Alabama, Mississippi, and Louisiana, in search of new trees. Competition with the northern-owned and well-financed southern lumber industry, which grew rapidly after the 1870s, forced turpentine operators to seek out the region's increasingly scarce timber supplies in the remotest areas. Their efforts to keep ahead of the timber cutters drove them southwards at a quicker pace than before the war. By the beginning of the twentieth century, naval stores men were well-established in south Georgia and north Florida, where the industry would remain centered. Destructive harvesting practices and turpentiners' southward movement were, however, but two of the industry's several features that persisted after the Civil War. Throughout the industry's migration, North Carolinians and their descendants continued to dominate production. Also, producers' reliance on factorage houses for financial support and marketing expertise persisted and in fact rose. At the same time the industry was clinging to antebellum characteristics, it faced new challenges in the

68. C. Dorsey Dyer, "History of the Gum Naval Stores Industry," *AT-FA Journal* 25 (January 1963): 7; "The Place 3," p. 24, Stephens Papers; Drew, "Early Days of the Naval Stores Industry," 16; "Naval Stores History," 6; Gamble, "Mining for Rosin in the Old North State," 37.

69. Gamble, "Mining for Rosin in the Old North State," 37–9.

early twentieth century. Pine acreage remained relatively scarce and expensive, especially after timber companies began efforts to conserve their remaining stands in the 1900s and 1910s. Other production costs, particularly labor, rose during the period, the greatest jump occurring during the First World War. Competition from the wood naval stores industry and from foreign gum naval stores production posed another serious threat to producers. After poor performance in its early years, wood naval stores plants proved capable of providing superior products possessing the specific qualities for individual consumers' needs. And foreign gum naval stores producers, especially the French, were able to supply European consumers with superior gum naval stores products while operating on a sustainable basis. Even though they admired the French example, American turpentine producers clung tenaciously to the old ways, the industry's labor system and working conditions, in part, among them.

CHAPTER 6

LABOR, FORCED AND FREE

THE LIVES OF NAVAL STORES LABORERS in the late nineteenth and early twentieth centuries in many respects remained unchanged from the antebellum period. In the absence of slavery, producers, who required cheap and reliable labor in the southern pine forests where few blacks lived, devised new methods to force recently freed African American men and women to work for them. With the passage of labor laws and the leasing of state and county convicts following Reconstruction, blacks found their decisions regarding work narrowed. Moreover, the tasks they performed and the living conditions in the camps did not depart significantly from those of antebellum days. Although prisoners leased to turpentine operations endured even harsher conditions than those held in either virtual or outright peonage, for both convicts and peons the life in the naval stores industry retained many old patterns.

The turpentine producers who moved into the pine forests of Georgia, Florida, Alabama, and Mississippi following the Civil War faced many challenges in securing adequate labor. Few native whites would agree to the hard work, so blacks remained the bulk of the industry's workforce. But few blacks lived in the piney woods because the area had contained little antebellum plantation agriculture. In Georgia's Wiregrass region, for example, the antebellum black population had been less than 5 percent of the total population in some cases and no more than 25 percent in others. By comparison, blacks represented over half the total population in many of Georgia's Black Belt counties.[1]

1. Carswell, *Holmesteading*, 143; Ann Patton Malone, "Piney Woods Farmers of South Georgia, 1850–1900: Jeffersonian Yeomen in an Age of Expanding Commercialism," *Agricul-*

Changes in black work habits following emancipation also challenged producers' search for labor. Freedmen reduced the pace and the number of hours they would work to levels closer to those of other free laborers. In addition, the amount of labor done by black women and children, who had performed such relatively light tasks as dipping, declined significantly as freedmen attempted to create the same domestic work pattern enjoyed by whites. As a result, by 1890 fully 98 percent of turpentine laborers were men and only 1.9 percent were women. Women and children might perform odd jobs to supplement the family income, but families typically did not work turpentine forests together. Their initiative created a severe labor shortage for turpentine operators, who, like other white southerners, expected blacks to work as long and as hard as they had as slaves and for almost as little compensation. A post-war *De Bow's Review* article bemoaned that "before the war negroe women and boys used to be employed to dip. It is very difficult now to find any hands willing to execute this branch of the business." The manager of several Florida turpentine camps in the late 1870s and 1880s explained that turpentine "work is severe to a degree almost impossible to exaggerate, and it is very difficult to control a sufficient quantity of free labor to properly cultivate any great number of trees."[2]

Laborers were not only hard to find, but difficult to keep. The postbellum turpentine industry suffered from challenges typical of southern manufacturing of the period. It was a highly competitive industry which required successful producers to control costs strictly, since profit margins remained low. Because labor was such a significant portion of the operators' cost, as much as 60 percent, the workers felt the brunt of the sharp competition through lower wages. Low wages undermined worker loyalty as naval stores producers competed with the piney woods' growing number of commercial farmers and lumber producers for the scarce labor. The migratory nature of the turpentine industry and the seasonal cycle of work also made it difficult for producers to maintain a steady and dependable labor force. During slack periods in the winter months and when an operator moved to fresh pine stands, some laborers took the occasion to seek other employment.[3]

tural History 60 (fall 1986): 51, 54, 75; Hilliard, *Atlas of Antebellum Southern Agriculture,* 32–4; J. C. Powell, *The American Siberia, or Fourteen Years' Experience in a Southern Convict Camp* (Montclair, N.J.: Patterson Smith, 1970), 27.

2. Dobson and Doyon, "Expansion of the Pine Oleoresin Industry," 49, 51; William Cohen, *At Freedom's Edge: Black Mobility and the Southern White Quest for Racial Control, 1861–1915* (Baton Rouge: Louisiana State University Press, 1991), 14; Armstrong, "Transformation of Work," 529; "Pine Forests of the South," 197; J. C. Powell, *American Siberia,* 27.

3. Jerrell H. Shofner, "Forced Labor in the Florida Forests, 1880–1950," *Journal of Forest History* 25 (January 1981): 14; Jerrell H. Shofner, "Mary Grace Quackenbos, A Visitor Florida Did Not Want," *Florida Historical Quarterly* 58 (January 1980): 273; Armstrong, "Georgia Lumber Laborers," 439, 444; Pete Daniel, *The Shadow of Slavery: Peonage in the South, 1901–1969* (Urbana: University of Illinois Press, 1990), 9; Hickman, *Mississippi Harvest,* 141; Wethering-

The turpentine operators who left the Carolinas and formed the back-bone of the industry in Georgia, Florida, Mississippi, and Alabama attempted to remedy one of these problems, that of the scarcity of blacks in the piney woods South, by bringing their laborers with them. Not just the dearth of available piney woods workers led producers to migrate with their laborers. Turpentining was very specialized labor, requiring skills learned in no other occupation. To increase their odds of success, producers preferred to bring along hands already familiar with the tasks, rather than train new ones. Turpentine workers, for their part, perhaps moved willingly as the industry in North Carolina declined. Trained in turpentine, not in agricultural production, they may have agreed to cast their lot with their employer rather than venture into a new occupation. It remains unclear as to whether their employers' compulsion played any role in their decision to head southward. In either case, the typical turpentine laborer in Wiregrass Georgia in the 1870s was a young, single, illiterate, black man from North Carolina.[4]

The influx of the turpentiners and their workers, along with the migration of poor upcountry and cotton belt whites and blacks, into the pine region helped alter the area's demographics. Between 1870 and 1890, the Georgia Wiregrass region's population doubled, and from 1890 to 1910, doubled again. In Georgia counties most active in naval stores production, the black population grew at a rate that surpassed both the increase in the state's white population and the overall rise in the state's black population. From 1860 to 1880 the black population in the state's southeastern counties that manufactured naval stores grew about 225 percent, while the state's overall black population rose 155 percent. In the same period, the number of naval stores laborers rose roughly 900 percent, from 307 to 3,743. A 175 percent growth in the white population in the important turpentine counties also exceeded the state's average of 138 percent. The increase from 1880 to 1900 was considerably more dramatic. During these years Georgia's naval stores–producing region saw an increase in black population of over 500 percent when the naval stores industry's labor force rose 700 percent. The state's African American population rose just 142 percent. Certain counties recorded increases in black population growth that far exceeded these averages. In Berrien County the black population increased 710 percent, in

ton, *New South Comes to Wiregrass Georgia*, 119; Bond, "Development of the Naval Stores Industry," 198; Eagan, *Florida Settler*, 20; Gavin Wright, *Old South, New South*, 187; Hervey Evans to Susan Murphy Evans, 22 July 1899, Patterson Papers; Malone, "Piney Woods Farmers of South Georgia," 79; Sarah F. Williams to Mother, 27 August 1867, Williams Papers.

4. Wetherington, *New South Comes to Wiregrass Georgia*, 86, 119; Armstrong, "Transformation of Work," 525; Armstrong, "Georgia Lumber Laborers," 440, 447; Tillman and Goodyear, *Southern Georgia*, 49.

Coffee County 634 percent, and in Irwin County 874 percent. Most amazingly, Colquitt County, which actually experienced a decline in black population from 1860 to 1880, saw a rise in its numbers from 1880 to 1900 of 3,430 percent, from 105 to 3,602. In 1900, most counties that produced naval stores had ten times the black population that they had in 1860. Since the expansion of the area's white population, although higher than the state's as a whole, proceeded at a lower rate than that of the African American population, by 1900 as much as 40 percent of Wiregrass residents were black.[5]

Not only were most workers in the Georgia turpentine industry black, but also the rate of labor participation in the business was higher among African Americans than was their proportion of the general population. As before the war, the vast majority of forest laborers were black, and the naval stores operators, distillers, and woodsriders were usually white. Black producers were not unheard of, however. One African American producer in Pierce County, Georgia, worked ten crops covering 2,500 acres, a relatively large operation which would have required the assistance of hired workers.[6]

A similar population shift occurred in other naval stores–producing states. Growth occurred in the black population of Florida's turpentine region, but because production took hold more slowly there than in Georgia, the rise in the number of African Americans in the population also began later. From 1860 to 1880 the black population of Florida's piney woods counties actually grew at a slower pace than the state's overall black population; some counties even saw a decline. After 1880 a few counties experienced a surge in their number of black residents. Following 1890, however, many piney woods counties saw a rise in black population of around 250 percent, well above the state average of 138 percent. The white population growth of the counties between 1890 and 1900, 131 percent, was about the state average. In southern Mississippi, the pattern was similar.[7]

5. Wetherington, *New South Comes to Wiregrass Georgia*, 76, 119, 162–3; Malone, "Piney Woods Farmers of South Georgia," 75; United States Department of the Interior, *Statistics of the Population of the United States at the Tenth Census* (Washington, D.C.: Department of the Interior, 1883), 385–6; United States Department of the Interior, *Twelfth Census of the United States Taken in the Year 1900* (Washington, D.C.: Department of the Interior, 1901), 533–4; Armstrong, "Transformation of Work," 525; U.S. Dept. of Interior, *Manufacturers of the United States in 1860*, 61–82; U.S. Dept. of Interior, *Report on the Manufactures*, 106; *Manufactures, 1905*, part II (Washington, D.C.: Department of Commerce and Labor, 1907), 170.

6. Wetherington, *New South Comes to Wiregrass Georgia*, 119; Armstrong, "Transformation of Work," 525; Armstrong, "Georgia Lumber Laborers," 440, 447; Tillman and Goodyear, *Southern Georgia*, 49.

7. U.S. Dept. of Interior, *Statistics of the Population*; U.S. Dept. of Interior, *Twelfth Census of the United States*; Hickman, *Mississippi Harvest*, 131; Nollie Hickman, "Black Labor in Forest

Although the black population grew in the naval stores region, competition for labor remained intense, and turpentine producers, along with other southern whites affected by the relative unavailability of reliable, cheap labor, sought to protect their businesses by assuming firm control over their employees. Although turpentine producers' involvement in the passage of vagrancy, enticement, emigrant agent, and false-pretenses legislation is unclear, such laws served them well. These acts were first passed by state legislatures during Reconstruction, then strengthened during the late nineteenth century, and by around 1900 reached mature development. Vagrancy laws represented one of the earliest and most widely adopted black codes. These statutes enabled law enforcement officials to force unemployed blacks to work during periods of labor scarcity and to sign and adhere to contracts. To ensure that blacks signed labor contracts, vagrancy laws criminalized the failure to make such agreements, and those individuals convicted of the offense were hired out. Enticement acts outlawed one employer hiring a laborer away from another. This legislation intensified the employer's control over a worker by establishing an owner-type relationship between the parties. It also outlawed whites from competing with each other in the labor market and thus driving up the cost. As companion legislation to the enticement acts, emigrant-agent laws imposed prohibitively high fees on labor agents who attempted to move workers from one state to another. Such laws first appeared in states that believed themselves most threatened by black outmigration. Like enticement legislation, emigrant-agent laws regulated black labor by controlling the activity of whites. Resourceful whites, however, attempted to skirt the law by using black agents and informal recruiters, who not only could enter and leave black areas with less notice than whites, but knew the best places to find black workers willing to leave for a new employer.[8]

Circumstances in the late nineteenth and early twentieth centuries resulted in intensified labor legislation. Producers feared that workers might desert them for another employer who offered substantial upfront incentives. Also, as labor costs rose after the turn of the century, producers grew increasingly concerned about preventing the loss of their own capital outlay and debts owed to them by workers when they left. Evidence suggests that

---

Industries of the Piney Woods, 1840–1933," in *Mississippi's Piney Woods: A Human Perspective*, ed. Noel Polk (Jackson: University Press of Mississippi, 1986), 29.

8. Cohen, *At Freedom's Edge*, 31, 202, 228, 245–6; William Cohen, "Negro Involuntary Servitude in the South, 1865–1940: A Preliminary Analysis," *Journal of Southern History* 42 (February 1976): 33–6, 39–42, 47–51; Shofner, "Forced Labor," 16, 18; Sylvia H. Krebs, "Will the Freedmen Work: White Alabamians Adjust to Free Black Labor," *Alabama Historical Quarterly* 36 (summer 1974): 158–9.

the operators' fears were not totally unfounded. In their struggle to secure adequate labor, producers increasingly violated the law and the industry's gentlemen's agreement not to "steal" each other's workers. Operators attempted to lure workers to their camps, usually relying on their most trusted black employees to perform the risky task. Itinerant preachers were often in the best position to move in and out of neighboring camps on recruiting missions without causing suspicion. They promised better pay and living conditions and commonly offered advances to encourage dissatisfied workers to leave their employers. Operators even left trade meetings early to have an untethered opportunity to steal absent neighboring producers' workers. Both the worker and the recruiter faced considerable danger. If the recruiter made a slip and was discovered, he might face a severe whipping or even death. His employer would usually deny any association and take no responsibility for the recruiter's actions. On the occasions when a producer permitted his indebted employee to move to another operator, the new employer was required to pay the worker's account. Some recruiters received a commission for each man they attracted to their employer's camp. In the early twentieth century one reporter explained that "each well-equipped place has 'cruiters' on the road looking up laborers from other camps to bring them in by any means—by allurement, by threat, by arrest. Labor is so precious and so necessary that the getting of it gilds a crime with virtue." As the scramble for labor intensified, the cost of securing it rose, both in terms of recruiting expenses and lost advances. By the turn of the century it cost roughly $15 to $20 per worker to recruit labor for twelve months. For 1912 the four turpentine operations run by the Ten Mile Lumber Company of Ten Mile, Mississippi, recorded an average total "recruiting expense" of $110.72, which most likely went toward advances. In 1922, Johnston, McNeill and Company, a turpentine operation in Okeechobee, Florida, had operating expenses of $53,026.41. Of that, $20,554.72, or nearly 40 percent, went toward salaries and wages. The company spent another $851.57 on recruiting and suffered the loss of $1,411.92 in advances to workers who apparently left its employment. The company's loss of advance payments represented over 2.5 percent of production costs, a significant amount in an industry with narrow profit margins.[9]

9. "Wisconsin to Check Fraud on Employers," news clipping, and Frederick C. Cubberly to H. L. Anderson, 17 August 1906, Frederick C. Cubberly Papers, Department of Special Collections, George A. Smathers Libraries, University of Florida; Tegeder, "Prisoners of the Pines," 196–9; Shelton, *Pines and Pioneers*, 202; Hickman, *Mississippi Harvest*, 125, 141–2; Albert Pridgen, "Turpentining in the South Atlantic Country," in *Naval Stores: History, Production, Distribution, and Consumption,* ed. Thomas Gamble (Savannah: Review Publishing and Printing, 1921), 103; C. W. Wimster, "Life History of C. W. Wimster, Turpentine Man," inter-

Compounding the producers' frustration over scarce labor was their persistent belief that blacks were unwilling to work.[10] One newspaper article explained that white workers could be counted on to complete a labor contract and work off their debt. "Others, and they are found largely among the negroes," the article explained, "seek to shirk the work to slip out of the duty; to neglect it and to scrap it, hoping that the creditor-employer will become disgusted and tell them to be gone."[11]

Under tight labor conditions and with racist perceptions, naval stores men in the Lower South's piney woods region joined the Georgia-Florida Sawmill Association at the turn of the century in demanding more effective labor legislation, a demand with which the states complied. The centerpieces of the strengthened early-twentieth-century compulsory labor system were new false-pretenses laws and stronger vagrancy acts. Beginning with Georgia and Alabama in 1903 and Florida in 1907, southern states passed false-pretenses laws making the refusal to work or repay advances prima facie evidence of intent to defraud. Before this legislation, laborers could only be held to their work if their employer could prove they intended to defraud at the time they contracted to work. Producers, however, could not easily establish liability even in sympathetic local courts. The new false-pretenses laws shifted the burden of proof to the workers. They had to demonstrate that they did not plan to defraud at the time they received cash or merchandise advances with a labor contract. The other important area of legislation, vagrancy laws, strengthened local law enforcement's ability to arrest anyone not working. From 1903 to 1909 Alabama, Arkansas, Florida, Georgia, Mississippi, North Carolina, Texas, and Virginia adopted strict new vagrancy laws. Florida's 1905 vagrancy act defined the offense so broadly that anyone deviating from the white South's acceptable social standards could be arrested.[12]

Many turpentine operators not only used advances to begin their workers' indebtedness as soon as they were hired, but encouraged their continua-

---

view by [Lindsay M. Bryan?], *American Life Histories: Manuscripts from the Federal Writers' Project, 1936–1940*, Library of Congress Internet Website; Richard Barry, "Slavery in the South To-Day," *Cosmopolitan Magazine* 42 (March 1907): 490; Maguire, interview by author; Ten Mile Lumber Company ledger, 1912, Dantzler Lumber Company Papers; Gay Goodman Wright, "Turpentining," 118; Report, Johnston McNeill Company, 2 April 1923, Powell Papers.

10. R. P. Brooks, *The Industrialization of the South* (Athens, Ga.: Bureau of Business Research, 1929), 5; Barry, "Slavery in the South To-Day," 488.

11. Untitled newspaper article, Correspondence, Department of Justice Central Files, General Records of the Justice Department, Record Group 60, National Archives.

12. Cohen, *At Freedom's Edge*, 231, 239, 243; Shofner, "Forced Labor," 15; Tegeder, "Prisoners of the Pines," 112; Cohen, "Negro Involuntary Servitude," 43; Shofner, "Mary Grace Quackenbos," 283; Drobney, *Lumbermen and Log Sawyers*, 176.

tion in debt and used it to coerce them to remain. When a laborer began work for a new employer, he typically received an advance of tokens with which to purchase supplies, and his payroll account was debited. At month's end the worker's earnings were applied to his account; if the credit for wages exceeded the debit for commissary purchases, he received the difference in commissary script. Many workers, however, borrowed on their account as fast as they earned wages. If a laborer broke even he had to borrow again to cover the next month's expenses. Turpentine workers commonly owed their employers between $200 and $300, the balance of which they were required to pay to end their employment. As long as the indebted laborer continued to work, his debt was of little concern to him or his employer. It only became an issue when the worker attempted to leave. In such an instance an employer could make one of three general responses. He could allow the labor to leave peacefully as long as the new employer paid off the account. The producer could threaten the employee with violence and forced return, but then not carry out the action. Or the employer might physically prevent the worker from leaving or might return him against his will if he did escape. The latter response constituted peonage and was not uncommon.[13] The turpentine workers' plight under peonage is captured in the late-nineteenth-century work song "I'se Gwine to Georgy":

> When I left old South Ca'lina,
> I left in the winter-time.
> "Where you gwine, nigger?"
> "I'se gwine to Georgy, I'se gwine to Georgy,
> To work in the turpentine."
>
> When I gits in Georgy,
> They gimme a hack and stock
> And put me in a crop; they say,
> "If you wants to see that double line,
> You shorely got to chop."
>
> You see that Woodsman comin, ridin through the pine;
> He turns round and 'gins to peep;
> You hear him say to the black man,
> "Old nigger, sink emin deep!"
>
> The nigger pull off his hat,
> And throwed it on the ground;
> You hear him say to the Woodsman,
> "Do you want me to cut em down?"

---

13. Shelton, *Pines and Pioneers*, 201; Hickman, *Mississippi Harvest*, 143–4.

They worked this nigger all year long;
It's time for him to go home.
You hear the Bossman say to the Bookkeeper,
"How do this nigger stand?"

The Bookkeeper goes in the office,
He sit down and 'gin to figger;
Then he say to the Bossman,
"That nigger's just even now!"

When I libbed in Georgy I heard a lion sing,
And I didn't have long to stay;
I got in debt, and I had to run away.
The Woodsman went to the Bossman,
And begin to fret; he said,
"I'll bet that nigger has left in debt!"

The Woodsrider caught me and brought me back;
He said, "If you don't work, I'll beat your back!"[14]

One of the characteristics of early-twentieth-century peonage was the involvement of white workers in the system. Some white southerners fell into peonage's grip, but recently arrived eastern European immigrants probably represented the largest percentage of whites ensnared in the practice. Labor-recruiting agencies opened in the northern cities and targeted immigrants who desperately needed work, would tolerate low wages, and lacked knowledge of the nature of labor conditions in the piney woods South. Many recruiters failed to divulge to workers the circumstances of their employment. Agents also neglected to explain that the transportation costs to the South and the advance wages they received to buy food from the commissary would start them off in debt. One such New York agent sent an average of three hundred men a month to work in the turpentine camps.[15]

It is often difficult to distinguish between the common situation of the indebted laborer and the peon, for only a thin line separated the two. Indebtedness to employers was the key component for holding laborers in peonage,

14. Another version of the song has the turpentine worker leaving "old Virginny." Stetson Kennedy, *Palmetto Country* (New York: Duell, Sloan and Pearce, 1942), 257–8; Florida Writers' Project, "Story of Naval Stores" (May 1943), 14.

15. "White Prisoners in Jail Sign Statement Telling of Arrest," *Pensacola Journal,* 30 December 1911; Shofner, "Mary Grace Quackenbos," 274–5; N. Gordon Carper, "Slavery Revisited: Peonage in the South," *Phylon* 37 (1976): 86–91; Barry, "Slavery in the South To-Day," 490; Tegeder, "Prisoners of the Pines," 119–20, 125–9; Sam Fink Affidavit, 11 October 1906, Correspondence, Classified Subject Files, Department of Justice Central Files.

but as historian J. William Harris points out, debt did not necessarily lead to peonage. "It is important to remember," he explains, "that debt pervaded every level of postbellum southern agriculture, not just the bottom level of sharecroppers." Laws supporting peonage in no way indicate its widespread practice. Many sharecroppers were poor and indebted but were never tied to the plantation by their condition. Merely becoming indebted to an employer did not constitute peonage. Pete Daniel maintains that "peonage occurred only where the planter forbade the cropper to leave the plantation because of debt." He explains that three general labor divisions emerged in the post-war South. Most southern workers were free and moved about selling their labor on a free market. Another group languished in debt peonage and was coerced to work to repay what they owed. Daniel identifies a third group that lived in a perplexing state somewhere between freedom and forced labor. In this middle ground a laborer who ended the year indebted to his employer and who voluntarily agreed to stay on and work off his debt was technically free. But if the employer used coercion to force the worker to remain, the worker then entered a state of peonage. Daniel argues that "the line was that thin. No doubt many workers drifted from freedom to peonage often in their lifetimes, never realizing that they had crossed the line." He adds that because of this uncertain status, it is difficult to determine how many of the South's laborers were caught between slavery and freedom. It is probably within this uncertain gray area between freedom and compulsion that most naval stores workers labored.[16]

Whether "free" or "forced," white or black, once in an operator's employment, turpentine laborers were not paid by the hour but for piecework, the actual amount of labor they performed each day. It was a practice not unknown in southern agriculture, especially on sea-island cotton plantations. Such a wage system provided producers with more control over their workers than a pay system based on shares. The pay scale varied for different tasks, and the pay for each task depended on how much work was actually completed. Also, because of the practice of paying according to piecework, there could be considerable difference between individual laborers in the amount of work performed and the pay they received. Pay rates apparently differed by place, as well. In most cases operators in Mississippi, Louisiana, and Texas paid more than those in the East, probably because of a scarcer labor supply. Moreover, wages could vary depending on the worker's sex.

16. Daniel, *Shadow of Slavery*, 24; J. William Harris, "The Question of Peonage in the History of the New South," in *Plain Folk of the South Revisited*, ed. Samuel C. Hyde, Jr. (Baton Rouge: Louisiana State University Press, 1997), 104; Pete Daniel, "The Metamorphosis of Slavery, 1865–1900," *Journal of American History* 66 (June 1979): 74, 89.

Women, who after the war typically did little work in the forest, received about 80 percent of what a man would get.[17]

The payment turpentine workers received resembled farm wages. They declined in the late nineteenth century to around 80¢ a day but rose in the years before the outbreak of the First World War. During these years, wages paid to both farm and naval stores workers laboring for the same Florida employer averaged around $1 for a twelve- to fourteen-hour day. Between the outbreak of the World War I and the United States' entry into the war, turpentine wages dipped. Most naval stores workers during these years typically earned less than $1 a day. Wages rose to over $1.20 between 1917 and 1920 as labor grew scarcer with the United States' entry into the war, but in the 1920s they fell to prewar levels. It was not just economic forces that shaped wages. Some producers took measures to reduce pay either out of sheer greed or as punishment. Two partners in a Georgia turpentine operation docked workers' pay as a penalty for not completing their task, for performing sloppy work, or for losing work time. The most unscrupulous producers practiced a deception called "loading the boxes." They reduced their workers' pay by adding to the standard crop size of ten thousand boxes, thus making their employees perform extra work without added compensation.[18]

Most turpentine operators paid their employees in scrip—tokens, coupon books, or punch cards—redeemable only at the camp store. Coin-size tokens, often with the producer's name stamped on the face, were issued in values of five, ten, twenty-five, and fifty cents and one dollar. Coupon books and punch cards were more often used for issuing larger denominations.

17. Armstrong, "Georgia Lumber Laborers," 443; Ralph Shlomowitz, "'Bound' or 'Free'? Black Labor in Cotton and Sugarcane Farming, 1865–1880," *Journal of Southern History* 50 (November 1984): 584, 589; Ralph Shlomowitz, "The Origins of Southern Sharecropping," *Agricultural History* 53 (1979): 562; Wetherington, *New South Comes to Wiregrass Georgia*, 121; Hough, *Report upon Forestry*, 1:139; Gavin Wright, *Old South, New South*, 202; Matthew J. Mancini, *One Dies, Get Another: Convict Leasing in the American South, 1866–1928* (Columbia: University of South Carolina Press, 1996), 54; Hickman, *Mississippi Harvest*, 125; Armstrong, "Transformation of Work," 527; Sandra Jo Forney, "The Importance of Sites Related to the Naval Stores Industry in Florida" (paper presented at the thirty-seventh annual meeting of the Florida Anthropological Society, Daytona Beach, Fla., 1985), 2.

18. Paisley, "Wade Leonard," 387–8; Gavin Wright, *Old South, New South*, 202–3; Brower and La Fontisee, "Report of the Investigation on the Naval Stores Industry," 50; Otho Monroe, interview by Michael Garvey, 19 March 1975, Mississippi Oral History Program, McCain Library and Archives, University of Southern Mississippi, 5; Marshall, *Labor in the South* 94–5; Drobney, *Lumbermen and Log Sawyers*, 142; Ziegler, Spillers, and Coulter, *Financial Aspects of Growing Southern Pine*, 56–7; William Alonzo Register, interview, Florida State Archives; Armstrong, "Georgia Lumber Laborers," 443; Hickman, *Mississippi Harvest*, 125.

Workers either signed the coupon book authorizing the amount to be deducted from their pay after spending it at the commissary or had the purchase amount punched out on the card. The camps' isolation and lack of transportation to the nearest town ensured that most workers traded at the commissary. Even if a turpentine business failed to turn a profit, producers could usually count on their commissaries to operate in the black. In most moderately sized operations the commissary opened for but a few hours, sometimes only in the afternoons or on Fridays. At camps located closer to a town, however, workers had the option of shopping at some private stores that accepted tokens at 70 percent of their face value. In other cases merchants would exchange the scrip for United States currency at the same discount. Some operators opposed the use of their tokens at other stores and indicated on the coins that they were for commissary trade only. Conflicts often erupted between town merchants and operators when the turpentiner refused to redeem the tokens at face value or in some cases would not buy them back at all.[19]

The challenges of the southern naval stores industry and the resulting labor characteristics explain why a wage system based on piecework, not sharecropping, emerged following emancipation. Because far fewer blacks were familiar with the techniques involved in turpentine production than were knowledgeable about agriculture, naval stores producers had a far smaller pool of experienced labor from which to draw compared to farmland owners. Also, in the piney woods of the Deep South—into which the industry moved after the Civil War—the extremely small native black population offered virtually no hope of supplying adequate labor. Moreover, work in the naval stores industry was well known for a difficult and demanding schedule that did nothing to attract new workers. For turpentine producers the resulting labor scarcity necessitated the tight control of workers that a wage system facilitated. Farmland owners, on the other hand, who did not need to worry so about securing labor to plant, tend, and harvest their fields, could afford to compromise with a sharecropping system that gave workers more autonomy than a wage system, but not as much as cash renting. That a sharecropping arrangement was possible in turpentine production was demon-

19. Armstrong, "Transformation of Work," 529–30; Shelton, *Pines and Pioneers*, 199; Johnston McNeill Company, Report, 1922, Powell Papers; Register, interview; Paisley, "Wade Leonard," 386; Gay Goodman Wright, "Turpentining," 103; Kenneth H. Thomas, *McCranie's Turpentine Still, Atkinson County, Georgia: A Historical Analysis of the Site, with Some Information on the Naval Stores Industry in Georgia and Elsewhere* (Atlanta: Georgia Department of Natural Resources, 1975), C-3; T. G. Willis report, 16 February 1931, Classified Subject Files, Department of Justice Central Files; C. R. Clark, *Florida Trade Tokens*, 3–4, 6–8.

strated by that very practice in the French naval stores industry in the late
nineteenth century.

Combined with the piecework wage system, the seasonal variation in the
work schedule presented laborers with special challenges. Producers tried to
keep their workers busy throughout the year in an effort to prevent them
from leaving to find employment to carry them through the winter. A Florida producer advised to "keep all hands at work doing something. It never
will do to let them start to scattering." However, operators found it virtually
impossible to provide constant employment. Boom-and-bust economic cycles subjected workers to layoffs, pay reductions, and periods of only partial
employment. The seasonal nature of production also worked against laborers, who found employment opportunities scarce during the winter months
when only boxing and raking were performed. It was not uncommon for
producers to contract with workers for only the ten busiest months. Bad
weather, however, could halt work even during the most active period. In
September 1889, for example, a series of storms and subsequent floods seriously hurt the industry in parts of Georgia. "Whatever dip was in the boxes
was washed out," one operator complained. "Nothing has been done for two
weeks and the bad condition of the woods will prevent work of any consequence being done for a week or ten days." During such times, workers received no wages, but had to continue buying supplies from the commissary.
Some turpentine workers attempted to stay busy by exercising considerable
versatility and mobility within the turpentine labor force. One Georgia laborer worked in December 1889 as a teamster, but in January 1890 as a
boxer. Another worker at the same operation labored at the still in early
November but by the end of the month was hauling barrels. In early December he was back at the still but then moved to cutting boxes for the remainder of the month.[20]

Although the introduction of a wage system and commissary represented
a significant break from the laborers' prewar years as slaves, other areas of
workers' experience changed in little significant respect. The actual work in
the naval stores industry saw minimal alteration after the war. The labor
remained hard and the standard of living low. Turpentine hands typically
awoke at around 4:30, began work at sunlight, and continued until sundown, with breaks for breakfast and lunch. The various jobs, the tools, and

20. Vance, *Human Geography of the South,* 122; Hervey Evans to Susan Murphy Evans, 6
January 1900, Patterson Papers; Armstrong, "Georgia Lumber Laborers," 411, 438–9, 444;
Shelton, *Pines and Pioneers,* 200–1; Account book, 1872, Thomas H. Osteen Papers, South
Caroliniana Library, University of South Carolina; Wimster, "Life History of C. W. Wimster,
Turpentine Man"; John Avery Gere Carson to J. P. Williams, 15 September 1888, Carson Pa-
pers.

the ten thousand box-size tasks all remained virtually unchanged from the early nineteenth century. Boxing, cornering, chipping, dipping, scraping, and distilling persisted as primitive processes, exposing workers to the same hazards as in the antebellum era. While the work remained strenuous and dangerous, it continued as well to be extremely dirty. The men working around the gum got so much of it spilled on their overalls that the cloth became stiff. When workers undressed at night they were unable to fold their overalls away and instead left them standing in the corner of their cabin.[21]

Technology changed but did not transform the role of coopers. Although many turpentine producers began buying factory-made spirit barrels, coopers retained their status as skilled workers. By the early twentieth century, few coopers' jobs included collecting the wood with which to construct barrels. Instead, turpentiners purchased machine-cut staves in bundles. They also bought hoop iron in spools. Despite the use of machine-made materials, the cooper's job persisted with little alteration from years earlier.[22]

Another of the industry's persistent features was the effort by camp managers, whether it was the producer himself, his foreman, or his woodsrider, to impose their full authority over laborers. In some cases the power of the manager over his workers even included the laborers' vote. Producers preferred to run their camps as they saw fit and resented intervention by outside authorities. Most used their authority with moderation, adopting policies that facilitated the camps' smooth operation and maximum production. Justice ranked a distant second in importance. Few workers, for example, were arrested for killing other blacks. Producers refused to call the sheriff, even for murder cases, because they did not want their workers sitting idly in jail. Moreover, the mere appearance of law officers could also cause a producer to lose many of his workers. Because a large number of the turpentine laborers had been in trouble with the law, just the sight of a sheriff or his deputies could cause many to leave and start work at another camp. Furthermore, the relatives of a murder victim often preferred to handle the

21. T. D. Clark, *Greening of the South,* 22; Vance, *Human Geography of the South,* 122; Armstrong, "Georgia Lumber Laborers," 443; Shlomowitz, "'Bound' or 'Free'?" 584, 589; Shlomowitz, "Origins of Southern Sharecropping," 562; Hough, *Report upon Forestry,* 1:139; Federal Writers' Project, *Florida: A Guide to the Southernmost State* (New York: Oxford University Press, 1939), 378; Schorger and Betts, *Naval Stores Industry,* 15–7; Blount, *Spirits of Turpentine,* 37–9; Maguire, interview by author; Berry, *Farm Woodlands,* 344–5; Wyman, *Florida Naval Stores,* 36; Brower and La Fontisee, "Report of the Investigation on the Naval Stores Industry," 8–9; Register, interview; Harvey, "Maguire Born into Turpentine Family," 9; Baker, "Summerall Turpentine Still," 7; Gay Goodman Wright, "Turpentining," 103.

22. Maguire, interview by author; A. V. Wood, "Notes on Glue for Sizing Turpentine Barrels," 5 June 1922, pp. 1–2, Cary Collection.

matter in their own way. They tended not to trust the authorities. Not only did many workers have criminal records, but also they knew from experience that the law would fail to take the matter seriously. To escape the vengeance of his victim's family and friends, a murderer had to run away. One camp manager explained that "we got rid of two people every time one man was shot."[23]

The use of brutality in an effort to maintain control also continued in the forest. Woodsriders attempted to rule the workers completely and harshly in order to gain their respect, maintain order, and extract efficient work. One former Florida camp manager explained that the foreman had to cause fear and instill respect in the workers: "in speaking to him they call him Capm, but among themselves they call him The Man. And believe me, he better be a man from the ground up! If he ever stands for any back-talk or shows a streak of yellow he's through, and might as well quit. For they lose all respect for him and won't mind him. Even though they keep up a pretense of respect to his face, they'll laugh at him behind his back and gang up to make his life miserable. They like to be ruled by an iron hand and no velvet glove." A Georgia overseer reportedly "ruled the roost where he stayed, and if one [worker] got out of line he took a black jack or somethin' and straightened him out." Every morning the overseer at the Jackson Lumber Company's turpentine operation near the Florida and Alabama border entered the quarters and struck those who moved too slowly for his liking with an ax handle. During the workday he punished unsatisfactory work by tying laborers to pine trees and beating them with a buggy whip. The screams of his victims could reportedly be heard through the woods for half a mile. Some managers did not hesitate to use deadly force to intimidate workers. At one eastern Louisiana turpentine operation the camp manager shot one of a group of blacks who had come to the camp only to gamble. Another company boss, Big Joe Watts, had seven notches on his gun by the late 1920s. Each notch represented a white man he had killed, his black victims apparently not worth commemorating. In 1915 one forester, after witnessing such actions, found that "life in the turpentine camps is often even tougher and more primitive than in the old time logging camp, yet some of the turpentine operators carry on their establishment in the spirit of the Old South."[24]

23. J. L. Herring, *Saturday Night Sketches: Stories of Old Wiregrass Georgia* (Tifton, Ga.: Sunny South Press, 1978), 112–6; Dobson and Doyon, "Expansion of the Pine Oleoresin Industry," 51; Hickman, *Mississippi Harvest*, 144–5, 152; Tegeder, "Prisoners of the Pines," 166, 240–1; Elwood R. Maunder, *Voices from the South: Recollections of Four Foresters* (Santa Cruz, Calif.: Forest History Society, 1977), 74–5.

24. Kennedy, *Palmetto Country*, 164, 168, 265–6; Gay Goodman Wright, "Turpentining," 119; "The Turpentiners," *Magnolia Monthly* 7 (October 1969); Tegeder, *Prisoners of the Pines,* 163; Monroe, interview, 6; Maunder, *Voices from the South,* 73; Paisley, "Wade Leonard,"

The turpentine operation at the town of Fargo, bordering the Okefenokee Swamp in southeastern Georgia, reveals the tough and lawless nature of some of these establishments. With ninety-six crops in the 1920s, it was one of the South's largest turpentine operations. The company served as its own law enforcement agency over the 210,000 acres it controlled and had agreements with the sheriffs in whose counties its operation extended not to come to Fargo unless sent for. Because the company manager tolerated any activity that did not directly interfere with the turpentine operation, an assortment of criminals on the run in Georgia and Florida sought refuge in and around the community, which soon became known as "Bad Man's Fargo." The absence of law enforcement attracted bootleggers during the days of Prohibition. With nineteen liquor stills hidden in the forest within ten miles of Fargo, the community was the center of Georgia's moonshine production.[25]

Although an unusually extreme case, the near-absolute power exercised by W. Alston Brown at his Cross City, Florida, camp provides another illustration of how camp managers and woodsriders wielded authority. Guards patrolled the camp at night and reported any trouble directly to Brown. They had orders to shoot anyone who attempted to escape. In the woods each guard, armed with a pistol and a double-barrel shotgun, oversaw between five and seven men. When relatives went in search of their family members, Brown prevented their contact. He read all incoming and outgoing mail and reportedly stopped some letters from reaching their intended recipients. The most common form of punishment at Cross City, even for unsatisfactory work, was severe beatings or whippings. Brown, however, occasionally employed even more brutal measures. He had some workers hanged by one thumb. In extreme instances, workers were brutally murdered. In one such case in the summer of 1921, James Powell, a black truck driver for Brown, quarreled with the boss of a nearby camp, and the next day they fought. A few nights later, the beaten camp boss, the county judge, who was the boss's brother-in-law, and another man tied Powell's hands, put him in their car and drove off. Two days later cattle drivers found the bloody remains of Powell's legs, arms, and clothing in an area away from the road.[26]

Although most woodsriders were white, some blacks held positions of importance in operations. The few black woodsriders in the business had

388–9; Buttrick, "Commercial Uses of Longleaf Pine," 901; Wimster, "Life History of C. W. Wimster, Turpentine Man."

25. Maunder, *Voices from the South*, 72.

26. John Bonyne reports, 10 June 1921, 14 November 1921, and 3 May 1922, Howard P. Wright report, 9 September 1921, E. J. Cartier reports, 16 May 1922, 5 May 1922, 18 May 1922, 23 May 1922, and Ben Doyle sworn statement, 17 May 1922, Cubberly Papers.

typically begun work in turpentine when they were young—dipping, raking, and helping around the still. As they gained experience they became dippers, teamsters, coopers, and distillers. The very best advanced to woodsriders. Some particularly trustworthy black youths worked as tallymen. For jobs that did not create a measured end product like boxing or chipping, producers used a tallyman to record each worker's progress. Camp managers assigned each worker a code made up of either a number or name. When a worker finished his task at one face, he called out his individual code loudly enough for the tallyman to hear him up to several hundred yards away. The different codes hollered throughout the forest reportedly took on a rhythmic chanting sound. Each tallyman could record the work of no more than ten to twelve hands. The tallyman needed to be competent, trustworthy, and of good hearing, but age and strength mattered little. At one camp a ten-year-old boy was promoted from toting water to keeping the tally.[27]

In many respects the general characteristics of camp life survived the Civil War. As during the antebellum period, turpentine camps of the late nineteenth and early twentieth centuries tended to be isolated and temporary. As railroad trunk lines spread across the southeastern pine belt and branch lines opened up the most uninhabited areas to turpentine production, workers found themselves living and working many miles from any community. Camp locations served primarily to place laborers near the forests in which they worked. However, the sites also served to keep laborers well away from other potential employers and free from the distractions offered by a more populated area. With the camp located far back in the unsettled forest, workers seldom traveled, and visitors were rare.[28]

With a still, cooperage shed, glue shed, pump house, spirit shed, stable, blacksmith shop, commissary, and workers' quarters, many camps represented self-contained piney woods enterprises. Usually quarters contained between twenty-five and forty houses arranged in a variety of patterns. At

27. Albert Pridgen, "Turpentining in the South Atlantic Country," in *Naval Stores: History, Production, Distribution, and Consumption,* ed. Thomas Gamble (Savannah: Review Publishing and Printing, 1921), 104; Kennedy, *Palmetto Country,* 264–6; Freeman Ashmore, "Looking Back: The Woodsrider," *Wakulla Area Digest* (September 1996): 13–4, 16, 24; Albert G. Snow, Jr., "Research on the Improvement of Turpentine Practices," *Economic Botany* 3 (October–December 1949): 379; Wyman, *Florida Naval Stores,* 9; Federal Writers' Project, *Florida,* 378; Blount, *Spirits of Turpentine,* 36–7; Thomas, *McCranie's Turpentine Still,* 33; Maguire, interview by author; Schorger and Betts, *Naval Stores Industry,* 15; "Pine Forests of the South," 196; Register, interview; Harvey, "Maguire Born into Turpentine Family," 9; Becky Vail, "Old-Timer Remembers 'Hard Old Days' in Woods," in News Clipping File, Lowndes County Historical Society, Valdosta, Ga.

28. S. G. Thigpen, *Boy in Rural Mississippi,* 177; Gene Burnett, "To Burn in a Turpentine Hell," *Florida Trend* (October 1976): 100.

some camps, shanties were erected about the woods to provide a moderate amount of privacy. Other camps had cabins spaced according to a grid pattern. Still other camp quarters lacked any organization at all, with houses built wherever the owner happened to choose. Producers often provided separate quarters for the single men away from the family cabins to prevent disruption caused by unattached men flirting with married women.[29]

Housing for turpentine laborers was among the poorest of all workers in the postbellum South. The workers' cabins, intended to serve only as temporary structures, were crudely and cheaply constructed, often costing no more than $200 apiece to build. Zora Neale Hurston explained in her novel *Seraph on the Suwanee* that "teppentine [*sic*] shacks are not built for beauty. They are temporary shelters. In a few years usually the woods are worked out, and the camp is moved. The houses are torn down and put up again at the new location." The typical turpentine laborer lived in a two-room cabin with batten siding, wide pine boards nailed together either horizontally or perpendicularly across the side with laths covering the cracks. Few cabins had screened windows, but shutters were common. None had indoor plumbing. Many possessed dirt floors, but it appears that, over time, more and more were built with wood floors. A stick-and-clay fireplace sat at one end of the cabin. For heating and cooking, workers burned wood gathered from the neighboring forest and, sometimes, dross, the residue that collected in rosin strainers. When a family grew too large for their cabin, another room, really nothing more than a lean-to, was added. Evidence suggests that, despite such arrangements made for large families, living space remained cramped. At one Florida operation, for example, nearly six people on average lived in each house. Despite their modest character, most houses were reportedly neatly kept, with the yards swept clean and vegetables cultivated in backyard gardens. The most-skilled workers tended to live in somewhat better housing. Dwellings for distillers, foremen, and woodsriders often had more room and were better constructed than those of the regular workers.[30]

29. Maguire, interview by author; Forney, "Importance of Sites," 3; Gay Goodman Wright, "Turpentining," 109–10; Baker, "Summerall Turpentine Still," 7; Kennedy, *Palmetto Country*, 265; Wimster, "Life History of C. W. Wimster, Turpentine Man."

30. Zora Neale Hurston, *Seraph on the Suwanee*, in *Novels and Stories*, Library of America (New York: Literary Classics of the United States, 1995), 651; Maguire, interview by author; Forney, "Importance of Sites," 3; Gay Goodman Wright, "Turpentining," 109–10; Baker, "Summerall Turpentine Still," 7; Kennedy, *Palmetto Country*, 265; Sandra Jo Forney, "Naval Stores Industry in North Florida Pine Flatwoods" (paper presented at the sixteenth annual meeting of the Society for Historical Archaeology, Denver, Colo., 1983), 4; Thigpen, *Boy in Rural Mississippi*, 174–7; Carswell, *Holmesteading*, 143; Bond, "Development of the Naval Stores Industry," 200; Wilson, interview; Wetherington, *New South Comes to Wiregrass Georgia*, 238; Hickman, "Black Labor in Forest Industries," 88; Account Book, Osteen Papers; Hickman, *Mississippi Harvest*, 146–7; Armstrong, "Transformation of Work," 531; Davis, ed., *Encyclopedia*

Camp living quarters were typically racially segregated. The black work-ers' cabins were located at one end of the camp, and the white owner, man-ager, woodsriders, and their families lived in finer homes at the other end. In many camps the whites lived beside the only road into the camp, usually a two-rut path, to monitor who came and went. As a general rule, white children did not play with black children and black and white adults did not socialize. Each race had constant contact with the other, however. White men had close association with the black workers, whom they managed, and the white women and children saw black men and women at work about the camp as well as in and around their homes. One white woman recalled that, as a child in a turpentine camp, "I didn't have any fear of the colored families. We didn't socialize with them, but we knew them all. They had gardens and brought fresh vegetables to my mother. We shared with them, too."[31]

Molasses, pork, and cornbread or maybe biscuits provided the bulk of the turpentine laborer's and his family's diet. To these staples workers added coffee, mackerel, peas, beans, rice, sugar, and occasionally beef, mutton, and cheese. All these foods they obtained from the commissary. On occasion fresh fish or salted mullet arrived in the commissary or from peddlers who traveled as far as fifty to sixty miles inland from the coast. Turpentine work-ers reduced their reliance on the commissary, and thus their indebtedness, by hunting, cultivating, and gathering some of their own food. They hunted the woods for squirrels, opossums, raccoons, rabbits, turtles, and other wild game. They fished in local rivers and streams as well. Women, when not tending to children, tended gardens, in which they grew turnips and col-lards; raised, killed, cured, and cooked pigs and chickens; and foraged in the woods for edible herbs and berries. Palmetto buds were reported to taste like cabbage, and banban twigs like snap beans. Evidence suggests that the intensity of this female-dominated domestic food production was related to the wage level in the camp: the better the pay, the less work required for additional food procurement.[32]

Turpentine workers usually ate three meals a day, all usually prepared by their wives over primitive cabin fireplaces. Workers ate their breakfast and

of American Forest, s.v. "naval stores"; Vance, *Human Geography of the South*, 122; Armstrong, "Georgia Lumber Laborers," 445.

31. Kennedy, *Palmetto Country*, 265; Monroe, interview, 3–4; Gay Goodman Wright, "Tur-pentining," 110; Wimster, "Life History of C. W. Wimster, Turpentine Man."

32. Thigpen, *Boy in Rural Mississippi*, 177; Hickman, *Mississippi Harvest*, 150. Account book, 1872, Osteen Papers; Forney, "Importance of Sites," 2; Carswell, *Holmesteading*, 143; Shelton, *Pines and Pioneers*, 202; Bond, "Development of the Naval Stores Industry," 198; Ziegler, Spillers, and Coulter, *Financial Aspects of Growing Southern Pine*, 562.

lunch in the forest. Every morning they carried their food in half-gallon lard cans and their water in gallon-sized bottles wrapped in a wet sack and tied with baling wire to keep it cool. Arriving around daylight by wagon, or after the 1910s by truck, workers might build a fire and eat breakfast as they waited for light. They usually used these breakfast sites as a "hang-up place," somewhere to leave their coats, lunch buckets, and water bottles. If the area had ants, workers employed a sapling as a "hang-up tree." Before hanging their lunch from the small tree's branches, they shaved six inches of bark off the trunk, exposing the gummy wood which would trap hungry ants that attempted to raid the lunch. If the breakfast site was inconvenient, workers might make a hang-up place closer to the day's work area. Woodsriders and producers knew that if they wanted to find a man in the forest, they need but arrive at the hang-up place around lunchtime. In the early afternoon, when the day's heat was at its greatest, workers broke for lunch. Lunch items included black-eyed peas, collard greens, slabs of fat sowbelly, and cornbread or biscuits with cane syrup. Other lunch entrées included canned salmon mixed with rice, tomatoes, and beans as well as a dish called dooby, a mixture of meat, onions, and cornbread. Lunches were usually eaten cold, but in chilly weather the workers might build a fire and heat them. Supper, the heaviest meal of the day, was eaten after work.[33]

Women did not usually work at turpentining, except maybe dipping gum, but they often supplemented their family's income by cooking, cleaning, and washing for the producers' and woodsriders' wives. The women selected for these jobs reportedly considered themselves fortunate to have the steady work. Still other women found jobs planting trees and cleaning tools at the season's end. In many cases women were limited to jobs at the camp because of its isolated location. However, if other white families lived nearby, the women could find jobs as domestics in homes outside the camp. At one less-remote Florida camp, some women and older children worked in nearby potato fields. Chloe Lud, married to a South Carolina turpentine worker in the 1870s, labored between four and twelve days each month at such jobs as spreading manure, planting potatoes, dipping gum, chopping cotton, and, most commonly, washing clothes to contribute to her household's income. With her earnings she purchased bacon, flour, mackerel, sugar, potatoes, cheese, and tobacco. Along with working outside the home, tending to children, and raising, canning and cooking food, women nursed the sick and injured and boiled the hardened gum out of stiffened overalls.[34]

33. Gay Goodman Wright, "Turpentining," 100–1; Maguire, interview by author.

34. Vail, "Old-Timer Remembers 'Hard Old Days'"; Robert N. Lauriault, "From Can't to Can't: The North Florida Turpentine Camp, 1900–1950," *Florida Historical Quarterly* 67 (January 1989): 326; Gay Goodman Wright, "Turpentining," 109–12; Monroe, interview, 4; Maguire, interview by author; Thomas, *McCranie's Turpentine Still*, C-3; Genevieve W. Chandler,

Producers encouraged marriages at turpentine camps, but few unions were legal. Marriages facilitated good camp government and economical use of housing. Therefore, turpentiners pushed single men and women to marry in a "commissary wedding." The producers or camp managers would decide with a couple that they should marry, would assign them a cabin, and would open an account for them at the commissary. Despite the informality of the arrangement, such unions were respected, considered binding, and could last for decades. Husbands and wives generally grew up in either the same camp or in neighboring camps, and they usually married young. The camp community did not regard boys as adults until they wed, and until then, their pay was collected as part of their fathers' household income. If a couple had some extra money—a rare occurrence—they might go to the county courthouse and get a marriage license. To gain a divorce the couple also consulted with the boss, who then assigned each to different quarters.[35]

Few camps offered much by way of diversions for the men and women living there. Because of the long daily work hours, on weekday evenings there was little time for rowdiness. Families in the close-knit communities would visit and make their own music. On Sundays part of the camp community attended worship services. Some camps contained a church, which during the week might serve as a schoolhouse. If a camp lacked a church, religious services were held in one of the cabins. In most camps a worker served as a preacher. Turpentine laborers also filled leisure time by celebrating holidays. At at least one Florida camp the black workers, for an uncertain reason, celebrated May 20 as "Freedom Day" by slaughtering hogs and having a large barbecue. On weekend nights, which offered the majority of free time, most entertainment centered around the camp juke joint, a house where men and women gathered to dance, drink moonshine, and flirt. Men gambled, some playing skin, a popular card game. Producers and woodsriders tried to limit the revelry and keep the peace on weekends. Some attempted to control the amount of moonshine that came into the camp. Others required that all activity end at midnight on Sundays so the men would be fit to work the next morning.[36]

"An Old Man from Horry," American Life Histories: Manuscripts from the Federal Writers' Project, 1936–1940, Library of Congress Internet Website; Bond, "Development of the Naval Stores Industry," 198; Gay Goodman Wright, "Turpentining," 109–12.

35. Kennedy, Palmetto Country, 266; Federal Writers' Project, Florida, 37; Gay Goodman Wright, "Turpentining," 113; Maguire, interview by author; Tegeder, "Prisoners of the Pines," 183; Hickman, Mississippi Harvest, 148–9; Hickman, "Black Labor in Forest Industries," 89.

36. "The Pine Plantation," New York Tribune, 17 March 1866; Thomas, McCranie's Turpentine Still, C-2, C-3. Blount, Spirits of Turpentine, 41; Federal Writers' Project, Florida, 377–8; Wyman, Florida Naval Stores, 9; C. R. Clark, Florida Trade Tokens, 7–8; Maguire, interview by

Payday, when workers received the balance of their monthly wages after their commissary accounts were deducted, was the most lively time. Many turpentiners arranged for their workers' transportation in the back of the camp wagon or truck to the nearest town. In town, workers received a break from the monotony of camp life, were able to purchase goods unavailable at the commissary, and could socialize with laborers from other turpentine operations. Although the camp's visit brought much-welcomed business to the town merchants, as well as to bootleggers, townspeople feared the black workers, considering them wild and unruly, and thought of the white woods-riders as outlaws. One laborer reported that "when we come to town folks would clear the streets." The frequent arrests of turpentine workers for rowdiness provided small communities with easy revenue, since producers and managers willingly bailed their workers out of jail, their labor too valuable to be sacrificed. Producers often found it very difficult to get any work done in the few days following payday. Some producers, although not all, recognized blue Mondays after the payday weekend because their workers were frequently too hungover to manage the strenuous labor with the precision necessary for successful operation.[37]

The white community perceived black turpentine workers as different from other African Americans, but disagreed as to whether turpentine workers were "good" blacks or "bad." Many such laborers had been born and raised in the isolated camps and knew little of the world beyond the forest. They had limited education and generally lacked skills in anything except turpentine production. When whites encountered them on their monthly trips to town, workers appeared ignorant, crude, and indolent, despite showing the respect toward whites demanded by the racial climate. Many whites believed that black turpentiners were indeed lazy and dangerous. In 1905 the state of Florida explained that its rising crime rate resulted in part from

author; Forney, "Importance of Sites," 3, 5; Kennedy, *Palmetto Country*, 265; Vail, "Old-Timer Remembers 'Hard Old Days'"; Gay Goodman Wright, "Turpentining," 119–20, 123–4; Monroe, interview, 3; Tegeder, "Prisoners of the Pines," 192, 158; Wimster, "Life History of C. W. Wimster, Turpentine Man."

37. Bond, "Development of the Naval Stores Industry," 198; Hickman, *Mississippi Harvest*, 149–50; "Peculiar to the South," *Indianapolis Sentinel*, 15 November 1896, Turpentine News Clipping File, Forest History Society, Durham, N.C.; Hervey Evans to Mattie McNair Evans, 16 August 1899, and Hervey Evans to Mattie McNair Evans, 30 July 1899, Patterson Papers; Hurston, *Seraph on the Suwanee*, 599; Gay Goodman Wright, "Turpentining," 119–20, 123–4; Maguire, interview by author; Thomas, *McCranie's Turpentine Still*, C-2, C-3; Blount, *Spirits of Turpentine*, 41; Federal Writers' Project, *Florida*, 377–8; Wyman, *Florida Naval Stores*, 9; C. R. Clark, *Florida Trade Tokens*, 7–8; Forney, "Importance of Sites," 3, 5; Kennedy, *Palmetto Country*, 265; Vail, "Old-Timer Remembers 'Hard Old Days'"; Monroe, interview, 3; Tegeder, "Prisoners of the Pines," 192, 158.

"the rapid growth of the turpentine and lumber industries in Florida" which had "caused an influx of a floating population that follow this class of work." Because a large number of whites shared the view that turpentine blacks were dangerous, not all communities allowed operations in their vicinity. John Carson, the president of one of the most powerful naval stores factorage houses, agreed that turpentine workers were indolent, but identified this laziness as a phenomenon of the early 1920s. Carson maintained that "Sambo is not as strong, vigorous or healthy as he was thirty to forty years ago. Disease has made inroads into his constitution and he cannot give the service now as then even should he so desire. Today the producer pays exceedingly high wages for very poor work, the result being that it takes from two to two and one-half men to do one man's work and the expense of operating the average turpentine farm is ten times more than in the period mentioned."[38]

Not all whites, however, were prepared to wholly condemn them. One white man explained in 1910 that despite their shortcomings, black turpentine laborers were hard workers. "The negro of the pineries," he reported, "is careless, often brutal, always happy-go-lucky, but the men who employ him say that he works well with [the] right management; in fact, is the best labor that can be had for the place, and that the business would not know what to do without him. He surely fits the scene and one would be sorry to miss him from it." Writing in the early 1920s, a naval stores man argued that turpentine workers were the same as other blacks, whom he believed were harmless when under a white man's control. He did not believe that "a turpentine negro is any worse than others of his race under similar conditions. The country at large has somehow gotten the idea that the turpentine negro is worse than other kinds of negroes. This impression is an erroneous one, and one which in justice to the turpentine negro, should be corrected."[39]

Just as American turpentine workers lived an existence unlike that of other southern blacks and were viewed as somehow different by the larger

38. Maunder, *Voices from the South,* 36; Kennedy, *Palmetto Country,* 265; I. F. Eldredge, *The 4 Forests and the Future of the South* (Washington, D.C.: Charles Lathrop Pack Forestry Foundation, 1947), 41; Paisley, "Wade Leonard," 386; Maguire, interview by author; Register, interview; Hickman, *Mississippi Harvest,* 146–7; Tegeder, "Prisoners of the Pines," 184; Wimster, "Life History of C. W. Wimster, Turpentine Man"; *The Eighth Biennial Report of the Commissioner of Agriculture, State of Florida, for the Period Beginning January 1, 1903, and Ending December 31, 1904* (Tallahassee: L. B. Hilson, State Printer, 1905), 318; Kennedy et al., eds., *History of Lake County, Florida,* 108; Carson, "Increased Cost of Naval Stores Production," 73.

39. Winthrop Packard, *Florida Trails: As Seen from Jacksonville to Key West and from November to April Inclusive* (Boston: Small, Maynard, 1910), 281; Pridgen, "Turpentining in the South Atlantic Country," 104.

southern society, so were many white producers. Operators and woodsriders were considered by many southern whites as tough pioneer types. Not only did they have to maintain order in their camps, a potentially dangerous duty requiring a heavy hand, but, like their laborers, they lived in the isolated forest and moved frequently. They lost regular contact with the outside world, and although they had a better standard of living than their workers, the turpentine producers' existence was not particularly high, measured against that of the larger white community. Their diet differed relatively little from their laborers', and their houses, which admittedly contained more room than anyone else's in the camp, were rather primitive. The only church to attend was often one for the workers, and there were few schools for producers' children. School-age children either had to attend a small, poorly funded school, learn from a tutor, or attend school away from home. Frequent camp moves challenged the access to and the stability of their education.[40]

Wives of producers and woodsriders faced many challenges in the isolated locations. The experience of Ida Willis illustrates the difficulties of white women in turpentine camps. Mrs. Willis met her husband, Allen, in the early 1910s through his sisters, with whom she attended Columbia College in South Carolina. At this time, Willis was a young turpentiner, just two years in the business. He worked an 11,000-acre operation twenty miles up the New River from Carrabelle, Florida, a small community on the Gulf and south-southwest of Tallahassee. When they married, Ida joined Allen at this location. Upon her arrival at the camp in June 1915, the curious stares of the black workers, who rarely if ever left the area and wanted to see the owner's new wife, unnerved her. Moreover, the camp's isolation and primitive nature immediately left her troubled. The only other human habitations in the vicinity were other turpentine camps, but even they were a fair distance away. The journey to Carrabelle, the nearest town, required a three-hour boat trip. Because the boat was old and broke down frequently, however, it was an unreliable means of transportation. Ida's house sat next to the river. It had no running water, but had an outhouse in the yard. Her days were spent embroidering tablecloths and napkins, cleaning the house with the help of a washerwoman, and preparing meals, which consisted of a monotonous round of cabbage, venison, pork and beans, and poultry. Ida saw little of the laborers. As was typical of turpentine camp layouts, the workers' quarters were located far away from the owner's house. Nevertheless, she feared the laborers, many of whom were ex-convicts. In fact just before she arrived,

40. Kennedy, *Palmetto Country*, 265; Ashmore, "Looking Back: The Woodsrider," 13–4, 16, 24.

one had attempted to kill Allen. She slept with a pistol when her husband
was away. She also claimed that the workers stole from her.[41]

Along with white turpentine producers, woodsriders, and black wage laborers, a fourth group, leased convicts, represented an important human
component of the southern naval stores industry. Like the employment of
paid workers, who, if not held in outright peonage, commonly languished
somewhere between forced and free labor, the use of convicts began after
the Civil War. During Reconstruction, first southern counties and then
states began to lease their convicts as a solution to rising prison populations
and empty treasuries. They sought the maximum amount of punishment at
a minimum cost to the government. By 1880 all of the former Confederate
states except Virginia leased their convicts, and in 1890 over 27,000 convicts
performed labor in the South.[42]

Georgia and Florida, the two principal naval stores–producing states during the late nineteenth century, quickly established the practice after the
war. With nowhere to house its prisoners once federal troops burned the
state penitentiary, Georgia passed its first convict lease act in December
1866. But it was not until 1868, when a hundred black prisoners went to
work constructing rail lines, that the provisional governor leased the first
convicts under this new legislation. In 1897 the Georgia General Assembly
passed a new convict lease law that made the system more flexible. It prohibited the leasing of convicts for longer than five years, permitted subleasing,
and placed bidding on a per-convict basis instead of on the entire population. Because convicts could now be sublet, employers no longer had to pay
for unneeded ones when business slowed. Also, because lessees paid for each
convict, the state could boost its revenue by increasing its number of convicts. Between 1870 and 1910, consequently, the number of convicts in Georgia grew ten times faster than the general population. Most of the increase
came from a sharp rise in the number of incarcerated young black men who
served increasingly lengthy sentences.[43]

41. Thomas, *McCranie's Turpentine Still*, C-1–C-4.

42. N. Gordon Carper, "The Convict-Lease System in Florida, 1866–1923" (Ph.D. diss.,
Florida State University, 1964), 3–5; Jonathan M. Wiener, "Class Structure and Economic De-
velopment in the American South, 1865–1955," *American Historical Review* 84 (October 1979):
981; Jeffrey A. Drobney, "Where Palm and Pine Are Blowing: Convict Labor in the North
Florida Turpentine Industry, 1877–1923," *Florida Historical Quarterly* 72 (April 1984): 413, 416;
Cohen, "Negro Involuntary Servitude," 55; Edward L. Ayers, *Vengeance and Justice: Crime and
Punishment in the Nineteenth-Century American South* (New York: Oxford University Press,
1984), 212.

43. E. Merton Coulter, *James Monroe Smith, Georgia Planter: Before and after Death* (Athens: University of Georgia Press, 1961), 64; Alex Lichtenstein, *Twice the Work of Free Labor:
The Political Economy of Convict Labor in the New South* (New York: Verso, 1996), 123; David

Florida, like Georgia, lacked the facilities in which to house its convicts. The state's first solution was to incarcerate them at the old U.S. armory at Chattahoochee, which by 1869 held three hundred convicts. The next year, however, Florida experimented with leasing when it contracted out fifteen convicts to cut and hew 200,000 feet of lumber for a railroad trestle. Over the next ten years, instead of developing its penitentiary system, Florida gradually moved toward full-scale convict leasing. Under the Bourbons, the system received a boost from the allowance of subleasing. White support for the institution intensified with the discovery of phosphate in the state in the 1880s, which spurred further demand for convict labor. It was during this decade that convicts probably began work in the state's naval stores industry.[44]

The same factors that strengthened peonage around the turn of the century—a tight labor market and the belief that blacks would not work unless compelled—encouraged convict leasing. A 1910 Florida report explained that convicts were employed "in the most remote places and their labor used where free labor is hard to get or control." At the same time, a reporter added that "the convict is a very desirable workman. He can be counted on for six days a week from dawn till dark, and that is more than can be said of any but a very few negroes, most of whom obey their own sweet, wayward, indifferent will."[45]

Convict leasing was especially popular among turpentine producers. Although only a small percentage of convicts leased out by the state of Georgia worked in naval stores, a substantial portion of its county convicts labored in the industry. Where only between 5 and 10 percent of state convicts worked in turpentine, approximately two-thirds of county convicts not working on roads labored in the industry. In Florida, turpentiners were the principal lessees of convicts. The use of convicts in Florida turpentine operations grew from 27 percent of the state prison population in 1899 to over 90 percent in 1910. Those businesses that worked the convicts found leasing very lucrative. In 1912 the average profit for a naval stores operation working

M. Oshinsky, "Worse Than Slavery": Parchman Farm and the Ordeal of Jim Crow Justice (New York: Free Press, 1996), 63.

44. Mancini, One Dies, Get Another, 184; Drobney, "Where Palm and Pine Are Blowing," 415; Carper, "Convict-Lease System in Florida," 25–6, 36, 45–6, 109; J. C. Powell, American Siberia, forward.

45. Mancini, One Dies, Get Another, 192; Barry, "Slavery in the South To-Day," 484, 486; Drobney, Lumbermen and Log Sawyers, 168; Marc N. Goodnow, "Turpentine: Impressions of the Convict Camps of Florida," Survey 34 (1 May 1915): 107; Eleventh Biennial Report of the Commissioner of Agriculture of the State of Florida for the Period Beginning January 1, 1909, and Ending December 31, 1910 (Tallahassee: T. J. Appleyard, State Printer, 1911), 567–8.

convicts was reportedly $25,000. But although a large percentage of convicts labored in turpentine production, especially in Florida, their number remained a relatively small part of the overall industry workforce. In 1890, when turpentining in Florida had only just begun and a mere five hundred Floridians worked in it, state convicts made up 39 percent of the labor force. Even then, fewer than 10 percent of producers worked state convicts. Eight years later, 71 percent of the state's prison population labored in the turpentine industry. That amounted, however, to only 734 convicts. On average, between 1880 and 1910 only 7 to 8 percent of naval stores workers were state convicts. A similar situation was true in Georgia in 1900, where 620 state and county convicts labored in turpentine camps. Although turpentine work represented only 14 percent of the overall number of convicts, they represented an even smaller percentage of the overall naval stores workforce, 3.2 percent. Thus, whereas naval stores production played a large role in the world of convict leasing, the reverse cannot be claimed; prisoners represented only a small portion of workers.[46]

Like virtually all wage laborers in the naval stores industry, the great majority of convict workers were black. Whereas before the Civil War whites represented the majority of southern prisoners, afterwards blacks made up 90 percent of the convict population. Historian Edward Ayers points out that this transformation in the southern prison population resulted from the states' assumption of control over blacks after emancipation freed them from their masters' control. The shift rested on southern whites' belief that blacks were innately criminal, would never work unless compelled, and that the

46. *Fourth Annual Report of the Prison Commission of Georgia, from October 1, 1900, to October 1, 1901* (Atlanta: J. F. Lester, 1901), 6, 36–8; *Fifth Annual Report of the Prison Commission of Georgia, from October 1, 1901, to October 1, 1902* (Atlanta: Lester Book and Stationery Co., 1902), 29–31; *Seventh Annual Report of the Prison Commission of Georgia, from June 1, 1903, to May 31, 1904* (Atlanta: Lester Book and Stationery Co., 1908), 19–26; *Eighth Annual Report of the Prison Commission of Georgia, from June 1, 1904, to May 31, 1905* (Atlanta: Lester Book and Stationery Co., 1905), 20–3; *Ninth Annual Report of the Prison Commission of Georgia, from June 1, 1905, to May 31, 1906* (Atlanta: Lester Book and Stationery Co., 1906), 18–21; *Tenth Annual Report of the Prison Commission of Georgia, from June 1, 1906, to May 31, 1907* (Atlanta: Lester Book and Stationery Co., 1907), 21–2; *Eleventh Annual Report of the Prison Commission of Georgia, from June 1, 1907, to May 31, 1908* (Atlanta: Lester Book and Stationery Co., 1908), 23–6; Clarissa Olds Keeler, *The Crime of Crimes, or The Convict System Unmasked* (Washington, D.C.: Clarissa Olds Keeler, 1907), 11; Drobney, "Where Palm and Pine Are Blowing," 417–8, 426–7; *Eighth Biennial Report*, 307, 309; *Tenth Biennial Report of the Commissioner of Agriculture of the State of Florida for the Period Beginning January 1, 1907, and Ending December 31, 1908* (Tallahassee: Union Label, 1909), 395, 473; *Eleventh Biennial Report*, 532, 567; Blount, "Spirits in the Pines," 162–3; *Report of the Commissioner of Agriculture of the State of Florida for the Period Beginning January 1, 1897, and Ending December 31, 1898* (Tallahassee: Tallahasseean Book and Job Print, 1899), 93–9; U.S. Dept. of Commerce and Labor, *Manufacturers, 1905*, 170.

white South was entitled to cheap black labor for society's good. To this end the white legal establishment targeted blacks. J. C. Powell, a former turpentine camp captain, observed that in the 1870s and 1880s "it was possible to send a negro to prison on almost any pretext, but difficult to get a white man there, unless he committed some very heinous crime." Because it required a serious offense for whites to be sentenced, white convicts tended to be more dangerous criminals than black prisoners and more difficult to work. They worked less, complained more, and rebelled with greater frequency than black convicts. Their resistance took the form of assaulting guards, escaping, attempting suicide, performing low-quality work, and mutilating themselves in the hope of receiving a hardship pardon.[47]

An analysis of the Florida state convicts who labored in the turpentine industry in 1898 reveals a profile that changed little during the leasing program's existence. The great majority of prisoners, over 80 percent, were black men. Fifteen percent were white men, 4 percent black women, and less than 1 percent white women. Over two-thirds of the convicts sentenced in 1898 were between the ages of sixteen and thirty. One was as young as eleven, and the oldest was sixty-seven. More than half of Florida's convicts were sentenced for some type of theft or breaking and entering, and around 22 percent were serving time for either murder or attempted murder. Only 1 percent were committed for rape or attempted rape. Just over 60 percent were sentenced for less than three years. Nearly a quarter received sentences of ten years or more. It appears that Florida convicts leased to turpentine operators differed little from the overall state convict population or the twenty-nine Georgia convicts who labored at a Berrien County turpentine operation around the turn of the century. Georgia's records reveal that around half the convict population was wholly illiterate, and slightly less than half were married.[48]

A sample of Florida turpentine camps that employed state convict laborers in 1913 reveals that the typical camp held between thirty and fifty convicts. Some camps contained no white convicts; in no case were more than

47. Ayers, *Vengeance and Justice,* 150, 197, 199; Lichtenstein, *Twice the Work of Free Labor,* 25, 29; Cohen, "Negro Involuntary Servitude," 34; Cohen, *At Freedom's Edge,* 227; *First Annual Report of the Prison Commission of Georgia from October 1, 1897, to October 1, 1898* (Atlanta: Geo. W. Harrison, State Printer, 1898), 26; *Fifth Annual Report,* 30–1; Powell, *American Siberia,* 332; Carper, "Convict-Lease System in Florida," 212–3, 290; Oshinsky, *"Worse Than Slavery,"* 72, 165.

48. *Eighth Biennial Report,* 340–5; *Tenth Biennial Report,* 473–95; *Report of the Commissioner of Agriculture, 1897–1898,* 81–5, 93–9; Lichtenstein, *Twice the Work of Free Labor,* 130; *Second Annual Report of the Prison Commission of Georgia, from October 1, 1898, to October 1, 1899* (Atlanta: Foote and Davies, 1899), 12.

10 percent of the convicts white. Only one black woman was held in a camp. The number of convicts at any one camp could vary widely through the year. In 1914 the population of the Waller Turpentine Company camp, for example, fluctuated between sixty and thirty-four convicts. At the Belmore Naval Stores Company camp as many as forty-five convicts and as few as thirty-four worked that same year. Convict work camps in general averaged one guard for every five convicts and one bloodhound per every twelve convicts. Each camp had one captain. The pattern for turpentine camps employing convicts was strikingly similar. Georgia's pattern appears to have been similar, too.[49]

Convict turpentine laborers performed the same tasks as free workers, almost always at separate camps, and usually at a quicker pace. Convicts rose at 4:30 A.M. and by 5:00 A.M. were on their way to the forest. They trotted to and from work on a squad chain, by which the men were attached together at the waist. A mounted guard set the pace, and other guards brought up the rear with drawn guns. Once in the woods, a few miles from the camp, convicts worked under the task system in squads, each squad watched by one or two guards mounted on horseback. After resting for thirty minutes for lunch, convicts resumed work until completing their tasks, which often kept them busy until dusk. They then marched back to camp the same way they had left. Not all convicts could withstand the quick march, especially after a long, hard day's work, and many collapsed. Some guards allowed these stragglers to follow in the rear at their own pace, while other guards meted out brutal punishment for falling behind. Powell reported that convicts "kept this gait up all day long, from tree to tree, and as the labor is exhausting in the extreme, I have frequently seen men on their way back to camp drop of fatigue, and their comrades on the squad-chain drag them a dozen yards through the dirt before the pace could be checked so as to enable them to regain their feet." It was not uncommon for convicts to endure this brutal schedule six and even seven days a week.[50]

49. Provision Registers for Waller and DeLeon turpentine camps, 1914, F. J. Titeaub to W. A. McRae, 30 September 1913, R. R. Tomline to W. A. McRae, 31 October 1913, T. D. Titeaub to W. A. McRae, 1 November 1913, T. D. Titeaub to W. A. McRae, 1 November 1913, and Inspectors' reports, September 1913 to February 1914, Convict Lease Program Subject Files, 1889–1916, Board of Commissioners of State Institutions Papers, Florida State Archives, Tallahassee; *Eleventh Annual Report*, 23–6; *Second Annual Report*, 30, 41.

50. C. J. Sullivan to G. J. Whitefield, 21 May 1914, Commissioner of Agriculture to Florida Naval Stores and Com. Company, 5 April 1902, N. A. Blitch to N. B. Broward, 5 April 1906, and J. D. Ferrell to W. A. McRae, 28 March 1913, Board of Commissioners of State Institutions Papers; Goodnow, "Turpentine," 104; Barry, "Slavery in the South To-Day," 487; Drobney, "Where Palm and Pine Are Blowing," 419–21; Powell, *American Siberia*, 22, 29; Lichtenstein, *Twice the Work of Free Labor*, 128–30; Shelton, *Pines and Pioneers*, 202; Hickman, *Mississippi Harvest*, 141–2, 420.

To complete their job during the week, convicts worked extremely hard. Some camps expected convicts to reach production levels as much as 50 percent above that of wage workers. The labor expectations and the nature of the work at turpentine camps were enormously burdensome compared to even the other businesses that employed convict labor. In 1901 a group of desperate convicts, apparently just leased to a naval stores operation, wrote the governor of Florida explaining that "we the undersigned, convicts at Mr. Buttgenbacks' Floral City camp, beg to state, that we would like to remain at the phosphate mines in preference to going to the turpentine farms. Some of the men here have worked at both places, and they are all unanimous in stating, that they prefer the mines." Certain convicts found their tasks especially taxing. Prisoners serving shorter sentences, thirty days for example, reportedly were worked harder than those serving for several years. Because a camp only had men with short sentences for a limited time, it lost nothing by working them to exhaustion. New convicts were often unable to keep up the prescribed pace and entered a period of depression and despondency. But within time, most reportedly developed the physical stamina to endure. Teenage boys also experienced special hardships in meeting their assigned tasks. Despite their small size, boys were expected to dip as much gum as grown men, fifty-two buckets each day.[51]

Like turpentine camps that employed wage labor, convict camps tended to be found in isolated locations. Of Florida's twenty-eight camps employing convicts in 1903, the least remote was two miles away from the nearest town and the most was fifteen miles from a community. A high stockade typically surrounded turpentine convict camps. Inside the yard little vegetation grew. During particularly wet seasons, such barren areas could quickly turn into muddy quagmires. Most buildings were constructed of rough pine boards and whitewashed. The bunk house resembled a warehouse and was the largest building in the camp. As much as one hundred feet long, they usually had uncovered rafters and boards and, except for barred windows and postings of the state prison authority's rules, bare walls. Some even lacked floors, and in cold weather a fire was built on the ground and the smoke allowed to escape however it could. At many camps the bunkhouse was divided into a dining hall and sleeping quarters. The dining section contained a heating stove, tables, and boxes and broken chairs for sitting. It appears that at some

51. John B. Kertzinger et al. to Governor Jennings, 20 May 1901 and C. J. Sullivan to G. J. Whitefield, May 21, 1914, Board of Commissioners of State Institutions Papers; Goodnow, "Turpentine," 104, 107; Drobney, "Where Palm and Pine Are Blowing," 425; Drobney, *Lumbermen and Log Sawyers,* 170; Barry, "Slavery in the South To-Day," 487; Powell, *American Siberia,* 17, 122–3, 332–3; Carper, "Convict-Lease System in Florida," 259.

camps, however, convicts came directly from work to the bunkhouse, chained at their portion of the bedding platform, and ate their supper there. Convicts ate their fare using dishes, pans, and spoons. Knives and forks were forbidden, since they could be used as weapons. In the bunkhouses' sleeping section, arrangements varied greatly; convicts at some camps had individual cots, but most slept on long platforms covered with hay and blankets, with no sheets. In some cases unchanged bedding grew disgustingly filthy. At one Florida camp bedding went unwashed for nearly a year. Sleeping convicts were chained by their waist chains to a chain that ran the length of the bunkhouse. At night guards inspected each link to ensure its security. If a convict wished to change his sleeping position, he had to call to the night guard and get his permission. For bathing, convicts used barrels of water placed in the sleeping quarters. Twenty-five to thirty convicts used each barrel, which led to the spread of disease and infection. In addition to the bunkhouse, camps contained a commissary, kitchen, pig pen, and garden plot.[52]

Segregation policies appear to have varied among camps, despite state legislation that forbade housing black and white convicts together. In the mid-1880s, Alabama forbade the chaining of black and white convicts together when not at work. The rule applied to both state and county convicts. The Georgia legislature, in 1891, went one step further and made it a crime for convict lessees to chain blacks and whites together, even at work. Compared to Georgia, Florida was slower and less radical in its requirement of separating prisoners. In 1905, it simply forbade chaining men of the two races together and four years later required counties to house the races separately. Florida said nothing about work. Mississippi's legislature in 1906 and in 1908 prohibited housing or feeding convicts together and stated that the races should work separately when a separate arrangement was feasible. In his recollection of experiences as a convict turpentine camp boss, however, J. C. Powell makes no mention of separating convicts by race except in the case where a sublessee requested an all-black work unit. It also appears that if a camp contained female convicts, special quarters were reserved for them.[53]

52. Mancini, *One Dies, Get Another*, 65; Goodnow, "Turpentine," 104–6; J. D. Ferrell to W. A. MacRae, 29 March 1913 and 30 June 1913, Commissioner of Agriculture to Florida Naval Stores and Com. Company, 5 April 1902, and N. A. Blitch to N. B. Broward, 5 April 1906, Board of Commissioners of State Institutions Papers; Drobney, "Where Palm and Pine Are Blowing," 418–9; "Horrible Treatment of Convicts," *Jacksonville Times-Union and Citizen*, 20 May 1899; *Tenth Biennial Report*, 383–4; Powell, *American Siberia*, forward, 18, 21, 39, 123–4, 289, 338–9; Drobney, *Lumbermen and Log Sawyers*, 156–7; Carper, "Convict-Lease System in Florida," 130.

53. Franklin Johnson, *The Development of State Legislation Concerning the Free Negro* (New York: Arbor Press, 1918), 64–5, 93–4, 88, 90, 135.

As with housing arrangements, the quality of food in convict camps could vary from adequate to condemnable. Most convicts, it appears, subsisted on a monotonous diet that differed little from that of free turpentine workers and dated to at least the early nineteenth century. Registers of provisions issued to convicts in 1914 reveal that biscuits and cornbread made up the staples of convicts' diets. Prisoners also received regular servings of rice, beans, molasses, and coffee. Seasonal variation existed in convict diet, though, with more varieties of vegetables—Irish potatoes, squash, green beans, melons, corn, green peas, okra, and fresh tomatoes—available during the summer months. Many of these fresh vegetables were grown in camp gardens. Irregular servings of meat, whether it be ham, sausage, salt pork, or fresh beef or pork, were also issued to prisoners. Some months they might receive one serving of meat every day, yet at other times there would be none at all. There were also slight variations from this general pattern between camps. At one camp, for example, convicts received peas and sweet potatoes, where another camp did not provide these. The latter camp did serve ham and fresh pork more often than the former. Pork remained the typical meat. But, at some camps in the early twentieth century, convicts complained of being fed very poor grades of pork and also not receiving enough food for breakfast. On occasion, convicts took the initiative themselves to supplement their diet. Because fresh pork was rarely included as part of camp meals, convicts sometimes killed and ate hogs stolen from either the camp or neighboring farmers. They also foraged in the woods for ground tortoise, raccoons, opossums, and other wild game.[54]

In addition to suffering the hardships caused by a demanding work pace, primitive living quarters, and an often inadequate diet, convicts leased to turpentine outfits were usually at the mercy of incompetent guards. The typical camp employed between seven and eight guards. Guards did not have to perform physically exhausting labor, as did the convicts, but they did have to keep the same long hours guarding the prisoners both in the camp and in the woods. They also lived in the rustic and isolated camps. Because producers needed to keep costs low in order to make a profit in the frequently depressed industry, guards received little compensation for their long work

54. "Horrible Treatment of Convicts"; F. J. Titeaub to W. A. McRae, 10 April 1913, J. D. Ferrell to W. A. McRae, 28 March 1913, F. J. Titeaub to W. A. McRae, 13 May 1913, J. D. Ferrell to W. A. McRae, 28 May 1913, R. R. Tomlin to W. A. McRae, 31 July 1913, De Leon Naval Stores Company and Waller Turpentine Company, convict provision registers, 1914, Commissioner of Agriculture to Florida Naval Stores and Com. Company, 5 April 1902, and N. A. Blitch to N. B. Broward, 5 April 1906, Board of Commissioners of State Institutions Papers; Drobney, "Where Palm and Pine Are Blowing," 419; Powell, *American Siberia*, 21, 123–4, 338–9; Goodnow, "Turpentine," 105–6.

and primitive living conditions. The occupation, therefore, attracted generally unreliable workers. Most guards were young men, often no more than nineteen years old, who lacked better prospects in the area surrounding each camp. Many worked sloppily, caused trouble, and stayed at the job only a short time. There was, consequently, a constant turnover in personnel. One observer described the guards he observed as "husky young men, mounted upon horses and wearing large black slouch hats, with long barreled pistols protruding from their hip pockets." The inability to attract reliable white men as guards led some producers to use trusted convicts to oversee other prisoners. Known as the trustee system, the practice was relatively common but had its shortcomings. One camp manager found that trustees earned the guards' confidence by preventing other convicts from escaping, only to later use that trust and the loosened restrictions it brought to run away themselves.[55]

Although captains might have proved overall more experienced and reliable than guards, many of them were shown to be inadequate as well, despite relatively good salaries. In 1905 captains, or camp wardens, made approximately $150 a month, or between $1,200 and $1,800 annually. In a few cases they could make as much as $2,500. Guards, by comparison, made only $25 a month, but if they owned their own horse they could receive as much as $35.[56]

Camp discipline, administered largely by incompetent guards, rested squarely on a system of punishment that centered on the strap. It appears that, beginning in the 1870s, most convict camps replaced the whip with a strap of tough leather measuring one and a half feet by three inches and attached to a wooden handle. A whipping boss usually administered the licks, ideally in moderation. Some wardens appear to have adopted the philosophy of restraint. The captain of one camp claimed that "'tisn't necessary to handle the men roughly except when they get incorrigible or commit some act that requires punishment. . . . Yes, we use a strap; but not very much. I don't have much trouble." Others had different ideas. One boss found severe punishment necessary because of the rough nature of the con-

---

55. Goodnow, "Turpentine," 103; Powell, *American Siberia*, 29, 41–2, 304–5; Mancini, *One Dies, Get Another*, 74; Carper, "Convict-Lease System in Florida," 116, 230–1; Drobney, "Where Palm and Pine Are Blowing," 418.

56. Commissioner of Agriculture to Florida Naval Stores Comm. Co., 5 April 1902, Inspectors' reports, September 1913 to February 1914, Board of Commissioners of State Institutions Papers; *The Ninth Biennial Report of the Commissioner of Agriculture of the State of Florida for the Period Beginning January 1, 1905, and Ending December 31, 1906* (Tallahassee: Capital, 1907), 293; Goodnow, "Turpentine," 107; Barry, "Slavery in the South To-Day," 486.

victs, whom he characterized as "'cracker outlaws' and cut-throat negroes." The Florida commissioner of agriculture report for 1903 and 1904 explained that new convicts, especially those from larger towns, required considerable punishment. "They have never learned the lesson of obedience, are indisposed to labor and are more insolent," the report stated. "For a time they disturb the temper of those who are working smoothly. Nothing but corporal punishment, sometimes repeated and more severe, will have any effect on them."[57]

Until the turn of the century there was no legal restriction on the number of blows a convict could receive or on the frequency they could be administered. Under unrestrained circumstances whippings could easily become uncontrolled, sadistic forms of torture and even death in which a warden turned the event into a cruel game for his amusement. After 1900, however, each convict camp was required to keep a monthly prison punishment record to be submitted to the Board of Commissioners of State Institutions and the commissioner of agriculture in Tallahassee. For each punishment, camps were to provide the prisoner's identification number, name, and the date on which the punishable offense occurred. They were also to note the number of licks the prisoner received, whether the convict's skin was lacerated from the beating, whether it was that individual convict's first or second offense, who performed the whipping, and who recommended it. Georgia demanded similar information.[58]

The punishment reports submitted to the state of Florida reveal that approximately 10 percent of the convicts were whipped each month an average of nine licks. The number of licks, however, depended on the convict's offense and varied among camps. An analysis of three different turpentine camps' punishment reports from 1914 illustrates the types of offenses captains found punishable in the early twentieth century. At the Lemon Bay Turpentine Company camp in Sarasota County, Florida (then Manatee County), the Noma Naval Stores Company camp in Holmes County, and the Waller Turpentine Company camp, the most common punishable offense was "bad work" or "not working." Convicts were also punished for "laziness," "missing task," "fighting," "refusing to work," "sassing," "bunching timber," "impudence," "slipping out mail," "gambling," "idleness," "disobe-

57. Commissioner of Agriculture to Florida Naval Stores Comm. Co., 5 April 1902, Board of Commissioners of State Institutions Papers; Drobney, *Lumbermen and Log Sawyers*, 171; Goodnow, "Turpentine," 106; Powell, *American Siberia*, 30; *Eighth Biennial Report*, 302.

58. Drobney, "Where Palm and Pine Are Blowing," 430; Prison Punishment Report, Lemon Bay Turpentine Company, 1914, Board of Commissioners of State Institutions Papers; Drobney, *Lumbermen and Log Sawyers*, 170; *First Annual Report*, 38–9.

dience," "bad conduct," "cursing," and even "selling [a] hat." Escaping, apparently a more serious offense, brought fifteen licks.[59]

Although each camp maintained somewhat different punishment policies, closer analysis reveals common patterns. Although poor work precipitated the great majority of disciplinary action, this infraction was among the most lightly punished. Disruptive behavior, whether classified as "sassing," "disobedience," or "impudence," was also not tolerated. But although punishment for these three violations occurred far less frequently than for work-related offenses, convicts received more licks for them. Fighting was a common, if not pervasive, problem among all camps. Gambling was permitted in some camps, but in others, such as the Waller Turpentine Company camp, it was considered a moderately serious offense. Lacerations were reported to have occurred only a surprising three times out of the total of 251 punishments for 1914 at all three camps, a rate just over 1 percent and so low that it calls into question the accuracy of the punishment reports with respect to the severity of whipping.[60]

The most-abusive uses of the strap went unnoted by camp wardens and only came to light during inspections. At a camp in Manatee County, Florida, an inspector found that convicts received beatings too frequently and of too severe a nature. The convicts, consequently, appeared to be in poor condition. At an Orange County camp, when the inspector had the convicts strip for observation, he found that seven of the forty-five convicts showed signs of the strap. Two possessed extremely large scars. At some camps, convicts reportedly received random beatings for no offense, and at others they were beaten so severely they could not work.[61]

Beating was not the only systematic method of discipline in turpentine convict camps. Some wardens devised more cruel and unusual forms of punishment. They had convicts strung up by their thumbs and left teetering on their toes for hours. Others endured the especially cruel "ordeal by water" in which guards strapped down a prisoner, forced a funnel into his mouth,

59. Drobney, "Where Palm and Pine Are Blowing," 430; Drobney, *Lumbermen and Log Sawyers,* 170; Lemon Bay Turpentine Company, Noma Naval Stores Company, and Waller Turpentine Company, Prison Punishment Reports, 1914, Board of Commissioners of State Institutions Papers.

60. Lemon Bay Turpentine Company, Noma Naval Stores Company, and Waller Turpentine Company, Prison Punishment Reports, 1914, Board of Commissioners of State Institutions Papers.

61. N. A. Blitch to N. B. Broward, 6 March 1906 and 5 April 1906, Board of Commissioners of State Institutions Papers; Barry, "Slavery in the South To-Day," 486; Carper, "Convict-Lease System in Florida," 290.

and poured water down his throat. The victim's expanded stomach caused great pain and sometimes death.[62]

Spontaneous and brutal methods of punishment were employed on an individual basis as guards attempted to force convicts to work at a quicker pace in the forest. One convict, for example, experienced difficulty carrying his dip bucket in his sore, raw hand, but could not work rapidly enough while carrying it on his arm. A guard threatened him with death unless he worked to standard, and when he failed, the guard shot and killed him. At the largest turpentine business in Florida, a sick convict who failed to work was hung by handcuffs from a tree branch so that his feet dangled above the ground. When he screamed from the pain after twenty minutes, a guard severely beat him with a grape vine. In another incident, three convicts persisted in dipping inadequately after receiving warnings from the captain. Two submitted to punishment, but the third drew his hack and threatened the captain. The captain responded by striking him on the head with a tree limb. In yet another instance a convict fell from exhaustion on the march back to camp. The other convicts found him too heavy to carry. Ordering the other convicts on, the guard tied the exhausted prisoner to his saddle and dragged him for three miles along the road. The convict died the next morning. Evidence suggests that such brutality occurred more frequently at camps employing county convicts. Seventy-five percent of the reports of cruel and inhumane treatment originated in the county convict camps.[63]

Convicts suffered health problems, not only from abusive punishments, but associated with the demanding turpentine work and difficult life at the camp as well. The relentless hard labor with heavy, wooden-handled tools caused sore and blistered hands. Moreover, camp records indicated that convicts working in the naval stores industry suffered from respiratory diseases, bilious fever, intestinal ailments, and cuts. Contagious diseases could spread easily through the crowded camp quarters. For example, one-half of the convicts hospitalized at Camp Magnolia in Clinch County, Georgia, in 1895–96 had influenza. Prisoners suffered the greatest amount of illness and death during the summer months, when the heat was most intense. The rainy months of July and August also adversely affected convicts, who caught chills, fever, and pneumonia after working in water. "Dats de time it gits

62. Carper, "Convict-Lease System in Florida," 115; Drobney, "Where Palm and Pine Are Blowing," 429.

63. Carper, "Convict-Lease System in Florida," 115, 290; Drobney, "Where Palm and Pine Are Blowing," 429; N. A. Blitch to N. B. Broward, 6 March 1906 and 5 April 1906, and J. D. Ferrell to Park Trammell, 30 April 1913, Board of Commissioners of State Institutions Papers; Barry, "Slavery in the South To-Day," 486–7; *Eighth Biennial Report*, 308.

yo," one convict explained. "Mah Gawd, man, hit's sho' awful, standin' in watah an' runnin' all day long in the wet grass up to yo' waist." Failure of camps to provide adequate footwear in the wet environment appears to have been a persistent problem. At one camp in 1906 a prisoner cut his foot and preferred to work with it wrapped in a cloth rather than confined in an ill-fitting boot. Convicts at another camp were forced to work barefoot when their shoes wore out and the camp manager delayed acquiring new ones. In 1907 it was reported that at one turpentine camp no convict possessed a whole pair of shoes. There, the men had cut feet from working among the sharp saw palmetto. Such exposed cuts became infected from constant exposure and, in some instances, caused blood poisoning. Goodnow noticed that the convicts' feet at the camp he visited were "swollen and misshapen." "They were spread out, broken down, cut, gouged, blistered and scratched," he reported, "and the nails of many of their toes were gone." One convict explained that when men who were not used to the work first got to camp, their feet swelled so much that once in the stockade they went barefoot because their shoes no longer fit. Convicts also contended with diseases they brought with them into the camps, especially tuberculosis and venereal disease. In 1910 the governor of Florida estimated that 75 percent of black convicts suffered from various stages of syphilis.[64]

Georgia records for 1895 and 1896 indicate that turpentine camps had a much lower rate of hospitalization, 12 percent, than did the overall convict population, 39 percent. However, this statistic no doubt says more about the primitive and isolated nature of turpentine camps—which were notorious for lacking hospital facilities—than about the frequency of illness or injury. In fact the Georgia penitentiary physician complained that "under the present management the prisoners are frequently moved to places where there is no preparation to care for them, and on this account they suffer a great deal."[65]

Although it is difficult to know the exact rate of mortality for convict laborers in turpentine, it appears to have been twice as high as the overall prisoner population's. In general, mortality among all leased convicts varied depending on their treatment and the business in which they worked. Convicts leased to plantations tended to have a better chance of surviving to the

64. J. D. Howe to W. A. McRae, 30 August 1913, and N. A. Blitch to N. B. Broward, 5 April 1906, Board of Commissioners of State Institutions Papers; *Annual Report of the Principal Physician of the Georgia Penitentiary from October 1, 1895, to October 1, 1896* (Atlanta: George W. Harrison, State Printer, 1896), 109, 117–42; Goodnow, "Turpentine," 105–6; Barry, "Slavery in the South To-Day," 487; Drobney, "Where Palm and Pine Are Blowing," 428–9; Blount, "Spirits in the Pines," 164.

65. *Annual Report of the Principal Physician*, 110, 117–42.

end of their sentence than those who worked in coal mines, railroad camps, and turpentine operations. At their very worst, death rates could run as high as 25 percent. The annual death rate for Georgia's and Florida's convicts appears to have hovered just below 5 percent. But at some camps the frequency was higher. In 1899 twelve out of fifty-five convicts who labored at a Padgett, Florida, turpentine camp died. Located in a low palmetto flat, the camp was wet much of the year. Diseases—especially lung infections and intestinal problems—and inadequate medical treatment along with being shot while attempting to escape were the most common causes.[66]

Convicts who endured these difficult and sometimes fatal working and living conditions had limited means of voicing complaint. In the first years of Florida's lease program, the state had no knowledge, except for the name of the lessee, of exactly who was in charge of the convicts, under what conditions they worked and lived, or how often or brutally they were punished. By the late 1890s, however, the state began limited efforts to bring convict leasing under tighter state control. The commissioner of agriculture, who had charge of the Florida convict lease system, a state legislative committee, inspection agents who reported to the commissioner of agriculture, and a prison chaplain all made periodic visits to the convict camps. Every twelve to fifteen months the commissioner of agriculture made a short visit to each camp and interviewed the convicts to see if they had any complaints. Only rarely, though, did prisoners report any problems, knowing that, although their discussions with the commissioner were conducted in the warden's and guards' absence, the trustees would report the conversation. Convicts also understood all too well that the captain and guards would tell a different story and that they would more likely be believed. The same circumstances prevented convicts from discussing grievances with the legislative committee that visited camps every two years. In the days preceding the committee's visit, which was announced in advance, camp conditions underwent a transformation. Living quarters and clothes were cleaned, the food got better, and whippings decreased. State inspectors made more frequent visits than the legislative committee, but their observations were typically superficial and uncritical. One agent, for example, found all camps in generally good condition but at one recommended that a new bunkhouse be built. Another reported that he made "a tour of inspection of the several convict

66. Keeler, Crime of Crimes, 7; Oshinsky, "Worse Than Slavery," 67; Drobney, "Where Palm and Pine Are Blowing," 428; Blount, "Spirits in the Pines," 164; Mancini, One Dies, Get Another, 66; Carper, "Convict-Lease System in Florida," 130, 237–9; Eighth Biennial Report, 251–352; Goodnow, "Turpentine," 106; Commissioner of Agriculture to Florida Naval Stores and Com. Company, 5 April 1902, and N. A. Blitch to N. B. Broward, 15 April 1906, Board of Commissioners of State Institutions Papers; Seventh Annual Report, 15.

camps of the State, to correct certain abuses and improper use of authority which had been reported. In every camp except one—of which due report was made—we found the convicts well cared for, well fed and clothed, and but little sickness among them." The fact that at least one agent was a naval stores manufacturer himself calls into question the reliability of both the inspectors and monitoring system. Not only were inspectors less than thorough, one chaplain faced the daunting task of single-handedly visiting all the Florida camps. Even he admitted that "owing to their [the camps'] scattered condition under subleases, [I] cannot effect much good." During the second half of the 1890s, the chaplain visited fifteen of the sixteen camps every nine weeks, requiring him to travel annually between 2,250 and 2,500 miles, and preached between eighty-five and ninety sermons.[67]

Although they possessed severely limited ability to complain to officials, convicts in turpentine camps combated harsh conditions in other ways. One convict feigned insanity to avoid work. He began speaking gibberish and cut down a tree which he was supposed to be boxing. In response he was whipped "until he admitted the ruse and promised to drop it in the future," the camp manager reported. He had no more attacks after that. In a more dramatic attempt to avoid the hard work, another convict, while cutting boxes, drove his ax through his foot, cutting a severe gash. The wound healed well enough for him to get about sufficiently to split wood. Still miserable, he again cut his foot, but this time the deep wound refused to heal and he died of gangrene after suffering in agony. Other more desperate convicts attempted suicide. When a guard threatened to whip a convict for not working hard enough, the distraught prisoner, a black preacher sentenced for stealing cotton, used a boxing ax to slit his throat. He missed his jugular vein but severed his windpipe so severely that his tongue dropped through the gaping cut. He recovered after receiving stitching for the wound. In yet another instance a poor white man sent to prison for murdering his brother-in-law refused in disgust to chip faces. When threatened with a whipping, he defiantly ordered a guard to shoot him, then attempted to break his skull with the weighted end of his hack. He, too, survived his self-inflicted wound.[68]

67. Carper, "Convict-Lease System in Florida," 116; Drobney, *Lumbermen and Log Sawyers,* 156; *Tenth Biennial Report,* 384; "White Slavery in Florida," *New York Evening Post,* 12 February 1898; W. J. Hillman to W. D. Bloxham, 25 July 1903, Board of Commissioners of State Institutions Papers; *Report of the Commissioner of Agriculture of the State of Florida for the Period Beginning January 1, 1895, and Ending December 31, 1896* (Tallahassee: Florida Printing Co., 1897), 78–9; *Report of the Commissioner of Agriculture of the State of Florida for the Period Beginning January 1, 1889, and Ending December 31, 1890* (Jacksonville: DaCosta, 1891), 141; *Report of the Commissioner of Agriculture, 1897–1898,* 92.

68. Powell, *American Siberia,* 60–4.

Escape, however, was the most common form of resistance. Escapees represented a double loss for the camp. Not only did the producer lose the labor for which he had already paid, but if the convict was not caught within two months, the operator had to pay a two-hundred-dollar fine. Some convicts appear to a have attempted escape spontaneously out of desperation. One Florida convict in the 1890s tried to escape after the entire camp received fifty lashes one night for not chipping their required task. When they were threatened with the same punishment the next day, he tried to get away. Another convict used more cunning in escaping from a Florida turpentine camp. One night he succeeded in cutting his chain and sneaked off his bunk and toward the cell house door. When the patrolling guard turned his back, the convict pushed the backdoor wide open, blocking the guard's view of him, slipped around the side of the building, and left the camp never to be seen again. Other prisoners took advantage of the circumstances under which they labored to attempt escape. Because prisoners were not shackled while they worked and the forest in which they labored obstructed the guards' view of their activity, prisoners could, with relatively little difficulty, clear the range of the guards' rifles. Armed guards notwithstanding, the greatest deterrent from escape in the woods was reportedly the prisoners' fear of the hounds. On average, county camps kept four dogs for tracking escapees.[69]

The relatively high success rate for escape attempts did nothing to discourage the practice. In Georgia, where figures are relatively complete, 1,174 convicts escaped during the lease's forty-year existence. Florida's recapture rate was only about 50 percent. In some cases prisoners were able to slip away only to be captured a short time later. Some escapees were caught within a matter of days, but remaining on the run for half or a whole year was more common. One convict even eluded authorities for four years before being recaptured.[70]

Once they successfully made it out of the camp, four conditions aided convicts in eluding authorities. First, there existed no procedural method for

69. Inspectors' reports, September 1913 to February 1914, J. D. Ferrell to W. A. McRae, 29 March 1913, and R. R. Tomlin to W. A. McRae, 31 July 1913, Board of Commissioners of State Institutions Papers; Goodnow, "Turpentine," 104–6; *Eighth Biennial Report,* 330; *Ninth Biennial Report,* 285; Drobney, "Where Palm and Pine Are Blowing," 424.

70. Coulter, *James Monroe Smith,* 69; Carper, "Convict-Lease System in Florida," 118; Powell, *American Siberia,* 79; Mancini, *One Dies, Get Another,* 68; *Report of the Commissioner of Agriculture, 1897–1898,* 90; Drobney, "Where Palm and Pine Are Blowing," 424; Drobney, *Lumbermen and Log Sawyers,* 162; Goodnow, "Turpentine," 106; F. J. Titeaub to W. A. McRae, 28 February 1914, and N. A. Blitch to N. B. Broward, 5 April 1906, Board of Commissioners of State Institutions Papers; *Eighth Biennial Report,* 347–50.

capturing convicts; camp bosses and guards coordinated the effort as best they could. If a convict successfully slipped away from a camp, guards and hounds—trained to track prisoners during mock escape attempts—began searching for his trail. Many convict camps used foxhounds for this task because their slower speed enabled the mounted guards to keep up with them. However, if the hounds failed to track an escapee within a few hours of his departure, the likelihood of his recapture dropped to less than 30 percent. Second, within the piney woods South there was a great demand for black labor, especially workers who already possessed skills in turpentining. Escaped convicts found little difficulty in securing employment in out-of-the-way naval stores operations, which hid them from recapture. Third, the area's poor white citizens, who tended to despise the black convicts but often hated the convict-lease system even more, sometimes agreed to assist escapees in an effort to discredit the practice. Fourth, the wild, inhospitable countryside surrounding camps offered a safe haven for runaways. Some parts of the turpentine belt, especially the area closest to the Gulf, were vast swamps with virtually impenetrably thick vegetation and very little settlement, even by the standards of the sparsely populated piney woods region. The escapees who lived in this coastal region survived off what the wilderness provided. They occasionally emerged from their hideouts only to purchase such supplies as powder and shot. Historian Matthew Mancini concludes that "literally thousands of escaped convicts must have inhabited the late-nineteenth-century Southern landscape." Because recapturing convicts proved difficult once they made their way away from camp, if guards happened to see them on the run, they shot them. Apparently guards used little restraint with their aim, shooting to kill rather than merely to halt the fleeing prisoner. At one Florida camp, for example, a guard shot an escaping convict twice and, once he was down, shot him a third time. The convict died a lingering death. In Florida from 1874 to 1920, an average of seven state convicts died each year from gunshot wounds they received while trying to escape.[71]

Despite the long hours of hard work and the less-than-ideal living conditions, convicts at some camps found time for recreation. State rules forbidding card playing and profane language notwithstanding, Florida convicts amused themselves with games of poker, dirty jokes, dancing, and singing. One visitor to a camp witnessed convicts singing and telling jokes in the dining room. While he was there, the convicts entertained him with an orig-

71. Drobney, *Lumbermen and Log Sawyers*, 162; Powell, *American Siberia*, 24, 31, 324–5, 324–6; Mancini, *One Dies, Get Another*, 68; Carper, "Convict-Lease System in Florida," 118; Blount, "Spirits in the Pines," 164; "Horrible Treatment of Convicts."

inal skit, "The Old Plantation." Another day they played a six-inning baseball
game. "It was crude, of course, but full of life," the observer explained, "each
side bantering and joking with the other over an error or a 'strike-out.'" The
catcher and the first baseman used gloves fashioned of hemp sacking stuffed
with straw. The other men used their bare hands.[72]

Although peonage and convict labor each represented an entirely different method of forced labor, in places lines between the two systems blurred.
At some camps convicts and peons worked together and occasionally lived
together. Many peons were threatened with the chain gang if they misbe-
haved. When workers were given a choice, peonage was the logical preference over the lease. Peonage at least allowed the worker to remain with
family and friends and permitted him relatively more autonomy at work and
in the quarters. Peonage and convict leasing were also linked in that both
depended on the collusion of local officials and large operators. If paid workers complained or tried to escape from their employer, the latter could have
them charged for a petty crime, pay their fine, and thus gain legal rights to
their labor while they worked off the debt. In some counties where the turpentine operators were especially powerful, they could have their workers
arrested on trumped-up charges and, once they were convicted and sentenced, lease them as convict labor. Such a circumstance became easier to
create in the first part of the twentieth century, when Florida passed an act
making it a misdemeanor to accept money or goods for labor and fail to
perform the work; the violation carried a $500 fine. Thus, workers charged
with violating labor contracts faced stiff fines, as well as court costs which
were far too high for them to pay and would ultimately lead them into a
convict work camp. Twenty percent of the Florida convicts working on
county farms or turpentine camps in 1907 had been sentenced for violating
labor contracts.[73]

Despite convict leasing's characteristically brutal nature and distinction
as a form of forced labor, the practice, whether used in industrial pursuits
or in agriculture, represented neither a form of slavery nor a functional replacement for it. Although both systems were forms of forced labor, they
each operated quite differently. First, slaveholders carried the cost of sus-

72. *Eighth Biennial Report,* 330, 347–50; Goodnow, "Turpentine," 105–6; Drobney, "Where
Palm and Pine Are Blowing," 425.

73. Mancini, *One Dies, Get Another,* 196; Carper, "Slavery Revisited," 97; Shofner, "Forced
Labor," 20–2; Register, interview; E. V. Meadows to John E. Wilkie, 5 September 1906, and
A. J. Hogh to United States Attorney General, 4 February 1907, Correspondence, Classified
Subject Files, Department of Justice Central Files; "Peonage in the South," 1617; Barry, "Slav-
ery in the South To-Day," 488–9; John Bonyne Report, 3 May 1922, Cubberly Papers; Tegeder,
"Prisoners of the Pines," 223, 109; Drobney, *Lumbermen and Log Sawyers,* 172.

taining the entire slave community, which included such relatively unproductive members as the elderly, the sick, and young children. Convict employers concerned themselves almost exclusively with productive men. A second difference is the low financial interest that the lessee had in the convict. Whereas each slave represented a considerable investment to his owner, a lessee had little long-term financial stake in an individual convict. The latter's death, release, or escape consequently did not represent a significant loss. One early-twentieth-century reformer found that "the lessee has no interest in the convict except to secure the largest amount of labor in a given time. What matters it to him if the convict's health is broken down? There are plenty of more convicts." This endless supply reinforced the cruel treatment of convicts, who were important to their employer only as a group not as individuals. By contrast each slave was valued as capital. But despite the smaller value of individual convicts compared to slaves, financial cost of convict leasing could present a greater problem than slave ownership when seasonal work cycles or economic downturns created periodic idleness, during which time the maintenance cost for the entire convict workforce continued. Whereas individual slaves could be sold or hired out, convicts were leased in lots and, until changes in state legislation, could not be subleased.[74]

This particular economic drawback aside, analysis of convict leasing in the turpentine industry largely supports recent scholarship that argues that convict leasing helped to modernize the southern economy by providing a cheap and reliable labor force for a region short of investment capital. Edward Ayers contends that the convict-lease system helped in the transition from an agricultural economy to one of fuller capitalist development by providing reliable labor at a fixed and predictable price and therefore helping produce quick profits. Convicts could be driven to work at a more rapid pace and for longer hours than free workers would tolerate and at difficult jobs that free workers shunned. Charles K. Dutton, a New Yorker and head of a large naval stores company, explained that he leased Florida convicts because "turpentine culture was exhausting work, and it was difficult to obtain enough labor for the proper cultivation of any great number of trees. Natives of Florida's piney woods would quickly abandon the work when any other type of livelihood became available."[75]

74. Mancini, *One Dies, Get Another*, 20–4; Keeler, *Crime of Crimes*, 14.
75. Carper, "Convict-Lease System in Florida," 49–50, 143–4; Drobney, *Lumbermen and Log Sawyers*, 151; Jerrell H. Shofner, "Negro Laborers and the Forest Industries in Reconstruction Florida," *Journal of Forest History* 19 (October 1975): 183; Clark, *Greening of the South*, 22; Oshinsky, *"Worse Than Slavery,"* 70; Ayers, *Vengeance and Justice*, 4, 185, 191–3.

Alex Lichtenstein agrees that convict leasing supplied a reliable and pre-dictable labor force required of the South's developing iron mines, railroad construction projects, brickyards, sawmills, and turpentine camps. Instead of repressing the region's industrial economy, he argues, "convict labor was a central component in the South's modernization." The region was poor in capital and rich in natural resources, and convict labor offered a solution for industrial growth. Lichtenstein finds that economic modernization is com-monly tied to forced labor as producers attempt to control workers who re-sist entering wage labor relationships, a situation that was especially so among naval stores producers. He explains that "the combination of labor uncertainty, production on a narrow margin, destructive methods of extrac-tion, seasonality, geographic mobility, and isolation encouraged many tur-pentine operators to look to the county courts for their labor supply." Forced labor, he argues, is also often a necessary phase in the process of capital accumulation that enables capitalist development. Finding itself at an eco-nomic disadvantage with so little investment capital, the South used forced labor to spur its economic progress without upsetting the traditional racial order. Lichtenstein concludes that "progress is not necessarily progressive for all peoples, and that the bearers of modernity frequently carry with them its antithesis." But whereas the manner in which producers employed con-victs in the naval stores industry certainly fits this argument, the relatively small number of such workers involved in turpentine manufacture, less than 10 percent, calls into question the degree to which the industry owed its continuation to convict leasing.[76]

When combined with similar findings by other scholars who examine the restricted freedom of wage laborers, however, the broader argument that varying forms and degrees of forced labor helped the South develop econom-ically appears valid with regard to the naval stores industry. David L. Carlton maintains that although peonage was not unique to the South, the practice was more widespread in the region because of the undercapitalized economy that consisted primarily of export agriculture and extractive industries and required routinized and relatively unskilled labor. It is therefore not surpris-ing, Pete Daniel adds, that the cotton belt, especially the Mississippi Delta; the turpentine region, particularly south Georgia, north Florida, and south-ern Alabama and Mississippi; and railroad construction camps throughout the South produced the most peonage complaints. Michael Tegeder, in his doctoral dissertation on Florida turpentine workers who labored as peons in the early twentieth century, finds no contradiction between forced labor and

76. Lichtenstein, *Twice the Work of Free Labor*, xv–xvii, 4–5, 11–3, 19–20, 170–1, 187–8, 195.

economic development as well as no significant divide between planters and industrialists or antebellum and postbellum economies. He maintains that "continuities in the development of forced labor in southern turpentine production were not incompatible with the postbellum process of modernization." Turpentiners, who commonly struggled under debt themselves and could expect low profit margins at best, sought financial relief by reducing their labor costs to barely more than subsistence wages. Labor expenses accounted for between 50 and 60 percent of production costs, and unlike costs of leases, tools, and supplies, which were fixed, the producer had some control over them. Forced labor offered the turpentiner the ability to pay low wages and still enjoy a relatively reliable labor supply.[77]

Both the naval stores industry's pre- and post-war reliance on forced labor and the workers' antebellum and postbellum experiences represent a relative degree of continuity. Labor laws—enticement, emigrant agent, vagrancy, and contract legislation—and the movement of free labor that they restricted, combined with convict leasing, forced many southern blacks to toil at turpentine production against their will. Although most such workers received wages, often low and based on piecework, the legal system and close surveillance by camp managers commonly left laborers little choice in terms of their employment. They continued to work at the same tasks as before the war and to live in camps that remained isolated, primitive, and transient. Unbridled revelry at the juke joint and an occasional trip to the nearest town broke the monotony. For convicts, work requirements were greater, the living conditions more isolated and crude, and the brutality visited upon them more intense than those of wage laborers. Although these conditions could also be found in other areas of southern business such as agriculture and especially the lumber industry, they were perhaps more broadly characteristic of the naval stores industry. So entrenched were the labor practices that early-twentieth-century government reform efforts met strong opposition and enjoyed only limited success.

77. Carlton, "Revolution from Above," 447; Daniel, *Shadow of Slavery*, 21; Tegeder, "Prisoners of the Pines," 13–5, 21–2, 49, 52.

Burning a tar kiln in North Carolina. From Porte Crayon, "North Carolina Illustrated: The Piney Woods," *Harper's New Monthly Magazine* 14 (May 1857): 774.

"Box" cutting near Ocilla, Georgia, 1903. U.S. Forest Service, courtesy Forest History Society.

Worker chipping a face, ca. 1900. Courtesy North Carolina Collection, University of North Carolina Library at Chapel Hill.

"Turpenting in the South Atlantic Country," by Albert Pridgen. From *Naval Stores: History, Production, Distribution, and Consumption*, ed. Thomas Gamble (Savannah: Review Publishing and Printing, 1921), 103.

Scraping the face, ca. 1910. Courtesy Florida Photographic Collection, Florida Bureau of Archives and Records Management.

A North Carolina turpentine distillery. From Frederick Law Olmsted, *A Journey in the Seaboard Slave States* (New York: Dix and Edwards, 1856), 344.

Naval stores dock, Savannah, Georgia. Author's collection.

Plant and yards of Yaryan Naval Stores Company, Brunswick, Georgia. Author's collection.

Homes of turpentine workers
near Godwinsville, Georgia.
Dorothea Lange, 1937.
Courtesy Library of Congress.

Tracking a runaway convict through a Florida pine forest. From Richard Barry,
"Slavery in the South To-Day," *Cosmopolitan* 42 (March 1907): 483.

Gutters and cup unraised. From U.S. Forest Service, *A Pictorial Album of the Naval Stores Industry* (U.S. Government Printing Office, 1937), courtesy Forest History Society.

Attaching cups and gutters, 1930s. Courtesy Florida Photographic Collection, Florida Bureau of Records and Management.

CHAPTER 7

GOVERNMENT, FRIEND AND FOE

DURING THE FIRST DECADES of the twentieth century, increased government involvement in the naval stores industry proved a mixed blessing. On the one hand, the business, with considerable assistance from the newly formed federal Bureau of Forestry, at long last began to adopt less destructive production methods than those employed since production began in the American colonies centuries earlier. University-trained researchers pioneered practices that not only yielded a higher-grade gum than the older practice of boxing, but also caused less harm to the tree. Their successes then fostered a more receptive environment for scientific forestry among many producers, thus allowing for further improvements. The naval stores industry benefited from federal forestry efforts as well as from research and experiments conducted by the Bureau of Chemistry. Where the Bureau of Forestry focused on improving gum harvesting, the Bureau of Chemistry worked to advance the distilling and marketing of turpentine and rosin. At the same time that federal agencies introduced significant beneficial changes to the conservative industry, the government led a series of attacks on the systems of forced labor that supported it. The United States Department of Justice began investigations of suspected producers for violation of the Thirteenth Amendment. Press coverage of the investigation focused national attention on the widespread use of peonage and spurred public outcry that drove the institution underground. With the same zeal, reformers also attacked convict leasing. Although not as widely practiced within the naval stores industry as peonage, convict leasing proved less capable of withstanding organized national opposition and state government Progressive reform efforts.

By the 1890s, North Carolina's southern neighbors could foresee forest devastation similar to what had already occurred in the Tar Heel State. In fact, South Carolina entered an advanced stage of depletion as early as the 1880s. The rapid destruction of that state's longleafs was reflected in a pessimistic South Carolinian's comment in 1884 that "the turpentine business [is] almost at an end as the trees are skinned to death so our future is not *rose-colored*." Even in Georgia some producers by the 1880s were moving on after exploiting the original acres they had come to turpentine. In 1881 Joseph A. Backer and Company, which had collected turpentine from forests served by the Brunswick and Albany Railroad, had already exhausted fourteen thousand acres and was then working ten crops on about two thousand acres with twenty laborers. In states where turpentining remained vigorous, increases in production came at the expense of younger and younger pines as the old virgin stands disappeared. In an 1897 report prepared for the Department of Agriculture's new Division of Forestry, forester Charles Mohr explained that turpentine orchards were commonly abandoned after four years because the gum quality was not thought to be profitable enough to justify working the older boxes. As a result, larger trees were disappearing and producers were forced to use smaller pines. Before the late 1890s, producers rarely boxed trees with diameters smaller than fourteen inches. But by 1897 they commonly worked trees smaller than ten inches across. The disease, decay, and fire that often killed abandoned turpentine trees prevented these smaller worked trees from maturing and reproducing.[1]

Although the destruction associated with turpentining as well as lumbering was widely recognized by nineteenth-century southerners, many at the time viewed the forest clearance as a sign of spreading civilization and as the inevitable price of progress. Thomas Clark explains that a large percentage of the population held the centuries-old folk belief that untamed forests represented a barrier to civilized society. Agriculture, not forest-product production, they believed, was the way to regional development. In 1912 the *Weekly Naval Stores Review* declared that "the pine forests must be swept away in a large measure to make way for the agriculturalist." Many southerners, in fact, viewed the timber almost as a nuisance. One booster explained that "to utilize the land for agriculture the timber must be cut off. . . . It is fortunate that our timber has great commercial value, because the process of clearing the land brings a handsome return to the land owner; but if the timber was

1. T. P. Baily to Doctor, 16 February 1884, Thomas J. Makie Papers, Special Collections Library, Duke University; Tillman and Goodyear, *Southern Georgia*, 49; Mohr, *Timber Pines of the Southern United States*, 69, 70, 72.

commercially valueless, we should then be forced to cut it down and burn it."[2]

Furthermore, many southerners saw the rapid and complete exploitation of timber as their only means of raising their standard of living. Even if they viewed large northern-owned lumber companies as encroaching resource exploiters, lumber products were so central to the late-nineteenth-century way of life that both the public and the federal government saw no choice but to tolerate their practices. James C. Cobb maintains that "in cases where residents of the New South were expected to choose between conservation and economic gain, the latter almost always won out." While ignoring the problems of forest depletion, southerners, like the forest-product producers, accepted the fatalistic view that exploitation was inevitable. A pamphlet promoting Georgia commented that turpentine orchards "already cover large areas, and the industry is not likely to slacken till the pine is exhausted." The pamphlet admitted that "timber once cut from these lands cannot be replaced. It is the growth of centuries."[3] As late as 1921 Thomas Gamble, the editor of the *Weekly Naval Stores Review,* argued that although lumbermen and turpentiners might have exploited the Deep South's timber resources, their activity was necessary to build up the region.

> The pine trees of Georgia and Florida and Alabama brought fortunes to many among the factors and operators. There is a feeling, more sentimental than practical, that this section gave away its heritage in the sacrifice of its forests and the sale of its timber and lumber and naval stores at low values. It is true that in some reasons the financial returns were unsatisfactory. But the states in question could not remain a wilderness of pines. The advancing wave of humanity demanded homes and the fact that while the lands were being cleared thousands and tens of thousands derived a livelihood from turpentining and saw milling, while many acquired a comfortable competence and some large fortunes, and that the wealth thus derived was used for the upbuilding of this section in railroad construction and in agriculture and industrial development, compensated for this passing of the pine.[4]

2. T. D. Clark, *Greening of the South,* 14; "At Other Naval Stores Ports of the South," *Weekly Naval Stores Review* 22 (27 June 1912), 66; Tillman and Goodyear, *Southern Georgia,* 59.

3. M. Williams, *Americans and Their Forests,* 20; Cobb, *Industrialization and Southern Society,* 125; Tillman and Goodyear, *Southern Georgia,* 48, 59.

4. Gamble, "Savannah as a Naval Stores Port," 61.

Some southerners dealt with the region's timber disappearance by simply failing to admit that the problem existed. They ignored the reality of the pine's consumption, incorrectly believing that ample resources remained and complete depletion lay only in the distant future. For instance, prospective settlers to south Georgia were assured that although "the lands about Hoboken and Schlatterville have been turpentined and partially denuded by cutting for the mill, . . . there is still a superabundance of timber for all practical and desirable purposes."[5]

It appears to have been some nonsoutherners who were the first to begin viewing the loss of the southern pine forest as an avoidable disgrace. In the mid-1870s, concerned Americans, many of them from the North who had watched their own timber disappear into sawmills, began efforts to conserve the nation's forests. Conservation pioneer George Perkins Marsh advocated the preservation of large timbered areas in a "natural" or "primitive" condition. At the same time, the American Association for the Advancement of Science established a committee for the promotion of federal and state legislation to protect forests and encourage timber cultivation. Partly as a result of the association's efforts, Congress in 1876 appropriated funds for a forestry agent at the Department of Agriculture, and by 1886 forestry advocates had their own division. In 1884 the Department of the Interior issued its first ever *Report on the Forests of North America* as part of the Tenth Census. With a sympathy for conservation issues, northern readers of turn-of-the-century muckraking periodicals were horrified to learn of the southern pine forest's rapid disappearance. Writing in 1891 for the magazine *Garden and Forest*, published in New York City for a popular audience, C. G. Pringle revealed that "of the extravagant methods which prevail in the United States none certainly exceeds in extravagance that under which the turpentine industry of the south is conducted; and there is no business connected with the products of the soil which yields so little return in proportion to the destruction of material involved." Pringle explained how the harvesting of gum to supply one still for three years used up fifteen thousand acres. At the time, 266 turpentine stills operated in Georgia. Therefore every three years nearly four million acres in Georgia alone was consumed for turpentine. In a 1903 issue of *The World's Work*, Overton W. Price, assistant forester for the Bureau of Forestry, explained to reform-minded readers that "there is no more deplorable sight to the man who has a sense of the value of trees than the abandoned turpentine orchard—a grim array of mutilated trunks, scorched and charred where the box is made, broken by the wind, infested

---

5. Martin, "American Gum Naval Stores Industry," 92–3, 101–3; M. Williams, *Americans and Their Forests*, 279, 283–4; Tillman and Goodyear, *Southern Georgia*, 52.

by insects, and worthless except to illustrate the futility of killing the goose which lays the golden eggs. The South is full of such pictures."[6]

Roughly twenty years after it arose in the North, interest in conservation began expanding across the South. Environmental historian Albert Cowdrey identifies three late-nineteenth-century developments that pushed the region toward support of conservation: depletion of resources, growth of organization, and the development of science. The South by 1900 could find much about the conservation movement to support. It offered the region improvements in agriculture, forestry, river basin planning, and public health. These improvements fit well with the New South Creed, which sought efficient resource use and development and was not shy about accepting outside help or leadership to accomplish these ends. Gifford Pinchot, as director of the Bureau of Forestry, won the region's timber product industries over to scientific forestry by offering considerable assistance to their resource management efforts, help they readily accepted.[7]

As influential men with business interests in southern forests warmed to conservation and the new field of forestry, state efforts, aimed at the wise use of remaining stands, began. In 1894, North Carolina produced a report on the condition of the timberlands in the eastern portion of the state, and two years later Alabama began a similar study. The most important and sustained effects, however, originated in the early twentieth century. In 1904, progressive Louisiana lumberman Henry E. Hardtner, who in the late nineteenth century began purchasing cutover land and reseeding it, convinced the Louisiana state legislature to create a Department of Forestry, although the state failed to fund the project. By the 1910s the pace of southern forestry development quickened. Virginia, Texas, North Carolina, and Louisiana organized divisions of forestry. Some southern colleges began offering forestry courses, and in 1914 Georgia established the region's first school of forestry. Later that same year, the Southern Pine Association was organized, and in 1916 the Southern Forestry Congress held its first meeting. Organized by the North Carolina state geologist Joseph Hyde Pratt, forester John S. Holmer, and Hardtner, the Southern Forestry Congress sought to address the region's forest problems. In an effort to encourage the regrowth of for-

6. M. Williams, *Americans and Their Forests,* 18–9; Cowdrey, *This Land, This South,* 103, 119–20, 135–6; United States Department of the Interior, *Report on the Forests of North America, Exclusive of Mexico* (Washington, D.C.: 1884); Pringle, "Waste in the Turpentine Industry," 49–50; Overton W. Price, "Saving the Southern Forests," *World's Work* 5 (March 1903): 3214.

7. M. Williams, *Americans and Their Forests,* 18–9; Cowdrey, *This Land, This South,* 103, 119–20, 135–6.

ests, between 1924 and 1927 all the naval stores–producing states established forest extension services.[8]

Alarmed by the rapidly approaching disappearance of the longleaf pine forest, both the federal and state governments, as well as some individual producers, made attempts, beginning in the late nineteenth century, to improve the turpentine industry's use of the South's declining timber supply. One of the first efforts was to determine the appropriate use of turpentined timber for lumber. Both lumbermen and consumers believed that turpentined pines were unfit for lumber because the drain of resin from the wood reduced its strength. The lumber and naval stores industries consequently used different timber tracts. The annual loss of wasted boxed timber in *each* of the states of North Carolina, South Carolina, Georgia, Florida, Alabama, and Mississippi amounted to between three and ten billion board feet, worth several million dollars. In an effort to end the timber loss, during the 1890s the Department of Agriculture conducted investigations on the mechanical, physical, and chemical attributes of turpentined and unturpentined wood. Tests showed that turpentined trees were just as strong as round timber and that turpentining did not affect the wood's weight or cause shrinkage. Thus the Agriculture Department concluded that turpentined trees were appropriate for the same uses as round ones. The discovery made more timber available for sawmills, but did nothing to reduce the destructiveness of gum harvesting.[9]

In a small area of the old naval stores–manufacturing region, producers attempted to remedy the industry's characteristic forest degradation by adopting sustainable harvesting practices based on the traditional methods. The change was forced by necessity more than by choice. North Carolinians had almost completely eliminated the longleaf stands in the southeastern corner of their state, but by the 1890s, the few remaining turpentiners had turned to more conservative practices. In the Cape Fear area, small producers were said to work their trees for ten or more successive years, all the while protecting them from fire. After allowing the trees to rest for a few years, operators then cut new boxes in the space left between the old boxes. These orchards had been harvested for between twenty to thirty-five years.

8. Vinson, "Conservation and the South," 124–5; Cowdrey, *This Land, This South,* 137; Davis, ed., *Encyclopedia of American Forest,* s.v. "naval stores"; Martin, "American Gum Naval Stores Industry," 139–40.

9. Martin, "American Gum Naval Stores Industry," 91–2; Schorger and Betts, *Naval Stores Industry* (Washington, D.C.: United States Department of Agriculture, 1915), 40; Brown, *Forest Products,* 181–3; Charles Mohr, "Effect of 'Boxing' or 'Bleeding,'" 1–2, Cary Collection; Martin, "American Gum Naval Stores Industry," 92; Brower and La Fontisee, "Report of the Investigation on the Naval Stores Industry," 26–7.

Some stands in Sampson and Bladen Counties were said to have been worked intermittently since 1845 and by the early 1890s continued to yield considerable quantities of gum.[10]

In areas where longleaf depletion was not yet as widespread as in North Carolina, a search was on for a way to harvest gum intensely without destroying the tree. Some efforts were less practical than others. An invention by a Savannah man in the early 1880s, consisting of a steam boiler mounted on a set of wheels with ten forty-yard-long flexible hoses attached to it, proved far too technical and cumbersome to receive producers' consideration. A more promising improvement appeared at the 1895 Atlanta Cotton States and International Exposition, where several exhibits focused on southern trees and the naval stores industry. At one booth, J. C. Schuler, a German-born turpentiner who had been producing in the South since the Civil War, displayed a method of using clay cups to collect turpentine. The method was said by a reporter to have "the advantage of reducing considerably the danger which 'boxed' trees are subjected to by fire, while the quality of the product is improved and the individual tree is less injured than it is by the method now generally adopted in the United States." The Exposition's exhibit judges awarded Schuler's invention the silver medal.[11]

Despite its acclaim, Schuler's system was not new; French turpentiners had made regular use of a similar method for over thirty years. Until 1860, French producers collected resin in small holes that they dug in the sand at the base of the tapped trees. Not surprisingly, this method resulted in an inability to collect all the resin as well as the contamination of what portion was gathered with sand and debris. The replacement of sand holes with clay cups began in 1840, but failed to gain much attention until the early 1860s, when world turpentine prices soared because of the interruption in the United States' trade. As French production expanded, the drive for greater productivity made the cup system popular. The system followed roughly the same production schedule as the box system. But instead of cutting a box, the French made an incision at the tree's base into which they hammered a gutter used to guide the gum into a one-quart clay pot, or sometimes a zinc cup, hung at the end of the gutter. The French chipped the faces above the cup from forty to fifty times each season, around fifteen more times than U.S. producers. The extra chipping did not lead to a higher face, since the

10. Mohr, *Timber Pines of the Southern United States*, 70; Ashe, *Forests, Forest Lands, and Forest Products*, 85–6.

11. "A New Idea in Turpentine Orcharding," *Manufacturers Record*, 6 October 1883, clipping in Turpentine News Clipping File; "Exhibitions," *Garden and Forest* 8 (November 1895): 449.

French made smaller scars with each chipping; in both countries the face rose about twenty inches a season. The French system had two distinct advantages over the American one. It prolonged the tree's use for turpentine by reducing injury to the trunk, and it gave a higher-grade product because the cups could be raised each year, preventing the gum from having to run down the ever-increasing length of the face.[12]

Americans learned about the French innovation soon after the Civil War ended and made sporadic efforts to emulate it. In all, between 1868 and 1895 inventors, including Schuler, registered eleven patents for turpentine-collecting devices. But by 1895, Schuler's Atlanta exhibit represented the only sustained effort to develop the cup system in the United States. Beginning his experiments around 1870, Schuler finally met relative success in 1893. Working on a tract of land owned by a railroad company and located about twenty-five miles north of Lake Charles, Louisiana, he was able to collect 25 percent more gum from his cup than from a box; moreover, the gum was of a higher quality. This method of turpentining was, however, more expensive than the traditional box method. The cost of working a crop for two seasons using the cup method was $460 instead of $190. But this increased cost was expected to be offset by the cups' increased yield and the higher turpentine and rosin grades that the gum produced. Moreover, Schuler claimed that his less-damaging method made turpentining a sustainable practice.[13]

Although Schuler received some coverage in timber industry periodicals, his limited means left him unable to continue his experiments or promote his system. He claimed to have made money in turpentining but lost these profits in "other investments." In 1894 he wrote to Bernhard E. Fernow, the Division of Forestry director in Washington, describing his new process. Schuler apparently received no support. By 1895 he was making his best effort to promote his system himself. His Atlanta exhibit was one method. It must have made somewhat of an impression, for one visitor wrote that his

12. Schorger and Betts, *Naval Stores Industry*, 19, 32; Ashe, *Forests, Forest Lands, and Forest Products*, 94, 96–9; Charles H. Herty, "New Method of Turpentine Orcharding," 15–6.

13. Dyer, "History of the Gum Naval Stores Industry," 7; Hough, *Report upon Forestry*, 1:140–2; Davis, *Encyclopedia of American Forest*, 475–6; Germaine M. Reed, *Crusading for Chemistry: The Professional Career of Charles Holmes Herty* (Athens: University of Georgia Press, 1995), 19; Ashe, *Forests, Forest Lands, and Forest Products*, 100–3; Herty, "New Method of Turpentine Orcharding," 15; Schorger and Betts, *Naval Stores Industry*, 19; Butler, *Treasures of the Longleaf Pines*, 44–5, 227; J. C. Schuler to B. E. Fernow, 5 October 1894, Turpentine News Clipping File; "Turpentine Orchards in South-West Louisiana—A New Process," *Southern Lumberman* (April 1895), clipping in Turpentine News Clipping File; Mohr, *Timber Pines of the Southern United States*, 71–2.

system "either in its present form or with some further modifications seems destined to add millions of dollars to the productive value of the Pine forests of the southern states." Schuler also printed his own pamphlets advertising the benefits of his "Great Timber Process of the South." But despite Schuler's attempts, his cup system failed to attract wide attention. By the end of the nineteenth century, the old destructive box method remained alive and well. In 1897 the *Jacksonville Citizen* reported that "many inventors have tried to devise an artificial box to be tacked or glued to the tree . . . but all these inventions have proven a failure, and have been discarded by practical men."[14]

The difficulty that the turpentine industry experienced in improving its technology was typical of other southern industries. Inadequate investment capital, absence of industry researchers and engineers, and conservative producers who preferred traditional and proven methods made innovation unlikely. Most turpentine producers lacked the capital to invest in equipment like cups. By the 1890s especially, narrow profit margins prevented the accumulation of money necessary to purchase new technology. Furthermore, turpentine producers lacked the resources required to hire scientists and engineers to develop, demonstrate, and endorse improvements. In 1921, naval stores researcher Robson Dunwody recounted that "the advancement or reward of individuals because of better methods introduced or results obtained, was seldom encouraged. As a consequence, few men of technical or other training particularly fitting them for this work, were attracted to the industry, and this has no doubt accounted for the slow progress along these lines, that has always characterized the manufacture of naval stores." Although the newly created U.S. Bureau of Forestry and the state of North Carolina expressed interest in developing a new system, they failed to follow through with experiments. Schuler lacked the means to convince an understandably skeptical group of producers to pay a large sum and go through the difficulty of converting to the system. Schuler had no special training in forestry or biology. The fact that he eventually went broke did nothing to enhance his argument for the cup system's financial feasibility.[15]

Despite the failure of late-nineteenth-century efforts to develop a less destructive gum-harvesting technique, an inventor in 1900 attempted to find a new way. Born in Milledgeville, Georgia, in 1867 and educated at the Uni-

14. J. C. Schuler to B. E. Fernow, 5 October 1894; J. C. Schuler, "The Great Turpentine Saving Process of the South" and "Big Florida Industry," *Jacksonville Citizen*, 7 September 1897, clippings in Turpentine News Clipping File; "Exhibitions," 449; Dunwody, "Proper Methods of Distillation," 127.

15. Dunwody, "Proper Methods of Distillation," 129.

versity of Georgia and the Johns Hopkins University, Dr. Charles H. Herty sailed to Germany in 1899 to continue his chemistry studies. Although trained as a "pure" chemist in the United States, his experiences in Germany led him to believe that he could best use his education for practical ends. He was especially interested in advancing his native South's economic condition by improving the region's existing industries and helping it develop the technology to start new ones. His interests in the turpentine industry were stirred by his favorite lecturer in Charlottenburg, Germany, who described the American turpentine industry as "butchery" and insisted that, without change, it would disappear. The most conservative estimates of the day predicted that, at the then current rate of boxing, virgin timber supplies would disappear before 1920. The reduced timber acreage by the turn of the century was not only reflected in higher prices, but was visually obvious as well. In 1901, one Georgia resident recalled that "in 1864 when I first went over the railroad from Savannah to Thomasville there was an almost unbroken forest of magnificent pines extending from Bryan to Thomas Co. through which the railroad cut its way like a ditch—but now one may go over the same rout [sic] and scarcely see a merchantable pine." Saving the industry from the wasteful practices that created such a scene was just the crusade Herty had sought.[16]

Herty spent the academic year of 1900–01 serving on the faculty at the University of Georgia and contemplating the problems of American turpentine production methods. He corresponded with producers and visited South Georgia to view firsthand the effects that traditional gum-harvesting practices had on the pine trees. He learned how the destructive methods had driven the industry southward, and he closely examined the problems boxing caused. Along with making field observations, Herty studied literature that fully explained the French system of gum collection and reviewed the U.S. Patent Office records to determine what had already been tried. He was fully aware that French turpentine producers had used the cup and gutter system for decades and that American inventors had attempted similar methods. What was needed and previous experimental processes had lacked,

16. Herty, *New Method of Turpentine Orcharding*, 9–10; Schorger and Betts, *Naval Stores Industry*, 1–2; T. D. Clark, *Greening of the South*, 37, 162; J. P. Williams to Charles H. Herty, 20 November 1900, and Archibald Smith to Charles H. Herty, 7 June 1901, Charles Holmes Herty Collection, Special Collections, Robert W. Woodruff Library, Emory University; "Turpentine Industry," *New York Tribune*, 26 January 1902, clipping in Turpentine News Clipping File; Gerry Reed, "Saving the Naval Stores Industry: Charles Holmes Herty's Cup-and-Gutter Experiments, 1900–1905," *Journal of Forest History* 26 (October 1982): 168; Reed, *Crusading for Chemistry*, 12, 14.

he believed, was an economical system that allowed the harvesting practices to remain as little changed as possible.[17]

In the spring of 1901 Herty began to lay the groundwork for his initial experiment. He first contacted the leading naval stores factors in Savannah for permission to experiment on their land. Not all were encouraging. One part owner of a Savannah factorage house responded that he "had no confidence in the project." J. P. Williams, a cotton and naval stores factor, believed differently and granted his permission to conduct experiments in his company's forest near Statesboro, in southeastern Georgia. With a test area secured, Herty next visited Gifford Pinchot, the head of the recently created Bureau of Forestry, in his Washington, D.C., office. After listening to Herty's plan, Pinchot agreed to lend assistance, beginning a pattern of cooperation between federal agencies and the naval stores industry that would last for over half a century. He offered Herty a position as collaborator with the bureau, an appointment that paid only three hundred dollars a year but came with invaluable fringe benefits: access to scientific instruments, a travel allowance, bureau stationery—which lent greater prestige to Herty's efforts—and a chance to publish his results. Another $150 raised by the Savannah factors helped pay for equipment. Herty also sought broad support from producers through a presentation on his plan before the actual work began.[18]

Although similar to the French system, the method of collecting gum that Herty discovered did not require unfamiliar tools, new techniques, or expensive retraining of workers. It permitted chipping to continue as usual. The only changes in turpentining came when, instead of boxing, workers hung cups and gutters, and, rather than dipping gum from boxes with spade-shaped dippers, laborers scraped gum out of cups with trowels. To install the system, two workers used cornering axes, just as they would in cornering a box, to remove the bark and create a smooth face. Then, swinging the ax sideways, the laborers removed just enough bark and sapwood to create a flat surface half the width of the smooth face. Next, they used broad axes to cut incisions about one-fourth inch deep at the top of the flat surface. Both incisions inclined toward the center, but they did not meet: one extended an inch beyond the end of the other. Into these incisions workers inserted

17. Herty, "Turpentine Industry in the Southern States," 346–7; Herty, *New Method of Turpentine Orcharding*, 12–3; Reed, *Crusading for Chemistry*, 16–8; Charles H. Herty to John M. Egan, 18 January 1901, Herty Collection.

18. J. B. Chestnett to Charles H. Herty, 5 September 1901, Herty Collection; Reed, *Crusading for Chemistry*, 19, 21; Herty, "Turpentine Industry in the Southern States," 348; Maxwell Taylor Courson, "Here Began a Revolution," *Southerner* 1 (fall 1979): 33.

the gutters—galvanized iron strips about two inches wide and from six to twelve inches long. The upper gutter declined to the center of the face and the lower gutter extended a little beyond, forming a spigot that channeled gum into the cup hung by a nail below.[19]

On July 20, 1901, Herty and his team hung the first cup and gutters. Because he could not find a pottery manufacturer to make his small order of earthen cups, Herty used galvanized iron cups instead. Under the eye of a local woodsrider hired by Herty, baffled and amused workers hung the equipment on two hundred trees. They boxed another two hundred pines in the same area. Herty kept records of the quantity and quality of gum collected using the two different systems. He also noted the effect that temperature and rain had on resin flow. Within days of the experiment's start, southern newspapers reported "that no more important public work than this has been undertaken in Georgia in many years, and that if Prof. Herty accomplishes the task he has set for himself the state will be 'incalculably benefited.'" By the fall, Herty's data indicated that his method held great promise. The cupped trees produced 186.06 barrels of gum, while the boxed ones yielded only 86.06 barrels. However, scrape from the boxed trees brought their total yield to 177.06 barrels. Although the cupped trees thus provided only ten barrels more of resin, the benefits of the cup remained significant. Because the cups yielded far more spirit-rich soft gum than boxes, their use resulted in more turpentine produced at the still. Not only that, but the rosin was of a higher quality. Furthermore, cupped trees proved able to withstand the wind better than boxed ones.[20]

Most informed observers expressed great faith in Herty once his results indicated initial success. Pinchot, in fact, offered him a full-time position at the Bureau of Forestry, which Herty joined at the beginning of 1902 after resigning from the University of Georgia. Many turpentiners also supported Herty's efforts, as did the American Forestry Association, which endorsed Herty's project, stating that "his work, in line with the movement for practical forestry in the United States, promises to preserve a source of great wealth for the South. That he has the support of the national bureau of forestry [sic] is a source of encouragement." But given the history of failed efforts at innovation, not all were convinced Herty could succeed in saving the industry. In October, Georgia's assistant commissioner of agriculture argued that the pine forest was certain to disappear. "There is no help for it. The trees cannot live longer than four years after they have been tapped. If we could preserve the forest it would accomplish a great deal, but the de-

19. Reed, *Crusading for Chemistry,* 19–21.
20. Courson, "Here Began a Revolution," 10, 12; Herty, *New Method of Turpentine Orcharding,* 16; "Destroying Pine Trees," *Tampa Tribune,* 26 July 1901, clipping in Turpentine News Clipping File.

mand for naval stores calls for wholesale and almost indiscriminate destruction of the pines."[21]

With growing industry support and the resources of the Bureau of Forestry behind him, Herty began a larger-scale experiment in 1902. The bureau financed the needed equipment, and a large turpentine-producing outfit, Powell, Bullard and Company, allowed the use of its timber, located near the town of Ocilla in southeastern Georgia. Using the company's own labor to determine how easily the transition to cups could be made, Herty outfitted one-, two-, and three-year old crops, half with his cups and gutters and the other half with boxes. Workers were instructed to chip, dip, and scrape normally. The gum collected using the two different systems was distilled separately. To render accurate dipping results, measurements were made of distilled products, not dip, which contained trash and water. The company sent the rosin to the Southern Naval Stores Company in Savannah for grading. The land-owning company kept the yield and profit records, which they later furnished to the bureau.

Problems plagued the experiment from the beginning. The cup manufacturer was slow to deliver. Herty had placed an order for 31,500 clay cups with the Chattanooga Pottery Company of Downing, Tennessee. However, the cups arrived a week late and with freight costs that nearly doubled their expected price. They were also not of the design Herty had specified; he requested oval bottoms, but instead received cups with flat ones. Labor problems also troubled the experiment's launch, a difficulty that was anticipated but not for the particular reason it occurred. Producers, and Herty himself, suspected that the industry's all-black labor-force "could not be taught to work in any but the orthodox way." With proper instruction, however, Herty found early on that workers could learn the new tasks well in only a few hours. But difficulties arose because the laborers had little faith in the strange new system that they were asked to install and felt it was beneath the dignity of good turpentine workers. Those who reluctantly performed the task condescendingly termed themselves "cup niggers." Herty, in exasperation, found that "the Negro laborers proved even more conservative than the white operators." Eventually the workers were convinced to cooperate, squads were organized, and the work proceeded smoothly.[22]

Once the experiment was under way, there were early indications that

21. Herty, *New Method of Turpentine Orcharding,* 17; Herty, "Turpentine Industry in the Southern States," 348; Reed, *Crusading for Chemistry,* 21; "Guarding the Forests," *Macon News,* 28 October 1901, and "Can Forests Be Saved?" *Augusta Herald,* 20 October 1901, Turpentine News Clipping File.

22. Herty, "Turpentine Industry in the Southern States," 348–51; Herty, *New Method of Turpentine Orcharding,* 18–9; Reed, *Crusading for Chemistry,* 21–6.

the new system was not performing as hoped when the boxes showed greater output than the cups. By the end of the season, however, records indicated that the cup system performed far better than the box. The virgin cups yielded 16 percent more gum than the virgin boxes, and the cup-collected gum produced 18 percent more spirits than that harvested from boxes. When amounts of spirits derived from scrape were also considered, the difference was even greater—23.43 percent more spirits derived from gum collected in a cup. Based on Herty's Ocilla experiments, producers could expect to net $412.54 more from each crop of first-year faces, $341.54 from second-year, $513.38 from third-year, and $516.48 from fourth-year. The cup system promised operators greater income for several reasons. New faces showed increased yield because of the cupped trees' greater vitality over boxed ones. The increase in the third- and fourth-year faces was largely explained by reductions in the distance the gum had to travel to reach the receptacle, since cups, unlike boxes, could be raised. Moreover, emptying cups was more efficient than dipping boxes. When removing the gum from a box, workers scooped out the contents and transferred it to a bucket sitting several feet away, inevitably leaving some of the gum in the box and dripping and spilling some on the way to the bucket. With cups, however, laborers removed the cup, held it directly over the bucket, and scraped virtually all the contents out. Furthermore, the ability of chippers to replace full cups with empty ones between dippings enabled more efficient collection from particularly productive trees. The experiment also demonstrated that cupping proved less fatal to pines than boxes. Fewer than half the number of trees cupped blew down or died compared with boxed ones. Because it cost around $350 per crop to purchase and install cups and gutters, the expense could be made back in the first year of use.[23]

Moreover, subsequent years proved that the cup method permitted turpentiners to manufacture rosin of so high a quality that it could not have been imagined before the twentieth century. Where No. 1 rosin was the very best that producers could have hoped for before, by the 1910s there were at least five grades above that. The best quality, Window White, sold for around 25 percent more than No. 1. Around 1910, this improved grade raised returns by one to two dollars per barrel. In years when depressed markets drove profit margins down, the use of cups could make the difference between a net profit and a loss for the year.[24]

23. Herty, "Turpentine Industry in the Southern States," 353, 356; Herty, *New Method of Turpentine Orcharding*, 20, 24–5, 31–2; Charles H. Herty to Vickers and McKenzie, 30 December 1903, and Charles H. Herty to J. E. North Lumber Company, 31 December 1903, Herty Papers.

24. Berry, *Farm Woodlands*, 336–7, 343; Brower and La Fontisee, "Report of the Investigation on the Naval Stores Industry," 22–4; "How Improvements in Industry Affected Various Rosin Grades," *Gamble's International Naval Stores Year Book, 1930–31*, 11.

Excited by the results, Pinchot encouraged Herty to prepare a report on his success. Herty eagerly complied, hoping to put his beneficial information in as many producers' hands as quickly as possible. The bureau, however, was slower to publish his report than Herty wished. Finally, in May 1903, *A New Method of Turpentine Orcharding* was issued. A forty-three-page Department of Agriculture bulletin with illustrative plates and drawings, it guided producers through the basic principles of the cup and gutter method. In it, Herty described the current boxing method and carefully identified its faults. He then gave an overview of his own experiments before detailing the directions and cost for installing, using, and raising cups and gutters.[25]

Most of Herty's time in the years following his Ocilla experiment was consumed with efforts to manage the company he co-founded to manufacture cups. Herty, John H. Powell—manager of the firm on whose land Herty conducted his 1902 experiment—and other naval stores interests in Savannah and Jacksonville, principally Consolidated Naval Stores Company, put up the money for a turpentine cup plant to be built in the naval stores region. Because Herty, a modestly paid Bureau of Forestry researcher, lacked investment capital, Powell loaned him $1,000. In the end, however, the group did not construct a new plant but instead bought Chattanooga Pottery, the outfit that manufactured the cups for the 1902 experiment. Herty continued for a brief period as a researcher with the bureau, which showed a continued interest in improving the naval stores industry, but persistent problems with the new company and conflicts with Pinchot over royalty payments for his patent strained Herty's position there, and he respectfully resigned in March 1904. Becoming a full-time employee of Chattanooga Pottery, not only did Herty enjoy a far more lucrative position than he had held at the Bureau of Forestry, but he could work at the same project as he had under Pinchot.[26]

Herty saw the company through several crises involving the cups. First, in January 1905, a bitter freeze hit the southern naval stores belt causing the water in hanging cups to turn to ice, cracking them. The company faced a problem filling the sudden flood of orders from turpentiners hoping to re-

25. Reed, *Crusading for Chemistry*, 22, 27–8; A. Sessoms to Charles H. Herty, 4 October 1902, A. G. Paul to Charles H. Herty, 26 September 1902, Denton Brothers and Company to Charles H. Herty, 16 March 1903, A. G. Paul to Charles H. Herty, 8 October 1904, Charles H. Herty to John C. Powell, 21 October 1902, Charles H. Herty to A. G. Paul, 15 October 1902, Charles H. Herty to A. G. Paul, 20 January 1903, Mixon Lucas to Charles H. Herty, 26 February 1903, A. H. Norwell to Charles H. Herty, 1 September 1903, A. G. Paul to Charles H. Herty, 15 September 1904, and Charles H. Herty to C. A. Howell, 10 January 1905, Herty Collection.

26. Reed, *Crusading for Chemistry*, 23–4, 26–9, 34–7, 41–3; Charles H. Herty to C. A. Howell, 10 January 1905, Herty Collection.

place their broken cups before the next season. Lacking the capacity to fill the orders, Chattanooga had to turn to other potteries for help. After the 1905 freeze, the company recommended that producers remove the cups and set them inverted on the ground during the winter months. Second, following the 1905 freeze, the American Can Company began marketing galvanized metal cups as winterproof substitutes for clay ones. Chattanooga reached an agreement with American Can, which claimed to know nothing of Herty's patent, whereby American Can sold metal cups through Chattanooga to those operators who preferred them to earthen ones. Each type of cup possessed both benefits and disadvantages. Clay cups cost half as much as metal cups, but clay cups were more likely to break. Clay cups were also heavier and therefore more expensive to ship from the factory to the producer. But although metal cups were cheaper to ship and did not break as easily, they tended not to perform as well as clay ones. Because the gum clung more stubbornly to their sides, workers used a metal knife to scrape the cups, which wore away the galvanizing, allowed rusting, and shortened the cups' lives. The rust also, no doubt, colored the gum, lowering its grade. Producers also complained that the metal cups heated more on sunny days, causing the evaporation of some of the spirits.[27]

After a slow initial start, producers began a steady adoption of the cup and gutter system. In the first year, only a few producers had access to the limited supply of equipment, but by 1904, cups and gutters were more readily available. Several events in the first decade of the twentieth century helped the situation. The endorsement of the system by several forestry organizations and the support of factors, who agreed to lend the capital for investment in cups and gutters, aided sales. By around 1910, the use of cups showed promising expansion in first-year crops, especially among large producers, whose substantially sized operations were the most threatened by the reduction in large timber tracts. Where only 14 percent of all spirits produced in 1908 and 1909 came from cupped trees, in the following year about a quarter of the spirits from virgin crops did. In his 1910 account of his travel in Florida, Winthrop Packard expressed relief that "the old crude method of boxing the trees is fortunately, rapidly passing and in the place of the great hole cut in the base of the trunk one often passes through miles of trees that have flower-pot like receptacles hung beneath them to catch the

27. John Henderson to Charles H. Herty, 19 January 1905, Herty to Brower, 23 January 1905, John Henderson to Charles H. Herty, 18 January 1905, J. F. Dusurberry to Charles H. Herty, 30 January 1905, D. R. Stewart to Chattanooga Pottery Company, 3 February 1905, Charles H. Herty to D. R. Stewart, 10 February 1905, and Charles H. Herty to East Coast Lumber Company, 2 March 1905, Herty Collection; Reed, *Crusading for Chemistry*, 41–3; Brower and La Fontisee, "Report of the Investigation on the Naval Stores Industry," 13–4.

pitch." By the mid-1910s, two industry experts found that "the damage to standing timber due to turpentine operations has been considerably reduced." Across the South from 1909 to 1914 the system's use increased 395.7 percent. By 1916 an estimated 75 percent of crops used the cup and gutter method, and in 1919 over 80 percent did.[28]

Some producers, however, negated the benefits of the cup by putting too many faces on their trees. Twice as many faces did not yield twice as much gum per tree. On pines measuring eleven to thirteen inches in diameter two feet from the ground, two faces yielded only 50 percent more gum than one face. In one crop this reduced the yield per cup by ten to fifteen barrels. Overcupped trees also suffered from the extra chipping, which reduced the amount of cambium tissue. At best, the trees' growth was severely reduced. At worst, pines were essentially girdled and died. Moreover, the larger surface of the wounded trunk left weakened trees more vulnerable to insects and disease. Weakened pines were also more susceptible to wind. Only trees sixteen inches in diameter or larger could yield enough gum to justify the cutting of two faces.[29]

The worst abuse of the cup system, however, was the effort to harvest gum from trees under six inches in diameter. As the amount of virgin timber declined and second-growth appeared in some areas, desperate producers fitted saplings, which were far too small to box, with cups and gutters. Not only did the yield from such small trees rarely cover the expense of their operation, but also the shock halted their growth and weakened many to the point of death. Furthermore, in cupping small pines, producers were ensuring that second-growth stands of sufficient size would never permit the industry's continuation. Even by the late 1920s this abuse remained a persistent problem.[30]

For a variety of reasons some producers refused to use the cup and gutter system. Even if the equipment would pay for itself within a year, its adoption required a large initial capital outlay that some financially strapped producers could not afford. And although Herty developed his system to deviate as little as possible from the traditional turpentining method, a number of

28. Brower and La Fontisee, "Report of the Investigation on the Naval Stores Industry," 17, 54–8; "Turpentine Makers Advocating Conservative Methods," 1, clipping in Turpentine News Clipping File; Schorger and Betts, *Naval Stores Industry*, 40, 43; Packard, *Florida Trails*, 281–2; Martin, "American Gum Naval Stores Industry," 116–7.

29. Brower and La Fontisee, "Report of the Investigation on the Naval Stores Industry," 24–5; *Good Naval Stores Practice*, 3; Charles H. Herty to Thomas Gamble, Jr., 12 July 1904, Herty Collection.

30. Schorger and Betts, *Naval Stores Industry*, 40; Herty, "Turpentine Industry in the Southern States," 364; Davis, ed., *Encyclopedia of American Forest*, s.v. "naval stores."

producers objected to the training their workers required to use the cups. These operators believed cupping represented too great a departure and realized that inadequately trained laborers could cause the near complete loss of gum by improperly installing the system. Also, many workers complained about the extra work of hanging and removing cups. Chippers did not like the added burden, required by some producers, of placing a shield over each cup to prevent pieces of bark and wood from falling in them. There were also problems with the cups themselves. Careless workers broke them accidentally, and despite manufacturers' warnings, freezing temperatures continued to cause many to crack. One Georgia producer even had to remove his clay cups from roadside trees after passing travelers used them for target practice.[31]

Such drawbacks notwithstanding, the success of Herty's experiments inspired interest among turpentiners in searches for other improvements. Since the naval stores industry itself failed to create any association strong enough to address effectively its specific problems, much of the research during the first decades of the twentieth century continued to originate from the Bureau of Forestry. Herty himself found it "strange that an industry as large as this one has no organization of any kind, no meetings for the discussion of subjects pertaining to its welfare." This situation arose not from a dearth of organizing initiatives, but from the failure of producers to maintain interest in such organizations once formed. Since the late nineteenth century, efforts to establish regional associations that would work to limit production had produced only short-lived groups. This pattern continued with the 1901 formation of the Turpentine Operators Association, which hoped to respond to the diminishing supply of virgin timber, to overproduction, and to soaring labor expense. The association, like the organizations that preceded it, met with very limited success in its short life. Other attempts at organization met similarly disappointing results. In 1909, Texas and Louisiana producers created the Western Naval Stores Association, headquartered in Beaumont, Texas. Producers, factors, and dealers in 1914 created the Turpentine Farmers Association, headquartered in Savannah. In the late 1910s the Turpentine and Rosin Producers Association of New Orleans was formed. All of these groups lasted for but short periods and suffered from the turpentiners' inability or unwillingness to cooperate in lowering production. When naval stores prices declined, makers were more likely to increase production, the greater output seeming the best way to

31. Ostrom, "History of Gum Naval Stores Industry," 221; Brower and La Fontisee, "Report of the Investigation on the Naval Stores Industry," 15-6, 24.

preserve cash flow. Because of paternalistic labor policies, which mandated that turpentiners keep their jealously guarded workforces active, and multi-year timber leases, even financially independent operators faced difficulty curtailing production.[32]

In the 1920s, turpentiners experienced somewhat more success in addressing their own concerns. Founded in 1925 and based in New Orleans, the Pine Institute of America conducted experiments to discover the chemical properties of turpentine and rosin and to develop new uses for these products. It also sought improved marketing, encouraged scientific forestry, and lobbied for government experiment stations. But it closed within a decade because of insufficient financial support. Turpentiners also benefited from such groups as the Georgia Forestry Association, which focused a portion of its attention on naval stores production. Organized in 1921, the association worked to encourage cup use and set a minimum size of trees worked. It also advocated fire protection.[33]

Thus in the absence of a strong, independent organization to focus on improving the naval stores industry, most efforts were initiated by the federal government. The government-supported conservation agenda marked a new pattern of cooperation between business, state, and federal agencies in the South, an alliance also seen in the first decades of the twentieth century with efforts to fight the boll weevil and improve public health. Herty's experiments helped to promote conservation in the South. His success inspired continued applied research at the Forest Products Laboratory in Madison, Wisconsin, established in 1910, and at government experiment stations set up in Florida and Mississippi. And because Herty had developed such a useful system with which the producers' needs were made central and since he had proved so genuinely eager to work with them in improving the industry,

32. Charles H. Herty to John M. Eagan, 18 January 1901, and A. Vizard to Charles H. Herty, 19 December 1900, Herty Collection; Tindall, *Emergence of the New South*, 130–4; Butler, *Treasures of the Longleaf Pines*, 247; Herty, *New Method of Turpentine Orcharding*, 9; Martin, "American Gum Naval Stores Industry," 14–5, 107; Brower and La Fontisee, "Report of the Investigation on the Naval Stores Industry," 50.

33. Butler, *Treasures of the Longleaf Pines*, 247–8; Priest, *Naval Stores*, 3; Armstrong, "Georgia Lumber Laborers," 438; Brower and La Fontisee, "Report of the Investigation on the Naval Stores Industry," 1, 70; Campbell, Unkrich, and Blanchard, *Naval Stores Industry*, 77; Martin, "American Gum Naval Stores Industry," 112, 140; L. F. Hawley, "Forest Service Investigations of Interest to the Naval Stores Industry," in *Naval Stores: History, Production, Distribution, and Consumption*, ed. Thomas Gamble (Savannah: Review Publishing and Printing, 1921), 139; "Welcome to Annual Meeting Georgia Forestry Association, at Savannah," 8 May 1942, Georgia Forestry Association Papers, Special Collections Division, University of Georgia Libraries, University of Georgia.

more naval stores men were afterward willing to consider other conservative methods developed by foresters.[34]

At the federal level, one early method used to encourage improved practices was the demand for strict adherence to improved methods when public pineland was leased for turpentining. Then, in 1908, an Agricultural Appropriations Bill allotted ten thousand dollars for a study of how the turpentine industry contributed to the death of the southern forest. More studies followed. By 1917, the United States Forest Service had published seventeen bulletins on naval stores production. Moreover, during the 1920s, the Forest Service operated three experiment stations in the South, in Asheville, North Carolina, in New Orleans, and in Starke, Florida. The first two worked on efforts to reduce forest destruction caused by turpentining. In 1923, tests began at the third station on private second-growth tracts granted for the Forest Service's use. Here foresters experimented with methods that would result in more profitable turpentining and conservation of the harvested pines. The men who worked for the Forest Service at this time received pay from the government, but large naval stores companies and factors had to cover the cost of their travel and accommodation when they worked in the field. On many occasions foresters stayed in private homes.[35]

Besides Charles Herty, Austin Cary was arguably the most influential federal forester to bring improved scientific management to the turpentine industry during this new era of government involvement. Born in Massachusetts in 1865, he studied biology at Bowdoin College, where he received his undergraduate and graduate degrees. He also attended the Johns Hopkins University and Yale University. Cary entered the new field of forestry after an 1892 chance meeting with Bernhard E. Fernow, the head of the U.S. Division of Forestry, who briefly employed Cary as a forestry surveyor and investigator. In 1904, with practical knowledge of forestry and an academic mastery of natural sciences, Cary went to teach at Yale, and the next year at Harvard. He also authored a *Manual for Northern Woodsmen*, a well-known, straightforward guide to land surveying, forest mapping, timber estimating,

34. Reed, *Crusading for Chemistry*, 47; Courson, "Here Began a Revolution," 12–3; Clark, *Greening of the South*, 49.

35. Cowdrey, *This Land, This South*, 127–35; Dereland Turpentine Company, C. B. Ferden, and Doe and Roe naval stores lease agreements, and sample crop inspection report, Cary Collection; United States Forest Service, "U.S. Government's Turpentine Experience in the Florida National Forest," in *Naval Stores: History, Production, Distribution, and Consumption*, ed. Thomas Gamble (Savannah: Review Publishing and Printing, 1921), 227; Schorger and Betts, *Naval Stores Industry*, 44–6; Vinson, "Conservation and the South," 154; Wyman, *Experiments in Naval Stores Practice*, 5; G. P. Shingler, interview by R. White, 30 June 1959, p. 4, Oral History Interview, Forest History Society; Clark, *Greening of the South*, 67.

and log and wood measurement. As an advocate of private enterprise and believer that economic motivation was the best road to conservation, Cary drew strong opposition from Pinchot, who promoted government ownership and control of forest resources. With Pinchot removed from office in 1910, Cary's sputtering career at the Forestry Service advanced; he would remain with the Service for twenty-five years, until his retirement.[36]

His first assignment was on the West Coast, but his graceless and unsociable behavior, combined with his resentment of government overregulation, caused him to clash with his supervisors and eventually led to a transfer. From several options he chose the South. Here Cary could operate on his own as the Forest Service concentrated most of its efforts in the West. Headquartered in Florida, he set about achieving his goal of stabilizing the southern forestry industry. His straightforward manner (which had caused problems in the West), his support for private property rights, and his opposition to government regulation helped him win southerners over to forestry, his greatest career achievement. Cary understood how to approach individual producers and gradually convince them to accept his scientific ideas. First he asked producers if they had any problems with their operation, then he walked into the woods with them, evaluated their situation, and suggested solutions. Through his efforts, turpentine operators learned the best size of streaks, the most productive chipping frequency, the optimal tree diameter for gum production, the appropriate number of faces per tree, the effects of turpentining on tree growth, and the benefits of the cup and gutter system. Producers came to trust Cary and his recommendations so much that, at their request, the Forest Service sent him on a trip to France in 1924 to observe the conservative management of the maritime forests there. Cary continued his work in the South even after his retirement in 1935. By this time many in the region considered him the father of southern forestry. He was visiting forestry students at the University of Florida when he died of a heart attack in 1936.[37]

Whereas Austin Cary is perhaps most notable for his successful efforts to

36. "List of Materials in the Austin Cary Memorial Forestry Collection," p. i, Cary Collection; Gloria Hutchinson, "Pioneer Maine Forester, Austin Cary: A Diamond in the Rough from East Machias, He Wrote the Book on Modern Forestry," 51–3, 68, 71–2, Austin Cary File, Forest History Society; Vinson, "Conservation and the South," 159–60; Cowdrey, *This Land, This South,* 137–8; Shingler, interview, 6; Koch, *Utilization of the Southern Pines,* 1478; "Austin Cary," 28–9, Cary File; Berry, *Farm Woodlands,* 345.

37. "List of Materials in the Austin Cary Memorial Forestry Collection," i; Hutchinson, "Pioneer Maine Forester," 51–3, 68, 71–2; Vinson, "Conservation and the South," 159–60; Cowdrey, *This Land, This South,* 137–8; Shingler, interview, 6; Koch, *Utilization of the Southern Pines,* 1478; Davis, *Encyclopedia of American Forest,* s.v. "Cary, Austin."

advance applied conservative methods, another federal forester made the most numerous research contributions. Eloise Gerry, who sometimes worked with Cary, pioneered studies into a problem that continued to plague turpentine producers well after the development and wide adoption of the cup system. Although the cup reduced the damaging effects of turpentining a tree, the wound created by chipping continued to harm the pine. Herty himself recognized that "if the tree is not wounded, turpentine is not produced; if it is girdled, the tree dies. Somewhere between these extremes lies the most efficient operation."[38]

Gerry, who held a Ph.D. from the University of Wisconsin, undertook research to find this balance. Trained as a wood anatomist and specializing in the study of wood formation and development, she focused on discovering what caused gum to flow from turpentined trees. Working at the Forest Service's Forest Products Laboratory in Madison, Wisconsin, Gerry provided a scientific basis to explain the benefits of lighter chipping, a justification some operators required before altering their practices. One of the greatest obstacles to light chipping was a persistent belief, which originated with the naval stores industry's introduction into America, that gum was tree sap. By the early twentieth century, American scientists understood from Gerry's work that unlike sap, which was water-based and circulated between the roots and the needles, gum was made by the resin ducts in the layers of new wood just below the bark. At the time a tree was chipped, it contained no gum. Rather, the trees' exterior wood cells manufactured gum following the wound as a way to protect the exposed wood from insects, disease, and evaporation. Deep chipping, therefore, did nothing to encourage gum yield.[39]

Gerry further proved what European researchers already suspected, that resin ducts grew much more numerous in the trunk two to three feet from the point that chipping began each year. Thus narrow streaks were important because they kept the face in the maximum area of production throughout the year. If producers chipped three-fourths to one inch upwards each time, the face would rise out of the region with the largest number of resin ducts. Moreover, narrow streaks also protected the layer of sapwood behind

38. Herty, "Turpentine Industry in the Southern States," 363.

39. Dyer, "History of the Gum Naval Stores Industry," 7; Ostrom, "History of the Gum Naval Stores Industry," 221; Maunder, *Voices from the South*, 124; Herty, "Turpentine Industry in the Southern States," 360–2; Schorger and Betts, *Naval Stores Industry*, 10; Eloise Gerry, *Improvement in the Production of Oleoresin through Lower Chipping* (Washington, D.C.: United States Department of Agriculture, 1931), 3; T. F. P. Veitch and V. E. Grotlisch, "What Uncle Sam Does for the Naval Stores Industry," in *Naval Stores: History, Production, Distribution, and Consumption*, ed. Thomas Gamble (Savannah: Review Publishing and Printing, 1921), 136; L. F. Hawley "Forest Service Investigations," 140.

the face, which kept the tree vibrant by severing only a few of the passages used to carry sap between the roots and the needles. Such streaks as well helped protect the resin-producing cells from the damaging effects of drought. If chips were cut too deeply or the gutter or apron driven too far into the trunk, the sapwood could be cut through. Gerry's continued experiments showed that one-fourth-inch chips yielded the best results. Thus, there was no need, she believed, for the lengthening of faces to exceed eight to twelve inches per season. The prescribed narrow chipping led to the introduction of the O hack, with a 0.75-inch-wide blade, and OO hack, with a narrower, 0.625-inch-wide blade. As an increasing number of producers adopted Gerry's recommendations, workers had to adjust the chipping practices. For all the previous years they had worked in turpentine, they were taught that "the deeper you go into the meat, the more blood you get." Gerry's work destroyed this myth.[40]

Although involved in a field almost completely dominated by men, Gerry was highly respected by the foresters and producers with whom she worked. They took her research and publications seriously and adopted her recommendations. Her presence in the field, however, caught the foresters of the 1910s and 1920s, who politely referred to her as "Miss Gerry," off guard. And the southern racial climate demanded that special arrangements be made when Gerry journeyed to the region for her research. On one trip, for example, her studies required that she collect fresh wood chips by following a black chipper through the woods for a day. The forestry supervisor, however, "couldn't hear to that. A girl would have been in great danger right off the bat." So, for several days, Gerry followed the black worker under the watchful eye of a white ranger who accompanied her to ensure her safety.[41]

Along with Herty, Cary, and Gerry, other government-supported researchers made many new discoveries during the 1910s and 1920s that helped the industry. For one, their studies showed that lighter methods of chipping could reduce the frequency of dry face and the fungi that often accompanied the ailment. Researchers also found that older trees with crown lengths less than one-third the total tree height were the most susceptible to dry face, and producers were advised to avoid them. If dry face did occur, operators should let the pine rest for a few weeks and thereby enable it to

40. Eloise Gerry, "The Goose and the Golden Eggs, or Naval Stores Production a la Aesop," *Southern Lumberman* (25 August 1923): 1–3; L. A. Ivanov, "Scientific Principles Underlying the Technique of Streaking Pines," 49, Cary Collection; *Good Naval Stores Practice*, 2; Butler, *Treasures of the Longleaf Pines*, 23; Eloise Gerry, *More Turpentine, Less Scar, Better Pine*, Leaflet 83 (Washington, D.C.: United States Department of Agriculture, 1931), 1–4; Gerry, *Improvement in the Production of Oleoresin*, 3, 17–23; Maunder, *Voices from the South*, 36.

41. Shingler, interview, 6; Eldredge, interview, 6–8.

better resist the condition. After the period, producers could either double-chip the face each week to rapidly raise the face above the affected area before it expanded further, or they could ignore the dry-faced area and begin the next streak above it. Foresters also made significant strides in understanding the variation in gum yields among different timber stands and among individual trees within those stands. They found that ground moisture, temperature, sunlight, soil, fertility, and tree size all contributed to resin production.[42]

Foresters also explored the problems associated with fire. Fire damage to pines remained a widespread problem in the first decades of the twentieth century. Although destruction caused by fire was less on average per acre in the southern piney woods than in forests of other areas of the country, such a large percentage of the southern pine forest was burned that overall damage in the region was much more extensive. Work by foresters in the 1920s demonstrated that persistent burning practices seriously harmed the pines and hurt their gum yield. Researchers discovered what producers had been unable to realize from casual observation: burning slowed the growth of trees not directly affected by the fire. Not only did burning consume the debris, it also damaged the humus layer which otherwise provided nutrients to the trees. Studies showed that longleafs grew 80 percent faster on unburned land than on burned. On unburned land gum production rose between 25 and 100 percent. Thus, in the most conservative estimates, producers could increase profits by 25 percent if they kept fire out. Foresters were willing to concede that the practice of yearly raking and burning of the pine straw, chips, and spilled gum reduced the amount of flammable material on the forest floor and, in turn, the later likelihood that accidental fire would rage out of control. For some producers, the 25 percent loss of potential profits was an acceptable sacrifice for greater insurance that a conflagration would not consume their entire stand.[43]

42. Schopmeyer and Maley, *Dry Face of Naval Stores Pines*, 1, 5, 7; True, "Dry Face of Turpentine Pines," 11, 14; Ivanov, "Scientific Principles," 28, 43–6; Wyman, *Experiments in Naval Stores Practice*, 8–9, 33, 36; Karl Petraschek, "The Further Development of the Technique of Turpentining Pines," 16–7, Cary Collection; Eloise Gerry, "A Study of Externally Matched Southern Pines Which Produce Widely Different Yields of Oleoresin," 2–4, Cary Collection.

43. Forbes and Stuart, *Timber Growing*, 3, 6, 14, 26; O. H. L. Wernicke, *Piney Wood Sense*, Pine Institute of America General Bulletin (Gull Point, Fla.: Pine Institute of America, 1926), 2–3, copy in Forest Service News Clipping File, Forest History Society; Harry Lee Baker, "Fire in the Turpentine Orchard" (paper presented at the Get-Together Conference of the Pine Institute of America, Pensacola, Fla., February 1929), 1–2, copy in Cary Collection; Wyman, *Florida Naval Stores*, 36; Eloise Gerry, "Oleoresin Production from Longleaf Pine Defoliated by Fire," *Journal of Agricultural Research* 43 (1 November 1931): 827, 830–3.

Although many turpentiners valued their traditional fire practices, foresters recommended that they replace their raking and burning practices with organized fire-prevention methods. According to the foresters' strategy, rather than reduce the risk of large fires by burning away the small deposits of flammable debris each year, turpentiners would contain fires and suppress them before they grew too large. Producers were to construct a network of fire lanes and breaks, which foresters assured them would cost less to construct than the expenditure for annual raking. Where raking cost between 7¢ and 15¢ per acre, fire prevention cost just 4¢ to 6¢. Although a risk of a large, disastrous forest fire was present even with the new protective methods, foresters promised producers that the increased profits from not burning offset it.[44]

In reducing their own firing practice, however, turpentiners were placing themselves at the mercy of local tradition that demanded periodic burning. Cattlemen—invoking custom—believed grass growing on the forest floor was rightfully theirs to use. They demanded burning to keep down undergrowth and encourage grass for their livestock. Even if the forest owners did not want their property burned over, they raked their trees in anticipation of the cattlemen setting fire to it anyway. "The cattleman was your friendly enemy," explained the son of one Florida turpentiner of the period. Some cotton farmers contributed to the problem; believing that the boll weevil thrived in wooded areas surrounding their cotton fields, they demanded eradication of the pests through fire. A 1926 Pine Institute of America bulletin explained that "the turpentine farmer, where fires are allowed to run wild, is really in a vicious predicament, for when he does not burn the woods others may do so at the wrong time with great damage to him. Yet any burning at any time costs him heavily."[45]

As a means of controlling fire and other resulting forms of tree damage, foresters advocated an end to the practice of free-ranging livestock. Timberland owners possessed the right to use the stands and had the obligation of paying taxes on the property, but beyond these legal rights and obligations they had little control over the acreage. The way many piney woods southerners saw it, an investor bought land for the timber and until he harvested it and put the cutover to some other productive use, local inhabitants had a right to the range. Because there were no fences, livestock was permitted to roam over the countryside, grazing on the native grasses. The number of animals involved was considerable. For example, in Washington County,

44. Forbes and Stuart, *Timber Growing*, 36; H. L. Baker, "Fire in the Turpentine Orchard," 2–3, 36.

45. Kayton, interview, 1; Maguire, interview by author; Wernicke, *Piney Woods Sense*, 3.

Florida, alone, the forest provided grazing for around ten thousand head of cattle and twenty thousand hogs. Sheep and goats also browsed the forest, especially during the spring and summer months, when the grasses' lushness peaked. Goats and pigs damaged stands considerably. Goats were fond of the tender tips of young pine stems and branches. Although hogs obtained most of their forage from acorns and low-growing plants, they did not hesitate to dig up and devour the starchy roots of longleaf pine seedlings. Sometimes they even dined on large saplings. In sufficient numbers hogs could destroy longleaf reproduction over a sizable tract. Foresters concluded that hogs could seriously injure between 46 and 85 percent of an area's young pines.[46]

Not only did foresters encourage the suppression of fire and conservation of young pines, they addressed the problem of the growing number of acres of cutover wasteland in the South. Much of the land fell into the hands of the states and county governments, seized for delinquent taxes. Some states attempted to sell the cutover acres as potential farmland. Foresters, however, pushed to reforest denuded timber tracts through reseeding. The more easily cultivated slash pine, however, and not the once dominant longleaf, was their chosen favorite. Without periodic burning, which the forestry establishment then shunned, the longleaf would be quickly shaded out by faster-growing species. And its long taproot, which even very young longleafs sent down, made it difficult to grow in nurseries. Although less hearty at a young age, the slash pine grew faster than the longleaf, making it marketable at an earlier age. And best of all, studies showed it could actually yield more gum than the longleaf. Only in the poorest soils, where no other species could thrive and where vegetation cover was much needed to curb erosion, did most foresters believe the longleaf had a place.[47]

The combination of the improved methods and the conservation efforts made between 1900 and 1920, both facilitated by federal intervention, averted the depletion that forestry experts had been forecasting, although timber supplies remained a fraction of what they had been several decades earlier. Turn-of-the-century technological changes also helped by reducing the nation's overdependence on wood. Treated railroad ties lasted thirty-five to fifty years instead of the previous five to ten. Building materials such as

46. Maunder, *Voices from the South*, 76; Ziegler, Spillers, and Coulter, *Financial Aspects of Growing Southern Pine*, 60; Vance, *Human Geography of the South*, 140; "Annual Report of the Starke Branch for the Year 1929–1930," 6, Cary Collection.

47. Georgia Department of Agriculture, *Georgia Historical and Industrial* (Atlanta: George W. Harrison, State Printer, 1901), 355; Vance, *Human Geography of the South*, 135; T. D. Clark, *Greening of the South*, 29–30; Kennedy et al., eds., *History of Lake County, Florida*, 43, 74; *Good Naval Stores Practice*, 3; Gerry, *Improvement in the Production of Oleoresin*, 2; Forbes and Stuart, *Timber Growing*, 8; Buttrick, "Commercial Uses of Longleaf Pine," 908.

brick, stone, cement, iron, and steel replaced wood in the construction of buildings, ships, bridges, freight cars, and farm implements. American wood consumption consequently declined rapidly after 1905, and timber supply estimates became more optimistic. Greater confidence in the forests' re-growth resulted as well from improved understanding of the growth rates for different trees, and the effect of climate and topography. One naval stores industry observer found as early as 1910 that "young trees grow where the old ones have been taken out and in many a once-plowed field stands to-day a young growth that will soon be big enough to yield a 'crop of boxes.'" In the mid-1920s, Georgia, for example, possessed only one million acres of virgin pine growth, but had nine million acres of second-growth timber.[48]

Where federal forestry efforts led to great advances in gum harvesting and forest management, another federal agency, the Bureau of Chemistry, worked as well to improve the quality of the turpentiners' product and de-velop more reliable marketing standards. Beginning in 1915, the bureau con-ducted demonstrations on better distilling methods, developed both privately and by the bureau, which would give higher yields. It exhibited a still thermometer, invented by a physician and turpentine producer from Cordele, Georgia, in 1908, which allowed for better regulation of heat. A decade later it publicized the new recording thermometer that gave a charge's temperature history. G. P. Shingler, who worked for the Chemical Bureau in the 1920s, invented a ten-ounce "nursing bottle" marked to indi-cate when water should be added, the temperature raised or lowered, or the rosin discharged, by measuring the water and spirit consistency of the fluid exiting from the condensing tube. Because many distillers could not read, these gauging devices were designed to be used by the illiterate. The bureau also sent agents into such important naval stores centers as Savannah to work with factors as well as to individual producers to advise on distilling problems. It printed and distributed posters and circular letters warning of wasteful losses through careless handling of gum, distilling, and treatment of the spirits and rosin.[49]

48. Donald J. Pisani, "Forests and Conservation, 1865–1890," in *American Forests: Nature, Culture, and Politics,* ed. Char Miller (Lawrence: University Press of Kansas, 1997): 25, 27; T. D. Clark, *Greening of the South,* 51, 129; Packard, *Florida Trails,* 277; Gerry, "Goose and the Golden Eggs," 3; Pikl, *History of Georgia Forestry,* 20; Thomas Gamble, "The Naval Stores Industry of the South," in *The South's Development: Fifty Years of Southern Progress: A Glimpse of the Past, the Facts of the Present, a Forecast of the Future* (Baltimore: [Manufacturers' Record], 1924), 325.

49. Dunwody, "Proper Methods of Distillation," 132–3; Shingler, interview, 1–3; Butler, *Treasures of the Longleaf Pines,* 81; Veitch and Grotlisch, "What Uncle Sam Does," 138; "Part

Perhaps the bureau's greatest contribution to production came in the late 1920s, with the introduction of a new kind of refining process, steam distillation, whereby steam-heated coils within the still raised the gum's temperature. Although first performed in a crude fashion in 1868 in Georgetown, South Carolina, and improved by the French eight years later, steam distillation in the United States did not mature until the bureau's Naval Stores Research Division worked out an acceptable facility design. Early difficulties with the original process involved the discoloration of rosin, which was by that time the most valuable of the naval stores products. Naval stores researchers solved the problem by developing a method of cleaning the gum before it entered the still. This process heated the gum and diluted it with spirits to make it more fluid, then filtered it and finally sprayed it into water, where it settled. The improvement led to the rapid proliferation of steam distilleries in the South.[50]

The Bureau of Chemistry also established better naval stores production standards and put inspectors in the major ports to ensure that products were accurately labeled. At the turn of the twentieth century, no uniform industry classification of purity and grade existed, and individual ports tended to follow different requirements. In 1912, the Bureau of Chemistry created industry-wide standards for both rosin and turpentine based on color. W.W. (Water White) and W.G. (Window Glass) represented the two palest and thus most valuable grades of rosin. Lower grades included N. (Extra Pale), M. (Pale), K. (Low Grade), I. (Good No. 1), H. (No. 1), F. (Good No. 2), E. (No. 2), D. (Good Strain), C. (Strain), B. (Common Strain), and A. (Black). The Bureau of Chemistry issued sets of glass standards by which inspectors could grade rosin. The original set was held at the bureau office in Washington and matching sets were kept at the major naval stores ports. The four turpentine grades included water white, standard one shade, two shades, and unmarketable.[51]

Although the Bureau of Chemistry's classifications and inspections helped the industry by providing added assurance to consumers that the

VII, 1932–49: Establishment of the Naval Stores Station," 6, Naval Stores Collection, Georgia Historical Society, Savannah, Ga.

50. Ostrom, "History of the Gum Naval Stores Industry," 222.

51. Davis, *Encyclopedia of American Forest,* 476, 479; John E. Register, "The Naval Stores Inspector—His Work and How He Does It," in *Naval Stores: History, Production, Distribution, and Consumption,* ed. Thomas Gamble (Savannah: Review Publishing and Printing, 1921), 69; Martin, "American Gum Naval Stores Industry," 108–9; Veitch and Grotlisch, "What Uncle Sam Does," 137–8; A. Sessoms, "To Factors and Operators," 1–2, Cary Collection; Campbell, Unkrich, and Blanchard, *Naval Stores Industry,* 49; Brower and La Fontisee, "Report of the Investigation on the Naval Stores Industry," 10, 47–8; Butler, *Treasures of the Longleaf Pines,* 119.

products they purchased were in fact of the standard they expected, some in the business viewed the government's increased role with suspicion. The head of one factorage house believed that "when the Government takes hold of the naval stores business at all it will take hold of it effectively, and we will have Governmental inspection and supervision from the tree to the trade. . . . [S]uch work will require a very large number of petty Government officials, whose stamp will be necessary before a barrel of rosin or turpentine can be marketed or shipped. Of course the turpentine operator will have to foot the bill." The government's involvement did not, however, prove to be so intrusive as suspected. By around 1920, Savannah had four naval stores inspectors who each examined 1,200 barrels of rosin and 300 barrels of turpentine each day at the season's height. However, as the suspicious factor predicted, producers paid for the service. Inspectors' fees cost nine cents per barrel of rosin and twelve cents per barrel of turpentine. Factors paid the fee, which was then charged to the producers' accounts. At the urging of both consumers and producers, the bureau in 1918 began collecting and publishing statistics on production, stocks on hand at stills, ports, dealers, and the principal consuming industries.[52]

The system of turpentine and rosin standards and inspections reached maturity in the federal Naval Stores Act of 1923. Designed with consumer interests in mind, it prohibited interstate commerce or foreign export of adulterated or mislabeled naval stores. The law reaffirmed the Bureau of Chemistry's grades for turpentine and rosin, but authorized the secretary of agriculture, who oversaw the bureau, to establish new ones and modify the existing standards if needed. Enforcement of the act was the duty of the Food, Drug, and Insecticide Administration, and violations were to be reported to the Department of Justice. The act also provided for inspectors to check products ready for shipment.[53]

But whereas early-twentieth-century federal involvement in production improvements—the cup and gutter system, light chipping, the appropriate response to dry face and fire control, and the demonstration of these innovations—and quality standardization served ultimately to help naval stores manufacturers, the government investigation and indictment of operators for violation of the Thirteenth Amendment seriously challenged the foundation of forced labor on which the industry had rested. At the same time,

52. C. Downing to W. C. Powell, 13 February 1914, Powell Papers; Register, "Naval Stores Inspector," 69; Veitch and Grotlisch, "What Uncle Sam Does," 138; Shingler, interview, 1.

53. Campbell, Unkrich, and Blanchard, *Naval Stores Industry*, 81–2; Thomas, *McCranie's Turpentine Still*, 7–8; Blount, *Spirits of Turpentine*, 28; "Naval Stores Act, March 3, 1923," 13, Naval Stores Collection.

southern states played an ambiguous role, working to preserve peonage but dismantling convict leasing.

At the turn of the century, Fred Cubberly, the Justice Department's commissioner for the northern district of Florida, noticed a large number of arrests under the state's "false provision law" of 1891. At the request of employers, local officials had charged workers with obtaining goods and money and refusing to deliver the labor promised under their contact. Curiously, none of these cases ever went to trial; instead "compromises" were worked out under which laborers agreed to return and work off their debt and the cost of their arrests. Cubberly also learned that some employers enforced the law without help from officials, making their own arrests and holding their own courts.

In February 1901, Cubberly witnessed this extralegal action firsthand at a turpentine distillery in Meredith, Florida, in Levy County. While speaking with the owner, a Mr. Meldon, another naval stores operator, J. O. Elvington from Otter Creek—about eleven miles southwest of Meredith—arrived in search of a white man named Higgins, the man's wife, and his six-year-old daughter. Higgins was indebted to Elvington for forty dollars. Meldon informed Elvington that the family was staying on his place, and within a few minutes Elvington had found the Higginses and begun their forced return to Otter Creek. Back in his Bronson, Florida, office, Cubberly studied the issue and approached the U.S. attorney of the Northern District with the suggestion that a test case be tried under the federal peonage statute of 1867, which outlawed all debt slavery. With the attorney's approval Elvington was indicted. After Secret Service operatives located missing witnesses in 1905, Elvington pleaded guilty to the peonage charge and received a one-thousand-dollar fine.[54]

Soon after observing the incident between Elvington and Higgins in Meredith, Cubberly received word of a more egregious example of peonage. A naval stores producer named J. R. Dean contacted him about the illegal arrest of some laborers at his camp. According to Dean, a prominent Tifton, Georgia, citizen, Samuel M. Clyatt, served warrants for the arrests of five black workers—who had left his employment and gone to work at Dean's camp near Rosewood, Florida—charging them with gambling. When Clyatt arrived in Levy County he turned his Georgia warrants over to a Florida deputy, who reportedly did not read them. The deputy dutifully arrested the four men whom Clyatt pointed out. Clyatt eventually released two of them

54. Frederick C. Cubberly to H. L. Anderson, 17 August 1906, Cubberly's description of Clyatt case, 17 August 1906, and Frederick C. Cubberly to Alexander Irvine, 31 January 1907, Cubberly Papers; Carper, "Slavery Revisited," 87.

but retained the others, Mose Ridley and Will Gordon. To Dean's protest, Clyatt responded that the men owed him money and that he was taking them back to Georgia to serve as examples to others who might try to leave. After Clyatt rejected Dean's offer to pay what the men owed him, Clyatt forced one of Dean's team drivers to take him and his men, along with Gordon and Ridley in leg chains, to the railroad. The men then went directly back to Georgia, with no court proceedings in Florida.

Cubberly quickly set to work. First he arrested the deputy. Then after gathering the facts from him, Cubberly summoned Clyatt as a witness and had him arrested when he returned to Florida. In building his case, however, Cubberly faced considerable obstacles. Despite efforts by the Secret Service, the two victims, Gordon and Ridley, were never found. Also, the case created considerable interest in the South, and by the time of the trial, $90,000 had been contributed for Clyatt's defense, $5,000 of which was raised in a single night by the Georgia-Florida Sawmill Association. Nevertheless, Clyatt became the first person tried and convicted for violating statutes outlawing peonage. But in March 1905, the Supreme Court overthrew the Clyatt conviction, arguing that the defendant's intentions were clear, but that the government had failed to establish Gordon and Ridley's indebtedness before their abduction. At the same time, it upheld the federal peonage statute and ordered that Clyatt be retried. The Justice Department, however, was unable to secure the necessary witnesses to make its case. Clyatt went free; Gordon and Ridley were never heard from again.[55]

Cubberly was not alone in his fight against peonage. As immigrants who escaped the institution in the South made their way back to New York, reports about the brutality in the southeastern turpentine camps spread through the ethnic communities. By 1906, Russian Jews, Hungarians, Italians, and Greeks, as well as some native New Yorkers, contacted Mary Grace Quackenbos about male family members held against their will in both southern lumber and turpentine camps. An economically independent, reform-minded woman with legal training, Quackenbos ran the People's Law Firm in Manhattan, which helped immigrants adapt to life in the United States. With a three-hundred-dollar grant from S. S. McClure, publisher of *McClure's Magazine,* and additional funds from the Jewish Aid Society, she assumed her maiden name, Winterton, and traveled through Florida

55. Authorities had made an attempt in 1899 to enforce the peonage law only to have a judge dismiss the indictment. Afterwards, no further action was taken until the Clyatt case. Frederick C. Cubberly's description of Clyatt Case, 17 August 1906, Frederick C. Cubberly to Russell, 18 December 1906, and Alexander F. Irvine to Roosevelt, 1 December 1906, Cubberly Papers; Carper, "Slavery Revisited," 87–8; "Peonage in the South," *Independent* 55 (9 July 1903): 1618; Tegeder, "Prisoners of the Pines," 90–9.

posing as a reporter. Afterwards, she conveyed her shocking findings to the Department of Justice and received its support for an investigation.

As a result of her pressure, F. J. O'Hara, a partner in a lumber and naval stores business in Florida, along with some of O'Hara's supervisors, were arrested for peonage. The trial took place in Jacksonville, headquarters of the Turpentine Operators Association, home office of the United Grocery Company, which supplied turpentine camp commissaries, and home of the *Florida Times-Union*, a major state newspaper sympathetic to producers. All three institutions opposed the peonage investigations and created an environment that made conviction difficult. Moreover, the defense attorney in the case was W. M. Toomer, president of the Turpentine Operators Association, and the jury foreman, C. B. Rogers, served as president of United Grocery Company. After a nine-day trial the jury took just seventeen minutes to find all parties innocent. Despite the disappointing outcome, Quackenbos continued her campaign against peonage as an associate of the Justice Department.[56]

Although not all peonage cases in the piney woods South ended with acquittals, many did. Not only were local juries unsympathetic to the plight of workers held against their will, but also, as the U.S. Attorney General was informed, "it is extremely difficult to get evidence in cases of this kind. The guilty parties are white men, and, in nearly every instance, the persons held in peonage are negroes." In many instances the local prosecutors were slow to act on peonage complaints, and when indictments were handed down, victims and witnesses commonly received death threats.[57]

Although the attack on peonage was certainly fueled by the same reformist zeal that initiated attacks on child labor, illiteracy, and convict labor, it was also probably a response to the increase in the practice of forced labor. William Cohen maintains that the fact that opposition to the practice came at the same time that racism was on the rise indicates that peonage was becoming more widespread. "Had peonage and other forms of involuntary servitude been constant across the decades," he explains, "it would be far more likely that white southern opposition would have surfaced earlier, rather than in 1903, when racism was at floodtide." Because the practice tended to be well-hidden and involved the informal use of law enforcement, no documentation with which to quantify its frequency exists. Assistant At-

56. Shofner, "Mary Grace Quackenbos," 275–9; "Verdict of Acquittal Ends First of the Peonage Cases," *Jacksonville Florida Times-Union*, 25 December 1906.

57. John M. Chevey to United States Attorney General, 21 April 1906, and Professor Livingston to Lock, 14 October 1906, Correspondence, Classified Subject Files, Department of Justice Central Files; Charles W. Russell, *Report on Peonage* (Washington, D.C.: Department of Justice, 1908), 7.

torney General Charles Russell admitted in 1908 that the government had no idea how many workers were held in peonage. He explained that "where we have found several cases we may conclude that there are, or have been, or are likely to be, others; but this is speculation." In fact, the Justice Department most certainly prosecuted only a tiny portion of the peonage violations. Most workers were unable to complain to department officials, and when officials did hear of possible violations, department attorneys often lacked sufficient evidence to prosecute because of threats, intimidation, and disappearance of witnesses.[58]

Widely read periodicals brought support for the Justice Department's fight against the expanding phantom institution. In the early twentieth century, the national press began publishing exposés on peonage and the difficulty of trying the cases, outraging Progressive northern readers. Reporters used extraordinary means to expose the evil. One went undercover as a worker but grew exhausted from the hard manual labor and returned home. Such writers appealed to desires for law and order by explaining that the institution flew in the face of the Thirteenth and Fourteenth Amendments, and that both producers and corrupt authorities employed extralegal measures in their attempts to return escaped workers. In July 1903, the *Independent,* a nationally read magazine, informed readers that "we find the South relapsing into a state of virtual slavery, in which the negro and the poor white man find their condition worse than that of the average slave of *antebellum* days." Another, more shocking article, appeared in *Cosmopolitan* in 1907. Richard Barry, author of the piece "Slavery in the South To-Day," assured readers that he did not use the term "slavery" figuratively but rather described "the actual physical slavery that keeps men worse than animals." In fact, he argued, this early-twentieth-century "slavery" was far worse than the antebellum version. "Where in negro slavery there was often sentiment, a marked exchange of affection between master and slave, there is nothing in this new form except the basest and most cold-blooded calculation joined with an indifference to human life which transcends anything that has gone before it."[59]

In an appeal reminiscent of abolitionists' claims of a slaveholders' conspiracy, readers learned that tyrannical labor lords ignored the federal laws against peonage. Reporters also explained how a small but powerful interest group—turpentine producers—exerted undue power to have its way. In De-

58. Daniel, *Shadow of Slavery,* 9–10; Cohen, *At Freedom's Edge,* 292; Russell, *Report on Peonage,* 8; Tegeder, "Prisoners of the Pines," 213, 215–6.

59. Alexander Irvine to Frederick C. Cubberly, 13 April 1907, Cubberly Papers; "Peonage in the South," 1617; Barry, "Slavery in the South To-Day," 481–2.

cember 1904, for example, the *Independent* ran an article telling of how twenty-six indictments for peonage had been returned by a federal grand jury against seven of Georgia's most prominent citizens, three of them members of the McCree family of Valdosta. One of the McCrees, Edward, pleaded guilty to thirteen charges and was fined one thousand dollars. The piece implied that, as a wealthy and powerful man who owned 37,000 acres in south Georgia and served as a member of the state legislature, Edward McCree had received a light sentence. The article went on to describe how the Turpentine Operators Association raised thousands of dollars with which to defend the forced-labor practices. It also appealed to the Progressive era's concern for family by explaining how families lived in the camps and that if a worker ran away, his wife and children were detained. In one case, the piece added, an employer withheld "young children from both father and mother for the purpose of forcing the payment of a debt." In the event such a story failed to draw sympathy because the victims were black, the writer recounted an incident of "a whole family of white persons, including young children, forced at the muzzle of a gun to leave their home and return to the swamp labor camp of the father's former employer some miles distant, there to remain until a small indebtedness due the employer was worked out by the father at wages which the employer arbitrarily fixed."[60]

Reports of peonage in popular magazines rarely failed to emphasize the abomination of whites held in "slavery." Barry jolted readers by claiming that northern businessmen, not southerners, were the root of a system so evil that it dared to cross the color line and prey upon whites. The inclusion of whites, he argued, resulted from a dearth of adequate labor for the new businesses entering the area. He maintained that black workers were too few and lazy and that whites could not be attracted to the region because they could not endure the climate. Desperate employers, according to his interpretation, therefore resorted to keeping whites in debt peonage to support their fortunes. Barry candidly admitted that as long as only blacks fell victim to producers' greed, few whites cared, but when members of their own race, even if most were recent immigrants, became caught in the system, whites demanded action. In 1911, readers of the *American Magazine* were likewise informed that "under the guise of a contract for labor many negroes and, indeed, some white men have been held—and illegally held—in a form of peonage not essentially different from slavery."[61]

60. "Peonage in the South," 1616–8; "Peonage in Georgia," *Independent* 55 (24 December 1903): 3079–80.

61. Barry, "Slavery in the South To-Day," 482–4; Ray Stannard Baker, "A Pawn in the Struggle for Freedom," *American Magazine* 72 (September 1911): 608.

Reporters tended to draw a distinction between how whites and blacks fell into debt bondage. Black workers were usually described as getting themselves into peonage because of their innate tendencies to be lazy, steal, and suffer from what reporter Herbert Ward called a "borrowing mania." Whites, in contrast, became victims of peonage despite their diligence and hard work, because the corrupt system trapped them. Ward's account of Bob English from Coffee County, Georgia, proved typical. He described English as a poor white man who rented a small farm on which he grew cotton. The landlord had English and his two grown boys arrested and charged with criminal negligence for failing to extinguish a fire that they did not start but that burned some of the landlord's turpentine trees. For their release the men agreed to work for the owner to repay the damage. "Thus Bob signed himself and his two boys into slavery." After three months of work, during which they received scant rations, they had only worked off $3.28, by the owner's accounting. The three peons broke out of the stockade where they were kept and walked five nights until they reached the Florida state line, eighty miles away. The landlord was indicted for peonage.[62]

Like many northerner readers, southern blacks, either victims or potential victims of the peonage system, supported the investigations and aided the fight. Peon Jack Richburg wrote the U.S. attorney general explaining his plight at the hands of the Taylor Company turpentine operation near Perry, Florida, and requesting the Justice Department's assistance. Richburg called on the attorney general, "as a legal advisor of the government for protection," to conduct a comprehensive investigation in the area, and he assured him that there were many cases like his that could result in prosecutions. In April 1909, a group of black petitioners from Polk County, Florida—located in the center of the peninsula—also asked the attorney general to investigate "the way colored people are mistreated and Odious Impositions and Severe punishment Imposed on the Colored Race and also Some White People." They felt sure that the county officials were taking action outlawed by the Constitution and added that the county's jail and convict camps were full of African American people who could provide evidence. The petitioners offered to assist in any investigation. It is unclear what became of the group's offer.[63]

Even some white southerners opposed the institution of peonage. In

62. Herbert D. Ward, "Peonage in America," *Cosmopolitan Magazine* 39 (August 1905): 427. Similar stories appeared describing like situations in other piney woods industries. "The Life Story of a Hungarian Peon," *Independent* 63 (5 September 1907): 559–63.

63. Jack Richburg to United States Attorney General, 10 September 1908, and O. C. Buey et al. to United States Attorney General, 22 April 1909, Correspondence, Classified Subject Files, Department of Justice Central Files.

1905, the *Independent* reported that "the best people of the South are opposed to the peonage system and condemn it in unmeasured terms. Many employers are opposed to it, but have been compelled to lean toward it in self defense, the local courts as a rule not protecting the laborer, and in some instances the officials receiving compensation from one employer for annoying and harassing other employers." In the Florida state legislature, a Representative Reese led opposition to that state's 1907 contract-labor bill, arguing, as the *Tallahassee Morning Sun* reported, that "the measure is unconstitutional and would give the unscrupulous employer an opportunity to intimidate and bind an employee to servitude against his will, which practically amounts to peonage, or imprison for debt." Other white critics focused on the institution's inclusion of their own race. The attorney general learned from one southerner that "peonage is a species of slavery that is endangering the liberties of the people. At first only colored men were subjected to it—but now it operates without regard to race or color." A few whites opposed the practice because of the harm it caused all its victims. They sometimes helped provide legal assistance for blacks who where trapped in peonage. In 1908, for example, a white man wrote a letter to the Justice Department on behalf of Sam Taylor, a turpentine worker who owed his employer a debt. The operator was holding Sam's wife Jamie in peonage at Albrin, Florida.[64]

Not even all those involved in the naval stores industry supported peonage. One turpentine man believed that, although peonage legislation was originally intended to serve the honest purpose of protecting the employer's advances, in practice the legislation had become a curse. Writing with twenty years of hindsight, he argued that the laws had left employers with such a feeling of legal protection that they had made more generous advances than earlier, resulting in huge debts among the workers that could never be paid off. Turpentine producers who were desperate for labor, however, would sometimes pay the debt to gain the laborers' services, thus greatly increasing their production costs.[65]

Although some southerners did in fact oppose peonage, the loudest voices that arose from the region either denied the practice's existence or supported it, especially after 1906. That year, the conviction of five officials of the Jacksonville Lumber Company, which manufactured naval stores among its other timber products, shook the southern pine belt. Jacksonville

64. "Peonage in the South," 1618; "'Pernicious Measure' Passed in House," *Tallahassee Morning Sun*, 7 May 1907; Mary Grace Quackenbos to United States Attorney General, 18 May 1907, E. W. Reeves to United States Attorney General, 6 June 1907, and Neil Sinclair to Department of Justice, 20 May 1908, Correspondence, Classified Subject Files, Department of Justice Central Files.

65. Pridgen, "Turpentining in the South Atlantic Country," 104.

Lumber was the largest business of its kind in the United States, and its general manager was well-connected, wealthy, and held in high regard in his community. Months later, in early 1907, three other events outraged the Florida political and business power structure. First, recently appointed U.S. Attorney General Charles J. Bonaparte announced his intention to continue his department's attack on peonage. Second, Mary Grace Quackenbos was appointed assistant U.S. attorney to help in prosecuting peonage cases. Third, Richard Barry's exposé of peonage, focusing on Florida, appeared in *Cosmopolitan* and another version in the *New York Evening Journal*.

In the wake of high-profile convictions, renewed investigations, and negative press, Florida business and political leaders denied that peonage existed in the state and began a campaign to discredit the federal officials who had brought the charges. The Turpentine Operators Association, United Grocery Company, the Georgia-Florida Sawmill Association, and newspapers across Florida, especially the *Jacksonville Florida Times Union*, began a campaign to convince the public that the peonage investigations amounted to nothing more than unfounded accusations and commotion stirred up by trouble-making outsiders who threatened the area's labor system.[66]

For its part, Florida's political establishment, especially U.S. Congressman Frank Clark, rushed to address the peonage accusations. Clark denounced the attorney general on the House floor, and in February 1907 he drafted a resolution requesting that the House investigate the peonage investigations and that the attorney general disclose how much money his department had spent on the Florida cases. Clark also wanted the Justice Department to explain Quackenbos's connection to the department—what official position she held, what salary she drew, and what her official duties were. He further demanded an explanation for why the department used special attorneys to prosecute peonage cases instead of the regularly appointed U.S. attorneys in Florida's two judicial districts. Shortly thereafter, the Florida legislature passed a resolution condemning Richard Barry and his publisher, William Randolph Hearst, for the disclosing article. Then in April the *Florida Times Union* thanked both Clark and the Florida legislature for their defense of the state and assured its readers that the Barry articles amounted to nothing more than "false, malicious, and defamatory libel."[67]

66. Charles Russell to United States Attorney General, 24 November 1906, and Untitled peonage article, Classified Subject Files, Department of Justice Central Files; Shofner, "Mary Grace Quackenbos," 277–8; "Ask Congress for Peonage Investigation," *Jacksonville Florida Times Union,* 21 February 1907.

67. Shofner, "Mary Grace Quackenbos," 277, 279; Representative Clark, House Resolution No. 886 Submission, 25 February 1907, Correspondence, Classified Subject Files, Department of Justice Central Files; "Strong Resolutions Adopted Condemning Barry and Hearst," *Jacksonville Florida Times-Union,* 4 April 1907.

In January 1908, Clark submitted yet another resolution, much like his earlier measure, to the House Judiciary Committee. In it, he argued that "numbers of innocent men have been indicted upon the testimony of prejudiced witnesses, and put to great expense in defending themselves against charges that prove upon trial in open court to be entirely groundless." Despite such serious allegations, the committee apparently rejected the resolution. Later that month, the Tampa Chamber of Commerce complained to the U.S. secretary of state that recent magazine articles were filled with "the basest untruths" which misrepresented "the good people of the South." Floridians especially, it claimed, had suffered from the "injustice" of Quackenbos's long investigations and "'trumped-up charges'" brought by "such disinterested sleuths."[68]

However, it was not reporters or the Justice Department, but rather the U.S. Supreme Court, that dealt the peonage system and its defenders their most serious but by no means fatal blow. In 1911 the court ruled in favor of Alabama peon Alonzo Bailey. Three years earlier, Bailey, a black farm laborer, contracted to work for Riverside Company of Montgomery, Alabama. He was sentenced to 136 days hard labor and ordered back to work for Riverside for leaving his employment without paying his debt. On appeal to the Alabama Supreme Court he lost. But the U.S. Supreme Court overturned the state decision, arguing that the law's presumption of guilt violated the federal Peonage Act of 1867 and the Thirteenth Amendment. The court also found that only a state could impose involuntary labor sentences as punishment for a crime. No man could command another to labor for the payment of debt.[69]

Although the Bailey case declared unconstitutional the most important legal underpinning of the peonage system, the practice persisted in the South. A collection of new state laws and the failure of local law enforcement to uphold the ruling combined to perpetuate debt servitude. In the same year its prima facie law was overturned, Alabama replaced it with one that continued to uphold peonage but returned the burden of proof to the employer. The next year South Carolina took similar action, and North Carolina's Supreme Court ruled against that state's false-pretenses clause but found nothing wrong with the rest of its peonage statute. Georgia's high court let its statute stand, prima facie clause and all, noting that the Bailey

68. Representative Clark, House Resolution No. 115 Submission, 6 January 1908, and C. Fred Thompson to Elihu Root, 28 January 1908, Correspondence, Classified Subject Files, Department of Justice Central Files.

69. Carper, "Slavery Revisited," 92–3; Baker, "A Pawn in the Struggle for Freedom," 608–9; Cohen, "Negro Involuntary Servitude," 43.

decision did not apply to them because Georgia had no law restricting rebuttal testimony in such cases. In 1913, Florida also passed legislation that omitted false pretenses, but in 1919, the legislature enacted another statute that reinstated it. Until 1944, when the U.S. Supreme Court once again ruled against false pretenses, both Georgia's and Florida's laws remained in force. But whether a state had a prima facie peonage statute or not, the failure to enforce the Supreme Court ruling at the local level enabled the practice to continue unchanged. The fact that Georgia and Florida, the two most important turpentine-producing states, retained the clause made it much easier for officials in those states to maintain debt servitude.[70]

It is difficult to gauge how widespread practices of peonage were in the years following the initial flurry of Justice Department investigations and the Supreme Court's Bailey case decision. Complaints during the 1920s were fewer than in the first two decades of the century, and a higher level of black outmigration than before indicates that workers were freer to move as they chose. William Cohen maintains that the trend in lynching can serve as an indicator of peonage's extensiveness. Because intensive racism underlay each, he argues, it can be assumed that as lynching declined, so did the occurrence of peonage. While this may have been the case in the agricultural regions of the Mississippi Delta and the black belt, evidence suggests that in the isolated naval stores areas, peonage remained widespread.[71]

Once the First World War ended, the strong pull of black workers northward subsided, but tight labor conditions persisted—as did the practice of peonage as a remedy. Some turpentiners, like Frank Rose of South Georgia, were forced out of the business in the 1920s because labor was so hard to find. Those who remained in the business continued to use debt to force workers to remain with them. In 1921, one turpentine man complained that "now it costs, in accounts that have to be paid, recruiting expenses, and transportation, probably two hundred dollars per head for each head of family he brings in, and sometimes in addition to this a lawsuit and a heavy court fine for violation of a 'Labor Law.'" Two years later, three partners in a Calhoun County operation, two of them county commissioners, were charged with keeping workers in debt and using a whip and sweatbox to enforce their control. In 1929, Oscar Bailey, a black worker at a turpentine operation in Appling County, Georgia, escaped and made his way as far as the adjacent county, where his employer tracked him and had the sheriff arrest and return him to Appling County. Reportedly, as in Oscar Bailey's

70. Cohen, "Negro Involuntary Servitude," 44; Carper, "Slavery Revisited," 93.
71. Cohen, *At Freedom's Edge*, 292–3, 297; Daniel, *Shadow of Slavery*, 148; Shofner, "Forced Labor," 22.

case, it was still common for "the turpentine men who work many negroes in this vicinity [to] have a way of taking out some kind of warrant in addition to their warrant for debt and holding them in jail trying to force a settlement of debt or of forcing the laborer to go back to work."[72]

Although it is true that the number of peonage cases brought by the Justice Department declined during the 1920s, this situation is probably more indicative of the department's heightened care in selecting cases than a decline in the practice. At one turpentine operation near Hotopaw in Osceola County, south of Orlando, two workers attempted to escape, and one was shot to death. The Justice Department refused to act, claiming it lacked enough evidence for conviction. In late 1930, the Justice Department also refused to investigate the poor treatment of the Union Turpentine Company workers in south Georgia because "it does not appear from the facts stated that the persons in question are being held on account of a debt, and as this is an essential element of the peonage law, the same must be present to afford a basis for Federal Action."[73]

That the most egregious known case of the practice occurred in the early 1920s lends strong support to the argument that peonage continued. The case centered around W. Alston Brown, the previously mentioned manager of the Putnam Lumber Company's turpentine camp at Cross City, Florida, about forty-five miles west of Gainesville. The region and the turpentine operation there developed simultaneously. Around 1920 the area surrounding the company's 300,000 acres became Dixie County, splitting off from Lafayette County, and Cross City, an unincorporated community of only a few hundred residents, mostly black, and accessible only by railroad, became the county seat. Brown, in fact, served as one of the county commissioners.[74]

Brown's notoriously brutal camp relied on systematic violence and intimidation to hold the company's workers in debt peonage. Brown sent labor agents to Savannah, Jacksonville, and other southern cities to convince workers to come to Cross City by the promise of good wages. Once in Brown's clutches, however, laborers were forced to toil all day long every day, even on Sundays and holidays, rain or shine, sick or well. Brown maintained absolute control over his camp. At night all the workers were locked

72. Gavin Wright, Old South, New South, 207; Vail, "Old Timer Remembers"; Pridgen, "Turpentining in the South Atlantic Country," 103; Shofner, "Forced Labor," 22; Letter to United States Department of Justice, 16 December 1930, and H. J. Lawrence to United States Department of Justice, 1 July 1929, Correspondence, Department of Justice Central Files.

73. Cohen, At Freedom's Edge, 292–3, 297; Daniel, Shadow of Slavery, 148; Shofner, "Forced Labor," 22; Nugent Dodds to Frank Brown, 30 December 1930, Correspondence, Department of Justice Central Files.

74. Gary Moore, "Prisoner of Riverside," Folio Weekly 10 (28 May 1996): 15–7.

behind a high, barbed-wire fence. Everything they needed had to be purchased from the camp store owned by Brown. He forbade them to leave, claiming all the workers owed him money, usually between twenty and three hundred dollars. But the debts for which Brown kept his employees as prisoners were, for the large part, fabrications. He skimmed money from each worker's weekly pay and also skimmed money from the cash that laborers gave him to pay off their alleged debts. Workers who successfully slipped out of the camp stockade were tracked down by Brown and forcibly returned, often with the aid of Dixie County law enforcement officials. One of Brown's standard tactics was to have the runaway workers convicted of a crime and fined. Brown paid the fine, making the worker obligated to him for labor to work off the amount. Brown secured the desired legal rulings by forcing laborers to testify falsely. On many occasions he brought the captured workers before the judge, sometimes in the evening at the judge's home, and instructed the justice of the crime and the sentence. Brown typically had his escaped workers charged with assault and battery in the event that a conviction for violation of labor contract did not hold. Because Brown also worked convicts, he sometimes had laborers sentenced to the county chain gang, then leased them and worked them in that capacity. Except for different clothing, it mattered little whether one worked for Brown as a convict or peon.[75]

In 1921, Fred Cubberly discovered the widespread peonage practiced at the Brown camp, and the Bureau of Investigation began an extensive inquiry during June of that year. Putnam Lumber Company denied any knowledge of the atrocities at Cross City. It knew that Brown's camp never lacked for labor, while others had problems, but apparently company officials never bothered to inquire about labor practices as long as production continued efficiently. Although the company cooperated with federal efforts, local officials worked to impede the investigation. The county judge not only evaded an agent, but also delayed handing over copies of records. Even more damaging to the case, Dixie County law enforcement officials intimidated witnesses, who consequently proved far less than fully cooperative in the investigation. Brown, for his part, denied the charges against him, arguing that he maintained a strong labor force because of his kindness toward workers, whom, he claimed, actually begged to work for him. He blamed the investigation on competing employers in the Cross City area who feared that

75. John Bonyne Reports, 14 November 1921, 3 May 1922, 3 June 1922, E. J. Cartier Reports, 16 May 1922, 18 May 1822, 23 May 1922, Howard P. Wright Report, 9 September 1921, and Howard P. Wright to Frederick C. Cubberly, 26 May 1922, Cubberly Papers; Moore, "Prisoner of Riverside," 16.

their laborers would leave and come to work for him and were using the power of the Justice Department in their retaliation. The grand jury apparently accepted Brown's explanation. Despite the generally consistent accounts of over forty witnesses who bravely testified against Brown in the face of threats, the grand jury refused to indict him.[76]

A few years later another more successful case developed from peonage charges at Mood Davis's turpentine camps, one in Calhoun County and the other in Bay County, Florida. At these camps, laborers found it impossible to work themselves out of debt. Davis threatened that if they left, he would force them to return and beat them. In an act of desperation, four men, two of them accompanied by their wives, escaped. Davis's search patrol discovered all six, returned them to their camps, and threatened them with death if they attempted to leave again. Within days, however, Justice Department investigators descended on the operations and collected evidence that eventually resulted in peonage charges against Davis. The runaways and eight other witnesses were kept in protective custody in Pensacola. Their ordeal resulted in the conviction of Davis. But despite such successes, the peonage investigations failed to end the institution. Instead, by the late 1920s, producers practiced debt servitude with greater caution in an effort to disguise the labor system's reality.[77]

At the same time that peonage came under national attention and attack, convict leasing attracted widespread outrage, aimed at Florida especially. The authors of convict leasing exposés focused on the same issues that were used against peonage—corruption, white victimization, comparisons to slavery, and northern guilt. Richard Barry informed the readers of Cosmopolitan that the leasing system rested on political corruption. In Florida, for example, all the state's 1,200 convicts were leased to one man in 1906. No other bidder came forward, because all understood that state politics ensured that they had no chance. As with peonage, one of the most shocking facets of convict leasing for many reformers was that, as one put it, "many hundreds of white men, women + children (minor boys) are at present working out under the most revolting conditions imaginable." To convey the cruelty of the convict-lease system, writers used analogies to other, more commonly recognized atrocities. In a 1907 pamphlet, reformer Clarissa Olds Keeler explained that, in the southern portion of Georgia where turpentine operators were most prevalent, "there are the stockades, the blood-hounds, the whip-

76. Shofner, "Forced Labor," 20; Moore, "Prisoner of Riverside," 16, 18; E. J. Cartier Report, 18 May 1922, M. J. Cronin Report, 9 June 1922, Charles R. Jordan to Howard P. Wright, 9 July 1922, and "Peonage Charge Is Erroneous Declares W. Alston Brown," Cubberly Papers.

77. Tegeder, "Prisoners of the Pines," 202–15.

ping post and every adjunct of the slave trade." She went on to claim that in Florida "stories told of the ill-treatment of convicts working on railroad construction, and at turpentine culture in pine forests, would compare favorably with the torture practiced during the Spanish Inquisition." An exposé of both peonage and convict labor in Georgia argued that leasing was "a system which is in some respects a worse disgrace than Lynching, because it is created and protected by law." In an effort to induce guilt in reform-minded readers, Marc Goodnow asked them to recognize that "when you cut or burn your finger and run to the medicine cabinet for a bottle of spirits of turpentine, you seldom stop to think of the way in which this medicine is gathered; how much more of pain it involves than the pain which you seek to allay by its use; what bodily and mental travail; what cost in human life; what degradation of a great and beautiful state merely for the sake of a few paltry dollars—the continuation, in fact, of a slavery even blacker in its sin than before the war."[78]

Georgia and Florida, the principal naval stores–producing states, both of which continued to use the lease, responded to opposition differently. In Georgia, where state reformers were already turned against the lease, the increasing expense of leasing convicts helped further erode support for the practice and ultimately brought its end. Historian Matthew Mancini shows that the end of the lease system in Georgia coincided with a reduction in its profitability. When the state permitted subleasing in 1897, market demand drove up the price of convict leasing. Where producers could work a convict for $11.21 a year in 1897 and $225.52 in 1904, by 1907 the cost had reached $670, an amount not much different from a free worker's wage. That year, the Panic of 1907 made convict leasing especially unprofitable. As market prices sunk, producers found they were stuck with unneeded work crews whose fee they had already paid and who continued to require food, clothing, and the oversight of hired guards. Once cheap, convict labor had become an economic burden. Finally, in 1908, Georgia's General Assembly's Convict Investigating Committee recommended an end to leasing. The governor and legislature agreed, and with the expiration of the last contracts in 1909 the practice ended in that state.[79]

In Florida, where leasing costs were far less expensive than in Georgia, the initial response to wide public criticism was the creation of new stan-

78. Barry, "Slavery in the South To-Day," 484, 486; Shofner, "Forced Labor," 19; Reverend Leon Ray Livingston to United States Attorney General, 1 May 1912, Correspondence, Classified Subject Files, Department of Justice Central Files; Keeler, *Crime of Crimes*, 11, 13; "Peonage in Georgia," 3080–1; Goodnow, "Turpentine," 103, 107–8.

79. Mancini, *One Dies, Get Another*, 96–8, 224–7.

dards for convict treatment. Regulations required employers to provide insulated and ventilated bunkhouses rather than the crude shacks they had been using. Prisoners were to sleep in individual beds instead of sleeping together on long platforms, and the night chain was to be replaced by a guard. A building was to be set aside for use as a hospital, and a physician was to be called to tend the sick. Some regulations focused on sanitation, requiring clean prison facilities and clothes and the convicts to have a bath once a week. The state also called for closer scrutiny, restriction of convict activity, and detailed records of punishment and food distribution.[80]

In addition, Florida made efforts to oversee the quality of guards at camps. With the introduction of a new guard application and record system, the commissioner of agriculture's office in Tallahassee could check the background of all camp guards. The state also required that former guards have a letter from their previous employer stating their qualifications before another could hire them. In addition, state regulations prohibited hiring as a guard anyone "addicted to any kinds of stimulants," who had relatives in the state prison system, or who had been discharged for unseemly conduct. In an effort to attract more competent guards, the state also demanded that they be paid from $18 to $25, plus room and board, per month.[81]

In the first decade of the twentieth century, Florida also imposed regulations to reduce the chances of convict escape. State legislation required lessees to employ one guard for every five prisoners, to ensure that at least one of the guards was mounted for every twenty-five prisoners, and to keep two trained bloodhounds. In the event that a convict did escape, Florida formulated procedures to facilitate capture. Lessees were to keep a photograph and description of each convict. If one escaped, his picture and information were to be sent to the local sheriff and police, and the lessee was to post a $100 reward for his apprehension. In 1906, Florida also had a book of photographs and descriptions made of all escapees over the previous ten years.[82]

To ensure all its new requirements were met, Florida also improved its inspection system. In 1899, the state employed its first supervisor of state convicts, whose job was to enforce regulations set by the Board of Commissioners of State Institutions. By 1910, Florida had four investigators, who inspected all the camps monthly and submitted reports to the commissioner of agriculture.[83]

80. Drobney, "Where Palm and Pine Are Blowing," 422; Drobney, *Lumbermen and Log Sawyers*, 160; *Eighth Biennial Report*, 385–8; *Tenth Biennial Report*, 422; Mancini, *One Dies, Get Another*, 193.

81. *Eighth Biennial Report*, 303–7; *Ninth Biennial Report*, 295.

82. *Ninth Biennial Report*, 282–4.

83. Drobney, "Where Palm and Pine Are Blowing," 421–3, 431–2; Drobney, *Lumbermen and Log Sawyers*, 159–60; Commissioner of Agriculture to Florida Naval Stores and Com. Company, 5 April 1902, Board of Commissioners of State Institutions Papers.

Where some reformers pushed for improvements to the convict-lease system, others called for the practice to be replaced by state chain gangs and prison farms. The reform opposition to the convict lease did not imply a belief that convicts should not work hard. Progressives typically believed that the region's economic sluggishness could be corrected with better infrastructure, which convicts could help build up, and they offered little challenge to existing southern race or class relationships. Most, like the writer of a Florida newspaper piece who wanted "to see the convict lease system abolished" because it was "a disgrace to the state and age," felt prisoners should labor for the direct benefit of the state. Some suggested that convicts work at a state farm, the proceeds going to hire expert labor to build good roads. Others wanted convicts themselves to work on state roads. Both plans satisfied Progressives in two ways: they offered not only improved transportation infrastructure but allowed for well-ordered social control by placing the convicts under the direct supervision of the state, where their work and treatment could best be monitored.[84]

Nearly a decade after Georgia, Florida stopped leasing state convicts. By this time, many Floridians had joined the national outcry against leasing in their state. Newspaper editors, civic leaders, the Florida Humane Society, and national muckraking periodicals focused on the abuses of leasing. In 1917, Florida, which wanted to build good roads to boost tourism, sent three hundred convicts to the state roads department. Then, with the completion of a new penitentiary in 1919, Florida ended its leasing program and sent its convicts to work on its highways. Mancini explains that such a change represented a reallocation of forced convict labor from the private to the public sector. But even after Florida dismantled state convict leasing, county prisoners continued to labor in privately owned work camps, including those producing turpentine.[85]

In 1923, national publicity surrounding the death of a young North Dakota man in a Florida county convict timber camp helped to finally bring an end to the system. In the fall of 1921, twenty-one-year-old Martin Tabert

84. Drobney, "Where Palm and Pine Are Blowing," 431; "The Everglades and State Convicts," attached to Leon Ray Livingston to United States Attorney General, 6 March 1912, Correspondence, Classified Subject Files, Department of Justice Central Files; Cobb, *Industrialization and Southern Society*, 30; Alex Lichtenstein, "Good Roads and Chain Gangs in the Progressive South: 'The Negro Convict Is a Slave,'" *Journal of Southern History* 59 (February 1993): 87–91; Drobney, *Lumbermen and Log Sawyers*, 172–3; Shofner, "Forced Labor," 17.

85. Drobney, *Lumbermen and Log Sawyers*, 173–4; Shofner, "Forced Labor," 19; Mancini, *One Dies, Get Another*, 105, 116, 196, 221; Jerrell H. Shofner, "Postscript to the Martin Tabert Case: Peonage as Usual in the Florida Turpentine Camps," *Florida Historical Quarterly* 60 (October 1981): 161, 163; Drobney, "Where Palm and Pine Are Blowing," 433; Drobney "Forced Labor," 69.

wanted to see the country and left the Munich, North Dakota, farm where he lived with his parents. His strategy of working part-time while moving from place to place succeeded until he arrived in Florida and found he could not sell his labor in a market that preferred cheap forced black labor. Out of money, he hoboed his way across the Florida panhandle on a train until, on December 15, 1921, he reached Leon County, where a deputy sheriff arrested him. A jury found him guilty of vagrancy and fined him twenty-five dollars. Unable to pay, he received a sentence of ninety days and, like all Leon County convicts, was turned over to the Putnam Lumber Company, which leased the county's prisoners for twenty dollars each per month.

Two months later, the Putnam Lumber Company sent his family a letter saying Martin had died February 1. Only after the Tabert's attorney and a North Dakota state attorney investigated the incident and witnesses came forward did the whole story unfold. Martin, like other convicts at the Putnam camp, rose at four o'clock in the morning and boarded a flatcar, which they rode for fifteen miles through swamps. When the car stopped, they had to walk another several miles, sometimes through hip-deep swamp water. Martin's feet swelled, and the swamp water caused an infection which his ill-fitting, tight shoes made worse. His request for a larger pair of shoes was ignored. By late January, Martin was very ill. He suffered from headaches and occasional fever and had developed swollen areas in his groin so severe that one inflammation had to be lanced. When he grew too weak to keep up with the demanding work, Tabert received regular beatings. On one occasion, in front of eighty-five to ninety convicts, he was beaten forty-five to fifty times with a four-foot-long whip made of three-ply leather and weighing seven and a half pounds. By then Martin ate very little. He wasted down to 125 pounds, and his back was covered with cuts and scabs. Blind with fever by late January, he lay in a stinking bed with his own froth coating his pillow. The doctor only saw him a few times before he finally died. Martin was buried in a runaway convict's old clothes in an unmarked grave in Perry, Florida, of which no one could seem to remember the location. Putnam Lumber Company reported that his death was due to malaria and Martin's refusal to take his medicine.

At the North Dakota legislature's request, the Florida legislature began an investigation of the incident that eventually led to a trial. Testimony revealed that the Leon County sheriff used his office to supply convict labor for Putnam Lumber Company. In the seven months before the sheriff's deal with Putnam, he had arrested only twenty men for vagrancy. In the same period after the deal, 154 men were arrested on the same charge. With no defense attorney present, the sheriff typically instructed the suspect to plead guilty at a sham trial which sometimes occurred late at night in front of drunken officials. At the trial that resulted from the Florida legislature's investigation, the camp's whipping boss was found guilty of second-degree murder and sentenced to twenty years. However, he was acquitted on a technicality at a new trial ordered by the Florida Supreme Court. For its part, Putnam Lumber Company settled with the Tabert family for twenty thousand dollars and received public absolution of blame.[86]

National publications detailed the tragedy of Tabert's demise and the efforts by crooked county officials and the Putnam Lumber Company to conceal camp abuses. The *Literary Digest* covered the affair in a piece carrying the eye-catching title "A Victim of Convict 'Slavery.'" The article argued that the leasing of county convicts had continued, despite efforts by the governor, because the people of Florida had no knowledge of the practice. It also reminded readers that Putnam Lumber Company, the company at the center of the Tabert case, was owned and operated out of Wisconsin, and that Florida newspapers were calling for justice in the case. As newspapers and organizations across the country campaigned for the system's end, the Florida legislature agreed that it should be abolished and, in April 1923, voted to end county convict leasing. In less than a month, the legislature approved another bill ending corporal punishment in the prison system. The governor signed both acts. Thus, the same state government that fought to preserve one form of forced labor, peonage, worked to end another.[87]

The results of the federal government's involvement in the naval stores industry proved equally mixed, assisting producers on one level and threatening them with litigation on the other. The naval stores industry's successful efforts to alter production methods represented the convergence of two significant developments, the near-total loss of the southern pine forest and the emergence of federally backed scientific forestry in the United States. Whereas others had tried and failed at developing a cup-type system in the nineteenth century, Charles Herty's success was owed in large part to producers who feared a seemingly impending timber depletion and were thus made more receptive to alternative practices. His efforts also benefited from his formal training and the support of the nation's newly formed forestry establishment. The former advantage permitted Herty to develop a practical and affordable method, qualities that did not necessarily guarantee its adop-

86. "A Victim of Convict 'Slavery,'" *Literary Digest* 77 (21 April 1923): 41–3; N. Gordon Carper, "Martin Tabert, Martyr of an Era," *Florida Historical Quarterly* 52 (October 1973): 116–26.

87. Drobney, "Where Palm and Pine Are Blowing," 434; "Victim of Convict 'Slavery,'" 40–6; "Florida 'Comes Clean' by Ending Convict Camps," *Literary Digest* 77 (16 June 1923): 38–40; Carper, "Martin Tabert," 128; Carper, "Slavery Revisited," 98; Carper, "Convict-Lease System in Florida," 366–7.

tion. The endorsement of the Bureau of Forestry helped convince producers of its merits. Furthermore, Herty's demonstrated desire to work in cooperation with producers ushered in, by the 1910s, an era of federally supported forestry experimentation and study unlike anything seen before in the industry. Although Herty shifted his attention to other areas of southern economic improvement, Austin Cary, Eloise Gerry, and other foresters continued research and close work with turpentiners. Their efforts led to far greater understanding of the influences of deep chipping, burning, and free-range grazing on turpentine yield. Federal assistance through Bureau of Chemistry research also helped naval stores producers by developing distillery improvements and uniform marketing standards. The national government was perhaps more successful in its efforts to aid the industry than it was in its attempt to end labor abuses. As southern states strengthened peonage legislation with false-pretense and vagrancy laws and employers began drawing whites into the system, the Department of Justice initiated investigations and trials of employers for violating the Thirteenth Amendment. However, despite intense national interest and the practice's apparent widespread use, only a relatively small number of producers were tried for peonage, and fewer still were convicted. Although the fear of prosecution drove the practice out of full public view, peonage continued into the 1940s. The naval stores industry's other form of forced labor, convict leasing, proved less resilient. The hiring out of convicts succumbed to public pressure, the growing expense of leasing, and the demand for chain gang work on state projects. Thus in the early twentieth century, producers could not count on government involvement to work always to their benefit. During the Depression years, however, the relationship between the industry and government would grow far less complicated.

CHAPTER 8

GOVERNMENT TO THE RESCUE

WHERE GOVERNMENT INVOLVEMENT in the first decades of the twentieth century proved a mixed blessing for operators, helping them improve production techniques but at the same time attacking their labor practices, during the 1930s and 1940s government intervention shifted decidedly in the producers' favor. Over these decades, assistance for the naval stores industry increased over what it had been earlier in the century, both in terms of research and direct financial support, and interference with labor relations subsided. The aid became so great, in fact, that it temporarily sustained the struggling business as it teetered on the edge of collapse. Government studies led to significant advancements in harvesting, refining, and marketing. Most important, federal economic assistance programs substantially subsidized gum naval stores production, enabling the weak industry to weather the ravages of the Great Depression. But as turpentine producers enjoyed heightened government support, they actively and successfully worked to deprive their laborers of similar aid in the form of New Deal worker benefits.

The southern forests' slow regeneration and the continued timber scarcity remained a concern in the early 1930s. A survey at the time estimated that of the fifty-two million acres in the naval stores belt, fourteen million acres lay as cutover waste, over thirty-five million acres were crowded in second-growth trees of various growth stages and sizes, and virgin pine growth covered only three million acres. The largest portion of the new growth was young and not of sufficient size to use. Nevertheless, some desperate landowners attempted to squeeze any profit they could from the saplings. By 1935, 56 percent of all turpentine trees were smaller than seven inches in diameter. Thus the naval stores industry continued at the expense of its future well-being. If left alone the saplings that were emerging offered a chance for reforestation. If fully stocked with trees, protected from fire, and worked conservatively, it was estimated, the existing second-growth stands could in a few years support seventy thousand crops. And if the fourteen million acres of cutover waste area were replanted and protected, in forty years they would add an additional twenty-eight thousand crops.[1]

In the 1930s and 1940s, reforestation efforts in denuded areas quickened as success with rapidly growing second-growth forests demonstrated that the turpentine industry, if it used its resources wisely, could survive on such stands. Several factors contributed to the southern forest's resurrection. First, many cutover acres proved inadequately fertile to serve as farmland, despite earlier claims to the contrary made by some southern states, and remained available for reseeding. Second, despite some continuation of regular burning, the practice diminished as foresters' persistent sermons against it began to win converts. Finally, there was a gradual reduction in the use of small timber as the gospel of conservation began to take hold. The first plantings of any significance on cutover land began in 1924 by timber owners in southeast Georgia. They and the landowners who followed their example in the late 1920s transplanted slash pine seedlings lifted from low-lying areas where the young trees had volunteered. By the 1930s, federal, state, and private nurseries grew pines for restocking. Between 1935 and 1936 alone foresters and landowners planted six million seedlings, mostly slash pine, in Florida. The project cost landowners around $1.50 per acre. The Civilian Conservation Corps, which, in 1936, operated twenty-four camps and employed 4,776 workers in Florida, assisted in planting the stock. Administered by the U.S. Forest Service, the CCC's reforestation efforts largely took place in four national forests that together contained over one million acres. Reforestation also began in Mississippi during the 1930s, but made its greatest strides there after 1940 when the state legislature revised the state tax code to encourage the growth and protection of young trees.[2]

1. R. E. Benedict, "The Naval Stores Industry," 1, Cary Collection; Wahlenberg, *Longleaf Pine*, 9–11; Wyman, *Experiments in Naval Stores Practice*, 4; Ziegler, Spillers, and Coulter, *Financial Aspects of Growing Southern Pine*, 5–6, 16.

2. "Welcome" (presented at the annual meeting of the Georgia Forestry Association, Savannah, Ga., 8 May 1942), 5–6, Georgia Forestry Association Papers; "The First Forest," 4, Southern Forest Institute Papers; A. R. Shirley, *Working Trees for Naval Stores* (Athens, Ga.: Georgia Agricultural Extension Service, 1946), 36–8; Wyman, *Florida Naval Stores*, 43; Federal Writers' Project, *Florida*, 32; Robert S. Maxwell, "The Impact of Forestry on the Gulf South," *Forest History* 17 (April 1973): 35; Blount, *Spirits of Turpentine*, 45; P. L. Buttrick, "The Hopes and Dangers in the South's New Forests" (presented at the annual meeting of the Georgia

By the early 1930s, Florida producers harvested 80 percent of their product from second-growth trees. Of all the stands used, both old growth and second growth, longleaf represented 60 percent and slash 40 percent. But because most of the nonrenewable old-growth pines were longleaf and the increasing second growth was primarily slash, turpentine producers turned more and more to the latter. To their delight they found favorable results. Experiments conducted in the first half of the 1930s indicated that slash pine actually yielded 25 percent more gum than longleaf. Chipping affected the trunks of slash pine more than it did longleaf and led to greater resin duct formation above the face, which resulted in heightened gum production. Unlike longleaf, slash pine did not put forth the largest amount of gum the first day after chipping, but extended the flow more evenly across the seven-day interval between chippings, yielding its greatest portion on the second day. Because the streaks on slash pine oozed gum longer than those on longleafs, their optimal chipping interval was longer, requiring fewer streakings and thus lowering labor costs. And because slash pine gum ran more freely than longleaf, a lower portion of its yield was in the form of scrape. Since scrape contained less spirits and produced a lower quality of rosin than soft gum, its lower percentage of the harvest made the slash pine a more lucrative species to work.[3]

By the late 1930s relieved industry observers believed that the current rate of reforestation could sustain the gum naval stores industry. The pine forest, although only a fraction of its original size, appeared to be stabilizing. Some problems remained, however. One forester admitted that the new forests were not of the same quality as the older ones; their stands usually being thin. Most tracts supported half the number of trees they potentially could, and some grew no more than 30 percent.[4]

Because during the 1930s and 1940s turpentiners began turning to second-growth stands that covered previously worked acres, the naval stores industry began a new trend: ending its characteristic mobility, it anchored itself in the areas where it had dominated in the early years of the century. The bulk of production continued to come from south Georgia and north

---

Forestry Association, Savannah, Ga., 19 May 1939), 1, 8–9, Georgia Forestry Association Papers; Forbes and Stuart, *Timber Growing*, 2.

3. Campbell, Unkrich, and Blanchard, *Naval Stores Industry*, 27; Austin Cary, "Studies on Flow of Gum in Relation to Profit in the Naval Stores Industry: A Condensed Account of Experiments Conducted from 1920 to 1931," *Naval Stores Review* (July–September 1933): 4, 12, 15, copy in Olustee Experiment Station Files; Harper and Wyman, *Variations in Naval Stores Yields*, 20, 22, 29.

4. Federal Writers' Project, *Florida*, 31–2; Blount, *Spirits of Turpentine*, 24–5; Buttrick, "Hopes and Dangers," 2.

Florida, the two areas claiming 80 percent of the United States' annual production. The pattern of naval stores trade activity at southern ports reflected the end of the industry's regional migration. Through the 1930s, the same ports that became well-established in the handling of naval stores in the early twentieth century—Savannah and Jacksonville—remained the principal exporters.[5]

Besides stabilizing forest resources, both federal and state efforts had by the early 1930s improved the handling and grading of the rosin and turpentine that flowed through the ports and thus helped strengthen trade. At the state level, inspectors, none of whom could be financially connected with the industry and all of whom worked under an appointed supervisor, used the USDA grading system. Although most inspectors worked at the market, some graded products at stills. Supervising inspectors regularly visited each naval stores yard in their states, examining the stock, sampling the barrels, and reviewing the books. The owner of the product paid the inspectors' fees. In compliance with the 1923 U.S. Naval Stores Act, which prohibited the domestic and foreign trade of adulterated or mislabeled rosin and turpentine, federal inspectors performed the same procedures as their counterparts at the state level. Because most naval stores products left the south, nearly all received two inspections. Those producers caught violating the inspection laws faced stiff penalties.[6]

Not only did government strengthen quality standards, but during the 1930s it also helped intensify naval stores research. The Naval Stores Research Division of the Department of Agriculture's Bureau of Agriculture and Industrial Chemistry stepped up studies into production and grading improvements and new consumer uses. Whereas the Forestry Service focused attention on broad issues affecting woodland and forest products industries across the country, the Naval Stores Research Division concentrated exclusively on improving the turpentine industry. Agents working for the

5. Tar production persisted in scattered areas of the Southeast: eastern North and South Carolina, south Alabama and Mississippi, south Louisiana, and east Texas. By the Second World War, however, its manufacture, arguably the oldest form of manufacturing in America, ended. Benedict, "Naval Stores Industry," 1–2; Federal Writers' Project, *Florida*, 88, 189, 378; F. P. Veitch and C. F. Speh, "Second Annual Naval Stores Report on Production, Distribution, Consumption, and Stocks of Turpentine and Rosin of the United States," 2, American Turpentine Farmers Association Papers; John K. Cross, "Tar Burning, A Forgotten Art?" *Forests and People* 23 (second quarter 1973): 21; Davis, ed., *Encyclopedia of American Forest*, s.v. "naval stores"; Campbell, Unkrich, and Blanchard, *Naval Stores Industry*, 15–6, 51; Campbell and Cassel, *Foreign Trade of Florida*, 73–4, 51, 82.

6. Shirley, *Working Trees for Naval Stores*, 30; Campbell, Unkrich, and Blanchard, *Naval Stores Industry*, 81–4; *Production of Naval Stores* (Washington, D.C.: United States Department of Agriculture, 1942), 6.

division demonstrated pioneering methods and new still equipment in the field. The division distributed helpful literature to producers through the mail and offered individual assistance upon request as well. It also collected statistics on naval stores production and on stock on hand at the stills, ports, dealers, and the consuming industries. The division's ability to assist producers intensified with the opening of the Naval Stores Experiment Station, built in the Olustee National Forest in Florida on ten acres donated by the Forest Service and with $40,000 appropriated by Congress. The Olustee forest contained an equal mix of longleaf and slash pines and was accessible to producers from the most productive naval stores regions in Georgia and Florida. It thus offered convenient research opportunities on both of the most common species used in turpentining. When the station opened in 1932, it consisted of a fire still, auxiliary buildings, and a building that housed chemicals and processing equipment. Three years later a chemical laboratory was added. As the world's first naval stores research station, the Olustee facility worked in cooperation with the Bureau of Agriculture's naval stores research laboratory in Washington, which studied the composition and properties of pine gum and better ways to prepare, use, handle, and transport naval stores. In 1943, the division headquarters was moved from Washington, D.C., to New Orleans, and eight years later, to Olustee.[7]

Stepped-up government research produced further advances in forest use. One improvement was a better understanding of the complexity of burning practices. Researchers agreed with experts who, in the 1910s and 1920s, found that even small, low-burning fires could damage trees, especially if they swept through the forest in the late spring and summer. Moreover, burning away underbrush, it had been shown, exposed seedlings to frost in cooler months, excessive heat in warmer ones, and rapid drying of the soil. Given this understanding, foresters had encouraged producers to begin intensive fire-suppression efforts. But by the 1940s, after over a decade of diligent fire suppression, researchers realized that an accidentally set blaze in an area free of fire for several years might be even more damaging than frequent burns. With fire suppressed, debris built up to deep levels on

7. Campbell, Unkrich, and Blanchard, *Naval Stores Industry*, 76, 79–80; Forney, "Importance of Sites," 6–7; "Locate Naval Stores Station in Osceola Forest of Florida," Turpentine News Clipping File; G. E. Hilbert, "Twenty Years of Research by the Naval Stores Station," *AT-FA Journal* 15 (January 1953): 6; "25 Years of Help," *Naval Stores Review* [68?]([1958?]): 13–4; "Gum Naval Stores," Papers of Theodore Bilbo, Archives and Manuscript Department, McCain Library and Archives, University of Southern Mississippi; Davis, ed., *Encyclopedia of American Forest*, 476; "Report of President to the Georgia Forestry Association" (presented at the annual meeting of the Georgia Forestry Association, Savannah, Ga., 18–19 May 1939), 4, Georgia Forestry Association Papers.

the forest floor, providing enough fuel to turn any unintentional fire into a roaring and extremely destructive conflagration. In 1934, for example, the effect of a forest fire which burned through 15,000 acres in southeast Georgia varied greatly between previously burned and unburned plots. In areas where light, frequent burning had been permitted, none of the turpentined slash and longleaf pines died and only a few of the young round second-growth trees perished. In another part, protected from fire for fifteen years, 50 percent of the turpentine trees and 80 percent of the second-growth saplings died. Studies also showed that whereas fire could damage pines in various ways, it might improve growing conditions. Although fire consumed soil nitrogen, it added nutrients through ash that leached into the ground with rain. Moreover, the removal of forest floor debris exposed soil to the direct rays of the sun, increasing its temperature. Rises in soil temperature increased a pine's ability to absorb water and thus raised gum production. The absence of dead plant material and low-growing vegetation also increased the chances that pine seeds would reach the soil where they could sprout. Once the seedlings emerged, fires lowered the threat of brown spot needle disease and reduced competition from grass.[8]

Thus, foresters, by the mid-1940s, recommended carefully controlled burning over none at all. Producers could manage the intensity and spread of fire by plowing fire lanes and burning between sundown and eight in the morning, when the wind was less likely to shift to a new direction. It was also best to burn during the winter months, following rain, and to confine the fire to small, more easily controlled areas. For stands intended for new production, producers enjoyed optimal results of burning just before the installation of cups. Operators were also to follow a rotation pattern so that plots were burned every three to five years, with raking being done around the trees before each firing.[9]

Because free-range cattle and other livestock herders, not turpentiners, were responsible for a portion of the burning in the southern forest, their activity stood in the way of carefully managed firing. Researchers thus tried to coordinate forest and range research to demonstrate the mutual benefits of their recommendations. As late as 1950, livestock herders considered it

8. Forbes and Stuart, *Timber Growing*, 7; Ashmore, "Looking Back: The Woodsrider," 24; Florida Writers' Project, "The Story of Naval Stores . . . ," *Florida Highways* 11 (July 1943): 32; T. D. Clark, *Greening of the South*, 67; Cary, "Studies on Flow of Gum," 4; Harper, *Effects of Fire*, 7–9, 12–5, 18, 21–2, 26–7; Campbell, Unkrich, and Blanchard, *Naval Stores Industry*, 32; Wahlenberg, *Longleaf Pine*, 201–2; Norman R. Hawley, "Burning in Naval Stores Forest," in *Proceedings, Third Annual Tall Timbers Fire Ecology Conference* (Tallahassee: Tall Timbers Research Station, 1964), 87; Weaver and Anderson, *Manual of Southern Forestry*, 233.

9. Shirley, *Working Trees for Naval Stores*, 40–1.

their right to practice free-range grazing year-round with very little supplemental feeding and minimal control over the number of cattle feeding. Very little planning went into their forest-burning practices, either. Foresters showed that herders were actually harming their own interests with their haphazard burning. Studies found that the South's choice forage lands were indeed in the southern pine belt, but that between July and early March grazing was poor and could not be improved by burning. Researchers also showed that burning commonly killed an area's bluestem bunchgrass, which offered the best grazing, and left only innutritious weeds and wiregrass. Such findings contributed to the decline in burning by livestock grazers in the piney woods.[10]

Government researchers also thoroughly examined factors affecting gum yield, refining the work done in previous decades. Through their efforts, foresters were able to make more precise conclusions regarding the effect of turpentining on tree growth and forest depletion than ever before. Growth reduction proved more related to the size and number of faces on a tree than the actual volume of gum extracted. Discoveries led to better recommendations regarding the pattern with which pines should be turpentined and harvested. Earlier suggestions recommended long rest periods between the conclusion of work on the front face and the start of harvesting from the back. This lengthy interval, foresters concluded, permitted pitch-soaking, rot, and insect damage to work their way up the truck above the face. They thus began recommending the rapid working of trees, using safe methods, and cutting the stands promptly with the end of chipping.[11]

By far one of the greatest industry advancements made by government researchers working at the Naval Stores Research Division was the design of a central distillery. Costing between $20,000 and $250,000, depending on size and sophistication, central distilleries employed the most up-to-date and efficient methods to produce more standardized, high-quality naval stores grades and at a lower cost than could be achieved with old-style copper fire stills. With the new process, the raw turpentine arrived in sealed barrels that were turned upside down over receiving vats to drain. After the gum stopped oozing from its container, steam jets directed into each barrel melted the

10. Weaver and Anderson, *Manual of Southern Forestry*, 155, 158–61, 175; Federal Writers' Project, *Florida*, 32.

11. Wahlenberg, *Longleaf Pine*, 200–1, 205; T. A. Liefeld, "Relation of Naval Stores Yields to Frequency of Chipping," *Journal of Agricultural Research* 64 (15 January 1942): 92; Clements, *Manual*, 2–4, 9–10, 24, 10–1; Cary, "Studies on Flow of Gum," 14; R. P. True and R. D. McCulley, *Defects above Naval Stores Faces Are Associated with Dry Face*, reprint of 15 December 1945 *Southern Lumberman* article (n.p., n.d.), 1–3, copy in Olustee Experiment Station Files.

last bit of gum, which ran out into the vat. Then, from the bottom of the vat, raw turpentine was pumped into another chamber, where it was heated with steam before proceeding through two sets of screens that removed such trash as insects, dirt, bark, and straw. The filtered gum next entered a wash tank, where it was cleaned of water-soluble contaminants. Once cleaned, a carefully measured amount of gum entered the still. In the still, which could hold from one hundred to two hundred barrels of gum, heat was applied with submerged steam coils. Technicians carefully regulated the distillation process until the water-turpentine flow from the condenser reached a rate of nine to one. At that point, the molten rosin was pumped from the still and packaged. Central distilleries were capable of processing between 1,000 and 2,000 barrels of crude gum each week. By comparison, a typical fire still could manage only a maximum of 180 barrels a week.

With central distilleries, producers could enjoy the advantages of better and cleaner equipment operated by highly trained specialists, all at a lower cost than running their own stills. And because these outfits had storage capacity for up to fifty thousand barrels of crude gum, the product could be refined and marketed year-round, reducing the annual fluctuation in market prices.[12]

The introduction of central distilleries in the 1930s coincided with several developments that made their success possible. First, road improvements in the naval stores region and the wide availability of motorized trucks enabled producers to haul their gum many miles to a large distillery more cheaply than operating a badly equipped and poorly run fire still themselves. Second, an increasing number of new gum producers, many of whom could not afford their own still, created a demand for such facilities. Price increases after the First World War had attracted the smaller turpentiners who had steadily left the business in the first two decades of the century. Much of the industry's growth occurred in the more eastern reaches of the pine belt, where by 1930, some second-growth pines began to grow large enough in the older naval stores areas to enter production. Because this new regrowth tended to be sparsely scattered and less productive than the larger tracts of fully mature virgin trees, it attracted more smaller producers than large operations, the latter requiring greater contiguous acreage. It was difficult for a producer with fewer than five crops to justify the expense of owning and operating his own still. Third, stricter marketing requirements,

---

12. Davis, ed., *Encyclopedia of American Forest*, 477; Martin, "American Gum Naval Stores Industry," xiv, 227–8; Campbell, Unkrich, and Blanchard, *Naval Stores Industry*, 97–8; Panshin et al., *Forest Products*, 454; Shirley, *Working Trees for Naval Stores*, 34; Hilbert, "Twenty Years of Research," 8.

which the central distilleries could meet more easily than fire stills, enhanced the former's popularity. Finally, competition from wood naval stores manufacturers, who were growing more and more capable of producing finer standardized product grades, necessitated that gum producers turn to specialized distillers able to refine similar products. All four factors led to the rapid construction of central distilleries across the Southeast in the 1930s and 1940s.[13]

Large naval stores producers and consumers built most of the government-designed central distilleries, with factorage houses playing surprisingly little role in their construction. Several facilities were built around Jacksonville, but most were located in Georgia. In 1936, Glidden Company built the South's first central processing and distillation plant in Jacksonville, Florida, and later ones in Valdosta and Collins, Georgia. A group of large operators organized Filtered Rosin Products Company, which, by 1942, operated stills in Brunswick, Baxley, Douglas, Valdosta, and Jacksonville. The Langdale family of Valdosta began construction of a plant late during the Second World War, after it received authorization to acquire the steel and brass necessary for the project. It replaced the roughly twenty-five fire stills the family operated at its own operations and also served other producers in south Georgia and northern Florida. By the mid-to-late 1940s, approximately thirty central distilleries were in operation in the naval stores region, processing close to 80 percent of the crude gum. Many producers abandoned the use of their existing fire stills or, when constructing new camps, decided against building stills and instead relied on the central distilleries to process their gum. Whereas approximately 1,300 fire stills were operating throughout the southern pine region in the mid-1930s, by 1950 only around 63 continued running, most fired on an irregular basis. Thus, in the 1930s and 1940s, gum naval stores producers returned to the status of pre-1830 operators in that they became gum harvesters who relied on large distilleries to process their turpentine.[14]

Even as central distilleries gained popularity, the Olustee Station re-

13. Martin, "American Gum Naval Stores Industry," 91, 118–9, 125–6; Brower and La Fontisee, "Report of the Investigation on the Naval Stores Industry," 28, 44–5, 59; Monroe, interview, 6; "Turpentiners," *Magnolia Monthly* 7 (October 1969); Schorger and Betts, *Naval Stores Industry*, 18; Davis, ed., *Encyclopedia of American Forest*, 476–7; Shirley, *Working Trees for Naval Stores*, 30, 33–4; Eldredge, *4 Forests and the Future of the South*, 21; Brown, *Forest Products*, 185; *Naval Stores Statistics*, 1–2; Maguire, interview by author.

14. Harley Langdale, Jr., interview by Harold K. Steen, 1991, p. 9, Forest History Society; "Langdale's New Processing Plant Will Open July 1st," *AT-FA Journal* (June 1945): 5; Butler, *Treasures of the Longleaf Pines*, 91; M. E. Henegar, *Slash and Longleaf Pine Growers Handbook: Practical Information and Suggestions for Growing, Protecting, and Realizing Maximum Utilization* (Lake City, Fla.: Newton, n.d.), i, iii, copy in Olustee Experiment Station Files; Hosmer, *Economic Aspects of the Naval Stores Industry*, 1.

searchers also assisted producers with improvements to the old fire still design. Their new still used fuel more economically, heated the kettle more evenly, provided better fire protection, proved easier to regulate, and consequently produced better results than the previous design, which had remained virtually unchanged for a century. During the first several years of the 1930s, ninety such stills were reportedly built in Florida. By 1934, around 15 percent of stills in the South were of the government design and another 8 percent employed some of its features. Only a large operation could afford a still of such quality, so most stills in operation at the time used none of the improvements. An estimated 78 percent of fire stills continued to use sound rather than the recording thermometer to regulate the process. Some of these primitive facilities continued to operate as late as the 1960s.[15]

Intensified wartime government research resulted in yet other advances in turpentine production: the use of acid spray to increase chipping efficiency and bark chipping, which removed only the inner and outer bark but no wood. Although studies of acid's application began in 1936 at the Olustee Experimental Forest, serious research took off when the Second World War increased naval stores demand. Research showed that a 50 percent water and sulfuric acid solution, when applied to a streak made only through the bark, collapsed the wood cells lining the resin ducts, thus enlarging their openings and allowing for a longer period of gum flow. The acid held the resin ducts open for two weeks, after which new streaks and acid were necessary. Thus, labor costs could be cut because workers needed to visit trees only half as often. Another benefit was the faces' slowed movement up the trunk. And with only bark removed, pines could more easily survive turpentining. By the mid-1940s, the method was ready for the industry's adoption.[16]

15. Campbell, Unkrich, and Blanchard, *Naval Stores Industry,* 80; Wyman, *Florida Naval Stores,* 28; "Cross-sectional View of Turpentine Fire Still Layout at the Naval Stores Station," Bilbo Papers; Shirley, *Working Trees for Naval Stores,* 33; "Ten Mile Notes," *Baxley (Ga.) News Banner,* 3 February 1932; "Before Tourism-Turpentine," *Southern Living* (October 1986), copy in St. Augustine Historical Society Research Library, St. Augustine; Butler, *Treasures of the Longleaf Pines,* 79; Jo Meldrim, interview by author, tape recording, St. Augustine, 19 August 1996.

16. Carl E. Ostrom and Worden Waring, "Effect of Chemical Stimulation of Gum Flow on Carbohydrate Reserves in Slash Pine," *Journal of Forestry* 44 (December 1946): 1076; Panshin et al., *Forest Products,* 443; Kenneth B. Pomeroy, "Modern Trends in an Ancient Industry," *Journal of Forestry* 50 (April 1952): 297; Koch, *Utilization of the Southern Pines,* 1479–80; Norman R. Hawley, "A Summary of the History of the Naval Stores Conservation Program," in *Historical Background of the Naval Stores Conservation Program* (n.p.: Georgia Forest Research Council, n.d.), 14, copy in Olustee Experiment Station Files (hereinafter *HB*); Dyer, "History of the Gum Naval Stores Industry," 8; Clements, *Manual,* 11; Mobley and Haskins, *Forestry in the South,* 157; Butler, *Treasures of the Longleaf Pines,* 54, 56.

Despite the advances made possible by government-supported research, however, the Great Depression hit the naval stores industry hard, necessitating further federal assistance. Risky financial moves on the part of producers in the 1920s left the industry wholly unprepared for the sudden economic collapse. A brief rise in profitability in the mid-1920s led operators to borrow heavily in an effort to increase production and cash in. Timber grew somewhat more available following the First World War, when the southern lumber industry entered a challenging period that required it to squeeze as much profit from its timber holdings as possible. Before 1910, companies had purchased timber in anticipation of a predicted future shortage. However, the required capital outlay for their purchases, combined with increased taxes on the idle property, placed a strenuous financial burden on owners. The promised timber scarcity failed to materialize, and by 1920 the growing supply of timber from the Northwest and the increased use of other building materials—cement, steel, and brick—made southern timber less valuable. With no further reason to hold the tracts that were proving to be more of a burden than an asset, large timber owners relaxed their grip on forest resources. Lack of restraint on the part of producers who in the late 1920s moved to take advantage of the newly available stands resulted in overextension and overproduction. Furthermore, the United States' high protective tariff worsened the Depression's impact on the naval stores industry, since in raising the price of imported goods, the government crushed foreign trade and made it impossible for other nations to purchase American goods, including naval stores.[17]

Producers, attempting to remain in business, responded with desperate measures. Turpentiners slashed operating expenses as much as possible by reducing already low wages to bare subsistence levels and refusing to replace worn-out equipment. They also reduced their overall level of production, although in many cases not by choice. Producers either lost the means to operate on the scale they once had or went broke and saw factors foreclose on their operations. Many producers worked their reduced number of crops intensely in an effort to extract as much gum as possible over the short term. Despite increased forest exploitation, the drop in the number of producers resulted in the 1932–33 crop year being the smallest in the previous thirty-five years. Although the economy began to crawl slowly toward recovery in

17. Brower and La Fontisee, "Report of the Investigation on the Naval Stores Industry," 27–8; Martin, "American Gum Naval Stores Industry," 122–3, 144; Campbell, Unkrich, and Blanchard, *Naval Stores Industry*, 22, 89–90; J. E. McCaffrey, interview by Elwood R. Maunder, p. 92, Oral History Collection, Forest History Society, Durham, N.C.; Pikl, *History of Georgia Forestry*, 34; Robert M. Newton to P. N. Howell, 25 September 1937, Dantzler Lumber Company Papers.

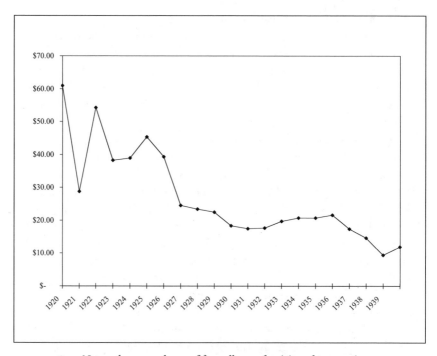

FIGURE 8.1. Net cash proceeds per fifty gallons of spirits of turpentine, 1920–1939. Based on data from Donald Fraser Martin, Jr., "An Historical and Analytical Approach to the Current Problems of the American Gum Naval Stores Industry" (Ph.D. diss., University of North Carolina, 1942), 338.

1933, the growing use of competing solvents, especially wood naval stores and mineral spirits, lessened the benefits of the improvement for the remaining gum naval stores producers.[18]

To make conditions worse for naval stores producers, just as the Depression was reaching its worst levels, a severe drought hit the southern pine belt. Problems began in 1930 with persistent warm winds and high temperatures, part of a weather pattern that contributed to the Dust Bowl in the plains states. Although rainfall remained relatively normal that year, the winds, heat, and low humidity caused rapid evaporation and a reduction in morning dews, all of which strained vegetation. Then, over the next two years, rainfall amounts dropped sharply. With drought conditions techni-

18. Martin, "American Gum Naval Stores Industry," 144, 195; Campbell, Unkrich, and Blanchard, *Naval Stores Industry*, 22, 89–90; McCaffrey, interview, 92; Pikl, *History of Georgia Forestry*, 34; Robert M. Newton to P. N. Howell, 25 September 1937, Dantzler Lumber Company Papers.

cally beginning when precipitation drops off 15 percent from the average, parts of the pine belt saw declines of from 20 percent to 30 percent. Under these extreme conditions, trees began dying. Longleaf pines, with their deep taproot, faired better than slash pines, yet even the former's mortality rate shot up. Overall tree loss amounted to 9.4 percent, or ten times higher than normal. With pines under considerable stress, gum yields sank, even in stands worked conservatively and for only a few years. Overall, the faces yielded 20 percent less gum in 1932 than they had the year before. As desperate turpentiners continued working the strained trees, the incidents of dry face and ips beetle attack rose. Moreover, partial defoliation, combined with enormous quantities of debris contributed by dead pines, greatly increased the risk of fire.[19]

A number of producers began sideline businesses as means to raise extra cash with which to weather the economic and environmental devastation. Some raised cattle and farm crops, such as sugar cane, sweet potatoes, corn, and hay. Those who owned their forests attempted to market their previously turpentined trees to lumber mills. But trees scarred with eight- and ten-foot faces produced at most only a few saw boards. Such pines' pitchy bottom sections, however, could be cut and sold as ties and poles. Because only a few pulpwood mills dotted the South in the 1930s, there was a limited market for the principal product of turpentined trees, wood chips.[20]

Many producers, however, recognized that new federal initiatives aimed at helping farmers, not sideline enterprises, offered their best chance for survival. Where earlier in the century the United States Justice Department's peonage investigations had led turpentiners to condemn federal involvement as a menace, the clear benefits of government-backed studies during the 1910s and 1920s, which in no way threatened the industry's labor system, eased fear over further aid from Washington. Before their petitions for funding under the farm assistance programs stood a chance, however, producers needed to convince government officials that the naval stores industry was, in actuality, agriculture. When the 1923 Naval Stores Act, which established product grades, passed Congress, it mentioned nothing about the status of naval stores as either industrial or agricultural products. The act gave the secretary of agriculture the duty of overseeing its enforcement, only because the Department of Agriculture administered the Forestry Service

19. John C. Hoyt, *Droughts of 1930–34*, 2, 11; "Report," Southern Forest Experiment Station, 11 May 1932, p. 2, Cary Collection; "Effect of 1931–32 Drought," pp. 1–7, Cary Collection; "Report on Survey of Conditions of Timber in a Portion of the Naval Stores Belt," Cary Collection.

20. Benedict, "Naval Stores Industry," 2.

and naval stores, no one denied, were forest products. But when producers requested relief under the federal Agricultural Marketing Act of 1929, which sought to stabilize farm prices through cooperatives that received low-interest federal loans and through sales to foreign countries, officials rejected them, ruling that turpentine and rosin were not defined as agricultural goods. Gum naval stores operators then began a campaign to reclassify their business, a task that required them to differentiate themselves from wood naval stores producers, who, with large, heavily capitalized and mechanized plants employing hundreds of workers, clearly represented a form of industry, but produced the same product as gum turpentine manufacturers.[21]

To this end, gum producers pointed out that the typical operator required relatively little capital to run his business, compared to wood naval stores operations, and that, unlike the technologically sophisticated wood naval stores industry—whose large plants and elaborate equipment permitted them to run year-round—gum producers used primitive methods and operated on a seasonal cycle. Furthermore, where wood naval stores were produced by only a few large operations widely scattered across the South, roughly 2,200 relatively small-scale operators made gum naval stores. Also, they maintained, a significant percentage of gum producers cultivated cropland in conjunction with their turpentine business, raising cotton, corn, tobacco, peanuts, and pecans with the same workers they employed in the forest. Producers further argued that they, like farmers, were subject to hazards such as uncooperative weather and seasonal overproduction, and they compared turpentining to maple syrup production, which was itself classified as agriculture.[22]

Once producers presented their reasonably valid case that gum collection was agriculture, they faced the slightly greater challenge of maintaining that distilling the gum, which many operators continued to do themselves, did not represent industry. Producers cleverly argued that, like changing any agricultural product from its "originally produced" state to its "first-processed" state, distilling did not change turpentine and rosin's nature as agricultural commodities. Converting a raw material into a primary raw material fit for future manufacturing purposes, like processing food products into a less-perishable form, producers argued, did not transform the essence of the product. Therefore, according to their logic, distilling gum was no

21. A. L. Brogden, Memorandum, 10 August 1940, Bilbo Papers; Martin, "American Gum Naval Stores Industry," 149–50.

22. Leon Henderson to T. F. Dreyfus, 1942, Bilbo Papers; "Gum Turpentine and Gum Rosin: Supporting Brief Filed by Producers Committee That Gum Naval Stores Are Agricultural Commodities," 20 November 1933, pp. 2, 4–6, 9, William M. Colmer Papers, Archives and Manuscripts Division, McCain Library and Archives, University of Southern Mississippi.

more an industry than ginning cotton, curing tobacco, or boiling maple sap into syrup. Like these processes, distilling neither added nor took away anything from the gum. It caused no transforming chemical process, but merely separated spirits and rosin. In distilling, producers were merely preparing the gum for market. Moreover, they maintained, naval stores products' ultimate use for industrial purposes changed nothing about their nature as agricultural commodities. Flax and linseed oil, for example, were agricultural commodities with industrial uses. As one industry observer explained, "the turpentine gum farmer is in exactly the same [class] as other American farmers. His residence, his terminology, his business, his standard of living and mode of thought places him in the same category as the producers of other agricultural commodities."[23]

The gum producers succeeded in persuading the government of their arguments' validity. In 1931 Congress amended the 1923 legislation to include as an agricultural commodity "crude gum from a living tree, and the following products as processed by the original producer of the crude gum from which derived gum spirits of turpentine and gum rosin as defined in the Naval Stores Act." The amendment made gum naval stores producers eligible for loans through the Federal Intermediate Credit Bank set up as part of the Federal Farm Board.[24]

With their new official definition, turpentiners immediately set to work to stabilize the naval stores market. In 1931, they attempted to raise prices by forming a cooperative, the Gum Turpentine–Rosin Marketing Association, which would use federal loans to purchase a large portion of the output. With a membership of around one thousand operators, who accounted for 70 percent of total production, as members, the association received government loans through the Federal Intermediate Credit Bank of Columbia, South Carolina. By July, after just three months of activity, the association stockpiled 62,000 barrels of spirits and 260,000 barrels or rosin. But at this point, the association exhausted its $2.5 million loan and, in the face of world industrial decline, failed to raise naval stores prices significantly. Over the next four years supplies accumulated by the association depressed the naval stores market even further until the surplus was fully disposed of.[25]

23. "Gum Turpentine and Gum Rosin," 6–10, Colmer Papers; Martin, "American Gum Naval Stores Industry," 17.

24. "Memorandum Concerning Senator George and Naval Stores," 29 June 1938, pp. 1–2, and R. H. Crosbey to Howell, 31 March 1939, Colmer Papers; Martin, "American Gum Naval Stores Industry," 150; Brogden, Memorandum, 10 August 1940, Bilbo Papers; Campbell, Unkrich, and Blanchard, *Naval Stores Industry,* 76.

25. Martin, "American Gum Naval Stores Industry," 150–1; Campbell, Unkrich, and Blanchard, *Naval Stores Industry,* 88; Butler, *Treasures of the Longleaf Pines,* 248.

Although the Gum Turpentine–Rosin Marketing Association's efforts failed, the producers' success in defining naval stores as an agricultural commodity enabled them to benefit from the Agriculture Adjustment Administration, which the Roosevelt administration created in 1933. The AAA sought to help the farm economy by reducing production and bringing supply and demand into balance. Its goal was to achieve parity, a point where farm products had the same purchasing power that they did from 1909 to 1914, when agricultural commodities presumably had a fair exchange value for nonfarm goods. Turpentine producers petitioned the AAA for a reduced-acreage plan whereby, like cotton, wheat, and tobacco farmers, they would be paid for land taken out of production. Given Congress's recent reclassification of naval stores, the Department of Agriculture ruled that turpentine was indeed an agricultural commodity and eligible for a marketing agreement with the AAA. But because turpentine and rosin were not basic commodities like other crops, the department decided that gum naval stores producers were not eligible for reduced production compensation in conjunction with the marketing plan. Despite being denied funds for taking trees out of production, turpentiners went ahead with an agreement to limit manufacturing.

Approved by the secretary of agriculture in February 1934, the plan provided for a compulsory restriction of output to prevent oversupply and assist in increasing prices. The agreement proposed to reduce the 1934–35 crop by 10 percent from the previous year in an effort to raise prices to the 1909–14 level of sixty cents per gallon for turpentine and thirty-eight dollars for three and a third barrels of rosin. Through the program, individual operators were allotted a production quota based on their previous four-year production averages. Also, restrictions were placed on the size of pines to be harvested. Under the plan, operators agreed not to harvest from trees less than nine inches in diameter four and one half feet from the ground or to work two faces on a tree less than fourteen inches in diameter. To maintain the program, producers paid to the committee assessed charges approved by the secretary of agriculture. At its inception, the plan called for a fee of fifteen cents for each barrel of turpentine and five cents for rosin. Any funds remaining after administrative costs would be used for industry research or product advertisement. A control committee elected by the producers ran the program. In the election for representatives, producers received one vote for each unit of naval stores produced in the preceding year. Thus large producers easily controlled decisions. Operators from all the naval stores–producing states were represented, as were factors, dealers, and industrial consumers. The wood naval stores industry created a similar agreement, which became effective in May 1934. As a designated *industry*, however, wood naval stores production fell under the jurisdiction of the National Industrial Recovery Administration.[26]

Despite its promised benefits, producers were unsatisfied with the allotment program; they wanted the same price-support payments that farmers received under the AAA. Using arguments similar to those made in 1931, turpentiners successfully asserted that gum naval stores were basic agricultural products, and in the second half of 1935, these goods were added to the list of commodities that benefited from price support. Thus producers became entitled to funds collected under customs laws for the purpose of encouraging exports and domestic consumption, and, most importantly, price adjustments. No sooner had the turpentine producers won this privilege, however, than the U.S. Supreme Court found the AAA unconstitutional.[27]

In the face of this enormous setback, efforts to bring control to the sagging naval stores market greatly intensified under the powerful leadership of Judge Harley Langdale of Valdosta, Georgia, the world's largest gum naval stores producer. Langdale's turpentine empire grew from a modest-sized operation his father started in the late nineteenth century. Born in South Carolina in 1860, the judge's father, John Langdale, moved as a young man to Statesboro, Georgia, then to Council, on the edge of the Okefenokee Swamp, where he began turpentining by 1894. Until his death in 1911, John Langdale produced gum naval stores, crossties, lumber, and cattle, which he grazed on the open range. His estate, consisting of eighteen to twenty thousand acres of property in south Georgia, was divided among his six children upon his death.[28]

Harley Langdale, born in 1888, graduated from Mercer University law school the year after his father's death and began practice in Valdosta, some forty miles to the west of the family home. Harley's law practice progressed rapidly, and he was soon elected a municipal judge. He retained an interest in naval stores production, having helped his father in the business since he

26. Proposed Marketing Agreement for Gum-Turpentine and Gum-Rosin Processors, 8–10, 27, Cary Collection; Campbell, Unkrich, and Blanchard, *Naval Stores Industry*, 84–92; Gilbert C. Fite, *Cotton Fields No More: Southern Agriculture, 1865–1980* (Lexington: University Press of Kentucky, 1984), 128; Memorandum, A. L. Brogden, 10 August 1940, Bilbo Papers; R. H. Crosbey to Howell, 31 March 1939, Colmer Papers; Thomas, *McCranie's Turpentine Still*, 8.

27. Brogden, Memorandum, 10 August 1940, Bilbo Papers; Blount, *Sprits of Turpentine*, 29.

28. "History of Gum Naval Stores," 2, American Turpentine-Farmers Association Papers; Harley Langdale, Jr., "Brief Facts on the Langdale Company," 1, Lowndes County Historical Society, Valdosta, Ga.; Downing Musgrove, "A Tribute to Judge Harley Langdale, Sr.," in *HB*, 1; Shelton, *Pines and Pioneers*, 184–5.

was ten. In 1922, he began purchasing timberland around Valdosta and, over the next few decades, expanded his holdings in Lowndes, Echols, and Clinch Counties. During the 1930s, he further increased his pine acreage by purchasing large quantities of reforested cotton land available at low prices following the boll weevil's destruction. Langdale relied on partners for efficient management of his far-flung operations. When beginning a new establishment, Langdale would find the most competent partner available, whether he could finance part of the venture or not, then borrow the money from a factor and set up the operation. By the late 1930s, Langdale, either by himself or in partnership with other operators, worked approximately 315 crops (3,150,000 faces) on nearly three million trees. His twenty-five camps and stills, which were scattered from the Carolinas to Florida, annually produced approximately 14,000 casks of spirits and 46,500 barrels of rosin, over 2.5 percent of the naval stores manufactured in the United States. As the chairman of the board of Langdale Companies, which produced and processed naval stores and dealt in gum turpentine products and production supplies, Langdale held a powerful position not only in the naval stores industry but in Georgia and the South. Guests for deer hunts on his vast property included Senator "Cotton Ed" Smith of South Carolina, Georgia senator Walter George, and Georgia governor and later senator Richard Russell. When producers met in Washington in the mid-1930s to secure financial help from the AAA, Langdale was among them, flexing his political muscle.[29]

What individual producers, including Langdale, feared in the wake of the AAA's defeat were continued low prices, ever-rising debts, and increased competition from substitute products. Langdale and other influential turpentiners understood that industry cooperation offered the only hope that the Depression would not swallow both large and small producers. They also recognized that, in a buyers' market in which they competed for customers with superior wood naval stores, improved gum products, tailored to meet the needs of the consumer, represented the only way to remain competitive.[30]

With the end of the AAA and the marketing agreement it had overseen, Langdale in 1936 founded the American Turpentine-Farmers Association,

29. Mary Beth Arceneaux, "Captains of the Naval Stores Industry," *Naval Stores Review* 90 (September–October 1980): 8–9; Martin, "American Gum Naval Stores Industry," 232–3; Langdale, "Brief Facts on the Langdale Company," 1; Shelton, *Pines and Pioneers*, 185; Musgrove, "Tribute to Judge Harley Langdale, Sr.," 1; Harley Langdale, Jr., interview, 1; Antwerp Naval Stores Company et al. to W. F. Holtsman, 20 October 1933, Cary Collection.

30. Frank W. Boykin to Aaron A. Lowenstein, 11 July 1936, Colmer Papers; J. Lundie, "A Few Words of Appreciation," 20 April 1966, American Turpentine-Farmers Association Papers; Martin, "American Gum Naval Stores Industry," 280.

whose mission was to unify gum naval stores producers into a cohesive force that could work to stabilize the market and industry. According to its charter, the AT-FA sought to provide improvements in production and marketing of gum turpentine, rosin, and their byproducts. It also hoped to achieve more economically efficient production and orderly marketing and distribution. Acting on its members' behalf, it would improve the industry's standing with government and business and cooperate in the planting and conservation of pines. Moreover, it claimed the power to purchase and store any surplus turpentine in an effort to control prices and to borrow money with which to make advances to members. A board of directors, elected by producers to serve one-year terms, administered the association. Although up for reelection every year, the board members rarely lost their posts. Langdale, for example, served as association president until 1966. Membership was open to both races, and reportedly some blacks did join. Blacks even served on some of the committees, but none held positions as officers or directors. To fund the association's project, members paid no more than five cents for each unit of naval stores they produced annually.[31]

Members received their money's worth and then some. The association significantly, if temporarily, improved the gum naval stores market. One of the greatest changes it brought was the marketing of turpentine in small containers. In the late 1930s, only 5 percent of gum turpentine was sold in small bottles or cans for individual household use. Most individual consumers simply took a bucket to a store, where they drew the spirits from a barrel. In 1939, however, the AT-FA began a $200,000 national campaign to promote the consumption of turpentine in association-approved containers which carried the "AT-FA Seal of Approval." As a result, by 1959, 80 percent of gum turpentine was sold in bottles and cans. The association also successfully encouraged the federal government to increase research into improved processing and new uses for gum naval stores which could keep the products in demand. The AT-FA itself also actively supported research. In 1937, it contracted with G and A Laboratories, Inc., of Savannah to develop new uses for naval stores. For the project it retained Charles Herty, the pioneer of the American cup and gutter system, as an advisor. The association too promoted efforts to reduce damage to trees caused by harvesting and provided members and their employees with group life and hospitalization insurance

31. Arceneaux, "Captains of the Naval Stores Industry," 8; Martin, "American Gum Naval Stores Industry," 155, 157; Downing Musgrove (paper presented at the Naval Stores Breakfast, 31 October 1961, Washington, D.C.), 1, and Charter, General Counsel and Assistant to the President [of the AT-FA] to John Slusser, 12 April 1966, American Turpentine-Farmers Association Papers; Blount, *Spirits of Turpentine,* 29; Davis, ed., *Encyclopedia of American Forest,* 476.

at about half the cost to individuals. Members received issues of its trade journal and invitations to its annual convention held each year in April, which after 1943 included the Miss Gum Spirits Competition.[32]

Perhaps the association's greatest achievement came immediately after its formation, when it successfully lobbied the federal government to include gum naval stores in a new government support program. In response to the Supreme Court's decision declaring the AAA unconstitutional, Congress repealed the legislation that created the administration and within six weeks replaced it with a new agricultural support plan, the Soil Conservation and Domestic Allotment Act, which substituted processing taxes and acreage quotas with benefit payments for soil conservation. Crops were taken out of production to be replaced with grasses and legumes, which could add fertility and stop erosion. On March 25, 1936, Georgia senator and Langdale friend Walter George, two other senators, several House members, and representatives of the AT-FA met to convince Department of Agriculture officials that turpentine was entitled to assistance under the program. The AT-FA argued that the Soil Conservation and Domestic Allotment Act afforded the naval stores industry the opportunity to adopt improved methods. According to their contrived argument, more conservative harvesting practices would facilitate greater tree growth, which in turn would provide a regular, yearly supply of needles on the forest floor that would decompose and restore soil fertility. In making the naval stores industry healthy, the Soil Conservation Service would, in turn, create a healthy forest. The AT-FA proposed that 20 percent of the then roughly 7,340,000 turpentined acres be removed from production and that the producers be reimbursed for their loss. In late June 1936, Congress passed a bill appropriating funds for gum naval stores price support under the Soil Conservation Act.[33]

During the first few years of government financial assistance, turpentiners received aid through two separate programs. The first was of a price-support program administered by the AT-FA. The association used support

32. Martin, "American Gum Naval Stores Industry," 279–80, xiii; A. R. Shirley, "Gum Naval Stores Long Linked with Industrial Development," *Valdosta (Ga.) Daily Times,* 18 November 1959; Maguire, interview by author; Harley Langdale to Secretary of Agriculture, 13 October 1947, Colmer Papers; Sherrie Farabee, "'Miss Spirits' Graced Turpentine Calendar," *Valdosta (Ga.) Daily Times,* 28 June 1989.

33. Tindall, *Emergence of the New South,* 404; Martin, "American Gum Naval Stores Industry," 157; Robert M. Newton, "Statement from American Turpentine Farmers Association to Agricultural Adjustment Administration" and "Memorandum Concerning Senator George and Naval Stores," 29 June 1938, Colmer Papers; Brogden, Memorandum, 10 August 1940, Bilbo Papers.

loans to stabilize the market at a base price by purchasing and stockpiling naval stores surpluses when prices weakened. The program ended the violent price fluctuations that had persistently plagued producers. Langdale considered this market stabilization to be the AT-FA's most substantial benefit to producers. The second, the Naval Stores Conservation Program, which began July 16, 1936, provided financial support to operators who reduced their production. It called for a 25 percent overall reduction in worked faces and the adoption of some moderate conservation practices. Participation was voluntary, and only around 924 producers, about 60 percent, signed up. Those who did adopt the plan were forbidden from cupping trees that measured smaller than nine inches in diameter and from placing more than one cup on trees smaller than fourteen inches. (That year 30 percent of worked trees were smaller than nine inches.) Producers who followed these guidelines were permitted to drop up to 40 percent of their total faces from production and receive reimbursement for their loss. They were paid twenty-five cents for each face no higher than sixty-six inches from the ground. This amounted to $2,500 per crop. The next year, however, in response to better naval stores prices, many producers opted to keep their trees in production. Only 664 turpentiners, representing just a third of the crops in operation, participated. However, the increased production and a renewed economic decline drove prices lower in 1938, and participation consequently rose to 1,799 operators, or 70 to 75 percent of total faces. Many new participants were small producers who worked less than two crops.[34]

After 1938, the two different programs merged into one. In the spring of 1939, naval stores prices dipped to a near forty-year low, and the AT-FA successfully applied for a loan to keep the summer production off the market. However, only members of the AT-FA *and* participants in the conservation program could benefit. After the crisis, the loan and conservation initiatives remained combined. Operators had to participate in the conservation program, removing from 15 to 30 percent of their faces from production, for which they were reimbursed, to enjoy the benefits of the price support program. Producers involved in the dual program enjoyed a better

34. Shirley, "Gum Naval Stores Long Linked"; A. R. Shirley, "Gum Naval Stores and the American Turpentine Farmers Association Cooperative," 4–7, American Turpentine-Farmers Association Papers; Arceneaux, "Captains of the Naval Stores Industry," 8; Dyer, "History of the Gum Naval Stores Industry," 8; Frank E. Fulmer, "'The First Voice Ordered: "Shoot Them." Then the Bullets Started!'" in *HB*, 5; Martin, "American Gum Naval Stores Industry," 158–60, 202; Koch, *Utilization of the Southern Pines*, 1478; Hawley, "Summary of the History of the Naval Stores Conservation Program," 14; Newton Naval Stores Company to P. N. Howell, 22 January 1940, Dantzler Lumber Company Papers.

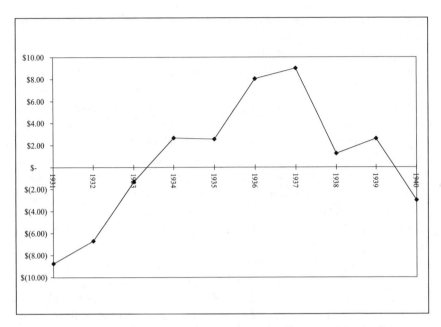

FIGURE 8.2. Profit or loss per gum unit for naval stores firms participating in government conservation programs, 1931–1940. Based on data from Martin, "American Gum Naval Stores Industry," 341.

chance of operating profitably, and consequently the number of participants rose from 1,799 in 1938 to 2,511 in 1939, to 2,785 in 1940, and to 4,264 the year after that.[35]

The U.S. Forest Service had the sometimes difficult task of ensuring that producers did indeed remove the required faces from production and that they did not excessively face trees. Oversight was organized out of the Forest Service's regional office in Atlanta and coordinated with smaller district offices in Savannah, Jacksonville, and Pensacola. (Later these three offices were combined into a single office centrally located in Valdosta.) Around forty men worked in the field for all three districts. The job of inspecting tended to attract men between twenty and forty years of age who wanted steady, relatively well-paying jobs funded by the federal government during the Depression. But although they enjoyed employment reliability, inspectors faced the daunting task of winning the trust of rural producers, many of whom had never had a Forest Service agent on their land and continued

35. Martin, "American Gum Naval Stores Industry," 159–64, 340–1; "Memorandum Concerning Senator George and Naval Stores," Colmer Papers, 3; Thomas, *McCranie's Turpentine Still*, 8.

to distrust government interference despite its benefits. Smaller producers especially resented someone coming onto their property and telling them what to do. The government vehicles assigned to inspectors did nothing to make their jobs easier. Many were worn-out cars confiscated by the Revenue Department, and some were riddled with bullet holes, said to be evidence of the kind of welcome some inspectors received when they attempted to perform their job. While taking a tree count at one operation in August 1936, for example, two inspectors working out of Vidalia, Georgia, were met with gunfire and forced to run for their lives from the forest. One inspector found that producers in his assigned area distrusted him because he drove a government car, a sure sign to the local people that he was in fact a revenuer looking for their liquor stills. Once the inspector explained his true mission to the sheriff, himself a moonshiner, word circulated and his inspections proceeded more smoothly. Inspectors also encountered difficulty in convincing operators and their woodsriders to keep the proper records, which would allow evaluation of the operation's compliance with the program. Although the inspectors themselves gained the trust of some producers in the NSCP, many were won over only after witnessing the success of more prosperous producers who followed the program. The inspectors' gentle but persistent push for conservation practices combined with the government's financial support propelled the wise-use practices well ahead of where they stood before the program began.[36]

Although the AT-FA actively and successfully sought government assistance for its members, it worked hard to deny turpentine workers the benefits of federal programs. The Social Security Act, when originally passed in 1935, excluded farmworkers and domestics but not turpentiner laborers. Langdale—who believed that the control of adequate labor was paramount for the industry's success—and the AT-FA argued to federal officials that the majority of gum turpentine producers also grew such agricultural commodities as cotton, corn, and tobacco, and commonly used the same labor in the

36. Thomas, *McCranie's Turpentine Still*, 8; Arthur G. Steedly, "Doctors, Lawyers, Teachers, Merchants, and Widows, Call to Ask Advice," in *HB*, 12; Charles T. Shea, "' . . The Ones on the Northside Are Northern Reds and the Ones on the South Are Southern Reds,'" in *HB*, 11, 16; Arthur A. Murphy, "'Good Forestry Has Advanced 25 Years, I Believe, Because of NSCP,'" in *HB*, 7; John K. Cross, "'Without a Doubt the Naval Stores Program Has Had a Profound Influence . . . ,'" in *HB*, 4; E. O. Powers, "'With Pearl Harbor Our World, of Course, Turned Upside Down,'" in *HB*, 8; Jim A. McArther, "'During the War, I Trained 22,000 German Prisoners-of-War to Work Naval Stores and Cut Pulpwood,'" in *HB*, 6; Fulmer, "'The First Voice Ordered: "Shoot Them."'" 5; Marion W. Ruffin, "'. . . I Had No Office, No Adding Machine, No Typewriter, and No Maps . . . ,'" in *HB*, 16; Gay Goodman Wright, "Turpentining," 92; J. Lundie Smith, "A Few Words of Appreciation," 20 April 1966, p. 7, American Turpentine-Farmers Association Papers.

fields that they used in the pine forest. The AT-FA further pointed out that state and federal legislation already recognized gum turpentine production as agriculture and, as such, it received price-support loans and crop-reduction payments. Because no final decision regarding naval stores workers' status was made by the time the program began in 1937, some operators began paying the Social Security tax, although others did not. Government investigators looking into producers who refused to pay discovered workers too frightened to cooperate, and investigators who entered camps without warrants found themselves in jail for trespassing. Finally in November, a district court judge in Georgia ruled that gum turpentine "is an agricultural pursuit and the labor employed by complainants therein is agricultural labor." Turpentine workers who had received their Social Security cards only six months earlier now found themselves excluded from the program. The AT-FA also succeeded in its efforts to exclude the industry from the Fair Labor Standards Act of 1938. The law's minimum-wage and overtime provisions would have sounded the death knell for the piecework payment method used since the end of slavery and driven wages to prohibitively high levels. With the exemption from the Social Security and minimum-wage laws, naval stores operators created exactly the relationship with the federal government for which they had hoped; they received financial assistance with minimal disruption of their labor practices.[37]

Where federal assistance failed to reach gum naval stores laborers, it found its way to producers in several ways. Government-funded forestry efforts began to pay off by the early 1930s with the stabilization of timber resources, allowing turpentine producers to settle firmly into south Georgia and north Florida. Intensified federal research into burning practices, gum yield, harvesting methods, and distillation further aided operators by allowing the most efficient use of the second-growth stands. Most significantly, the federal government provided economic assistance as the weakening industry faced collapse during the Great Depression. After several failed efforts by producers to gain financial support, the new and powerful American Tur-

37. Memorandum Relating to Status of Turpentine Farmers, 27 May 1938, Colmer Papers; Prince K. Reed, interview by author, 19 August 1996, St. Augustine; Brogden, Memorandum, 10 August 1940, Bilbo Papers; S. Kennedy, *Palmetto Country,* 263; Shelton, "Pines and Pioneers," 184; Campbell, Unkrich, and Blanchard, *Naval Stores Industry,* 92; Decision of George L. Shelton et al. *v.* Marion H. Allen, 16 November 1937, and American Turpentine-Farmers Association Resolution, passed 20 April 1938, Bilbo Papers; Gene Burnett, "To Burn in a Turpentine Hell," *Florida Trend* (October 1976): 102; Butler, *Treasures of the Longleaf Pines,* 174; John W. Langdale, interview by Harold K. Steen, 1991, p. 12, Forest History Society; "Rich and Lula Gray," American Life Histories, Manuscripts from the Federal Writers' Project, 1936–1940, Library of Congress Internet Website.

pentine-Farmers Association won both low-interest loans to stabilize the market and price-support payments to those individual producers who practiced conservation methods. But as the AT-FA secured federal assistance for its member operators, it worked to deny turpentine workers the benefits of federal aid. This action, part of a persistent pattern of labor exploitation, ultimately helped undermine the entire gum naval stores industry.

CHAPTER 9

DEMISE OF AN OBSOLETE INDUSTRY

THE GOVERNMENT'S INCREASED involvement in the gum naval stores industry during the 1930s and 1940s did not change the business's continued use of exploitative labor practices, which ultimately spelled its demise. Besides the adaptation of some new production methods, the lives and work routines of naval stores workers and producers' labor-management techniques remained relatively unaltered during the 1930s and 1940s from what they were decades earlier. Such continuing practices as low wages, debt peonage, brutality, and close worker oversight did little to attract laborers to the industry's employment, especially after the United States' entry into World War II. That conflict and post-war developments challenged the industry by loosening the binds of peonage and creating a labor scarcity, actions that prevented gum turpentine producers from effectively competing with the highly mechanized wood naval stores industry. By the 1950s, large industrial plants, not independent operators, manufactured the great majority of American naval stores.

As was the case since colonial times, producers in the 1930s and 1940s relied on cheap black labor, which they believed to be inherently unreliable. Almost all chippers, dippers, coopers, and ordinary still workers were black. In the early 1940s, an investigator explained that for "generation after generation they have followed its [the naval stores industry's] southward migration, and the majority of those engaged in it today are descended from a long line of turpentine workers." One industry observer expressed the prevailing understanding that "workers for the woods operation in naval stores production are almost entirely negroes, as the work is too severe and pay too small for white laborers. Too there is a feeling among the white workers that such disagreeable work is negroes' work and that white men would demean themselves by doing it."[1]

Although the labor force in the gum naval stores industry remained predominantly black, more whites worked in the pine forests beginning in the 1930s than during previous decades. The number of small, white producers who performed their own labor rose, as did that of poor, backwoods farmers who labored for operators to supplement their meager incomes. The latter group constituted around 4 or 5 percent of the workforce and performed the same tasks and received the same pay as black laborers. During the depths of the Depression, some unemployed whites, desperate for any work, threatened black turpentine laborers with death if they did not give up their jobs, and indeed the threats succeeded in frightening some people away.[2]

That whites would resort to such measures testifies more to the despair of the times than the economic attractiveness of naval stores work. Producers continued to pay by piecework, not by the hour, and wages remained low. During the Depression, wages fell to levels that allowed only the most frugal laborers to remain debt-free. Moreover, it was not possible to perform as much work as laborers had in earlier decades. By the 1930s and 1940s, tending the trees required more walking than previously. Many of the second-growth stands had been burned and cut, creating stands so thin that workers spent as much as two-thirds of their time in the woods walking from tree to tree. They then had time to tend only five thousand faces a week, half of the number that had been expected of workers since the eighteenth century. Experienced turpentine workers sometimes refused to work in such scattered stands where the piecework system ensured they would receive less pay. Under these conditions turpentine workers made only $30 a month at the same time a common laborer earned $40. Even John Langdale, Judge Langdale's son, admitted that, in terms of pay, the naval stores laborer was on the "bottom of the totem pole."[3]

1. S. Kennedy, *Palmetto Country,* 261; Campbell, Unkrich, and Blanchard, *Naval Stores Industry,* 32.

2. Reed, interview; Robert Cook, "Photographing the Turpentine Industry at Cross City, Florida," 1, in Writers Program, Florida, "Turpentine Camp at Cross City," Department of Special Collections, George A. Smathers Libraries, University of Florida; Florida Writers' Project, "Story of Naval Stores" (July 1943), 14; Lauriault, "From Can't to Can't," 315; Eldredge, *4 Forests and the Future of the South,* 42; E. F. Dean to Department of Justice, 1 June 1932, Correspondence, Classified Subject Files, Department of Justice Central Files.

3. Reed, interview; William P. Langdale, interview by H. K. Steen, 1991, pp. 4, 6, Forest History Society, Durham, N.C.; Paisley, "Wade Leonard," 390; Campbell, Unkrich, and Blanchard, *Naval Stores Industry,* 31; Helen S. Hartley, "Jim Lewis, Turpentine Worker," American Life Histories: Manuscripts from the Federal Writers' Project, 1936–1940, Library of Congress Internet Website; John W. Langdale, interview, 6.

The tasks for which workers received so little compensation in some regards grew more difficult than in earlier periods. The improved methods developed by government researchers challenged workers by requiring that they change the older harvesting practices to which they had been accustomed. Bark chipping proved especially difficult for some workers to master. Those who persisted in swinging the bark hack with great force could damage the blade, which was not designed to endure such pressure. Producers reported that, in many cases, it was easier to train brand-new laborers to bark hack than to reteach hackers experienced in the old method. Another innovation, acid spray, required that workers pay especially careful attention to their task. Laborers first chipped only enough bark to expose the wood. Then, holding the sprayer at a forty-five-degree angle, they moved the sprayer across the streak in a single steady motion, spraying the top of the streak and under the overhanging bark. Only enough acid to wet the streak completely was to be applied, but not enough to drip down the face.[4]

Acid use posed both a real and a perceived work hazard. Rumors associated with its use provoked fear among some producers as well as workers. It was said not only that acid attracted lightning to treated trees, but that the sprayed areas sprouted mushrooms that were fatal to cattle. Word also spread that acid runoff turned swamp water black and imbued it with properties that burned the feet and legs of workers who had to wade through it on their rounds. One worker expressed the reservations of many laborers when he concluded that "anything that will eat the parts off a man will surely kill a tree or a cow. And I bet it will give you cancer too." While all these rumors proved unfounded, acid burns did pose actual risks to laborers. Under normal circumstances there was very little worker contact with the acid. However, a nozzle improperly screwed onto a bottle or a bottle punctured by the sharp edges of gutters or by hack blades could ooze acid onto workers' hands. Exposure to the acid was not especially harmful if the area of contact was washed immediately, but in the forest that was often impossible. If not immediately removed, acid ate through clothing and seriously burned skin. Such incidents were apparently all too frequent. At a St. Johns

4. Ralph W. Clements, *The Bark Hack: Techniques of Using This Efficient Method,* reprint of January–March 1953 *Naval Stores Review* article (n.p., n.d.), copy in Olustee Experiment Station Files, Georgia Agrirama, Tifton, Ga.; Reed, interview; Ralph Clements, "Field Supervision Important When Using the Bark Chipping–Acid Stimulation Method," *Naval Stores Review* 61 (June 1951): 24–6; Clements, *Manual,* 13–5; H. L. Mitchell, "Information on the Use of Chemical Stimulants to Increase Gum Yields," *Savannah Weekly Naval Stores Review and Journal of Trade* 55 (7, 14, 21 April 1945), copy in Olustee Experiment Station Files, Georgia Agrirama; Mobley and Hoskins, *Forestry in the South,* 159–61; Shirley, *Working Trees for Naval Stores,* 25–9.

County, Florida, operation, workers had to buy their own soda to treat acid burns. One Florida laborer, known as "Red Eye," had seriously reduced vision from exposure to acid on his face.[5]

Many workers languished in debt. Older workers were especially susceptible to indebtedness during the Depression. As aging laborers grew less physically capable, and their work pace slowed, their income, based on piecework, declined accordingly. Older workers were, however, reportedly permitted to continue charging groceries and supplies even though producers knew they had no chance of paying their debt. Sick workers also grew deeply indebted, not only because they were unable to work, but because the cost of medicine and doctor visits were charged to the operator, who paid the bills and added the amount to the worker's account. When a member of the camp died, the burial expenses created even greater debt. Upon a death, everyone in the camp, including the boss, donated money, but rarely enough to cover the full costs. In at least one instance a dead man's family was unable to afford the funeral home's fifty-dollar charge and opted to bury their relative themselves. But despite the challenges posed by a low standard of living during the Depression, turpentine laborers often found their situation less desperate than that of some sharecroppers. Unlike these poor farmers, who were often turned off the land as a result of New Deal agriculture programs, turpentine workers could at least depend on receiving food, clothing, and shelter—even though it was sparse and resulted in greater personal debt. For many, the period offered no better option.[6]

The plight of Depression-era turpentine workers is reflected in portions of Georgia-born blues singer Hudson "Tampa Red" Whittaker's 1932 recording "Turpentine Blues":[7]

5. Gay Goodman Wright, "Turpentining," 103; Carl E. Ostrom, "Gum Yields Affected by Quality of Acid Applied to Streak," *AT-FA Journal* (June 1945): 6; Cross, "'Without a Doubt,'" 4; "Naval Stores Equipment," *Forest Farmer* 9 (September 1950): 9, copy in Olustee Experiment Station Files; Clements, *Manual,* 22; Mobley and Hoskins, *Forestry in the South,* 160–1; Stetson Kennedy, *Jim Crow Guide: The Way It Was* (Boca Raton: Florida Atlantic University Press, 1959), 139.

6. Maguire, interview, St. Augustine Historical Society; Federal Writers' Project, *Florida,* 452; Richard E. Smith, Federal Bureau of Investigation Report, 12 November 1936, Correspondence, Classified Subject Files, Department of Justice Central Files; Kennedy, *Palmetto Country,* 261; John W. Langdale, interview, 6, 13–4; Reed, interview; Ashmore, "Looking Back: The Woodsrider," 36; W. J. Kelly and A. L. Brogden to Our Turpentine Farmer Friends, 12 April 1940, Andrew D. Poppell Papers, Florida State Archives; Maguire, interview by author; Vail, "Old-Timer Remembers"; Gavin Wright, *Old South, New South,* 15, 199; Zora Neale Hurston, "Turpentine Camp—Cross City," 2, in Writers Program, Florida, "Turpentine Camp at Cross City," Department of Special Collections, George A. Smathers Libraries, University of Florida.

7. Lawrence Cohn, ed., *Nothing but the Blues: The Music and the Musicians* (New York: Abbeville Press, 1993), 164–5.

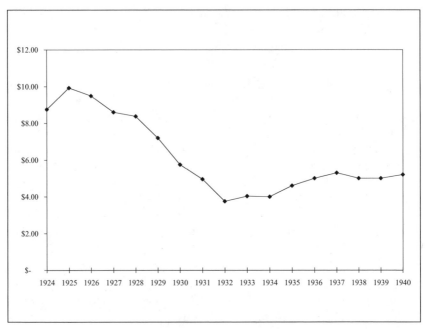

FIGURE 9.1. Average weekly wages per gum naval stores wage earner, 1924–1940. Based on data from Martin, "American Gum Naval Stores Industry," 339.

> Turpentine business ain't like it used to be
> Turpentine business ain't like it used to be
> I can't make enough money now to even get on a spree
>
> I ain't gone work no mo, I tell you the reason why
> I ain't gone work no mo, tell you the reason why
> Because everybody wants to sell, but nobody wants to buy
>
> You can work in the fields, you can work at the sawmill too
> You can work in the fields, you can work at the sawmill too
> But you can't make no money at nothing you try to do
>
> So Lawdy please tell me what we turpentine people are gone a do
> Lawdy please tell me what we turpentine people gone a do
> We may work one week, but we got lay off a mon or two.[8]

As they had done since the late nineteenth century, turpentine workers continued to make most of their purchases from the commissary. If commis-

8. Tampa Red, "Turpentine Blues," *Legends of the Blues*, vol. 2, audiocassette, Columbia Records.

saries lacked a needed item, it could be obtained by filling out an order. At one camp, workers could even acquire suits this way. However, women sewed most clothes with cloth they purchased by the bolt. Commissary prices remained typically higher than those at ordinary retail stores, between 10 and 100 percent more. According to one estimate, commissaries made a net profit of 20 percent at a time when retail stores earned between 5 and 8 percent. Producers justified the inflated prices in different ways. One maintained that "we weren't in the grocery business. We just wanted to make up for bad debts." Another explained that "of course we have to charge the niggers more, but they save in the long run. Just think how much it would cost them to drive thirty miles into town for vitals if they had cars." Despite price gauging, in many cases, commissaries remained a practical necessity, the nearest town was usually fifteen to twenty miles away from the camp. However, in areas where commissaries took business away from merchants, resentments could flare. In 1940, for example, Florida merchants unsuccessfully demanded that a judge order turpentine commissaries to pay the state sales tax required of all other retailers in the state.[9]

Whether their provisions came from the commissary, gardens, or the woods, workers' eating habits persisted with little change from earlier periods, and women continued to dominate food cultivation, purchases, and preparation. Staples of the turpentine workers' diet remained pork (mostly fat back), corn (prepared as cornbread), sweet potatoes, beans, peas, collards, mustard greens, eggs, chicken, and occasionally beef. Along with the goods and produce purchased at the commissary and grown in family gardens, workers continued to supplement their diet with small game and birds men hunted in the woods, and fish, especially bream and perch, caught by women and children. According to one report, however, during the depths of the Depression, some turpentine workers subsisted on a diet of bread, sugar, and water.[10]

As with their diet, workers continued to live in isolated quarters during the 1930s and 1940s, as they had done for decades. Most camps contained around fifteen cabins housing forty to sixty people. A WPA writer found the quarters at one Florida operation to be very primitive. "Weather-beaten and almost black," he explained, "the majority of these pine-board shacks are not

---

9. Gay Goodman Wright, "Turpentining," 114; S. Kennedy, *Palmetto Country,* 259; Reed, interview; Maguire, interview by author; Vail, "Old-Timer Remembers"; Gavin Wright, *Old South, New South,* 15, 199; Hurston, "Turpentine Camp—Cross City," 2.

10. Harley Langdale, Jr., interview, 13; Lauriault, "From Can't to Can't," 324; Ashmore, "Looking Back: The Woodsrider," 24; Reed, interview; Florida Writers' Project, "Story of Naval Stores" (July 1943), 14–5; S. Kennedy, *Palmetto Country,* 263; S. Kennedy, *Jim Crow Guide,* 139; "Rich and Lula Gray."

even equipped with shutters and porches. They are built on the low flat lands beneath tall pines, and the spacious yards are flooded during the rainy season." However, many quarters built during this period consisted of more substantial cabins than had been constructed in previous decades. Many contained two to three rooms. Some had glass and screened windows and painted interior walls. A few even possessed electric lights and running water. As in previous years, women did not typically work in turpentine but did live in the quarters with their families. Although single men lived two or three to a cabin, nuclear families each had their own dwelling. Families usually kept their houses neat and swept their yards clean of all debris and vegetation, save for a few flowers. Backyard garden plots yielded collards and yams. Many families also kept a few chickens and a coon dog. But not all workers lived in the quarters. Because automobiles and paved roads provided easier access to local communities than in previous periods, an increasing number of workers lived in adjacent towns and commuted to work.[11]

Although workers had increasing access to towns, the camp church and especially the juke joint remained the principal forms of distraction from the monotonous work routine. One worker explained of turpentine laborers "thats all they got to do beside work—go to church and drink shine." Camps usually contained a small church, where either a visiting preacher or a worker led services every Sunday. At some camps, Baptist and Methodist preachers conducted worship on alternating Sundays. On weekdays after work, a few laborers held prayer meetings. Turpentine workers who were religious tended to be very devout, but a larger number of laborers still reveled at the juke joint, particularly on Saturday nights. Typically operated by an entrepreneurial worker, jukes, as in previous decades, provided a place for laborers to drink moonshine, dance, and gamble. A few establishments also sold food such as hamburgers and fish. Along with food, sex could be purchased at some of these establishments. Prostitutes roamed from camp to camp, usually arriving on payday. The juke on Saturday night retained its character as a violent place where fights and even murders were not uncommon. When revelry at the juke continued through Sunday, many workers were too hungover to work the next day. On such occasions one innovative

11. "Rich and Lula Gray"; Maguire, interview, St. Augustine Historical Society; Eldredge, 4 Forests and the Future of the South, 43; Florida Writers' Project, "Story of Naval Stores" (July 1943), 14; Meldrim, interview; Thomas, McCranie's Turpentine Still, 34; Brown, Forest Products, 186; Duncan, "Report on Trip to Cross City," 6, in Writers Program, Florida, "Turpentine Camp at Cross City," Department of Special Collections, George A. Smathers Libraries, University of Florida, Gainesville; "Trends in the Production of Naval Stores in the U.S.," Gamble's International Naval Stores Yearbook, 1930–31, 57.

woodsrider administered his own hangover medicine consisting of a mixture of moonshine, 666 (a cold tonic), Raymond's Little Kidney Pills, Black Drought (a strong laxative), and any other medicine he had handy. The combination probably only exacerbated a hangover, but the woodsrider claimed it left his laborers fully recovered for work the next day.[12]

Despite child labor laws, throughout the 1930s and 1940s children performed a limited amount of work at turpentine operations. Most commonly they dipped to support their families' income. Producers even issued different sizes of nail kegs as dip buckets to correspondingly sized children. Children, along with women, also labored in nearby potato and cabbage fields, hundreds working at one time.[13]

When not contributing to their families' income, some children attended school. Although not available to children at all turpentine camps, schools did become more accessible during the 1930s and 1940s. Some camps had one-room schoolhouses, but most commonly the church served as a classroom during the weekdays. Whether supported by the producer or the local county government, camp schools were notoriously underfunded. At a camp in MacClenny, Florida, in the late 1930s, 1 teacher was responsible for 52 children crammed into one room. At another camp, 250 students and 8 teachers were crowded into a church. In many cases teachers were traveling instructors who visited several camps during the week. Only six to nine grades were available, and children were usually able to achieve a basic level of literacy at best. If, in the unusual case, a county school was nearby, children walked or were driven by a worker. No buses provided transportation. At some camps, however, no school of any kind was available within an accessible distance. Even where schools were available, several factors discouraged regular attendance. When the weather grew warm enough for gum to run, attendance rates dropped 30 percent as children began assisting with dipping. During cold weather, some children failed to attend because they lacked warm clothing.[14]

Along with poor living conditions in camps, decades-old labor practices persisted. Worker recruitment continued in the tight labor market. A camp

---

12. S. Kennedy, *Palmetto Country*, 263; Reed, interview; Florida Writers' Project, "Story of Naval Stores" (July 1943), 14–5; William P. Langdale, interview, 4–5; "Rich and Lula Gray."

13. Reed interview; W. W. Barber to Newton, 14 April 1945, Dantzler Lumber Company Papers.

14. Lauriault, "From Can't to Can't," 325; Florida Writers' Project, "Story of Naval Stores" (July 1943), 15; A. Philip Randolph to Homer Cummings, 5 March 1937, Correspondence, Classified Subject Files, Department of Justice Central Files; Hurston, "Turpentine Camp—Cross City," 15; Gavin Wright, *Old South, New South*, 113–4; S. Kennedy, *Palmetto Country*, 262; Reed, interview; Meldrim, interview; "Rich and Lula Gray."

manager would leave for a nearby community carrying moonshine and a black worker who knew other men in the area who might be persuaded to change employers. After giving a recruit some drinks and bragging about the superior working conditions at his camp and the availability of jobs, a manager would bring the new worker back to the camp. In some cases cash advances were required to coax laborers from their employers. Typical advances amounted to twenty-five dollars or less, although during the periods of greatest labor scarcity, advances reportedly could rise as high as five hundred dollars. Some recruiters employed more creative means of attracting laborers. One black Florida voodoo practitioner successfully used magic to attract labor for his employer. On a recruiting mission to Georgia when prospective workers proved unwilling to accept his offer, he rubbed two pebbles together, glared at the men, and threatened to hex them if they did not return with him. No matter the means used to hire workers, however, the following Monday morning, as was common, the manager would arrive at the recruited worker's former camp and, provided the camp manager cooperated, collect the new worker's belongings and pay off his account.[15]

Woodsriders remained an integral part of turpentine operations; they continued to ensure not only that tasks were completely and carefully executed but also that tools were maintained in good condition. The manager of a Georgia turpentine camp, in the 1940s, described his occupation as a fifteen-hour-a-day job. He hauled laborers to the woods, checked their work, took the sick to the doctor in Valdosta, paid their delinquent debts to local merchants, managed the commissary, and maintained law and order. Some woodsriders apparently continued to resort to brute violence to force unwilling workers to remain at their tasks.[16]

As part of the industry's characteristic paternalism, turpentiners attempted to control their labor by closely monitoring their quarters, an activity made possible by the camps' continued isolation in the pine wilderness. As had been the case since the antebellum era, many camps were located between twelve and twenty miles from the nearest road and could be reached only by a company road winding through murky swamps and dense

15. William P. Langdale, interview, 3; S. Kennedy, *Jim Crow Guide,* 137; Federal Writers' Project, *Florida,* 377; Richard E. Smith, Federal Bureau of Investigation Report, 12 November 1936, Correspondence, Classified Subject Files, Department of Justice Central Files.

16. Eldredge, *4 Forests and the Future of the South,* 42; Reed, interview; Maguire, interview, St. Augustine Historical Society; Florida Writers' Project, "Story of Naval Stores" (May 1943), 36; Hurston, "Turpentine Camp—Cross City," 4; William P. Langdale, interview, 4–5; Ashmore, "Looking Back: The Woodsrider," 24; Richard E. Smith, Federal Bureau of Investigation Report, 23 December 1936, Correspondence, Classified Subject Files, Department of Justice Central Files.

forests to an inaccessible spot. One member of the Florida Writers' Project found the area between Cross City and the Gulf, where many camps were scattered, to have no towns, the open pine flats broken only by small cypress swamps, and the region penetrated by only a few long dirt roads. Turpentiners and free-range hog and cattle raisers were commonly the only inhabitants in such regions. Many producers wanted to know the business of all who visited the camp and all details of outsiders' discussions with workers. One investigator of forced labor practices succeeded in gaining access to a camp in Front Cove, Florida, only after he told the manager he was there to record folk songs. Once the songs were recorded and the satisfied boss left, the investigator began his interview. With the white man gone, one worker admitted that "the only way out [of a turpentine camp] is to die out."[17]

Some producers went to considerable lengths to protect their precious labor force, and evidence suggests that peonage remained a common practice in the 1930s. An investigator with the Workers Defense League found that "peonage is nothing unusual in Florida. There are several sections in which it flourishes but these are veritable 'no-man's lands' where one must tread softly if wishing to live." When one turpentine worker, James Day, escaped from a turpentine camp in Manioh, Georgia, the owner falsely claimed that Day owed him two hundred dollars and held his four small children as ransom for his return. After unsuccessfully appealing to the U.S. district attorney and the FBI, Day went to court for the return of his children only to be jailed for abandoning them. The sheriff offered to release Day on the condition that he returned to work for the producer. In another instance, Lige James Johnson, a black turpentine worker for Charles A. Gaskins near Wewahitchka, Florida, left his job free of debt for employment in Panama City. But in 1938 Gaskins alleged that Johnson owed him thirty-five dollars and forced him to return to the turpentine camp for four more months of work. Three years later Gaskins claimed, after examining his books, that Johnson still owed him twenty-two dollars and wanted him to return to the camp. This time Johnson resisted, a struggle ensued, and Johnson was forced into Gaskins's car. During the thirty-mile-long ride back to the camp, Johnson jumped from the car and ran into the woods. Gaskins's subsequent trial for peonage attracted the attention of the American Turpentine-Farmers Association. Fearing that Gaskins's conviction might disrupt the industry's labor practices, the association lent the services of its own

17. Lauriault, "From Can't to Can't," 327; Cook, "Photographing the Turpentine Industry at Cross City," 5; Duncan, "Report on Trip to Cross City," 1, 4; Federal Writers' Project, *Florida,* 376; Maguire, interview, St. Augustine Historical Society; "Rich and Lula Gray"; S. Kennedy, *Jim Crow Guide,* 136; S. Kennedy, *Palmetto Country,* 262–3.

attorney to the defense. Despite their efforts, however, Gaskins was convicted of peonage. But on appeal, the U.S. District Court in Pensacola overturned the conviction, citing that Johnson had escaped from the car before returning to work at the camp. Thus Gaskins had attempted but not succeeded in placing Johnson in debt servitude and consequently was not guilty of the crime.[18]

Two powerful institutions historically associated with the naval stores industry—factorage houses and the criminal justice system—helped perpetuate the practice of peonage. Factors would only advance capital to producers whom they trusted to manage an operation profitably. The secret to success, as one former producer explained, "was that if you could handle the labor, most all turpentine labor was black, if you could handle those and knew how to get the work out of them, well then you could get along with the factors pretty good because you could operate." Moreover, although the leasing of convicts had officially ended in the early 1920s, a similar practice continued. If a worker left an operation, his employer could have him charged with a crime, taken to court, convicted, and then sentenced to the worker's choice of either twelve to eighteen months in prison or a fine. Workers typically chose the latter. The employer then paid the fine, obligating the convicted worker to labor for him to pay off the debt. The sheriff customarily threatened the worker with the chain gang if he left again.[19]

As had been the case earlier, the absence of labor union activity in the gum naval stores industry allowed such abuses to go largely uncontested. Although many of the white laborers, who dominated the skilled positions at pulp and paper mills, were organized, the majority of black workers involved in harvesting timber, stumps, and gum naval stores were not. A. Philip Randolph believed that workers such as turpentine laborers were exploited "because there is no labor organization in the South that has the strength and power to prevent the exploitation of Negro and white workers."[20]

The investigation and trial of turpentiner Will Knabb demonstrates the degree to which peonage and brutality persisted among some producers and

18. Richard E. Smith, Federal Bureau of Investigation Report, 12 November 1936, Correspondence, Classified Subject Files, Department of Justice Central Files; Shofner, "Postscript to the Martin Tabert Case," 169–72; S. Kennedy, *Jim Crow Guide,* 40; Shofner, "Forced Labor," 24.

19. Reed, interview; Harley Langdale, Jr., interview, 7; Shofner, "Postscript to the Martin Tabert Case," 164–7; Daniel, *Shadow of Slavery,* 180.

20. Eldredge, *The 4 Forests and the Future of the South,* 43; A. Philip Randolph to Homer Cummings, 5 March 1937, Correspondence, Classified Subject Files, Department of Justice Central Files.

the difficulty prosecutors had of convicting them of federal labor statute violations. On October 13, 1936, three black turpentine workers—Ed Baker, his
son-in-law Arthur Smith, and Alfred Smith—decided to quit work for Knabb
to find better wages. They came to R. T. Boyd's residence in Coleman, Florida, and requested work at his still. The three men also asked that a truck
be sent to MacClenny, Florida, to move their belongings and that Boyd pay
the balance of their accounts. The next day Boyd and a worker named William Simpson went to MacClenny to move the men and their families and
settle their debts. Boyd first settled the account of Alfred Smith for $9.22 at
a separate camp under the management of Knabb's son Earl, for which Boyd
received a receipt. He then loaded Smith's household goods onto his truck
and proceeded to MacClenny to Camp 17 to settle the other accounts and
load the other two workers' belongings. But upon entering the Camp 17 office, Boyd found the owner, Will Knabb; his woodsrider, Fred Jones; and
Earl Knabb, who had proceeded Boyd to MacClenny, all armed with pistols.
Knabb refused to let Boyd take the three workers and accused him of recruiting his labor, at the time a crime in Florida. The white men cursed and
threatened Boyd. Laying his hand on his pistol, Knabb informed Boyd that
he could not leave the office until he accepted the return of the $9.22 he
had paid Earl on Alfred Smith's account. Knabb also claimed that Arthur
Smith owed between thirty and forty dollars for burning part of a forest. The
three men forced Boyd to unload Alfred's belongings, and in the meantime,
Knabb called Alfred and Arthur into his office and asked if they were trying
to leave. Upon replying in the affirmative, they were threatened with severe
beatings, a response reported to be typical of Knabb when disciplining workers who attempted to leave. Several days after the incident, Ed Baker escaped and made his way to Boyd's camp, but his wife, daughter, and
belongings remained with Knabb. Knabb warned the two women that he
would have their shack guarded and if they left he would have them arrested.
Knabb's woodsrider thwarted the Smith men's escape, and they continued
to work for him in the woods.[21]

On October 23, 1936, Boyd, Simpson—who had accompanied Boyd to
Knabb's camp—and Ed Baker all visited the FBI Jacksonville Bureau office
and related the story. A week and a half later, Will and Earl Knabb, Fred
Jones, and Ed Hall were subsequently charged with peonage violations and
taken into custody by bureau agents and U.S. Marshals. All three men
pleaded not guilty and were each released on one-thousand-dollar bonds.

21. C. B. Winstead, Federal Bureau of Investigation Report, 19 March 1937; Richard E.
Smith, Federal Bureau of Investigation Report, 12 November 1936 and 13 December 1936,
Department of Justice Central Files.

Once the Knabbs were arrested, Arthur and Alfred Smith and Baker's wife and daughter were all moved to Boyd's camp, where they became his workers.[22]

The inquiry and trial of the Knabbs and their associates drew considerable attention from the press and concerned organizations. The NAACP and Workers Defense League sent investigators of their own. According to workers interviewed by the NAACP, all of Knabb's four hundred black laborers were held in peonage. Workers labored from sunup to sundown and received from 60¢ to $1.00 per day, although a few received $1.25. It was rumored in the community that, although Knabb kept accounts of wages owed to workers, they received smaller amounts than they were due on payday and met with serious consequences if they complained. Workers were forced to make all their purchases from the commissary, where prices were 100 percent higher than at retail stores. Thus their low wages had only half the buying power they would have had with area merchants. One woodsrider, in fact, discontinued his employment with Knabb after two years because he did not approve of the way the camps were operated. Knabb ran his various turpentine operations like small police states. He had all roads leading to the quarters watched, and two spies lived among the workers, even crawling under the shanties to discover dissatisfaction or escape plans. If workers attempted to leave, Knabb threatened their lives and had them beaten. Because labor was so scarce, it was Knabb's policy to punish workers but not dismiss them. When one of Knabb's woodsriders dismissed a worker for calling him a liar, an unhappy Knabb explained that it was "all right to whip them, but not to run them off." By the fall of 1936, newspapers across the country carried stories of Knabb's operation.[23]

The Knabb case illustrates the difficulty prosecutors found in securing convictions in peonage cases. When questioned about any fear of peonage charges, Knabb arrogantly responded that "I have been doing that for 19 years and there hasn't been any charge of peonage made against me, and

22. Richard E. Smith, Federal Bureau of Investigation Report, 12 November 1936, Federal Grand Jury Indictment of William Knabb, Earl Knabb, Fred Jones, and Edward Stuart Hall, February 1937, and Brien McMahon to Herbert S. Phillips, 7 November 1936, Department of Justice Central Files.

23. Shofner, "Postscript to the Martin Tabert Case," 168–70; W. G. Boyd to Dave Sholtz, 1 December 1936, Walter White to Attorney General, 8 December 1936, and A. Philip Randolph to Homer Cummings, 5 March 1937; W. G. Boyd to William Green, 1 December 1936; Richard E. Smith, Federal Bureau of Investigation Report, 12 November 1936, Aron S. Gilmartin to Homer T. Cummings, 24 November 1936, Richard E. Smith, Federal Bureau of Investigation Report, 23 December 1936 Correspondence, and C. B. Winstead, Federal Bureau of Investigation Report, 10 March 1936, Correspondence, Classified Subject Files, Department of Justice Central Files; Shofner, "Postscript to the Martin Tabert Case," 168.

nobody has tried to stop me." Knabb's powerful friends, including state senators, reportedly sought to interfere with the case. Will Knabb's brother, T. J.
Knabb, had been a state senator and turpentiner and had himself been the
subject of a peonage investigation. Another brother who was associated with
Will in the turpentine business was the president of the Bank of MacClenny.
Knabb's influential supporters made efforts to tamper with government witnesses, actions that Boyd explained were "very easy when negroes are offered money or either intimidated to forget what they know." Boyd wrote to
the governor requesting help, as well as to the U.S. attorney general, explaining the seriousness of the case. "I do know," he proclaimed, "that if the Federal Government fails in this attempt at this time to bring about justice what
will take place hereafter in the turpentine and operation of same, slavery
and servitude here in Florida. It will show that the Knabbs not only control
the territory surrounding McClenney [sic] but that they are bigger than the
Federal Government as they have often made their braggs."[24]

The trial's outcome did nothing to disprove Boyd's claim. The district
attorney, who decided the evidence did not involve Earl Knabb, dismissed
him from the case. Once the trial was under way, the defense argued that
the peonage charge represented nothing more than a rivalry between turpentine operators and had grown from Boyd's frustrated efforts to recruit
labor from Knabb's camp. The defense also intimated that the lawyers representing Boyd had demanded $16,000 in "hush money." Even after listening
to this implausible defense, the jury deliberated for less than thirty minutes
before acquitting Knabb and his men of all federal peonage charges.[25]

Thus, many conditions long associated with turpentine work persisted,
forced labor among them. Producers continued to organize labor according
to the task system and pay by piecework. The low-paid black men who dominated the labor force continued to work in rough terrain under the watchful
eye of woodsriders who considered violence and brutality necessary measures for labor management. Workers lived in isolated camps where they
remained indebted to the commissary. Driven from the open by U.S. Justice
Department investigations, peonage continued, as did efforts by producers
to recruit or "steal" workers from one another.

Not all industry patterns continued, however. Beginning in the late

24. C. B. Winstead, Federal Bureau of Investigation Report, 10 March 1936, Richard E.
Smith, Federal Bureau of Investigation Report, 12 November 1936, W. G. Boyd to J. Edgar
Hoover, 28 December 1936, W. G. Boyd to Homer S. Cummings, 1 December 1936, and W. G.
Boyd to Dave Sholtz, 1 December 1936, Correspondence, Classified Subject Files, Department
of Justice Central Files; Shofner, "Postscript to the Martin Tabert Case," 168.

25. Motion to Quash and "Witness Arrested As Perjurer, 2nd Held for Contempt," news
clipping, Department of Justice Central Files.

1930s, the number of small producers rose rapidly, a trend that had begun earlier but accelerated with the growth of central distilleries. These large gum processors eliminated the need for the considerable capital required to own and run a fire still and made it possible for owners of small timber tracts to enjoy a greater return by working their trees for turpentine themselves rather than leasing to large producers. Small owners thus began working their own pines, commonly employing their sons as laborers, and marketing the gum at the nearest central distillery. Men who possessed no land occasionally found timber owners willing to let them work land on shares. Blacks made up a substantial portion of these new share turpentine producers. Unlike black turpentine wage earners, share workers labored independently and, because their production expenses were low, did not rely on advances as did agricultural sharecroppers. Their rapid entry into naval stores production helped to greatly alter the industry's makeup. In 1934, the typical turpentiner worked nearly ten crops and employed thirty workers in gum production and just over two in distilling. Eighty percent of these producers had their own still, which, on average, produced 435 units annually. But from the early 1930s to the mid-1940s the number of turpentiners grew from six hundred to between four and five thousand, 70 percent working less than one crop of faces.[26]

In yet another change, the factorage houses entered a decline during the 1930s. In the early years of the decade, around 80 percent of naval stores were marketed through factors, just as they had since at least the early nineteenth century. Consolidated Naval Stores Company remained the largest factor in the United States, with a tangible net worth, in 1935, of eight million dollars, or 75 percent of all the other ten houses combined. By the late 1930s, however, growing dissatisfaction with the factorage system developed among producers. They complained that factors and dealers did not initiate any consumer marketing strategy, but instead only took orders for what was available. Because gum turpentine producers had competition from wood naval stores, gum producers demanded more aggressive efforts to retain their market share. They also alleged that factors encouraged overproduction because they benefited from commissions on the extra sales, regardless of the resulting low naval stores prices, and profited from the investment in additional loans and equipment sales. Producers especially resented the re-

26. Martin, "American Gum Naval Stores Industry," 223, 231–2; General Counsel and Assistant to the President to John Slusser, 12 April 1966, and J. Lundie Smith, "A Few Words of Appreciation," 20 April 1966, American Turpentine-Farmers Association Papers; Kayton, interview; Davis, ed., *Encyclopedia of American Forest*, s.v. "naval stores"; Brown, *Forest Products*, 86; Eldredge, interview; Reed, interview.

cent vertical integration of factorage houses like Consolidated, which controlled not only the marketing of products and the supplying of investment capital, but also manufactured the equipment, marketed the groceries needed to stock the commissaries, and even competed with producers by running their own operations. Another complaint was that factors were expensive at a time when economic efficiency mattered more than ever. The factor charged $2\frac{1}{2}$ percent commission for each transaction and 8 percent interest for all capital advances. Harley Langdale, Jr., the judge's son, likened factors to loan sharks. Some producers even began questioning the factors' honesty, suspecting that they conspired with bankers and exporters to manipulate prices for their own profit. But although producers resented the paternalistic relationship between themselves and their factors, many considered them necessary evils. Factors had, after all, helped numerous operators begin their businesses. Judge Langdale, who himself had experienced great difficulty working his way out from under his factor, saw them as a necessary, stabilizing force in the industry.[27]

With the government's entrance into market regulation and the rise of centralized distilleries, disgruntled producers found it somewhat easier to loosen ties to their factors. The factor was no longer the principal voice in an operator's production practices. Under the Naval Stores Conservation Program, turpentiners needed to satisfy the Forest Service's requests just as much as their factor's, although both parties were usually in agreement on recommendations. Also, in the American Turpentine-Farmers Association producers had a new, powerful voice with the political clout to influence national policy. But the shift from processing gum in fire stills to centralized distilleries undermined factors the most. Producers could now sell their gum directly to the central distillery and did not have to wait for the factor to find a buyer. Moreover, in reducing the operating expenses by eliminating the need for each producer to run his own still, the central facilities decreased producers' reliance on factors. The entry of new types of producers spurred by the central distilleries weakened the factors' position as well. The many new small operators harvested gum largely with their own labor and

27. Campbell, Unkrich, and Blanchard, *Naval Stores Industry*, 26, 51, 90–1; Baker, "Summerall Turpentine Still," 11–3; Turpentine and Rosin Factors, Inc., to A. D. Poppell, 31 January 1940, Turpentine and Rosin Factors, Inc., to Our Customers, 1 March 1940 and 26 March 1940, Poppell Papers; Antwerp Naval Stores Company et al. to W. F. Holtsman, 20 October 1933, and Commercial Reports of Naval Stores Factors, 20 October 1933, Cary Collection; Eldredge, *The 4 Forests and the Future of the South*, 20; Harley Langdale, Jr., interview, 7–9; Downing Musgrove (paper presented at the Naval Stores Breakfast, 31 October 1961, Washington, D.C.), 2–4, American Turpentine-Farmers Association Papers; Shelton, *Pines and Pioneers*, 185.

thus had very low production costs that did not require the factor's financial services. Also, smaller producers were usually able to secure loans from banks, relieving themselves of any need for a factor. Not only was the region's banking industry better developed by the 1940s than at any previous time, but small producers tended to own their own land, which banks accepted as collateral. Such producers required only small loans, just enough to cover the cost of the hardware needed to place their trees in production.[28]

Surprisingly, factors failed to lead the industry's construction of central distilleries, an inaction that ensured their obsolescence. The uncertain business climate of the 1930s caused factors' hesitation to invest in these expensive and technologically revolutionary facilities. By the time very large producers and consumers constructed enough of these plants to prove their profitability, the region was well on its way toward containing as many distilleries as its gum producers could keep in business. Desperate to have part of the market share, by the early 1940s such companies as Turpentine and Rosin Factors of Jacksonville and the giant Consolidated Naval Stores Company bought interests in existing stills, but they were too late to gain any control over processing. Because factors failed to adapt to changes in gum naval stores processing and marketing, their businesses rapidly declined, and by the second half of the 1940s, they played only a minor role in the industry.[29]

Whereas an increase in the number of small producers and the decline of the factorage houses' influence represented significant changes beginning in the 1930s, the Second World War set in motion circumstances that transformed the entire industry. When it began in Europe in 1939, the war created uncertainty in the gum naval stores market. Although many European buyers clamored for the products, interruption in shipping traffic made export difficult. But with American entry into the conflict, wartime demand for rosin turned naval stores supplies from surplus to shortage, and the Naval Stores Conservation Program, whose initial mission had been to reduce production, shifted to encourage manufacture for the war effort. NSCP foresters put on "Naval Stores for Victory Shows" to encourage production expansion. With a few musicians, a truck full of war equipment, and one or two wounded servicemen, they preached the message that "no ship can sail, no plane can fly, and no soldier can eat or fight without naval stores." Such companies as Filtered Rosin Products attempted to recruit new producers

28. Kayton, interview, 4–5; Eldredge, interview, 9–10; Shirley, "Gum Naval Stores Long Linked."

29. Martin, "American Gum Naval Stores Industry," 226–7, 273.

with a booklet explaining the basics of gum naval stores production and by offering assistance to anyone desiring to enter the business. The company assured operators that "crude gum production for turpentine and rosin is a vital necessity for victory. Produce more of it and buy victory bonds with your larger income." The Newton Company circulated a similar publication to help producers realize the maximum yield from their faces. By 1942, the U.S. Department of Agriculture estimated that of the approximately thirty million acres of pineland in the naval stores region, 60 percent was in production and 400,000 people depended, at least partially, on the products' manufacture for a living. But despite these large numbers, turpentine and rosin demand exceeded production throughout the war. With a yearly goal of 350,000 units, the industry could only supply 250,000.[30]

Two situations prevented turpentiners from meeting production goals. A greater demand for lumber and pulpwood, relative to naval stores, created part of the difficulty by consuming trees that potentially could have been tapped. From 1939 to 1942, lumber production and thus timber consumption in Georgia nearly doubled, from 1.09 billion board feet to 2.07 billion board feet. An acute labor shortage, however, explains most of the problem in meeting wartime demands for naval stores. Problems securing adequate labor persisted throughout the war. The federal government's wartime Office of Price Administration set prices of naval stores so low that producers were reportedly unable to raise wages to attractive levels without incurring a loss. The industry could not successfully compete for workers with other forest product industries in the naval stores belt or with the war industries that lured rural workers to the cities. In November 1941, Harley Langdale insisted to Washington officials that operators needed to increase wages dramatically in order to retain their current workers and attract others who had already left for better-paying jobs. He explained that where farmers could rely on machinery to increase production, gum turpentine producers relied completely on man power. The following year a producer lamented that he was making all he could, but because of the labor shortage his production was less than 50 percent of its potential. He complained that the army was

---

30. Continental Turpentine Company and Rosin Corporation, Incorporated, to Cordell Hull, 13 February 1940, Colmer Papers; Steedley, "Doctors," 12; Thomas, *McCranie's Turpentine Still*, 8; "Naval-Stores Trade Today," *Foreign Commerce Weekly* 10 (2 January 1943), 8–9; Powers, "'With Pearl Harbor Our World,'" 8; M. E. Henegar, *Gum Naval Stores Timber Land Use: Information and Suggestions* (Brunswick, Ga.: Filtered Rosin Products, n.d.), 6, copy in Olustee Experiment Station Files, Georgia Agrirama, Tifton, Ga.; Henegar, *Slash and Longleaf Pine Growers Handbook*; *Production of Naval Stores*, 8; Snow, "Research on the Improvement of Turpentine Practices," 380; Pikl, *History of Georgia Forestry*, 39.

drafting his turpentine workers, but worse, a "large part of our turpentine labor, both white and black are on WPA, and so far, my efforts to get them back in to the turpentine business has been a failure."[31]

As severe as the labor scarcity was, it could have been much worse. By the 1930s, changes in the industry had already eliminated the requirement for two historically important classes of laborers, coopers and distillers. The need for coopers gradually declined as the manner in which turpentine and rosin were packaged changed. Most producers purchased factory-made, tightly constructed spirit barrels, which were crafted of oak. Coopers were needed only to coat the barrels' inside with glue to properly seal them. At a few operations, coopers continued to construct wooden rosin barrels from machine-cut staves, but such barrels were growing prohibitively expensive and metal barrels did not possess several problems associated with wooden ones. Wooden barrels shrank as they dried and allowed the rosin to leak. Moreover, they did not last long. The wood barrels used to hold the NSCP loan stock could not endure more than two years in storage before decay required rebarreling at considerable expense. Wide weight variation in wood barrels made it difficult to determine prices, and central distilleries had a harder time sampling resin from wooden barrels. During the 1930s, producers therefore turned to metal rosin barrels, which arrived either ready-made or in two sections that had only to be crimped together. By 1941, all 130,503 barrels of rosin in storage were metal. A small percentage of rosin was packed in four- to six-ply paper bags weighing one hundred pounds. Thus, as the use of wooden barrels declined, producers lost the need for coopers. And as with coopers, the number of distillers declined as producers ended their use of old fire stills and began shipping resin to central distilleries.[32]

31. *Production of Naval Stores,* 8; Snow, "Research on the Improvement of Turpentine Practices," 380; Pikl, *History of Georgia Forestry,* 39, 41; T. D. Clark, *Greening of the South,* 115–6; Tindall, *Emergence of the New South,* 467; Albert G. Snow, *Turpentining and Poles,* reprint 15 December 1948 *Southern Lumberman* article (n.p., n.d.), 1, copy in Olustee Experiment Station Files; Jay Ward to Theodore G. Bilbo, 9 May 1945, Claude Pepper to Chester Bowles, 11 May 1945, Robert M. Newton to Office of Price Administration, 2 May 1945, William H. Davis, 28 May 1945, and Cliff Dees to Theodore G. Bilbo, 26 February 1942, Bilbo Papers; Harley Langdale, Memorandum Regarding Gum Naval Stores, 10 November 1941, Colmer Papers.

32. Maguire, interview by author; Hurston, "Turpentine Camp—Cross City," 12–4; Blount, *Spirits of Turpentine,* 43–5; Butler, *Treasures of the Longleaf Pines,* 114; Florida Writers' Project, "Story of Naval Stores" (July 1943), 31; Campbell, Unkrich, and Blanchard, *Naval Stores Industry,* 32–4; Shirley, *Working Trees for Naval Stores,* 35–6; Hosmer, *Economic Aspects of the Naval Stores Industry,* 23; Martin, "American Gum Naval Stores Industry," 32; Duncan, "Report on Trip to Cross City," 4.

Despite the decreased need for coopers and distillers, turpentiners still lacked a sufficient workforce; they reacted to the labor crisis in several ways, among them the continuation of peonage. In the 1940s, a convention of Georgia Baptists concluded that "peonage or debt slavery has by no means disappeared from our land. There are more white people involved in this diabolical practice than there were slaveholders. There are more Negroes held by these debt slavers than were actually owned slaves before the war Between the States. The method is the only thing which has changed." In 1942, the FBI received a letter from one young man's desperate mother and aunt requesting help in rescuing him from peonage. The two semiliterate women wanted "to see if there is enny wat(y) of getting you to get my boy out of the Hills of MacHenry- Miss Sippie. he have been there Six mears this coming September the First and I just heare from him now and then. he is on a tearptine Farm ant, that is a out Law Place and I am asking you for help if you Please. I want to see my Dear sun if there is enny possible chance enny more in life." The Justice Department, at J. Edgar Hoover's recommendation, decided not to investigate the case. In yet another incident in the 1940s, a producer recruited a family of dippers to whom he sent bus tickets. Their employer, however, stopped them on their way to town with their belongings and forced them to return. After the father went to the new employer by himself, his former one, with whom his family stayed, went to retrieve him only to be punched and held at gunpoint until the sheriff arrived. After an FBI investigation, the producer narrowly escaped peonage prosecution because of the leniency of a sympathetic Superior Court judge in Tifton, Georgia. A Florida Writers' Project participant found that turpentine workers "are the lowest strata of legally free humans," and a social worker remarked that "a negro who is foolish enough to go to work in a turpentine camp is simply signing away his birthright."[33]

Producers also responded to their labor shortage in more innovative ways than peonage. The state of Georgia paroled convicts to provide workers in rural areas. The program was begun in the spirit of patriotism on the argument that crop products were more essential to victory than road construction by chain gangs. Employers were to see to the ex-convicts' upkeep and to pay them the then current rate for rural help, but if the parolee left the camp, he was to be arrested and returned to prison to complete his sentence.

33. Stetson Kennedy, *Southern Exposure* (Garden City, N.Y.: Doubleday, 1946), 48; James Houser, 7 July 1942, John Edgar Hoover to Wendell Berge, 1 August 1942, and Wendell Berge to Director, Federal Bureau of Investigation, 12 August 1942, Correspondence, Classified Subject Files, Department of Justice Central Files; William P. Langdale, interview, 5–6; Duncan, "Report on Trip to Cross City," 6; S. Kennedy, *Palmetto Country*, 261.

Whereas many parolees went to farms, some found themselves in turpentine camps. In one instance a member of the governor's staff, who operated a large turpentine operation in Patten, Georgia, employed a dozen parolees, both white and black. They all lived together in a barn. At least one such worker objected to the turpentine work and complained that he was not adequately compensated. Other operators employed released Florida convicts. In the 1940s, Florida reportedly freed prisoners, even murderers, if they promised not to return to the state. Many took jobs at Georgia turpentine operations. German prisoners of war who worked at many jobs in the South—in agriculture, pulpwood, and at army bases—also labored in the naval stores industry. At Blountsville, Florida, foresters helped to train twenty-two thousand prisoners of war, many of them captured from Rommel's army, for harvesting turpentine and cutting pulpwood. Turpentiners apparently so valued and jealously guarded the use of these German workers that, upon repatriation following the war, they sought assurance that their prison laborers would not be withdrawn at a rate faster than in other businesses.[34]

The naval stores producers' willingness to employ former convicts and prisoners of war resulted from the challenging situation that the Second World War presented them; at the same time the war drove product demand to dizzying heights, it sapped the supply of low-cost workers on whose shoulders the labor-intensive business rested. Producers' concern therefore shifted from managing surplus quantities of turpentine and rosin to securing adequate timber stands and workers to meet government requirements for increased supplies. But the military, federal work programs, and wartime industries, all of which paid higher wages than work in turpentine, siphoned off the laborers needed to harvest gum.

With the war's end, the gum naval stores industry entered a rapid decline. As long as the war continued, naval stores demand exceeded supply, and the industry persisted despite its shortcomings. But because nothing about the gum naval stores industry changed substantially over the course of the conflict, its future was doomed. Gum producers continued to suffer from labor shortages. The hard, low-paying work that required laborers to toil in the summer heat while fighting bugs attracted few black southerners, who, with the rise of small manufacturing facilities in local communities,

34. J. Carlton Gatner, Federal Bureau of Investigation Report, 7 January 1943, Correspondence, Classified Subject Files, Department of Justice Central Files; Maguire, interview, St. Augustine Historical Society; William P. Langdale, interview, 5; Blount, *Spirits of Turpentine*, 29; McArther, "'During the War,'" 6; John W. Snyder to William Colmer, 29 May 1946, Colmer Papers.

could find better-paying and less physically demanding jobs. Moreover, by the early 1960s, the expansion of minimum-wage laws to cover agricultural workers, including those in naval stores production, forced operators to abandon the piecework system for hourly wages, which proved disastrously expensive.[35]

Just as alternative job opportunities began attracting workers away from the gum naval stores industry, widespread peonage diminished, although the practice by no means ended. First, two Supreme Court rulings in the first half of the 1940s found both Georgia's and Florida's labor laws, which continued to support peonage despite previous court decisions against similar statutes, unconstitutional, thus removing the legal underpinnings for the practice in those states. Second, the increasing availability of automobiles made escape easier, and the telephone put workers in better contact with legal assistance. Finally, as roads improved and cars became more accessible, community grocery stores began to attract the business of turpentine workers, undermining the role of the commissary, the linchpin of worker indebtedness. As early as 1943, one Florida observer found that "low-price cash and chain stores in nearby towns, improved transportation facilities and the fact that with few exceptions present-day camps are no longer isolated communities, have reduced commissary stocks to staple groceries, work clothes, tobacco, and soft drinks."[36]

The few workers who continued in the business had grown up in it, had little or no education, and knew only that trade. They had no way of leaving the industry, had no one to intercede for them, and had no choice but to accept whatever they were given. Wages in the naval stores industry remained so low that, as John W. Langdale, the judge's son, explained, "they could make as much on welfare as they could working the pine trees to get gum." But as this entrenched workforce aged, no one replaced it. In 1959,

35. Keith W. Dorman, "High-Yielding Turpentine Orchards: A Future Possibility," *Chemurgic Digest* 4 (29 September 1945): 295; "Firm Provides Constant Cash," *Valdosta (Ga.) Daily Times*, 26 June 1977; Davis, ed., *Encyclopedia of American*, 477; E. W. Carswell, "'Naval Stores' Industry Came to Northwest Florida in 1883," *Pensacola Florida News-Journal* File, Pensacola Historical Resource Center, Pensacola.

36. An investigation of peonage begun by the Workers Defense League in the second half of the 1940s uncovered potential forced-labor practices in turpentine camps. The League found that "more forms of forced labor are more widely practiced in Florida than in any other state." And as late as 1949 the Workers Defense League found fourteen turpentine camps in Alachua County, Florida, alone where peonage was openly practiced. Brown, *Forest Products*, 186; Duncan, "Report on Trip to Cross City," 5–7; S. Kennedy, *Southern Exposure*, 49; Shofner, "Forced Labor in the Florida Forests," 24–5; Shofner, "Postscript to the Martin Tabert Case," 172; Gay Goodman Wright, "Turpentining," 115; Daniel, *Shadow of Slavery*, 185; Cohen, "Negro Involuntary Servitude," 52; S. Kennedy, *Palmetto Country*, 259.

one retired forester explained that "today blacks don't want to work in turpentine. They can go to a little town and work at a manufacturing plant and make more money with shorter hours." Many of the few producers who continued worked on a very small scale, laboring with their families to harvest gum. In some instances, white women replaced black men in the forest. On one occasion an NSCP inspector came across a producer and his wife preparing trees for installing cups. The wife held a broad ax while her husband hit it with a maul. The same inspector also discovered a widow, whose livelihood depended on naval stores, using a hack after her chipper left. Such cases were reportedly not uncommon.[37]

Resumption of foreign naval stores production after the Second World War also hurt the American gum naval stores industry by decreasing export demands. Before the war, nearly half of all U.S.-produced rosin and close to 40 percent of turpentine was exported. By the late 1940s, less than a quarter of naval stores was sold overseas. U.S. production continued to outpace exports, however, causing price declines.[38]

Yet it was the wood naval stores industry, rather than foreign manufacturing, that hurt gum turpentine and rosin producers more. In 1933, Phoenix Naval Stores Company acquired and reopened the Yaryan wood naval stores plant at Gulfport, which Hercules had earlier shut down with the completion of its Hattiesburg facility. Three years later the Crosby Naval Stores plant began operations in Picayune, Mississippi, and the Alabama Naval Stores Company started production in Mobile. In 1938, the Chemical Products Company plant opened at Laurel, Mississippi. Newport Company, based in Pensacola, remained active during the period and, in 1939, opened a new plant. By the late 1940s, wood naval stores plants also went up in western Louisiana. A Crosby plant opened in DeRidder in 1946, and one year later, another Newport plant started operations in Oakdale. By the end of the 1940s, the South contained thirteen wood naval stores plants: one in Georgia, one in Florida, three in Alabama, six in Mississippi, and two in Louisiana. One Mississippi plant held the distinction of being the largest in the world. Although in 1940 gum naval stores operators manufactured the

37. Reed, interview; Kayton, interview, 5; Wilson, interview; Blount, *Spirits of Turpentine,* 30; "Langdale Company Sells Gum Process Machinery," *Valdosta (Ga.) Daily Times,* 27 August 1975; Meldrim, interview; McArther, "'During the War,'" 7; Senate Committee on Agriculture and Forestry, *Crude Pine Gum Act of 1967: Hearing before a Subcommittee . . . on S. 2511,* 90th Cong., 1st sess., 1967, 5, 10.

38. Campbell, Unkrich, and Blanchard, *Naval Stores Industry,* 19, 36–7, 92–3; Martin, "American Gum Naval Stores Industry," 193, 196–7; Harley Langdale and E. E. Holdman to Office of International Trade, United States Department of Commerce, 6 May 1948, and Harley Langdale to Secretary of Agriculture, 13 October 1947 [38], Colmer Papers.

majority of products—60.7 percent of U.S. turpentine and 53.6 percent of rosin—the domestic wood naval stores output that year was the largest on record. With the rise in demand during the Second World War, wood naval stores increased its share of the world market. As their customer base continued to expand, wood naval stores by 1945 exceeded gum naval stores in production. One industry observer remarked that, despite all of the gum naval stores industry's government support, "the steam solvent industry due to its efficient operation, competes with the gum industry and produces a better product at less cost, and is on a sounder financial and industrial basis."[39]

But just as gum naval stores production declined and wood naval stores manufacturing experienced impressive growth at its expense, the latter's consumption of huge quantities of stumps threatened to exhaust the supply, in the same way gum turpentine had nearly consumed the living pine stands generations earlier. Together, the thirteen wood naval stores plants that used the destructive distillation method had a capacity of nearly four thousand tons of stumps per day, requiring two hundred boxcars or five hundred trucks full to keep them supplied. Although the southern pine belt contained hundreds of thousands of acres of cutover land from which stumps were available, the growth in demand outpaced the replacement of the supply, especially since not all pine stumps made suitable processing material. Because they contained most of the heartwood, the stumps from old-growth longleaf were the most profitable to process, and like the virgin longleaf pine stands themselves, their number was finite.

Beginning in the late 1940s and continuing through the 1950s, plants employing destructive distillation suffered not only from a decline in available stumpage but also, and more importantly, from new, more-efficient production techniques developed by the pulpwood industry. At the South's increasing number of pulpwood plants, the trunks were debarked, chipped, and cooked in a weak sulfuric acid solution to extract the wood's cellulose for paper. During the process, turpentine spirits were released and, once condensed, formed sulfate turpentine. While the spirits vaporized from the cooked solution, rosin was emitted in the form of tall oil, a frothy substance that materialized on the top of the mixture and could be skimmed off after

39. R. E. Price, "Naval Stores in Southwest Louisiana," *McNeese Review* 2 (spring 1949): 10–1; Croft, "Twin Success Story," 9; Charlotte Wittwer, "Stumpwood to Resins—Oldest Pensacola Industry," *Pensacola Florida News-Journal* File; *Naval Stores Statistics*, 2–3, 5; Martin, "American Gum Naval Stores Industry," 21, 182, 186–8; "Naval Stores History We Never Knew," 4–5; Shirley, "Gum Naval Stores Long Linked"; "Waste Stumps from Dixie Cut-Over Land Become Hundreds of Products at Plant," *Pensacola Florida News-Journal*, 2 October 1949; Koch, *Utilization of the Southern Pines*, 1477.

cooking. During the early years of the pulpwood industry, no process existed to refine the tall oil into its usable component parts, and it had to be discarded or burned as fuel. But in the late 1940s, the Arizona Chemical Company, after a decade of research, developed a fractional distillation process whereby tall oil could be separated into fatty acids, rosin, and pitch. With this discovery, the sulfate naval stores industry, also considered part of the wood naval stores industry, quickly moved to conquer production. Sulfate naval stores could be made more cheaply than comparable gum or destructively distilled products. By 1955, sulfate naval stores production exceeded that of gum, and over the next thirteen years it almost completely replaced all other methods. Over the 1950s gum naval stores manufacture declined by nearly 65 percent. In 1950, it accounted for just 40 percent of the total production of naval stores products. By 1960, it dropped to close to 20 percent, then to around 16 percent in 1965, and, in 1970, to less than half of a percent. Forest researcher Albert Snow, with the Southeastern Forest Experiment Station, explained that "the naval stores industry must compete with newer industries for manpower, and its products must be marketed in competition with those of modern chemical industries." Although many plants using destructive distillation went out of business, a few innovative producers, such as Newport Company, began construction of tall oil processing plants. In the late 1940s, Newport built a facility at Bay Minette, Alabama, and later enlarged its capacity tenfold. In the early 1960s, it erected another such plant in Oakdale, Louisiana.[40]

By the early 1950s, many larger producers and businesses that supported the gum naval stores industry phased out production and turned to other activities. Foreseeing the industry's continued decline, producers like the Maguire family began selling their St. Johns County, Florida, timber for pulpwood in the early 1940s and started a timberland-management company that remains in operation today. The Langdales continued to prosper by restructuring their naval stores operation and simultaneously branching out into a wide range of businesses. In the mid-1940s, the Langdale turpentine operation consisted of eighteen to twenty separate partnerships, but, in 1947, the judge began buying out the partnerships and consolidating these

---

40. Davis, ed., *Encyclopedia of American Forest*, 477–8; Koch, *Utilization of the Southern Pines*, 1477; Snow, "Research on the Improvement of Turpentine Practices," 375, 380; Carswell, "'Naval Stores' Industry Came to Northwest Florida in 1883"; Blount, *Spirits of Turpentine*, 30; *Naval Stores Statistics*, 2–3; *Naval Stores: A Summary of Annual and Monthly Statistics, 1955–74* (Washington D.C.: U.S. Department of Agriculture, 1977), 5; Croft, "Twin Success Story," 9; R. E. Price, "Naval Stores in Southwest Louisiana," 10–1; Wittwer, "Stumpwood to Resins"; Martin, "American Gum Naval Stores Industry," 21, 182, 186–8; Shirley, "Gum Naval Stores Long Linked"; "Waste Stumps from Dixie."

different enterprises into the Langdale Company, with him and his sons as equal shareholders. At the same time, the family built a central distillery and a wood-treating operation. Through the 1960s, the Langdales remained a powerful force in Georgia and in what little remained of the gum naval stores industry. The judge continued as the AT-FA president until 1966. While a Georgia state congressman from 1949 to 1951, his son John sponsored an unsuccessful bill on behalf of the AT-FA to change Georgia from the Peach State to the Turpentine State. Over the next few decades, as the gum naval store industry continued to decline, the Langdales shifted their financial resources into other lines of business. When the judge died in April 1972 at the age of eighty-four, another son, Harley junior, became the head of Langdale Company, while yet another son, Billy, took on responsibility for organizing timber for the Langdale mills. Harley junior served as chairman of the Valdosta Savings and Loan and as the chairman of the board of Georgia's state university system. In the mid-1970s, the Langdale Company sold its gum turpentine processing plant, which had operated continuously since 1945, to a Guatemalan concern. By the 1980s, Langdale businesses in and around Valdosta included a sawmill, a building supply company, a Sheraton Hotel, a Ford car dealership, a tire company, a fuel company, and an insurance company. Outside of the Valdosta area, they owned a fence post processing plant in Homerville, Georgia, a pole-peeling operation and pole yards in both Chauncy and Blackston, Georgia, and a wood processing plant in Sweetwater, Tennessee.[41]

Companies supplying turpentine equipment also had to change their focus or go out of business. The Lerio Corporation of Valdosta, for example, began as a manufacturer of metal turpentine cups. Founded by the family patriarch, who had been in the naval stores industry since the turn of the century, the company produced its last cups in the early 1960s. The business continued, however, because a decade earlier the Lerios had the foresight to diversify and began manufacturing ice cans, draft beer pumps, garden hoses, and oil breather caps. By the late 1970s, their largest-selling product was metal containers used by nurseries for growing plants. Not all companies made such a successful transition, however. Consolidated Naval Stores Company, the vertically integrated gum industry giant, kept its factorage business during the Depression, but closed its subsidiaries. With the increasing popularity of central distilleries, it acquired a 25 percent interest in Filtered Rosin Products, which operated five plants in south Georgia and north Florida.

41. John Langdale, interview, 1, 7, 10–1, 15, 21–2; Arceneaux, "Captains of the Naval Stores Industry," 9; Georgia House of Representatives, Resolution Honoring John W. Langdale, 6 March 1998, SR 723; "Langdale Company Sells Gum Process Machinery."

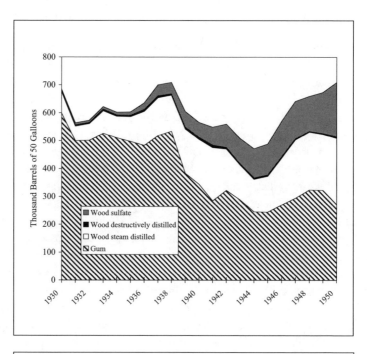

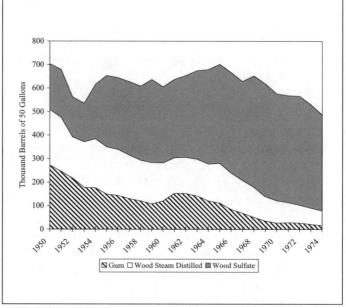

FIGURE 9.2. Turpentine production by method, 1930–1950 (top) and 1950–1974 (bottom). Based on data from *Naval Stores Statistics, 1900–1954* (Washington, D.C.: United States Department of Agriculture, 1956), 8; *Naval Stores: A Summary of Annual and Monthly Statistics, 1955–74* (Washington, D.C.: United States Department of Agriculture, 1977), 5. Figures for 1950–1974 do not include destructively distilled turpentine.

Unsatisfied with the arrangement, Consolidated divested itself within just a few years. By 1948, only forty operators used their factorage services. With such little demand for its business, Consolidated closed its factorage house at the end of 1949.

The very few gum turpentine producers who continued operations after the 1960s faced not only the challenge of low prices and high production costs, but the end of government support. In 1967, the government began liquidating its stockpile of gum naval stores held as part of the NSCP, and in 1972, it shut down the program. One year later the Olustee Experiment Station ended naval stores studies and began agricultural research. Remaining producers faced the difficulty of finding a still to process the gum. As the central distillation plants closed, operators were forced to truck their gum farther and farther away. In 1955, twenty-four central distilleries operated, most located in Georgia, but twenty-one years later, only seven plants remained. By the late 1970s, just two gum distilleries operated, and these were in the Valdosta area. Today only one facility, built in Baxley, Georgia, in 1949, continues to serve the very small number of remaining gum naval stores producers. Pulpwood plants using the sulfate method supply most naval stores.[42]

During the 1930s and 1940s, the labor conditions of naval stores workers remained remarkably similar to what they were many decades earlier. Although new gum-harvesting technology required workers to adopt different techniques, the routine and labor conditions changed relatively little. Producers persisted in their reliance on cheap, black labor and debt peonage, and woodsriders continued to monitor workers closely. Moreover, workers' lives remained centered on isolated camps where education was scarce. Hard work, low pay, and poor living conditions offered little to encourage workers' retention once greater employment opportunity rose in the World War II and post-war South. As employment related to the war effort attracted black men, naval stores producers found little means of encouraging or even forcing them to stay. The economic development and associated transportation and communication improvements that continued to sweep the South after the war further widened worker options and greatly eroded operator control of turpentine camps. As the pool of cheap and reliable black labor vanished, the wood naval stores industry grew at the expense of its

42. Harvey, "Maguire Born into Turpentine Family," 9; Kathy Hawk, "Turpentine: An Ancient Technology Almost Tapped Out in St. Johns County," *St. Augustine Ancient City Beacon,* 25 June 1982; "Quality Product, Good Service Key Lerio Success," *Valdosta (Ga.) Daily Times,* 26 June 1977; Blount, "Spirits in the Pines," 100; Butler, *Treasures of the Longleaf Pines,* 166; Davis, ed., *Encyclopedia of American Forest,* 477; "Location of Processing Facilities in Relation to Gum Output, Crop Year 1954–55," Naval Stores Collection.

gum counterpart. Just as destructive distillation made impressive gains, however, a newer, even more efficient method, sulfate naval stores, rose to take its place. Many large gum naval stores producers diversified into other businesses, leaving only a few very small operators who employed family labor. Today large industrial plants supply the demand for naval stores.

Conclusion: The New Old South

The fact that today's old naval stores belt possesses so few towns, a widely scattered rural population, and little sign of once having been the largest area of industrial employment in the South demonstrates that economic growth has not always followed the pattern seen in regions like the Carolina piedmont. Analysis of naval stores production, one of the most representative of southern industries, provides a different picture of southern development than that which scholars who concentrate on cotton cultivation and textile manufacturing typically offer. It reveals that antebellum southerners did indeed show an interest in manufacturing and, although they admittedly poured the majority of their resources into agricultural pursuits, that they were willing to invest in such enterprises as turpentine operations, especially in areas that failed to support plantation agriculture. Typical of both antebellum and postbellum southern industry, turpentining was closely linked to agriculture, operated in rural areas, required relatively little initial capital investment, and employed forced labor. As a transient, extractive industry that remained technologically primitive and whose low pay attracted few willing workers, naval stores production contributed little to the long-term economic development in the piney woods South.

After languishing as a marginally profitable business that no state save North Carolina would pursue, by the 1830s, the naval stores industry was boosted by increased demand from new uses for turpentine. Prices soon rose high enough to make gum and spirit production an appealing alternative to cotton cultivation. The poor whites and yeoman farmers who dominated colonial production remained in the business, but another type of producer entered it in the 1830s. With access to substantial capital resources and the control of large, slave labor forces, new entrepreneurs each invested in thousands, even tens of thousands of acres of previously undesirable pineland, constructed their own distilleries, and began production on a grand scale. At the same time, a transportation revolution in North Carolina—

improvements in river navigation and construction of plank roads and then railroads—facilitated the industry's expansion into areas previously too remote to permit profitable manufacture. Slaves performed the vast majority of work at these large turpentine operations. The various procedures involved in harvesting gum, the geography of the pine forests, and the ways that these three factors affected slave-management practices created distinct work patterns and manners of life for slaves in the naval stores industry.

Slave laborers were not the only victims of exploitation by the burgeoning naval stores industry. As North Carolina's mature longleaf pines yielded to windfall, rotting, fire, and insects, stands failed to regenerate. By the 1850s, destructive gum-harvesting methods led to severe depletion of the state's longleaf pine forests, causing the industry to begin a southward migration in search of fresh stands. Producers purchased fresh pine tracts in South Carolina, Georgia, Florida, and Alabama and moved their operations, including their slaves, to the new locations, but persisted with the same destructive harvesting practices that had forced them from North Carolina.

Although the Civil War devastated the turpentine market, interrupted the naval stores industry's southward movement out of North Carolina, and freed the slaves on whose labor production had relied, the business recovered rapidly and with it prewar patterns. Despite new labor arrangements and somewhat altered gum collection practices, the continuation of the antebellum businesses' basic characteristics—large-scale production, primitive harvesting methods that led to environmental degradation, and reliance on forced labor—demonstrates a relative degree of continuity between the Old South and the New. The New South's railroad building boom, especially in Georgia and Florida, provided access to more and more isolated longleaf pine tracts, just as had the antebellum transportation improvements in North Carolina. The old harvesting process, which dated back to colonial times, persisted and, consequently, destruction of turpentined timber continued. The unchanged practices and their effect on the forest perpetuated the industry's transient nature, ultimately forcing almost all turpentining out of North Carolina. North Carolinians and their descendants, however, continued their domination of production. By the beginning of the twentieth century, Tar Heels were firmly established in south Georgia and north Florida, where they helped pioneer middle-class business communities in the thinly settled pine forests. Turpentine operators who left the Carolinas brought their workers with them. The influx of turpentine laborers into the pine region contributed to a surge in the percentage of African Americans as part of the region's population.

Along with the southward migration, reliance on forms of relatively unfree black labor represented further continuation of the industry's antebellum characteristics. As before the war, producers, while not practicing slavery, relied on forced labor and employed various tactics to ensure that workers remained in the business. Convicts leased to turpentiners, especially in the state of Florida, provided cheap and reliable labor. The great majority of turpentine workers, however, lived in a state somewhere between freedom and forced labor. Whereas some workers were free to sell their labor on the market, enticement, emigrant agent, and vagrancy legislation limited the movement of many workers, casting them into a gray area of semifreedom. Others languished in actual debt peonage, coerced to work to repay what they owed their employer. The intensive work routine involved in naval stores manufacture and the laborers' Spartan daily existence in the isolated pine forest camps also persisted.

The industry's characteristic elements survived largely unchanged through even Progressive Era reform efforts. Around the turn of the century, as southern states strengthened peonage legislation with false-pretenses laws and expanded vagrancy statutes and employers began drawing whites—particularly recently arrived immigrants—into the system, the Department of Justice investigated and tried employers for violation of the Thirteenth Amendment. The national press coverage of the cases focused public attention on the use of forced labor and spurred public outcry. But despite intense national interest and peonage's apparent extensive use, only a small number of producers were ever tried and fewer still convicted. With the same zeal but more successful results, reformers also attacked convict leasing. Not as widely practiced but practiced more openly than peonage, convict leasing proved less capable of withstanding opposition pressure. The combination of public attack, the growing expense of leasing, and the demand for chain gang work on state projects finally brought convict leasing to an end. Peonage, however, survived. Although the fear of prosecution drove the practice out of public view, it continued beyond the 1930s.

Even though Progressive efforts failed to alter significantly the lives of turpentine workers, they did lead to the adoption of less destructive harvesting methods than had been employed since the naval stores industry began in the American colonies two centuries earlier. Researchers pioneered two new practices, shallow scarring of the tree trunk to make gum run and the attachment of a clay cup to collect it, methods that not only produced a higher-grade gum than the older practices of deep chipping and boxing but also caused less harm to the tree. The industry's ability to alter production methods in the early twentieth century resulted from the confluence of two significant events: the near total loss of the southern pine forest and the emergence of scientific forestry in the United States. The success of the new techniques fostered a more receptive environment for forestry among many producers, which allowed for further refinement of improved methods and ultimately greater involvement of forestry in the South. In this more cooperative atmosphere the federal Bureaus of Forestry and Chemistry were able to pioneer other improvements that aided the industry. But despite all these advancements, the basic system of production persisted.

Unlike destructive production methods, turpentiners faced business challenges during the Progressive Era that federal efforts did not address. Despite a stabilization of timber resources, due largely to forestry efforts, pine acreage remained relatively scarce and expensive, especially after lumber companies, fearful of a timber depletion, began buying up remaining stands. Other production costs, particularly labor, rose during this period, the greatest jump occurring during the First World War as African Americans began migrating to northern cities. Both higher timber and higher labor costs strained turpentine producers' ability to operate profitably. Competition from two new rivals, the wood naval stores industry and foreign gum naval stores production, posed another serious threat to operators. Foreign naval stores producers, especially the French, grew capable of supplying European consumers with quality turpentine and rosin, thus cutting into the U.S. naval stores export market. Moreover, wood naval stores production, a highly mechanized and technical process of extracting turpentine and rosin from ground-up pine stumps, enjoyed an advantage over gum naval stores manufacturing in its ability to provide superior products possessing specific qualities tailored to individual consumers' needs.

The persistence of these challenges, combined with the economic and social changes that affected the South in the 1930s and 40s, finally brought the gum naval stores industry to virtual collapse as the wood naval stores industry took its place. However, the transition occurred only after considerable efforts by producers and the federal government to save the dying industry. With the 1936 creation of the American Turpentine-Farmers Association, which successfully argued that turpentiners were in fact agriculturists, operators began benefiting from New Deal crop programs. Although their new status as farmers provided producers with a temporary reprieve from minimum-wage and social security legislation, New Deal work programs and especially the influx of young black men into the military during the Second World War drained available labor. Moreover, though peonage survived into the 1940s, improvements in transportation and communication made naval stores camps far less isolated than in earlier periods and significantly reduced the control exercised by producers over their workers. Producers were unable to operate without cheap labor, and as the supply declined, so did gum naval stores production. The wood naval stores industry, which did not rely on intensive labor but rather on heavy mechanization and a small number of well-trained technicians, made gains at the expense of the gum industry. By 1945, wood naval stores production exceeded that of gum and, ten years later, outpaced it by two and a half times, only to be replaced itself during the 1960s by the manufacture of naval stores at pulp-wood plants.

The demise of the gum naval stores industry in the post–World War II South ultimately represents the defeat of a poorly capitalized, technologically primitive, and labor-intensive business by a well-funded, sophisticated, and highly mechanized one. Retaining the basic characteristics it possessed as far back as the colonial era, the gum naval stores industry, despite significant government support, found itself unable to compete in the South's mid-twentieth-century business environment. It could not succeed against its rival, which offered far more attractive employment and produced a superior product at a lower price. With its failure to modernize, the gum segment of the naval stores industry fell victim to an advancing economy. That turpentine and rosin production could remain so primitive and not fully industrialize until the Second World War indicates that an important area of the post–Civil War southern economy constituted a continuation of basic antebellum patterns and suggests, as Henry Grady admitted to readers of the *New York Ledger* in 1889, that "the new South is simply the old South under new conditions."[1]

1. *The New South: Writings and Speeches of Henry Grady* (Savannah: Beehive Press, 1971), 107.

BIBLIOGRAPHY

PRIMARY SOURCES

Manuscripts and Manuscript Collections

American Turpentine Farmers Association. Papers. Georgia Agrirama, Tifton, Ga.

Basden, William. Papers. Special Collections Library. Duke University.

Bilbo, Theodore. Papers. Archives and Manuscript Department. McCain Library and Archives. University of Southern Mississippi.

Board of Commissioners of State Institutions. Papers. Florida State Archives, Tallahassee, Fla.

Buford, John. Papers. Special Collections Library. Duke University.

Carondelet, Francisco Luis Hector de. Papers. Fol. 83, microfilm. Archivo Central de Indias, Cuba.

Carson, John Avery Gere. Papers. Manuscripts Collection. Georgia Historical Society, Savannah, Ga.

Cary, Austin. File. Forest History Society, Durham, N.C.

———. Memorial Forestry Collection. Department of Special Collections. George A. Smathers Libraries. University of Florida.

Clark, Belton Decator. Papers. South Caroliniana Library. University of South Carolina.

Colmer, William M. Papers. Archives and Manuscripts Division. McCain Library and Archives. University of Southern Mississippi.

Cook, Robert. "Photographing the Turpentine Industry at Cross City, Florida." In Writers Program, Florida, "Turpentine Camp at Cross City." Department of Special Collections. George A. Smathers Libraries. University of Florida.

Cubberly, Frederick C. Papers. Department of Special Collections. George A. Smathers Libraries. University of Florida.

Dantzler Lumber Company. Papers. Special Collections. Mitchell Memorial Library. Mississippi State University.

Day, Henry C., to Judge Pierreporch, 29 February 1872, letter attached to a copy of James R. Butts's *150,000 Acres Yellow Pine Timber, Turpentine, and Cotton Lands*

(Macon: Georgia Land Agency, 1858). Special Collections Division. University of Georgia Libraries. University of Georgia.

Department of Justice Central Files. General Records of the Justice Department. Record Group 60. National Archives, Washington, D.C.

Duncan. "Report on Trip to Cross City." In Writers Program, Florida, "Turpentine Camp at Cross City." Department of Special Collections. George A. Smathers Libraries. University of Florida.

Fatio, Francis Philip. "Considerations on the Importance of the Province of East Florida to the British Empire," 14 December 1782. St. Augustine Historical Society Research Library, St. Augustine, Florida.

Forest Service News Clipping File. Forest History Society, Durham, N.C.

Georgia Forestry Association. Papers. Special Collections Division. University of Georgia Libraries. University of Georgia.

Germond, Gilbert Isaac. Work Journal. Department of Special Collections. George A. Smathers Libraries. University of Florida.

Grant, Dorothy Fremont. Collection. North Carolina State Archives, Raleigh, N.C.

Grist, James Redding. Papers. Special Collections Library. Duke University.

Harper, Francis. Papers. Special Collections Library. Duke University.

Harrington, John McLean. Papers. Special Collections Library. Duke University.

Herty, Charles Holmes. Collection. Special Collections. Robert W. Woodruff Library. Emory University.

Holland, George. Collection. North Carolina State Archives, Raleigh, N.C.

Hurston, Zora Neale. "Turpentine Camp—Cross City." In Writers Program, Florida, "Turpentine Camp at Cross City." Department of Special Collections. George A. Smathers Libraries. University of Florida.

Jones, Oliver H. Papers. Special Collections Library. Duke University.

Jordan, Daniel W. Papers. Special Collections Library. Duke University.

Judge, John. Papers. Southern Historical Collection. University of North Carolina at Chapel Hill.

Lee, Ransom. Papers. Special Collections Library. Duke University.

MacRae, Hugh. Papers. Special Collections Library. Duke University.

Maguire Land Corporation. Papers. Maguire Land Corporation, St. Augustine, Fla.

Makie, Thomas J. Papers. Special Collections Library. Duke University.

McDowell, Thomas David Smith. Papers. Southern Historical Collection. University of North Carolina at Chapel Hill.

McKay, John. Papers. Special Collections Library. Duke University.

Mercer Family. Papers. Southern Historical Collection. University of North Carolina at Chapel Hill.

Naval Stores Collection. Georgia Historical Society, Savannah, Ga.

Olustee Experiment Station Files. Georgia Agrirama, Tifton, Ga.

Osteen, Thomas H. Papers. South Caroliniana Library. University of South Carolina.

Patterson, Martha Virginia McNair Evans. Papers. Southern Historical Collection. University of North Carolina at Chapel Hill.

Pensacola Florida News-Journal File. Pensacola Historical Resources Center. Pensacola, Fla.

Poppell, Andrew D. Papers. Florida State Archives, Tallahassee, Fla.

Powell, William C. Papers. Special Collections Library. Duke University.

Probate Record 1511. Darlington County Historical Commission, Darlington, S.C.

Richardson, William A. B. and John H. Papers. Special Collections Library. Duke University.

Rodman, William Blount. Papers. North Carolina State Archives, Raleigh, N.C.

St. Johns County Court Cases. St. Augustine Historical Society Research Library, St. Augustine, Fla.

C. Schrack and Company. Papers. Special Collections Library. Duke University.

Seawell, Aaron Ashley Flowers. Papers. Southern Historical Collection. University of North Carolina at Chapel Hill.

Sharpe, Wilbur M. Papers. South Caroliniana Library. University of South Carolina.

Smedley, Joseph V. Papers. Special Collections Library. Duke University.

Smith, William R. Memorandum Book, 1852–1853. Special Collections Library. Duke University.

Southern Forest Institute. Papers. Special Collections Division. University of Georgia Libraries. University of Georgia.

Sparrow, Thomas. Papers. Southern Historical Collection. University of North Carolina at Chapel Hill.

Stephens, Erwin Duke. Papers. Special Collections Library. Duke University.

Stuckey, B. J. L., *v.* M. J. Outlaw and B. L. Outlaw, Civil Suit Testimony, c. 1890. Darlington County Historical Commission, Darlington, S.C.

Testimony regarding working boxes on shares, 30 May 1883. Sessions 805. Darlington County Historical Commission, Darlington, S.C.

Tillinghast Family. Papers. Special Collections Library. Duke University.

Turlington, A. J. Papers. Special Collections Library. Duke University.

Turlington, William H. Papers. Special Collections Library. Duke University.

Turpentine News Clipping File. Forest History Society, Durham, N.C.

Williams, Sarah Hicks. Papers. Southern Historical Collection. University of North Carolina at Chapel Hill.

Wise, William B. Papers. Special Collections Library. Duke University.

Wooten and Taylor Company. Papers. Special Collections Library. Duke University.

Interviews

Carraway, Michael G. Interview by author. Museum of the Cape Fear, Fayetteville, N.C., 6 April 1991. Notes in author's possession.

Chandler, Genevieve W. "An Old Man from Horry." American Life Histories: Manuscripts from the Federal Writers' Project, 1936–1940. Library of Congress Internet Website.

Eldredge, Inman F. Interview by Roy R. White. 9 July 1959. Austin Cary File. Forest History Society, Durham, N.C.

Gray, Rich and Lula. "Rich and Lula Gray." American Life Histories: Manuscripts from the Federal Writers' Project, 1936–1940. Library of Congress Internet Website.

Hartley, Helen S. "Jim Lewis, Turpentine Worker." American Life Histories: Manuscripts from the Federal Writers' Project, 1936–1940. Library of Congress Internet Website.

Jones, James H. Interview by Roy R. White. 9 July 1959. Forest History Society, Durham, N.C.

Kayton, Herbert L. Interview by Roy R. White. 7 October 1959. Forest History Society, Durham, N.C.

King, A. David, III. Interview by author. Georgia Agrirama, Tifton, Ga., 14 June 1996. Notes in author's possession.

Langdale, Harley, Jr. Interview by Harold K. Steen. 1991. Forest History Society, Durham, N.C.

Langdale, John W. Interview by Harold K. Steen. 1991. Forest History Society, Durham, N.C.

Langdale, William P. Interview by H. K. Steen. 1991. Forest History Society, Durham, N.C.

Maguire, Elliott. Interview. Oral History Collection, St. Augustine Historical Society Research Library, St. Augustine, Fla.

———. Interview by author. Tape recording. St. Augustine, Fla., 5 June 1996.

McCaffrey, J. E. Interview by Elwood R. Maunder. Forest History Society, Durham, N.C.

Meldrim, Jo. Interview by author. Tape recording. St. Augustine, Fla., 19 August 1996.

Monroe, Otho. Interview by Michael Garvey. 19 March 1975. Mississippi Oral History Program, Archives and Manuscripts Division, McCain Library and Archives, University of Southern Mississippi.

Perry, Percival. Interview by author. Wake Forest University, Winston-Salem, N.C., 9 April 1991. Notes in author's possession.

Reed, Prince K. Interview by author. Tape recording. St. Augustine, Fla., 19 August 1996.

Register, William Alonzo. Interview. Florida State Archives, Tallahassee, Fla.

Shingler, G. P. Interview by R. White. 30 June 1959. Oral History Interview, Forest History Society, Durham, N.C.

Tatum, Fitzhugh Lee. Interview by Ruth L. Stokes. 19 October 1974. Southern Oral History Program, Southern Historical Collection, University of North Carolina at Chapel Hill.

Wilson, Dwight. Interview. Oral History Collection. St. Augustine Historical Society Research Library, St. Augustine, Fla.

Wimster, C. W. "Life History of C. W. Wimster, Turpentine Man." By [Lindsay M. Bryan?]. American Life Histories: Manuscripts from the Federal Writers' Project, 1936–1940. Library of Congress Internet Website.

Census Reports and Government Publications

Coxe, Tench. *A Statement of the Arts and Manufactures of the United States of America for the Year 1810*. Philadelphia: A. Cornman, Jr., 1814.

Georgia House of Representatives. Resolution Honoring John W. Langdale. 6 March 1998, SR 723.

United States Department of Commerce and Labor. Bureau of the Census. *Manufactures, 1905.* Washington, D.C.: 1907 and 1908.

United States Department of the Interior. *Abstract of the Statistics of Manufactures, According to the Returns of the Seventh Census. 1850.* Washington, D.C.: Department of the Interior, 1858.

―――. *Eighth Census of the United States, 1860. North Carolina, White and Free Colored Population.* Washington, D.C.: National Archives and Records Service, 1967. Microfilm.

―――. *Manufactures of the United States in 1860.* Washington, D.C.: 1865.

―――. Census Office. *Report on the Forests of North America, Exclusive of Mexico.* Washington, D.C.: 1884.

―――. Census Office. *Report on the Manufactures of the United States at the Tenth Census (June 1, 1880).* Washington, D.C.: 1883.

―――. Census Office. *Report on Manufacturing Industries in the United States at the Eleventh Census: 1890.* Washington, D.C.: 1895.

―――. *The Seventh Census of the United States: 1850.* Washington, D.C.: 1853.

―――. *Seventh Census of the United States, 1850. North Carolina, White and Free Colored Population.* Washington, D.C.: National Archives and Records Service, n.d. Microfilm.

―――. Census Office. *The Statistics of the Wealth and Industry of the United States, Ninth Census, 1870.* Washington, D.C.: 1872.

―――. Census Office. *Statistics of the Population of the United States at the Tenth Census (June 1, 1880).* Washington, D.C.: Department of the Interior, 1883.

―――. Census Office. *Twelfth Census of the United States, Taken in the Year 1900, Population.* Washington, D.C.: 1901.

United States Department of State. *Compendium of the Enumeration of the Inhabitants and Statistics of the United States as Obtained at the Department of State, From the Returns of the Sixth Census, 1840.* Washington, D.C.: 1841.

―――. *Digest of Accounts of Manufacturing Establishments in the United States and of their Manufacturers.* Washington, D.C.: 1823.

United States Senate Committee on Agriculture and Forestry. *Crude Pine Gum Act of 1967: Hearing before a Subcommittee . . . on S. 2511,* 90th Cong., 1st sess., 1967.

Musical Scores and Recordings

Nicke, Warren, and Lucille De Mert. "De Woods of Pine." Chicago: De Mert and Dougerty, 1926.

Tampa Red. "Turpentine Blues." *Legends of the Blues.* Vol. 2. Audiocassette. Columbia Records.

Newspaper Articles

"Agency for the Sale of Timber, Lumber, and Naval Stores." *Wilmington Journal,* 5 January 1849.

"Ask Congress for Peonage Investigation." *Jacksonville Florida Times Union*, 21 February 1907.

"Big Florida Industry." *Jacksonville Citizen*, 7 September 1897.

"Camphine! Camphine!!" *Wilmington Journal*, 2 March 1849.

"Camphine Lamps." *Wilmington Chronicle*, 21 December 1842.

"Can Forests Be Saved?" *Augusta Herald*, 20 October 1901.

"Convict Camp Guard Is Charged with Assault." *Tampa Tribune*, 28 June 1907.

"Death from Camphine Gas." *Wilmington Journal*, 12 October 1849.

"Destroying Pine Trees." *Tampa Tribune*, 26 July 1901.

"Distillery for Sale." *Wilmington Chronicle*, 24 January 1849.

"18,000 Acres Turpentine Land for Sale." *Wilmington Journal*, 28 June 1850.

Farabee, Sherrie. "'Miss Spirits' Graced Turpentine Calendar." *Valdosta (Ga.) Daily Times*, 28 June 1989.

"Firm Provides Constant Cash." *Valdosta (Ga.) Daily Times*, 26 June 1977.

"For Sale." *Wilmington Journal*, 10 August 1849.

"For Sale." *Wilmington Journal*, 29 October 1852.

"For Sale, Valuable Turpentine and Farming Lands in Bladen County." *Wilmington Journal*, 21 March 1856.

"A Great Bargain." *Wilmington Journal*, 4 October 1850.

"Great Yield of Turpentine." *Wilmington Chronicle*, 9 May 1849.

"Guarding the Forests." *Macon News*, 28 October 1901.

"High Prices." *Fayetteville (N.C.) Observer*, 1 February 1853.

"Horrible Treatment of Convicts." *Jacksonville Times-Union and Citizen*, 20 May 1899.

"Land and Negroes for Sale." *Wilmington Journal*, 4 July 1851.

"Land for Sale." *Wilmington Journal*, 19 July 1850.

"Land for Sale." *Wilmington Journal*, 13 October 1854.

"Land for Sale on Cape Fear River." *Wilmington Chronicle*, 10 November 1841.

"Lands for Sale." *Wilmington Journal*, 27 June 1845.

"Lands for Sale." *Wilmington Journal*, 29 December 1848.

"Langdale Company Sells Gum Process Machinery." *Valdosta (Ga.) Daily Times*, 27 August 1975.

"Latest Improvement in the Camphene Lamp." *Wilmington Journal*, 26 February 1847.

"Naval Stores." *Wilmington Journal*, 15 May 1846.

"New York Market." *Wilmington Journal*, 20 November 1846.

"Notice." *Wilmington Chronicle*, 1 June 1849.

"Notice." *Wilmington Journal*, 30 May 1845.

"Notice." *Wilmington Journal*, 21 March 1856.

"Notice.—A Valuable Plantation for Sale." *Wilmington Journal*, 23 November 1849.

"Notice to Dealers in Turpentine & Tar." *Wilmington Journal*, 25 June 1847.

"Notice to Turpentine Makers." *Wilmington Journal*, 4 October 1844.

"Peculiar to the South." *Indianapolis Sentinel*, 15 November 1896.

"'Pernicious Measure' Passed in House." *Tallahassee Morning Sun*, 7 May 1907.

"The Pine Plantation." *New York Tribune*, 17 March 1866.

"Plantation for Sale." *Wilmington Journal*, 24 April 1846.

"Plea for Long Leaf Pine." *Charleston, South Carolina New Courier*, 25 July 1901.

"Quality Product, Good Service Key Lerio Success." *Valdosta (Ga.) Daily Times*, 26 June 1977.

"Real Estate for Sale." *Wilmington Journal*, 4 July 1845.

"Review of the Newbern Market." *New Bern (N.C.) Newbernian*, 6 January 1852.

Shirley, A. R. "Gum Naval Stores Long Linked with Industrial Development." *Valdosta (Ga.) Daily Times*, 18 November, 1959.

"Steam Mills and Turpentine Distilleries." *Tarboro Press*, 25 January 1845.

"Steam Saw-Mill, Turpentine Still, &c. Trust Sale." *Wilmington Journal*, 17 March 1854.

"Strong Resolutions Adopted Condemning Barry and Hearst." *Jacksonville Florida Times Union*, 4 April 1907.

"Ten Mile Notes." *Baxley (Ga.) News Banner*, 3 February 1932.

"10,000 Acres of Land for Sale." *Wilmington Journal*, 21 November 1851.

"The Tide Turned." *Fayetteville Observer*, 25 January 1853.

"To Lumber and Turpentine Companies." *Wilmington Journal*, 7 September 1849.

"To Save Forests." *New York Evening Sun*, 10 September 1902.

"To the Public." *Wilmington Journal*, 4 March 1853.

"To Turpentine Makers." *Wilmington Chronicle*, 27 December 1843.

"To Turpentine Makers." *Wilmington Journal*, 21 September 1844.

"To Turpentine Makers in Duplin." *Wilmington Journal*, 12 May 1848.

"Trade of Washington." *Tarboro, North Carolina Press*, 21 January 1846.

"Trouble Threatened." *Jacksonville Florida Times-Union*, 9 February 1896.

"A Turpentine Farm for Sale or Rent." *Wilmington Journal*, 29 August 1856.

"Turpentine Industry." *New York Tribune*, 26 January 1902.

"Turpentine in Texas." *Houston Post*, 16 September 1903.

"Turpentine Land for Sale." *Wilmington Journal*, 21 March 1856.

"Turpentine Lands in Florida for Sale." *Wilmington Journal*, 21 March 1856.

"Turpentine Manufacture." *Marion (S.C.) Star*, 15 July 1874.

"Turpentine Operating in Georgia Forests." *Atlanta Journal*, 31 October 1901.

"The Turpentine Region." *Tarboro Press*, 11 February 1846.

"Turpentine—The New Law." *Wilmington Journal*, 21 May 1847.

"12,000 Acres of Turpentine Land for Sale." *Wilmington Journal*, 10 January 1851.

"Valuable Cape Fear Plantation for Sale." *Wilmington Journal*, 24 June 1853.

"Valuable Farming and Turpentine Lands for Sale." *Wilmington Journal*, 2 March 1849.

"Valuable Land for Sale." *Wilmington Journal*, 11 May 1849.

"Valuable Lands for Sale." *Wilmington Journal*, 22 December 1848.

"Valuable Plantation for Sale." *Wilmington Journal*, 23 November 1849.

"Valuable Real Estate." *Wilmington Journal*, 26 February 1847.

"Valuable Real Estate for Sale." *Wilmington Journal*, 16 August 1850.

"Valuable Real Estate for Sale." *Wilmington Journal*, 4 November 1853.

"Valuable Real Estate for Sale." *Wilmington Journal*, 10 March 1854.

"A Valuable Tract of Land for Sale." *Wilmington Journal*, 4 January 1856.

"Valuable Turpentine Land for Sale." *Wilmington Journal*, 20 November 1846.

"Verdict of Acquittal Ends First of the Peonage Cases." *Jacksonville Florida Times-Union*, 25 December 1906.

"Waste Stumps from Dixie Cut-Over Land Become Hundreds of Products at Plant." *Pensacola News-Journal*, 2 October 1949.

"White Prisoners in Jail Sign Statement Telling of Arrest." *Pensacola Journal*, 30 December 1911.

"White Slavery in Florida." *New York Evening Post*, 12 February 1898.

"Wilmington—Business—The Turpentine Trade—How Turpentine Is Obtained—The Pine Trees—Pitch and Tar—Speculations in Lumber." *New York Tribune*, 17 March 1866.

"Wilmington Market." *Wilmington Journal*, 18 April 1845, 16 May 1845, 8 August 1845, 19 December 1845, and 17 April 1846.

Wittwer, Charlotte. "Stumpwood to Resins—Oldest Pensacola Industry." *Pensacola News-Journal* File, Pensacola Historical Resources Center, Pensacola, Florida.

"Would Preserve Pine Forests." *Atlanta Constitution*, 2 June 1901.

Journal Articles and Pamphlets

"At Other Naval Stores Ports of the South." *Weekly Naval Stores Review* 22 (27 June 1912): 66.

Baker, Ray Stannard. "A Pawn in the Struggle for Freedom." *American Magazine* 72 (September 1911): 608–10.

Barry, Richard. "Slavery in the South To-Day." *Cosmopolitan Magazine* 42 (March 1907): 481–91.

Buttrick, P. L. "Commercial Uses of Longleaf Pine." *American Forestry* 21 (September 1915): 896–908.

Cable, George W. "The Convict Lease System in the Southern States." *Century Magazine* 27 (February 1884): 582–99.

Cary, Austin. "Studies on Flow of Gum in Relation to Profit in the Naval Stores Industry: A Condensed Account of Experiments Conducted from 1920 to 1931." *Naval Stores Review* (July–September 1933): 2–18.

Clements, Ralph W. *The Bark Hack: Techniques of Using This Efficient Method.* Reprint January–March 1953 *Naval Stores Review* article. N.p., n.d. Copy in Olustee Experiment Station Files, Georgia Agrirama, Tifton, Ga.

———. "Field Supervision Important When Using the Bark Chipping–Acid Stimulation Method." *Naval Stores Review* 61 (June 1951): 24–6.

"Cotton Crop in North Carolina." *North-Carolina Planter* 3 (October 1860): 320.

"Cotton Growing in the Old North State." *North-Carolina Planter* 3 (August 1860): 263.

Crayon, Porte. "The Dismal Swamp." *Harper's New Monthly Magazine* 8 (September 1856): 441–55.

———. "North Carolina Illustrated: The Piney Woods." *Harper's New Monthly Magazine* 14 (May 1857): 741–55.

Dorman, Keith W. "High-Yielding Turpentine Orchards: A Future Possibility." *Chemurgic Digest* 4 (29 September 1945): 293–9.

"Exhibitions." *Garden and Forest* 8 (November 1895): 449–50.

"Florida." *De Bow's Review* 10 (April 1851): 404–12.

"Florida 'Comes Clean' by Ending Convict Camps." *Literary Digest* 77 (16 June 1923): 36–42.

Forbes, R. D. "The Passing of the Piney Woods." *American Forestry* 29 (March 1923): 131–6, 185.

Gerry, Eloise. "The Goose and the Golden Eggs, or Naval Stores Production a la Aesop." *Southern Lumberman* (25 August 1923).

———. *More Turpentine, Less Scar, Better Pine.* Leaflet 83. Washington, D.C.: United States Department of Agriculture, 1931.

———. "Oleoresin Production from Longleaf Pine Defoliated by Fire." *Journal of Agricultural Research* 43 (1 November 1931): 827–35.

———. "Recent Observations on the Effects of Turpentining on the Structure of Second Growth Slash and Longleaf Pines." *Journal of Forestry* 21 (March 1923).

Goodnow, Marc N. "Turpentine: Impressions of the Convict Camps of Florida." *Survey* 34 (1 May 1915): 103–8.

Hann, John H. "Translation of Alonso De Leturiondo's Memorial to the King of Spain." *Florida Archaeology*, n.s., 2 (1996): 165–225.

Harper, V. L., and T. A. Liefeld. "A New Day in the Naval Stores Industry." *Journal of Forestry* 36 (November 1938): 1128–30.

Herty, Charles H. "The Turpentine Industry in the Southern States." *Journal of the Franklin Institute* 181 (March 1916): 339–67.

Hilbert, G. E. "Twenty Years of Research by the Naval Stores Station." *AT-FA Journal* 15 (January 1953): 5–9.

"Journal of a French Traveler in the Colonies." *American Historical Review* 26 (July 1921): 726–47.

Liefeld, T. A. "Relation of Naval Stores Yields to Frequency of Chipping." *Journal of Agricultural Research* 64 (15 January 1942): 81–92.

"The Life Story of a Hungarian Peon." *Independent* 63 (5 September 1907): 556–64.

MacLeod, John. "The Tar and Turpentine Business of North Carolina." *Monthly Journal of Agriculture* 2 (July 1846): 13–9.

"The Manufacture of Turpentine in the South." *De Bow's Review* 8 (May 1850): 450–6.

McMillan, Dugall, to *Southern Cultivator.* 14 April 1846. *Southern Cultivator* 4 (November 1846): 174.

Mitchell, H. L. "Information on the Use of Chemical Stimulants to Increase Gum Yields." *Savannah Weekly Naval Stores Review and Journal of Trade* 55 (7, 14, 21 April 1945). Copy in Olustee Experiment Station Files, Georgia Agrirama, Tifton, Ga.

"Naval Stores Equipment." *Forest Farmer* 9 (September 1950).

"North Carolina, Its Resources, Manufactures, Etc." *De Bow's Review* 4 (October 1847): 256, 258.

"Notes on the Long-Leafed Pine." *Monthly Journal of Agriculture* 2 (July 1846): 12–3.

"Organizing an Agricultural Society in Onslow County." *North-Carolina Planter* 2 (October 1859): 311.

Ostrom, Carl E. "Gum Yields Affected by Quality of Acid Applied to Streak." *AT-FA Journal* (June 1945): 6.

Ostrom, Carl E., and Worden Waring. "Effect of Chemical Stimulation of Gum Flow on Carbohydrate Reserves in Slash Pine." *Journal of Forestry* 44 (December 1946): 1076–81.

"Peonage in Georgia." *Independent* 55 (24 December 1903): 3079–81.

"Peonage in the South." *Independent* 55 (9 July 1903): 1616–18.

"The Pine Forests of the South." *De Bow's Review: After the War Series* 3 (February 1867): 196–8.

Pomeroy, Kenneth B. "Modern Trends in an Ancient Industry." *Journal of Forestry* 50 (April 1952): 297–9.

Price, Overton W. "Saving the Southern Forests." *World's Work* 5 (March 1903): 3207–22.

Pringle, C. G. "Waste in the Turpentine Industry." *Garden and Forest* 4 (4 February 1891): 49–50.

"Product of Turpentine at the South." *De Bow's Review* 11 (September 1851): 303–5.

"Production of Turpentine in Alabama." *De Bow's Review* 7 (December 1849): 560–2.

Ruffin, Edmund. "Notes of a Steam Journey." *Farmer's Register* 8 (30 April 1840): 243–54.

———. "Observations Made during an Excursion to the Dismal Swamp." *Farmer's Register* 4 (January 1837): 517–8.

Schopmeyer, Clifford S. "Gum Yield and Wood Volume on Single-Faced Naval Stores Trees." *Southern Lumberman* (15 December 1955).

———. "Labor Requirements for Working Turpentine Faces." *Naval Stores Review* 64 (April 1954): 7.

Snow, Albert G., Jr. "Research on the Improvement of Turpentine Practices." *Economic Botany* 3 (October–December 1949): 375–94.

———. *Turpentining and Poles.* Reprint of 15 December 1948 *Southern Lumberman* article. N.p., n.d. Copy in Olustee Experiment Station Files, Georgia Agrirama, Tifton, Ga.

"The Southern Pine Forest—Turpentine." *De Bow's Review* 18 (February 1855): 188–91.

"Turpentine Business in Georgia." *De Bow's Southern and Western Review* 9 (July 1850): 118–9.

"Turpentine Business in North Carolina and Georgia." *Commercial Review of the South and West* 5 (April 1848): 364.

"Turpentine: Hints for Those about to Engage in Its Manufacture." *De Bow's Review* 19 (October 1855): 486–9.

"Turpentine Makers Advocating Conservative Methods." Clipping in Turpentine News Clipping File, Forest History Society, Durham, N.C.

"Turpentine Orchards." *Northern Lumberman* 2 August 1896. Turpentine News Clipping File, Forest History Society, Durham, N.C.

"Turpentine Orchards in South-West Louisiana—A New Process." *Southern Lumberman* (April 1895).

"Turpentine Product of the South." *De Bow's Review* 18 (January 1855): 61–3.

"25 Years of Help." *Naval Stores Review* [68?] ([1958?]): 13–6, 21.

"A Victim of Convict 'Slavery.'" *Literary Digest* 77 (21 April 1923): 40–6.

Ward, Herbert D. "Peonage in America." *Cosmopolitan Magazine* 39 (August 1905): 423–30.

Wernicke, O. H. L. *Piney Wood Sense.* Pine Institute of America General Bulletin. Gull Point, Fla.: Pine Institute of America, 1926.

Books

Andrews, Evangeline Walker, ed. *Journal of a Lady of Quality.* New Haven: Yale University Press, 1922.

Annual Report of the Principal Physician of the Georgia Penitentiary from October 1, 1895, to October 1, 1896. Atlanta: George W. Harrison, State Printer, 1896.

Ashe, W. W. *The Forests, Forest Lands, and Forest Products of Eastern North Carolina.* Raleigh: North Carolina Geological Survey, 1894.

Avirett, James Battle. *The Old Plantation: How We Lived in Great House and Cabin before the War.* New York: F. Tennyson Neely, 1901.

Baldwin, George H. "Jacksonville as a Naval Stores Port and Market." In *Naval Stores: History, Production, Distribution, and Consumption,* edited by Thomas Gamble. Savannah: Review Publishing and Printing, 1921.

Bartram, William. *Travels through North and South Carolina, Georgia, East and West Florida, the Cherokee Country, the Extensive Territories of the Muscogulges or Creek Confederacy, and the Country of the Choctaws.* In *William Bartram: Travels and Other Writings.* New York: Library of America, 1996.

Berry, James Berthold. *Farm Woodlands.* Yonkers-on-Hudson, N.Y.: World Book Co., 1923.

Biographical Souvenir of the States of Georgia and Florida. Chicago: F. A. Battey, 1889.

Brickell, John. *The Natural History of North-Carolina.* 1737. Reprint, New York: Johnson Reprint, 1969.

Brooks, R. P. *The Industrialization of the South.* Athens, Ga.: Bureau of Business Research, 1929.

Bureau of Chemistry. "The Principal Uses of Rosins and Spirits Turpentine." In *Naval Stores: History, Production, Distribution, and Consumption,* edited by Thomas Gamble. Savannah: Review Publishing and Printing, 1921.

Butts, James R. *150,000 Acres Yellow Pine Timber, Turpentine and Cotton Lands.* Macon: Georgia Land Agency, 1858.

Carman, Harry J., ed. *American Husbandry.* Port Washington, N.Y.: Kennikat Press, 1939.

Carson, J. A. G. "The Increased Cost of Naval Stores Production." In *Naval Stores: History, Production, Distribution, and Consumption,* edited by Thomas Gamble. Savannah: Review Publishing and Printing, 1921.

The Colonial Records of North Carolina. Vol. 4. Edited by William L. Saunders. Raleigh: P. M. Hale, Printer to the State, 1886.

The Colonial Records of North Carolina. Vol. 8. Edited by William L. Saunders. Raleigh: Josephus Daniels, Printer to the State, 1890.

The Colonial Records of North Carolina. Vol. 9. Edited by William L. Saunders. Raleigh: Josephus Daniels, Printer to the State, 1890.

Corsan, W. C. *Two Months in the Confederate States: An Englishman's Travels through the South.* Baton Rouge: Louisiana State University Press, 1996.

Cross, John K. "'Without a Doubt the Naval Stores Program Has Had a Profound Influence . . .'" In *Historical Background of the Naval Stores Conservation Program.* N.p.: Georgia Forest Research Council, n.d. Copy in Olustee Experiment Station Files, Georgia Agrirama, Tifton, Ga.

Dennett, John Richard. *The South as It Is, 1865–1866.* 1965. Reprint, Baton Rouge: Louisiana State University Press, 1995.

Downing, C. "Brunswick as a Naval Stores Port and Market." In *Naval Stores: History, Production, Distribution, and Consumption,* edited by Thomas Gamble. Savannah: Review Publishing and Printing, 1921.

Dunwody, Robson. "Proper Methods of Distillation and Handling in the Production of Turpentine and Rosin." In *Naval Stores: History, Production, Distribution, and Consumption,* edited by Thomas Gamble. Savannah: Review Publishing and Printing, 1921.

Eagan, D. *The Florida Settler; Or, Immigrants' Guide: A Complete Manual of Information Concerning the Climate, Soil, Products and Resources of the State.* Tallahassee: Floridian, 1873.

Eighth Annual Report of the Prison Commission of Georgia, From June 1, 1904, to May 31, 1905. Atlanta: Lester Book and Stationery Co., 1905.

The Eighth Biennial Report of the Commissioner of Agriculture, State of Florida, for the Period Beginning January 1, 1903, and Ending December 31, 1904. Tallahassee: L. B. Hilson, State Printer, 1905.

Eldredge, I. F. "How the French Turpentine System Looked to an American." In *Naval Stores: History, Production, Distribution, and Consumption,* edited by Thomas Gamble. Savannah: Review Publishing and Printing, 1921.

Eleventh Annual Report of the Prison Commission of Georgia, from June 1, 1907, to May 31, 1908. Atlanta: Lester Book and Stationery Co., 1908.

Eleventh Biennial Report of the Commissioner of Agriculture of the State of Florida for the Period Beginning January 1, 1909, and Ending December 31, 1910. Tallahassee: T. J. Appleyard, State Printer, 1911.

Federal Writers' Project. *Florida: A Guide to the Southernmost State.* New York: Oxford University Press, 1939.

Fifth Annual Report of the Prison Commission of Georgia, from October 1, 1901, to October 1, 1902. Atlanta: Lester Book and Stationery Co., 1902.

First Annual Report of the Prison Commission of Georgia from October 1, 1897, to October 1, 1898. Atlanta: Geo. W. Harrison, State Printer, 1898.

Forbes, R. D., and R. Y. Stuart. *Timber Growing and Logging and Turpentining Practices in the Southern Pine Region.* Washington, D.C.: United States Department of Agriculture, 1930.

Fourth Annual Report of the Prison Commission of Georgia, from October 1, 1900, to October 1, 1901. Atlanta: J. F. Lester, Printer and Stationer, 1901.

Fulmer, Frank E. "'The First Voice Ordered: "Shoot Them." Then the Bullets Started!'" In *Historical Background of the Naval Stores Conservation Program.* N.p.: Georgia Forest Research Council, n.d. Copy in Olustee Experiment Station Files, Georgia Agrirama, Tifton, Ga.

Gamble, Thomas. "Mining for Rosin in the Old North State." In *Naval Stores: History, Production, Distribution, and Consumption,* edited by Thomas Gamble. Savannah: Review Publishing and Printing, 1921.

————. "The Naval Stores Industry of the South." In *The South's Development: Fifty Years of Southern Progress: A Glimpse of the Past, the Facts of the Present, a Forecast of the Future.* Baltimore: [Manufacturers' Record], 1924.

————. "The Production of Naval Stores in the United States." In *Naval Stores: History, Production, Distribution, and Consumption,* edited by Thomas Gamble. Savannah: Review Publishing and Printing, 1921.

————. "Savannah as a Naval Stores Port, 1875–1920." In *Naval Stores: History, Production, Distribution, and Consumption,* edited by Thomas Gamble. Savannah: Review Publishing and Printing, 1921.

Gamble's International Naval Stores Year Book, 1930–31. Savannah, Ga.: Thomas Gamble, 1930.

Georgia Department of Agriculture. *Georgia Historical and Industrial.* Atlanta: George W. Harrison, State Printer, 1901.

Gerry, Eloise. *Improvement in the Production of Oleoresin through Lower Chipping.* Washington, D.C.: United States Department of Agriculture, 1931.

————. "The Production of Crude 'Gum' by the Pine Tree." In *Naval Stores: History, Production, Distribution, and Consumption,* edited by Thomas Gamble. Savannah: Review Publishing and Printing, 1921.

Good Naval Stores Practice. Washington, D.C.: United States Department of Agriculture, 1927.

Grady, Henry. *The New South: Writings and Speeches of Henry Grady.* Savannah: Beehive Press, 1971.

Hamer, Philip M., George C. Rogers, Jr., David R. Chesnutt, C. James Taylor, Peggy J. Clark, David Fischer, eds. *The Papers of Henry Laurens.* 16 vols. Columbia: University of South Carolina Press, 1968.

Harper, V. L. *Effects of Fire on Gum Yields of Longleaf and Slash Pines.* Washington, D.C.: United States Department of Agriculture, 1944.

Harper, V. L., and Lenthall Wyman. *Variations in Naval-Stores Yields Associated with Weather and Specific Days between Chippings.* Washington, D.C.: United States Department of Agriculture, 1936.

Hawley, L. F. "Forest Service Investigations of Interest to the Naval Stores Industry." In *Naval Stores: History, Production, Distribution, and Consumption,* edited by Thomas Gamble. Savannah: Review Publishing and Printing, 1921.

Hawley, Norman R. "A Summary of the History of the Naval Stores Conservation Program." In *Historical Background of the Naval Stores Conservation Program*. N.p.: Georgia Forest Research Council, n.d. Copy in Olustee Experiment Station Files, Georgia Agrirama, Tifton, Ga.

Henegar, M. E. *Gum Naval Stores Timber Land Use: Information and Suggestions*. Brunswick, Ga.: Filtered Rosin Products, n.d. Copy in Olustee Experiment Station Files, Georgia Agrirama, Tifton, Ga.

———. *Slash and Longleaf Pine Growers Handbook: Practical Information and Suggestions for Growing, Protecting, and Realizing Maximum Utilization*. Lake City, Fla.: Newton, n.d. Copy in Olustee Experiment Station Files, Georgia Agrirama, Tifton, Ga.

Herty, Charles H. *A New Method of Turpentine Orcharding*. Washington, D.C.: United States Department of Agriculture, 1903.

Hodgson, Adam. *Remarks during a Journey through North America in the Years 1819, 1820, and 1821 in a Series of Letters*. New York: Samuel Whiting, 1823.

Hough, Franklin B. *Report upon Forestry*. Vol. 1. Washington, D.C.: Government Printing Office, 1878.

———. *Report upon Forestry*. Vol. 2. Washington, D.C.: Government Printing Office, 1880.

Hoyt, John C. *Droughts of 1930–34*. Washington, D.C.: United States Department of the Interior, 1936.

Hurston, Zora Neale. *Seraph on the Suwanee*. In *Novels and Stories*. Library of America. New York: Literary Classics of the United States, 1995.

Johnson, Franklin. *The Development of State Legislation Concerning the Free Negro*. New York: Arbor Press, 1918.

Keeler, Clarissa Olds. *The Crime of Crimes, or The Convict System Unmasked*. Washington, D.C.: Clarissa Olds Keeler, 1907.

Keith, Alice Barnwell, ed. *The John Gray Blount Papers*. Vol. 1. Raleigh: State Department of Archives and History, 1952.

Lawson, John. *A New Voyage to Carolina*. 1709. Reprint, Chapel Hill: University of North Carolina Press, 1967.

Lefler, Hugh Talmage, ed. *North Carolina History Told by Contemporaries*. Chapel Hill: University of North Carolina Press, 1948.

"The Life of the Naval Stores Industry as at Present Carried on in the South." In *Naval Stores: History, Production, Distribution, and Consumption*, edited by Thomas Gamble. Savannah: Review Publishing and Printing, 1921.

Maunder, Elwood R. *Voices from the South: Recollections of Four Foresters*. Santa Cruz, Calif.: Forest History Society, 1977.

McArther, Jim A. "'During the War, I Trained 22,000 German Prisoners-of-War to Work Naval Stores and Cut Pulpwood.'" In *Historical Background of the Naval Stores Conservation Program*. N.p.: Georgia Forest Research Council, n.d. Copy in Olustee Experiment Station Files, Georgia Agrirama, Tifton, Ga.

Michaux, F. André. *The North American Sylva*. Philadelphia: D. Rice and A. N. Hart, 1857.

Mohr, Charles. *Timber Pines of the Southern United States.* Washington, D.C.: United States Department of Agriculture, 1897.

Murphy, Arthur A. "'Good Forestry Has Advanced 25 Years, I Believe, Because of NSCP.'" In *Historical Background of the Naval Stores Conservation Program.* N.p.: Georgia Forest Research Council, n.d. Copy in Olustee Experiment Station Files, Georgia Agrirama, Tifton, Ga.

Musgrove, Downing. "A Tribute to Judge Harley Langdale, Sr." In *Historical Background of the Naval Stores Conservation Program.* N.p.: Georgia Forest Research Council, n.d. Copy in Olustee Experiment Station Files, Georgia Agrirama, Tifton, Ga.

Ninth Annual Report of the Prison Commission of Georgia, from June 1, 1905, to May 31, 1906. Atlanta: Lester Book and Stationery Co., 1906.

The Ninth Biennial Report of the Commissioner of Agriculture of the State of Florida for the Period Beginning January 1, 1905, and Ending December 31, 1906. Tallahassee: Capital Publishing, State Printer, 1907.

Olmsted, Frederick Law. *The Cotton Kingdom.* 1861. Reprint, New York: Modern Library, 1984.

———. *A Journey in the Seaboard Slave States.* New York: Dix and Edwards, 1856.

Packard, Winthrop. *Florida Trails: As Seen from Jacksonville to Key West and from November to April Inclusive.* Boston: Small, Maynard, 1910.

Palmer, R. C. *New Standard for Turpentines.* Pine Institute of America Report, reprinted from *American Paint Journal.* Gull Point, Fla.: Pine Institute of America, 1926. Copy in Turpentine News Clipping File, Forest History Society, Durham, N.C.

Perry, G. W. *A Treatise on Turpentine Farming.* New Bern, N.C.: Muse and Davies, 1859.

Powell, J. C. *The American Siberia, or Fourteen Years' Experience in a Southern Convict Camp.* 1891. Reprint, Montclair, N.J.: Patterson Smith, 1970.

Powell, William S., ed. *The Correspondence of William Tryon and Other Selected Papers.* Vol. 1. Raleigh: Division of Archives and History, Department of Cultural Resources, 1980.

Powers, E. O. "'With Pearl Harbor Our World, of Course, Turned Upside Down.'" In *Historical Background of the Naval Stores Conservation Program.* N.p.: Georgia Forest Research Council, n.d. Copy in Olustee Experiment Station Files, Georgia Agrirama, Tifton, Ga.

Pridgen, Albert. "Turpentining in the South Atlantic Country." In *Naval Stores: History, Production, Distribution, and Consumption,* edited by Thomas Gamble. Savannah: Review Publishing and Printing, 1921.

Priest, George H., Jr. *Naval Stores: Production, Consumption, and Distribution.* Washington, D.C.: United States Department of Commerce, 1927.

Production of Naval Stores. Washington, D.C.: United States Department of Agriculture, 1942.

Purrse, Thomas. "How the Savannah Board of Trade Fixes Prices and Regulates the Trade." In *Naval Stores: History, Production, Distribution, and Consumption,* edited by Thomas Gamble. Savannah: Review Publishing and Printing, 1921.

Quinn, David B., and Alison M. Quinn. *The First Colonists: Documents on the Planting of the First English Settlements in North America, 1584–1590.* Raleigh: North Carolina Department of Cultural Resources, Division of Archives and History, 1982.

Register, John E. "The Naval Stores Inspector—His Work and How He Does It." In *Naval Stores: History, Production, Distribution, and Consumption,* edited by Thomas Gamble. Savannah: Review Publishing and Printing, 1921.

Reid, Whitelaw. *After the War: A Tour of the Southern States, 1865–1866.* 1866. Reprint, New York: Harper and Row, 1965.

Report of the Commissioner of Agriculture of the State of Florida for the Period Beginning January 1, 1889, and Ending December 31, 1890. Jacksonville: DaCosta, 1891.

Report of the Commissioner of Agriculture of the State of Florida for the Period Beginning January 1, 1893, and Ending December 31, 1894. Tallahassee: John G. Collins, State Printer, 1895.

Report of the Commissioner of Agriculture of the State of Florida for the Period Beginning January 1, 1895, and Ending December 31, 1896. Tallahassee: Florida Printing, 1897.

Report of the Commissioner of Agriculture of the State of Florida for the Period Beginning January 1, 1897, and Ending December 31, 1898. Tallahassee: Tallahasseean Book and Job Print, 1899.

Robin, C. C. *Voyage to Louisiana.* New Orleans: Pelican, 1966.

Romans, Bernard. *A Concise Natural History of East and West Florida.* Gainesville: University of Florida Press, 1962.

Ruffin, Marion W. "'. . . I Had No Office, No Adding Machine, No Typewriter, and No Maps. . . .'" In *Historical Background of the Naval Stores Conservation Program.* N.p.: Georgia Forest Research Council, n.d. Copy in Olustee Experiment Station Files, Georgia Agrirama, Tifton, Ga.

Russell, Charles W. *Report on Peonage.* Washington, D.C.: Department of Justice, 1908.

Russell, Robert. *North America: Its Agriculture and Climate.* Edinburgh: Adam and Charles Black, 1857.

Scarborough, William Kauffman, ed. *The Diary of Edmund Ruffin.* Vol. 1. Baton Rouge: Louisiana State University Press, 1972.

Schoepf, Johann David. *Travels in the Confederation.* 1788. Reprint, New York: Burt Franklin, 1968.

Schorger, A. W., and H. S. Betts. *The Naval Stores Industry.* Washington, D.C.: United States Department of Agriculture, 1915.

Second Annual Report of the Prison Commission of Georgia, from October 1, 1898, to October 1, 1899. Atlanta: Foote and Davies, 1899.

Seventh Annual Report of the Prison Commission of Georgia, from June 1, 1903, to May 31, 1904. Atlanta: Lester Book and Stationery Co., 1908.

Shea, Charles T. "'. . . The Ones on the Northside Are Northern Reds and the Ones on the South Are Southern Reds.'" In *Historical Background of the Naval Stores Conservation Program.* N.p.: Georgia Forest Research Council, n.d. Copy in Olustee Experiment Station Files, Georgia Agrirama, Tifton, Ga.

Shirley, A. R. *Working Trees for Naval Stores.* Athens: Georgia Agricultural Extension Service, 1946.

Smyth, John Ferdinand Dalziel. *A Tour in the United States of America*. 1784. Reprint, New York: Arno Press, 1968.

Somers, Robert. *The Southern States since the War, 1870–71*. 1871. Reprint, University: University of Alabama Press, 1965.

Steedly, Arthur G. "Doctors, Lawyers, Teachers, Merchants, and Widows, Call to Ask Advice." In *Historical Background of the Naval Stores Conservation Program*. N.p.: Georgia Forest Research Council, n.d. Copy in Olustee Experiment Station Files, Georgia Agrirama, Tifton, Ga.

Tenth Annual Report of the Prison Commission of Georgia, from June 1, 1906, to May 31, 1907. Atlanta: Lester Book and Stationery Co., 1907.

Tenth Biennial Report of the Commissioner of Agriculture of the State of Florida for the Period Beginning January 1, 1907, and Ending December 31, 1908. Tallahassee: Union Label, 1909.

Thigpen, S. G. *A Boy in Rural Mississippi and Other Stories*. Picayune, Miss.: S. G. Thigpen, 1966.

Tillman, Joseph, and C. P. Goodyear. *Southern Georgia: A Pamphlet*. Savannah, Ga.: Savannah Times Steam Printing House, 1881.

Twelfth Biennial Report of the Department of Agriculture of the State of Florida from the Years 1911 to 1912. Tallahassee: T. J. Appleyard, State Printer, n.d.

United States Forest Service. "U.S. Government's Turpentine Experience in the Florida National Forest." In *Naval Stores: History, Production, Distribution, and Consumption*, edited by Thomas Gamble. Savannah: Review Publishing and Printing, 1921.

Veitch, F. P., and V. E. Grotlisch. "What Uncle Sam Does for the Naval Stores Industry." In *Naval Stores: History, Production, Distribution, and Consumption*, edited by Thomas Gamble. Savannah: Review Publishing and Printing, 1921.

Williamson, Hugh. *The History of North Carolina*. Philadelphia: Thomas Dobson, 1812.

Woolsey, Theodore S., Jr. "Conservative Turpentining by the French." In *Naval Stores: History, Production, Distribution, and Consumption*, edited by Thomas Gamble. Savannah: Review Publishing and Printing, 1921.

Wyman, Lenthall. *Experiments in Naval Stores Practice*. Washington, D.C.: United States Department of Agriculture, 1932.

———. *Florida Naval Stores*. Tallahassee: State of Florida, Department of Agriculture, 1929.

Ziegler, E. A., A. R. Spillers, and C. H. Coulter. *Financial Aspects of Growing Southern Pine, Washington County, Florida*. Tallahassee: Florida Forest Service, 1931.

Secondary Sources

Dissertations, Theses, and Unpublished Papers

Baker, Hulda Summerall. "Summerall Turpentine Still." Museum of Coastal History, St. Simons Island, Ga.

Blount, Robert S. "Spirits in the Pines." Master's thesis, Florida State University, 1992.

Carper, N. Gordon. "The Convict-Lease System in Florida, 1866–1923." Ph.D. diss., Florida State University, 1964.

Croft, Janice. "A Twin Success Story: Pensacola and Newport." Pensacola Historical Resource Center, Pensacola, Fla.

Forney, Sandra Jo. "The Importance of Sites Related to the Naval Stores Industry in Florida." Paper presented at the thirty-seventh annual meeting of the Florida Anthropological Society, Daytona Beach, Fla., 1985.

———. "Naval Stores Industry in North Florida Pine Flatwoods." Paper presented at the sixteenth annual meeting of the Society for Historical Archaeology, Denver, Colo., 1983.

Hayes, Martha Green. "General History of the Turpentine Industry." Georgia Agrirama, Tifton, Ga.

John H. Appleyard Agency. "Draft . . . Newport Talk for Historical Society . . . April 19, 1984." Pensacola Historical Resource Center, Pensacola, Fla.

Langdale, Harley, Jr. "Brief Facts on the Langdale Company." Lowndes County Historical Society, Valdosta, Ga.

Martin, Donald Fraser. "An Historical and Analytical Approach to the American Gum Naval Stores Industry." Ph.D. diss., University of North Carolina, 1942.

Perry, Percival. "The Naval Stores Industry in the Ante-Bellum South, 1789–1861." Ph.D. diss., Duke University, 1947.

Tegeder, Michael David. "Prisoners of the Pines: Debt Peonage in the Southern Turpentine Industry, 1900–1930." Ph.D. diss., University of Florida, 1996.

Vinson, Frank Bedingfield. "Conservation and the South, 1890–1920." Ph.D. diss., University of Georgia, 1971.

Wright, Gay Goodman. "Turpentining: An Ethnohistorical Study of a Southern Industry and Way of Life." Master's thesis, University of Georgia, 1979.

Newspaper Articles

Carswell, E. W. " 'Naval Stores' Industry Came to Northwest Florida in 1883." *Pensacola Florida News Journal* File, Pensacola Historical Resource Center, Pensacola, Fla.

"Gum Naval Stores Long Linked with Industrial Development." *Valdosta (Ga.) Daily Times,* 18 November 1959.

Harvey, Karen. "Maguire Born into Turpentine Family: Industry Once Had Major Impact on County." *Compass,* 26 April 1990.

Hawk, Kathy. "Turpentine: An Ancient Technology Almost Tapped Out in St. Johns County." *St. Augustine Ancient City Beacon,* 25 June 1982.

Vail, Becky. "Old-Timer Remembers 'Hard Old Days' in Woods." News Clipping File, Lowndes County Historical Society, Valdosta, Ga.

"Waste Stumps from Dixie Cut-over Land Become Hundreds of Products at Plant." 2 October 1949, *Pensacola Florida News-Journal* file, Pensacola Historical Resource Center, Pensacola, Fla.

Wittwer, Charlotte. "Stumpwood to Resins—Oldest Pensacola Industry." *Pensacola Florida News-Journal* File, Pensacola Historical Resource Center, Pensacola, Fla.

Journal Articles and Pamphlets

Airaksinen, Mikko. "Tar Production in Colonial North America." *Environment and History* 2 (1996): 115–25.

Arceneaux, Mary Beth. "Captains of the Naval Stores Industry." *Naval Stores Review* 90 (September–October 1980): 8–9.

Armstrong, Thomas F. "Georgia Lumber Laborers, 1880–1917: The Social Implications of Work." *Georgia Historical Quarterly* 67 (winter 1983): 435–50.

———. "The Transformation of Work: Turpentine Workers in Coastal Georgia, 1865–1901." *Labor History* 25 (fall 1984): 518–32.

Ashmore, Freeman. "Looking Back: The Woodsrider." *Wakulla Area Digest* (September 1996): 13–6, 24.

Bateman, Fred, James Foust, and Thomas Weiss. "The Participation of Planters in Manufacturing in the Antebellum South." *Agricultural History* 68 (April 1974): 277–97.

"Before Tourism—Turpentine." *Southern Living* (October 1986). Copy in St. Augustine Historical Society Research Library, St. Augustine, Fla.

Bellamy, Donnie D. "Slavery in Microcosm: Onslow County, North Carolina." *Journal of Negro History* 62 (October 1977): 339–50.

Bond, Bradley G. "Herders, Farmers, and Markets on the Inner Frontier: The Mississippi Piney Woods, 1850–1860." In *Plain Folk of the South Revisited,* edited by Samuel C. Hyde, Jr. Baton Rouge: Louisiana State University Press, 1997.

Bond, Stanley C., Jr. "The Development of the Naval Stores Industry in St. Johns County, Florida." *Florida Anthropologist* 40 (September 1987): 187–202.

Buck, Paul H. "The Poor Whites of the Ante-Bellum South." *American Historical Review* 31 (October 1925): 41–54.

Buckner, Edward. "Prehistory of the Southern Forest." *Forest Farmer* 54 (July–August 1995): 20–2.

Burnett, Gene. "To Burn in a Turpentine Hell." *Florida Trend* (October 1976): 100–2.

Cain, Robert J. "Cotton for the Kaiser: James Sprunt, Contraband, and the Wilmington Vice Consulate." *North Carolina Historical Review* 74 (April 1997): 161–81.

Carlton, David L. "The Revolution from Above: The National Market and the Beginnings of Industrialization in North Carolina." *Journal of American History* 77 (September 1990): 445–75.

Carper, N. Gordon. "Martin Tabert, Martyr of an Era." *Florida Historical Quarterly* 52 (October 1973): 115–31.

———. "Slavery Revisited: Peonage in the South." *Phylon* 37 (1976): 85–99.

Cecelski, David S. "Oldest Living Confederate Chaplain Tells All? Or, James B. Avirett and the Rise and Fall of the Rich Lands." *Southern Cultures* 3 (winter 1997): 5–24.

———. "The Rise and Fall of the Rich Lands." *Coastwatch* (January–February 1997): 21–4.

Cohen, William. "Negro Involuntary Servitude in the South, 1865–1940: A Preliminary Analysis." *Journal of Southern History* 42 (February 1976): 31–60.

Cook, Richard C. "Early Industry Accounts through 1920." *Naval Stores Review* 77 (August 1967): 6–8.

———. "Naval Stores: The Forgotten Industry in Tar Heel State." *Naval Stores Review* 77 (July 1967): 8–9.

Courson, Maxwell Taylor. "Here Began a Revolution." *Southerner* 1 (fall 1979): 10–3.

Craighead, F. C. "Insects That Attack Southern Pines." Austin Cary Memorial Collection, Department of Special Collections, George A. Smathers Libraries, University of Florida.

Croker, Thomas C., Jr. "The Longleaf Pine Story." *Southern Lumberman* (December 1979): 69, 74.

Crosby, Richard C., Jr. "Captains of the Naval Stores Industry." *Naval Stores Review* 91 (September–October 1981): 14–6.

Cross, John K. "C-H-A-R-C-O-A-L . . . . . Charcoal." *NSCP Safety-Valve* 3 (June 1965): 1–3.

———. "Tar Burning, A Forgotten Art?" *Forests and People* 23, no. 2 (1973): 21–3.

Daniel, Pete. "The Metamorphosis of Slavery, 1865–1900." *Journal of American History* 66 (June 1979): 88–99.

Dew, Charles B. "David Ross and the Oxford Iron Works: A Study of Industrial Slavery in the Early Nineteenth-Century South." *William and Mary Quarterly,* 3d ser., 31 (April 1974): 189–224.

———. "Disciplining Slave Ironworkers in the Antebellum South: Coercion, Conciliation, and Accommodation." *American Historical Review* 79 (April 1974): 393–418.

Dobson, Jeffrey R., and Roy Doyon. "Expansion of the Pine Oleoresin Industry in Georgia: 1842 to Ca. 1900." *West Georgia College Studies in the Social Sciences* 18 (June 1979): 43–57.

Drew, John. "The Early Days of the Naval Stores Industry." *Naval Stores Review* 91 (November–December 1981): 14–7.

———. "Let's Face It." *Naval Stores Review* 92 (May–June 1982): 4.

Dreyfus, T. F. "Old Stumps Yield New Wealth." *Illinois Central Magazine* (May 1931): 13–4.

Drobney, Jeffrey A. "Company Towns and Social Transformation in the North Florida Timber Industry, 1880–1930." *Florida Historical Quarterly* 75 (fall 1996): 121–45.

———. "The Transformation of Work in the North Florida Timber Industry, 1890–1910." *Gulf Coast Historical Review* 10 (fall 1994): 93–110.

———. "Where Palm and Pine Are Blowing: Convict Labor in the North Florida Turpentine Industry, 1877–1923." *Florida Historical Quarterly* 72 (April 1984): 411–34.

Duhse, R. J. "Timber Pirates to Tree Farms." *North Florida Living* (March 1985): 44–5.

Dyer, C. Dorsey. "History of the Gum Naval Stores Industry." *AT-FA Journal* 25 (January 1963): 4–9.

Fenoaltea, Stefano. "Slavery and Supervision in Comparative Perspective: A Model." *Journal of Economic History* 44 (September 1984): 635–68.

Fisher, Diane. "Florida's Turpentine Industry." *Florida Living Magazine* 15 (October 1995): 29.

Florida Writers' Project. "The Story of Naval Stores . . . ." *Florida Highways* 11 (May 1943): 11–5, 35–7.

———. "The Story of Naval Stores . . . ." *Florida Highways* 11 (July 1943): 15–8, 31–2.

Forney, Sandra Jo. "Kin to Kant: Naval Stores Production Was a Major Industry of the Nineteenth Century." *Women in Natural Resources,* n.s., 1, no. 9 (1987): 17–9.

Franklin, W. Neil. "Agriculture in Colonial North Carolina." *North Carolina Historical Review* 3 (October 1926): 539–74.

Garcia-Estrada, Joaquin, Antonio Rodriguez-Segura, and Pedro Garzon. "Cerebral Cortex and Body Growth Development of Progeny of Rats Exposed to Thinner and Turpentine Inhalation." *General Pharmacology* 19 (1988): 467–70.

Golfarb, Stephen J. "A Note on Limits to the Growth of the Cotton-Textile Industry in the Old South." *Journal of Southern History* 48 (November 1982): 545–58.

Greene, S. W. "The Forest That Fire Made." Reprint from *American Forests.* Copy in Austin Cary Memorial Forestry Collection, Department of Special Collections, George A. Smathers Libraries, University of Florida.

Gregersen, Per, et al. "Neurotoxic Effects of Organic Solvents in Exposed Workers: An Occupational, Neuropsychological, and Neurological Investigation." *American Journal of Industrial Medicine* 5 (1984): 201–25.

Haller, John S., Jr. "Sampson of the Terebinthinates: Medical History of Turpentine." *Southern Medical Journal* 77 (June 1984): 750–4.

Hautala, Kustaa. "European and American Tar in the English Market during the Eighteenth and Early Nineteenth Centuries." *Annales Academiæ Scientiarum Fennicæ* 130 (1964): 1–195.

Hawk, Kathy. "Turpentine: An Ancient Technology Almost Tapped Out in St. Johns County." *St. Augustine Ancient City Beacon* (25 June 1982): 1, 12–3.

Hawley, Norman. "Naval Stores: America's First Widespread Forest Industry." *Southern Lumberman* (15 December 1966): 162–4.

Hendy, M. S., B. E. Beattie, and P. S. Burge. "Occupational Asthma Due to an Emulsified Oil Mist." *British Journal of Industrial Medicine* 42 (January 1985): 51–4.

Herndon, G. Melvin. "Naval Stores in Colonial Georgia." *Georgia Historical Quarterly* 52 (December 1968): 426–33.

Holmes, Jack D. L. "Naval Stores in Colonial Louisiana and the Floridas." *Louisiana Studies* 7 (winter 1968): 295–309.

Hutchinson, Gloria. "Pioneer Maine Forester, Austin Cary: A Diamond in the Rough from East Machias, He Wrote the Book on Modern Forestry." Austin Cary File, Forest History Society, Durham, N.C.

Kowal, R. J. *Ips Beetles Are Killing Pines: What Shall We Do about It?* Research Notes. Asheville, N.C.: United States Department of Agriculture, Forest Service, Southeastern Forest Experiment Station, 1955.

Kowal, R. J., and Harry Russell. *Beetles in Your Pines? How Good Cutting Practices and*

Management Stop Beetles from Killing Your Timber. Asheville, N.C.: United States Department of Agriculture, Forest Service, Southeastern Forest Experiment Station, n.d.

Krebs, Sylvia H. "Will the Freedmen Work: White Alabamians Adjust to Free Black Labor." *Alabama Historical Quarterly* 36 (summer 1974): 151–63.

"Langdale's New Processing Plant Will Open July 1st." *AT-FA Journal* (June 1945): 5.

"Larger Profits in Turpentine." *Progressive Farmer* (15 June 1903). Turpentine News Clipping File, Forest History Society, Durham, N.C.

Lauriault, Robert N. "From Can't to Can't: The North Florida Turpentine Camp, 1900–1950." *Florida Historical Quarterly* 67 (January 1989): 310–28.

Lichtenstein, Alex. "Good Roads and Chain Gangs in the Progressive South: 'The Negro Convict Is a Slave.'" *Journal of Southern History* 59 (February 1993): 85–110.

Lovel, Isabel Nelson. "Hammond, Louisiana, and Its Swedish Founder." *Swedish Pioneer Historical Quarterly*, n.s., 4 (1967): 221–6.

Malone, Ann Patton. "Piney Woods Farmers of South Georgia, 1850–1900: Jeffersonian Yeomen in an Age of Expanding Commercialism." *Agricultural History* 60 (fall 1986): 51–84.

Maxwell, Robert S. "The Impact of Forestry on the Gulf South." *Forest History* 17 (April 1973): 31–5.

McCorkle, James L., Jr. "Mississippi from Neutrality to War (1914–1917)." *Journal of Mississippi History* 43 (May 1981): 85–125.

Moore, Gary. "Prisoner of Riverside." *Folio Weekly* 10 (28 May 1996): 14–8.

Morriss, Margaret Shove. "Colonial Trade of Maryland, 1689–1715." *Johns Hopkins University Studies in Historical and Political Science*, n.s., 3 (1914): 1–157.

Nash, Gerald D. "Research Opportunities in the Economic History of the South after 1880." *Journal of Southern History* 32 (August 1966): 308–24.

"Naval Stores History." *Naval Stores Review* 100 (March–April 1990): 6–8.

"Naval Stores History We Never Knew 'Til Now." Olustee Experiment Station Files, Georgia Agrirama, Tifton, Ga.

"A New Idea in Turpentine Orcharding." *Manufacturers Record,* 6 October 1883. Turpentine News Clipping File, Forest History Society, Durham, N.C.

Ostrom, Carl E. "History of Gum Naval Stores Industry." *Chemurgic Digest* 4 (15 July 1945): 217–23.

Paisley, Clifton. "Wade Leonard, Florida Naval Stores Operator." *Florida Historical Quarterly* 51 (April 1973): 381–400.

Perry, Percival. "The Naval Stores Industry in the Old South, 1790–1860." *Journal of Southern History* 34 (November 1968): 509–26.

———. "The Naval Stores Industry in the Old South, 1790–1860." *North Carolina Forestry History Series* 1 (April 1967): 1–19.

Price, R. E. "Naval Stores in Southwest Louisiana." *McNeese Review* 2 (spring 1949): 9–12.

Reed, Gerry. "Saving the Naval Stores Industry: Charles Holmes Herty's Cup-and-Gutter Experiments, 1900–1905." *Journal of Forest History* 26 (October 1982): 168–75.

Romaine, Eldon Van. "Naval Stores, 1919–1939." *Naval Stores Review* 100 (July–August 1990): 6–16.

Schopmeyer, C. S., and Otis C. Maloy. *Dry Face of Naval Stores Pines.* Forest Pest Leaflet 51. Washington, D.C.: United States Department of Agriculture, 1960.

Sheridan, Richard C. "Chemical Fertilizers in Southern Agriculture." *Agricultural History* 53 (January 1979): 308–18.

Shlomowitz, Ralph. "'Bound' or 'Free'? Black Labor in Cotton and Sugarcane Farming, 1865–1880." *Journal of Southern History* 50 (November 1984): 569–96.

———. "Origins of Southern Sharecropping." *Agricultural History,* n.s., 53, no. 3 (1979): 557–75.

Shofner, Jerrell H. "Forced Labor in the Florida Forests, 1880–1950." *Journal of Forest History* 5 (January 1981): 14–25.

———. "Mary Grace Quackenbos, A Visitor Florida Did Not Want." *Florida Historical Quarterly* 58 (January 1980): 273–90.

———. "Negro Laborers and the Forest Industries in Reconstruction Florida." *Journal of Forest History* 19 (October 1975): 180–91.

———. "Postscript to the Martin Tabert Case: Peonage as Usual in the Florida Turpentine Camps." *Florida Historical Quarterly* 60 (October 1981): 161–73.

Smith, R. H. *A Control for the Black Turpentine Beetle in South Georgia and North Florida.* Research Notes. Asheville, N.C.: United States Department of Agriculture, Forest Service, Southeastern Forest Experiment Station, 1955.

Smith, Richard H. "Benzene Hexachloride Controls Black Turpentine Beetle." Reprint from *Southern Lumberman* (15 December 1954). Copy in Olustee Experiment Station Files, Georgia Agrirama, Tifton, Ga.

Smith, R. H., and R. E. Lee III. *Black Turpentine Beetle.* Forest Pest Leaflet 12. Washington, D.C.: United States Department of Agriculture, 1972.

Snow, Sinclair. "Naval Stores in Colonial Virginia." *Virginia Magazine of History and Biography* 72 (1964): 75–93.

Stauffer, J. M. "The Timber Resource of 'The Southwest Alabama Forest Empire.'" *Journal of the Alabama Academy of Science* 30 (January 1959): 52–67.

Taylor, Alan. "Unnatural Inequalities: Social and Environmental Histories." *Environmental History* 1 (October 1996): 6–19.

True, R. P. "Dry Face of Turpentine Pines." *Forest Farmer* 8 (August 1949): 6, 11.

"The Turpentiners." *Magnolia Monthly* 7 (October 1969).

Wiener, Jonathan M. "Class Structure and Economic Development in the American South, 1865–1955." *American Historical Review* 84 (October 1979): 970–92.

Williams, Justin. "English Mercantilism and Carolina Naval Stores, 1705–1776." *Journal of Southern History* 1 (May 1935): 169–85.

Books

Albion, Robert Greenhalgh. *Forests and Sea Power: The Timber Problem of the Royal Navy, 1652–1862.* Cambridge: Harvard University Press, 1926.

Averitt, Jack N. *Georgia's Coastal Plain.* 3 vols. New York: Lewis Historical, 1964.

Ayers, Edward L. *The Promise of the New South: Life after Reconstruction.* New York: Oxford University Press, 1992.

———. *Vengeance and Justice: Crime and Punishment in the Nineteenth-Century American South.* New York: Oxford University Press, 1984.

Ball, Douglas B. *Financial Failure and Confederate Defeat.* Urbana: University of Illinois Press, 1991.

Bennett, William H., Charles W. Chellman, and William R. Holt. *Insect Enemies of Southern Pines.* Washington, D.C.: United States Department of Agriculture, Southern Forest Experiment Station, 1958.

Berlin, Ira, and Philip D. Morgan. "Labor and the Shaping of Slave Life in the Americas." In *Cultivation and Culture: Labor and the Shaping of Slave Life in the Americas.* edited by Ira Berlin and Philip D. Morgan. Charlottesville: University Press of Virginia, 1993.

Blount, Robert S. *Spirits of Turpentine: A History of Florida Naval Stores, 1528 to 1950.* Tallahassee: Florida Agricultural Museum, 1993.

Brown, Nelson Courtlandt. *Forest Products: The Harvesting, Processing, and Marketing of Materials Other Than Lumber, Including the Principal Derivatives, Extractives, and Incidental Products in the United States and Canada.* New York: John Wiley and Sons, 1950.

Butler, Carroll B. *Treasures of the Longleaf Pines: Naval Stores.* Shalimar, Fla.: Tarkel, 1998.

Campbell, A. Stuart, and Alvin Cassel. *The Foreign Trade of Florida.* Gainesville: Bureau of Economic and Business Research, College of Business Administration, University of Florida, 1935.

Campbell, A. Stuart, Robert C. Unkrich, and Albert C. Blanchard. *The Naval Stores Industry.* Gainesville: Bureau of Economic and Business Research, College of Business Administration, University of Florida, 1934.

Carswell, E. W. *Holmesteading: The History of Holmes County Florida.* Tallahassee: Rose Printing, 1986.

———. *Washington: Florida's Twelfth County.* Chipley, Fla.: E. W. Carswell, 1991.

Cash, William Thomas. *The Story of Florida.* 4 vols. New York: American Historical Society, 1938.

Cecil-Fronsman, Bill. *Common Whites: Class and Culture in Antebellum North Carolina.* Lexington: University Press of Kentucky, 1992.

Clark, C. R. *Florida Trade Tokens.* St. Petersburg: Great Outdoors, 1980.

Clark, Thomas D. *The Greening of the South: The Recovery of Land and Forest.* Lexington: University Press of Kentucky, 1984.

Clements, Ralph W. *Manual: Modern Gum Naval Stores Methods.* Asheville, N.C.: United States Department of Agriculture, Forest Service, Southeastern Forest Experiment Station, 1960.

Cobb, James C. *Industrialization and Southern Society, 1877–1984.* Chicago: Dorsey Press, 1984.

Cohen, William. *At Freedom's Edge: Black Mobility and the Southern White Quest for Racial Control, 1861–1915.* Baton Rouge: Louisiana State University Press, 1991.

Cohn, Lawrence, ed. *Nothing but the Blues: The Music and the Musicians.* New York: Abbeville Press, 1993.

Cooper, William J., Jr., and Thomas E. Terrill. *The American South: A History.* New York: Alfred A. Knopf, 1990.

Coulter, E. Merton. *James Monroe Smith, Georgia Planter: Before and after Death.* Athens: University of Georgia Press, 1961.

Cowdrey, Albert E. *This Land, This South: An Environmental History.* Rev. ed. Lexington: University Press of Kentucky, 1996.

Cox, Thomas R., Robert S. Maxwell, Phillip Drennon Thomas, and Joseph J. Malone. *This Well Wooded Land: Americans and Their Forests from Colonial Times to the Present.* Lincoln: University of Nebraska Press, 1985.

Crittenden, Charles Christopher. *The Commerce of North Carolina, 1763–1789.* New Haven: Yale University Press, 1936.

Daniel, Pete. *The Shadow of Slavery: Peonage in the South, 1901–1969.* Urbana: University of Illinois Press, 1990.

Davis, Richard C., ed. *Encyclopedia of American Forest and Conservation History.* New York: Macmillan, 1983.

DeCredico, Mary A. *Patriotism for Profit: Georgia's Urban Entrepreneurs and the Confederate War Effort.* Chapel Hill: University of North Carolina Press, 1990.

Dew, Charles B. *Bond of Iron: Master and Slave at Buffalo Forge.* New York: W. W. Norton, 1994.

———. "Sam Williams, Forgeman: The Life of an Industrial Slave in the Old South." In *Region, Race, and Reconstruction: Essays in Honor of C. Vann Woodward,* edited by J. Morgan Kousser and James M. McPherson. New York: Oxford University Press, 1982.

Dorland's Illustrated Medical Dictionary. 25th ed. Philadelphia: W. B. Saunders, 1974.

Doyle, Rodger. *Atlas of Contemporary America: A Portrait of the Nation.* New York: Facts on File, 1994.

Drobney, Jeffrey A. *Lumbermen and Log Sawyers: Life, Labor, and Culture in the North Florida Timber Industry, 1830–1930.* Macon: Mercer University Press, 1997.

Dusinberre, William. *Them Dark Days: Slavery in the American Rice Swamps.* Athens: University of Georgia Press, 2000.

Eldredge, I. F. *The 4 Forests and the Future of the South.* Washington, D.C.: Charles Lathrop Pack Forestry Foundation, 1947.

Evans, William McKee. *Ballots and Fence Rails: Reconstruction on the Lower Cape Fear.* Chapel Hill: University of North Carolina Press, 1966.

Fite, Gilbert C. *Cotton Fields No More: Southern Agriculture, 1865–1980.* Lexington: University Press of Kentucky, 1984.

Fogel, Robert William, and Stanley L. Engerman. *Time on the Cross: The Economics of American Negro Slavery.* Boston: Little, Brown, 1974.

Gamble, Thomas. "Charleston's Story as a Naval Stores Emporium." In *Naval Stores: History, Production, Distribution, and Consumption,* edited by Thomas Gamble. Savannah: Review Publishing and Printing, 1921.

———. "Early History of the Naval Stores Industry in North America." In *Naval*

Stores: History, Production, Distribution, and Consumption, edited by Thomas Gamble. Savannah: Review Publishing and Printing, 1921.

———. "Pages from Wilmington's Story as America's First Great Naval Stores Port." In *Naval Stores: History, Production, Distribution, and Consumption,* edited by Thomas Gamble. Savannah: Review Publishing and Printing, 1921.

Genovese, Eugene D. *The Political Economy of Slavery: Studies in the Economy and Society of the Slave South,* 2nd ed. Middletown, Conn.: Wesleyan University Press, 1989.

———. *Roll, Jordan, Roll: The World the Slaves Made.* New York: Vintage Books, 1976.

Gold, Pleasant Daniel. *History of Duval County, Including Early History of East Florida.* St. Augustine: Record, 1929.

Gosselin, Robert E., Harold C. Hodge, Roger P. Smith, and Marion N. Gleason. *Clinical Toxicology of Commercial Products.* 4th ed. Baltimore: Williams and Wilkins, 1976.

Hahn, Steven. *The Roots of Southern Populism: Yeoman Farmers and the Transformation of the Georgia Upcountry, 1850–1890.* New York: Oxford University Press, 1983.

Hansbrough, Thomas. "Human Behavior and Forest Fires." In *Southern Forests and Southern People,* edited by Thomas Hansbrough. Baton Rouge: Louisiana State University Press, 1963.

Harris, J. William. "The Question of Peonage in the History of the New South." In *Plain Folk of the South Revisited,* edited by Samuel C. Hyde, Jr. Baton Rouge: Louisiana State University Press, 1997.

Harris, Wallace Leigh. *History of Pulaski and Bleckley Counties, Georgia, 1808–1956.* Macon: J. W. Burke, 1957.

Hawley, Norman R. "Burning in Naval Stores Forest." In *Proceedings, Third Annual Tall Timbers Fire Ecology Conference.* Tallahassee: Tall Timbers Research Station, 1964.

Heitman, John Alfred. *The Modernization of the Louisiana Sugar Industry, 1830–1910.* Baton Rouge: Louisiana State University Press, 1987.

Herring, J. L. *Saturday Night Sketches: Stories of Old Wiregrass Georgia.* Tifton, Ga.: Sunny South Press, 1978.

Hickman, Nollie. "Black Labor in Forest Industries of the Piney Woods, 1840–1933." In *Mississippi's Piney Woods: A Human Perspective,* edited by Noel Polk. Jackson: University Press of Mississippi, 1986.

———. *Mississippi Harvest: Lumbering in the Longleaf Pine Belt, 1840–1915.* University: University of Mississippi, 1962.

Hilliard, Sam Bowers. *Atlas of Antebellum Southern Agriculture.* Baton Rouge: Louisiana State University Press, 1984.

Historic Properties Survey of St. Johns County. St. Augustine: Historic St. Augustine Preservation Board, 1985.

Holvey, David N., ed. *The Merck Manual of Diagnosis and Therapy,* 12th ed. Rahway, N.J.: Merck, Sharp, and Dohne Research Laboratories, 1972.

Hosmer, Joseph B. *Economic Aspects of the Naval Stores Industry.* Atlanta: Georgia School of Technology, 1948.

Industrial Toxicology. 3d ed. Acton, Mass.: Publishing Sciences Group, 1974.

Innes, Stephen. *Creating the Commonwealth: The Economic Culture of Puritan New England*. New York: W. W. Norton, 1995.

Johnson, Guion Griffis. *Ante-Bellum North Carolina: A Social History*. Chapel Hill: University of North Carolina Press, 1937.

Joyner, Charles. *Down by the Riverside: A South Carolina Slave Community*. Urbana: University of Illinois Press, 1984.

Kay, Marvin L. Michael, and Lorin Lee Cary. *Slavery in North Carolina, 1748–1775*. Chapel Hill: University of North Carolina Press, 1995.

Kennedy, Stetson. *Jim Crow Guide: The Way It Was*. Boca Raton: Florida Atlantic University Press, 1959.

———. *Palmetto Country*. New York: Duell, Sloan and Pearce, 1942.

———. *Southern Exposure*. Garden City, N.Y.: Doubleday, 1946.

Kennedy, William T., et al., eds. *History of Lake County, Florida*. 1929. Reprint, Tavares, Fla.: Lake County Historical Society, 1988.

Kirby, Jack Temple. *Poquosin: A Study of Rural Landscape and Society*. Chapel Hill: University of North Carolina Press, 1995.

Knittle, Walter Allen. *The Early Eighteenth Century Palatine Emigration: A British Government Redemptioner Project to Manufacture Naval Stores*. Philadelphia: Dorrance, 1936.

Koch, Peter. *Utilization of the Southern Pines*. Washington, D.C.: United States Department of Agriculture Forest Service, 1972.

Kolchin, Peter. *American Slavery, 1619–1877*. New York: Hill and Wang, 1993.

Lamoreaux, Naomi R. *The Great Merger Movement in American Business, 1895–1904*. New York: Cambridge University Press, 1985.

Lee, Lawrence. *The Lower Cape Fear in Colonial Days*. Chapel Hill: University of North Carolina Press, 1965.

Lefler, Hugh Talmage, and Albert Ray Newsome. *North Carolina: The History of a Southern State*. Chapel Hill: University of North Carolina Press, 1954.

Lewis, Ronald L. *Coal Iron and Slaves: Industrial Slavery in Maryland and Virginia, 1715–1865*. Westport, Conn.: Greenwood Press, 1979.

Lichtenstein, Alex. *Twice the Work of Free Labor: The Political Economy of Convict Labor in the New South*. New York: Verso, 1996.

Mancini, Matthew J. *One Dies, Get Another: Convict Leasing in the American South, 1866–1928*. Columbia: University of South Carolina Press, 1996.

Marshall, F. Ray. *Labor in the South*. Cambridge, Mass.: Harvard University Press, 1967.

McDonald, Roderick A. *The Economy and Material Culture of Slaves: Goods and Chattels on the Sugar Plantations of Jamaica and Louisiana*. Baton Rouge: Louisiana State University Press, 1993.

McWhiney, Grady. "Antebellum Piney Woods Culture: Continuity over Time and Place." In *Mississippi's Piney Woods: A Human Perspective*, edited by Noel Park. Jackson: University Press of Mississippi, 1986.

———. "Crackers and Cavaliers: Shared Courage." In *Plain Folk of the South Revis-*

ited, edited by Samuel C. Hyde, Jr. Baton Rouge: Louisiana State University Press, 1997.

Merrens, Harry Roy. *Colonial North Carolina in the Eighteenth Century.* Chapel Hill: The University of North Carolina Press, 1964.

Miller, Randall M., and John David Smith, eds. *Dictionary of Afro-American Slavery.* New York: Greenwood Press, 1988.

Mobley, M. D., and Robert N. Haskins. *Forestry in the South.* Atlanta: Turner E. Smith, 1956.

Naval Stores: A Summary of Annual and Monthly Statistics, 1955–74. Washington, D.C.: United States Department of Agriculture, 1977.

Naval Stores Statistics, 1900–1954. Statistical Bulletin No. 181. Washington, D.C.: United States Department of Agriculture, 1956.

Oakes, James. *Slavery and Freedom: An Interpretation of the Old South.* New York: Alfred A. Knopf, 1990.

Oshinsky, David M. *"Worse Than Slavery": Parchman Farm and the Ordeal of Jim Crow Justice.* New York: Free Press, 1996.

Panshin, A. J., E. S. Harrar, J. S. Bethel, and W. J. Baker. *Forest Products: Their Sources, Production, and Utilization.* New York: McGraw-Hill, 1962.

Pikl, I. James. *A History of Georgia Forestry.* Athens: Bureau of Business and Economic Research, University of Georgia, 1966.

Pisani, Donald J. "Forests and Conservation, 1865–1890." In *American Forests: Nature, Culture, and Politics,* edited by Char Miller. Lawrence: University Press of Kansas, 1997.

Pomeroy, Kenneth B., and James G. Yoho. *North Carolina Lands: Ownership, Use, and Management of Forest and Related Lands.* Washington, D.C.: American Forestry Association, 1964.

Porcher, Francis Peyre. "Uses of Rosin and Turpentine in Old Plantation Days." In *Naval Stores: History, Production, Distribution, and Consumption,* edited by Thomas Gamble. Savannah: Review Publishing and Printing, 1921.

Powell, William S. *North Carolina through Four Centuries.* Chapel Hill: University of North Carolina Press, 1989.

Pyne, Stephen J. *Fire in America: A Cultural History of Wildland and Rural Fire.* Princeton: Princeton University Press, 1982.

Reed, Germaine M. *Crusading for Chemistry: The Professional Career of Charles Holmes Herty.* Athens: University of Georgia Press, 1995.

Schoenbaum, Thomas J. *Islands, Capes, and Sounds: The North Carolina Coast.* Winston-Salem, N.C.: John F. Blair, 1982.

Scott, Rebecca J. *Slave Emancipation in Cuba: The Transition to Free Labor, 1860–1899.* Princeton: Princeton University Press, 1985.

Sharrer, G. Terry. "Naval Stores, 1781–1881." In *Material Culture of the Wooden Age,* edited by Brooke Hindle. Tarrytown, N.Y.: Sleepy Hollow Press, 1981.

Shelton, Jane Twitty. *Pines and Pioneers: A History of Lowndes County, Georgia, 1825–1900.* Atlanta: Cherokee, 1976.

Silver, Timothy. *A New Face on the Countryside: Indians, Colonists, and Slaves in South Atlantic Forests, 1500–1800.* New York: Cambridge University Press, 1990.

Sitterson, J. Carlyle. *Sugar Country: The Cane Sugar Industry in the South, 1753–1950.* Lexington: University Press of Kentucky, 1953.

Smith, Julia Floyd. *Slavery and Rice Culture in Low Country Georgia, 1750–1860.* Knoxville: University of Tennessee Press, 1985.

Speh, Carl F. "The Naval Stores Industry in the Western Territory." In *Naval Stores: History, Production, Distribution, and Consumption,* edited by Thomas Gamble. Savannah: Review Publishing and Printing, 1921.

Stampp, Kenneth M. *The Peculiar Institution: Slavery in the Ante-Bellum South.* 1956. Reprint, New York: Vintage Books, 1989.

Starobin, Robert S. *Industrial Slavery in the Old South.* New York: Oxford University Press, 1970.

Stewart, Mart A. *"What Nature Suffers to Groe": Life, Labor, and Landscape on the Georgia Coast, 1680–1920.* Athens: University of Georgia Press, 1996.

Taylor, Rosser Howard. *Slaveholding in North Carolina: An Economic View.* Chapel Hill: University of North Carolina Press, 1926.

Thomas, Kenneth H. *McCranie's Turpentine Still, Atkinson County, Georgia: A Historical Analysis of the Site, with Some Information on the Naval Stores Industry in Georgia and Elsewhere.* Atlanta: Georgia Department of Natural Resources, 1975.

Thorndale, William, and William Dollarhide. *Map Guide to the U.S. Federal Censuses, 1790–1920.* Baltimore: Genealogical Publishing, 1987.

Tindall, George B. *The Emergence of the New South, 1913–1945.* Baton Rouge: Louisiana State University Press, 1967.

Tolles, Zonira Hunter. *Shadows on the Sand: A History of the Land and the People in the Vicinity of Melrose, Florida.* Gainesville: Storter Printing, 1976.

Trelease, Allen W. *The North Carolina Railroad, 1849–1871, and the Modernization of North Carolina.* Chapel Hill: University of North Carolina Press, 1991.

True, R. P., and R. D. McCulley. *Defects above Naval Stores Faces Are Associated with Dry Face.* Reprint of 15 December 1945 *Southern Lumberman* article. N.p., n.d. Copy in Olustee Experiment Station Files, Georgia Agrirama, Tifton, Ga.

United States Department of Commerce. *Historical Statistics of the United States, Colonial Times to 1970.* Bicentennial ed. 2 vols. Washington, D.C.: U.S. Dept. of Commerce, 1975.

Vance, Rupert B. *Human Geography of the South: A Study in Regional Resources and Human Adequacy.* Chapel Hill: University of North Carolina Press, 1935.

Vlash, John Michael. *Back of the Big House: The Architecture of Plantation Slavery.* Chapel Hill: University of North Carolina Press, 1993.

Wahlenberg, W. G. *Longleaf Pine: Its Use, Ecology, Regeneration, Protection, Growth, and Management.* Washington, D.C.: Charles Lathrop Pack Forestry Foundation, 1946.

Weaver, Howard E., and David A. Anderson. *Manual of Southern Forestry.* Danville, Ill.: Interstate Printers and Publishers, 1954.

Weir, Robert M. *Colonial South Carolina: A History.* Millwood, N.Y.: KTO Press, 1983.

Wetherington, Mark V. *The New South Comes to Wiregrass Georgia, 1860–1910.* Knoxville: University of Tennessee Press, 1994.

Williams, Ida Belle. *History of Tift County.* Macon: J. W. Burke, 1948.

Williams, Michael. *Americans and Their Forests: A Historical Geography.* New York: Cambridge University Press, 1989.

Wilson, Charles Reagan, and William Ferris, eds. *Encyclopedia of Southern Culture.* Chapel Hill: University of North Carolina Press, 1989.

Wood, Betty. *Slavery in Colonial Georgia.* Athens: University of Georgia Press, 1984.

Wood, Peter H. *Black Majority: Negroes in Colonial South Carolina from 1670 through the Stono Rebellion.* New York: W. W. Norton, 1974.

Woodman, Harold. *King Cotton and His Retainers: Financing and Marketing the Cotton Crop of the South, 1800–1925.* Lexington: University Press of Kentucky, 1968; reprint, Columbia: University of South Carolina Press, 1990.

Woodward, C. Vann. *Origins of the New South, 1877–1913.* Baton Rouge: Louisiana State University Press, 1951.

Wright, Gavin. *Old South, New South: Revolutions in the Southern Economy since the Civil War.* New York: Basic Books, 1986.

INDEX